Adomnán's Lex Innocentium *and the laws of war*

Adomnán's *Lex Innocentium* and the laws of war

JAMES W. HOULIHAN

FOUR COURTS PRESS

Set in 10.5 pt on 12.5 pt Bembo for
FOUR COURTS PRESS LTD
7 Malpas Street, Dublin 8, Ireland
www.fourcourtspress.ie
and in North America for
FOUR COURTS PRESS
c/o IPG, 814 N. Franklin St, Chicago, IL 60610.

© James W. Houlihan and Four Courts Press, 2020

A catalogue record for this title
is available from the British Library.

ISBN 978-1-84682-849-2

All rights reserved. No part of this publication may be reproduced, stored in or introduced into a retrieval system, or transmitted, in any form or by any means (electronic, mechanical, photocopying, recording or otherwise), without the prior written permission of both the copyright owner and the publisher of this book.

SPECIAL ACKNOWLEDGMENT

The author and publisher would like to acknowledge the support of the Heritage Office, Offaly County Council.

Printed in England
by TJ International, Padstow, Cornwall

To the people of Birr, from this generation to future generations, about something remarkable that happened in their native place, many, many generations ago.

To the people of Ireland, so that they may learn of one of the great treasures of their heritage.

To the custodians of the Geneva Conventions, so that they may know of, and be inspired by, one who went before them.

Contents

ABBREVIATIONS	9
ACKNOWLEDGMENTS	10

1 *Lex Innocentium:* the concept and its contexts — 11

    Introducing Lex Innocentium — 11
    The concept — 12
    Historical contexts — 15
    The concept in a modern context — 22
    Historiography — 25

2 Attitudes to warfare and violence in the early medieval West — 27

    Biblical tradition: the Christian and killing — 28
    Augustine — 37
    Interpretations of Augustine — 44
    The barbarian laws — 48
    Contemporary accounts — 55

3 Irish attitudes to violence — 59

    Late seventh-century Ireland — 59
    Empirical evidence — 65
    Normative texts — 70
    Literary texts — 81

4 Adomnán — 93

    Introduction — 93
    Biography and works — 95
    Adomnán and violence — 105

5 The Law — 115

    Birr — 115
    Surviving manuscripts: provenance and description — 119
    Dating — 121
    The core text: paragraphs 34–49 — 128

6   After 697: a law for women   141

    Did it make a difference?   141
    Changing emphasis   143
    Transition completed   151
    The Viking interlude   152
    Raphoe: Adomnán and his law endure   156
    Sixteenth-/ seventeenth-century afterlife   164

7   *Lex Innocentium* situated: its place in the medieval history of *jus in bello*   174

    The Peace of God   174
    Why Ireland? Why 697?   181
    Adomnán's jus in bello: *his concept, his inspiration and his achievement*   188

APPENDIX   192

BIBLIOGRAPHY   207

INDEX   227

Abbreviations

AL	*Ancient Laws of Ireland*
AU	*The Annals of Ulster* (to AD 1131)
CCSL	*Corpus Christianorum. Series Latina*
CIH	*Corpus Iuris Hibernici*
CSEL	*Corpus Scriptorum Ecclesiasticorum Latinorum*
DLS	*De Locis Sanctis*
eDIL	Electronic Dictionary of the Irish Language
GCS	*Griechischen Christlichen Schriftsteller*
HE	Bede, *Historia Ecclesiastica*
IHL	International Humanitarian Law
JHIL	*Journal of the History of International Law*
JRSAI	*Journal of the Royal Society of Antiquaries of Ireland*
LxI	*Lex Innocentium*
MGH	*Monumenta Germaniae Historica.*
	Epp Epistolae
	Legum Legum Nationum Germanicarum
	SRG Scriptores Rerum Germanicarum in usum Scholarum
	SRM Scriptores Rerum Merovingicarum
	SS Scriptores in folio
NHI	D. Ó Cróinín (ed.), *A new history of Ireland,* i: *prehistoric and early Ireland* (Oxford, 2005)
PL	*Patrologia Latina*
PRIA	*Proceedings of the Royal Irish Academy*
VC	*Vita Columbae*
ZCP	*Zeitschrift für celtische Philologie*

Acknowledgments

This work is based, to a large extent, on my PhD thesis, and I am hugely grateful to Elva Johnston of University College, Dublin who had the task of converting me from a lawyer into a historian. The old mould having been broken, I was able to benefit from her vast learning and scholarship, both the breadth and depth of which amazed me; all of which was delivered to me with such patience and kindness. I am also most grateful for the help and insightful assistance of Edward Coleman, Roy Flechner and, at a later stage, Damian Bracken. A special thank you to Dáibhí Ó Cróinín for his painstaking, comprehensive and learned critique of the final draft of this monograph, which I feel was above and beyond the call of duty.

I acknowledge, in particular, Máirín Ní Dhonnchadha without whose groundbreaking scholarship on *Lex Innocentium* my study would not have been possible.

Thank you to Martin Fanning of Four Courts Press for his help and professional guidance, which, I suspect, exceeded the norm. I am most grateful also to Amanda Pedlow and the Heritage Office, Offaly County Council, for their financial support.

My family have had to bear the brunt of, what can only be described as, my obsession, over the last number of years. My children, Desmond, Sorcha, Arthur and Aifric were always ready to drop what they were doing and help out. To all of them thank you for your understanding and encouragement.

Most of all I want to thank my wife Irene, not only for her practical help and encouragement, which were considerable, but for allowing me the space to pursue my task and, very particularly, for her understanding and empathy with my overall project.

CHAPTER I

Lex Innocentium: the concept and its contexts

INTRODUCING *LEX INNOCENTIUM*

In the year AD 697, a great gathering took place in Birr, in the middle of Ireland. The meeting was convoked by Adomnán, abbot of Iona. It was a joint lay–ecclesiastical assembly that included all of the most important leaders of the day from Ireland with representation, also, from those parts of northern Britain under Irish influence. The purpose of the meeting was to promulgate a law for the protection of, broadly speaking, women, children and clerics primarily, but not exclusively, in time of war.[1] In today's terminology, it was a law for non-combatants. Historians know of the enactment of this law from an entry in the Annals of Ulster for the year 697:

Adomnanus ad Hiberniam pergit et dedit Legem Innocentium populis.[2]

Adomnán proceeded to Ireland and gave the *Lex Innocentium* to the peoples.

---

1 K. Meyer (ed. and trans.), *Cáin Adamnáin: an Old Irish treatise on the Law of Adamnán* (Oxford, 1905); T. O'Loughlin (ed.), *Adomnán at Birr AD 697: essays in commemoration of the Law of the Innocents* (Dublin, 2001) and D.N. Dumville's review of this work in the *Catholic Historical Review*, 89:2 (2003), pp 283–4. See also G. Márkus (trans.), *Adomnán's 'Law of the Innocents': Cáin Adomnáin* (Kilmartin, 2008); M. Ní Dhonnchadha (ed. and trans.), 'An edition of *Cáin Adomnáin*' (PhD, University College, Cork, 1992); eadem, 'The guarantor-list of *Cáin Adomnáin*, 697', *Peritia*, 1 (1982), pp 178–215; J. Grigg, 'Aspects of the *cáin*: Adomnán's *Lex Innocentium*', *Journal of the Australian Early Medieval Association*, 1 (2005), pp 41–50; J.W. Houlihan, 'Adomnán's *Lex Innocentium* and the jurisprudence of warfare' (PhD, University College, Dublin, 2019). See references to *Cáin Adomnáin* in more general works such as: D. Ó Cróinín, *Early medieval Ireland, 400–1200* (2nd ed., London, 2017), p. 80; T.M. Charles-Edwards, *Early Christian Ireland* (Cambridge, 2000), p. 208, and p. 568; idem, 'Early Irish law' in D. Ó Cróinín (ed.), *A new history of Ireland*, i: *prehistoric and early Ireland* (Oxford, 2005) (henceforth *NHI*), pp 334–7; J.E. Fraser, 'Adomnán and the morality of war' in J.M. Wooding et al. (eds), *Adomnán of Iona: theologian, lawmaker, peacemaker* (Dublin, 2010), pp 95–111. See Houlihan, 'Jurisprudence', pp 24–30 for detailed historiography and Chapter 5 below for a discussion of who attended the meeting. 2 S. Mac Airt and G. Mac Niocaill (eds and trans.), *The Annals of Ulster* (Dublin, 1983), s. a. 697. Also W. Stokes (ed. and trans.), 'The Annals of Tigernach', *Revue Celtique*, 16 (1895), pp 374–419; 17 (1896), pp 6–33 and pp 119–263 and pp 337–420; 18 (1897), pp 9–59 and pp 150–97 and pp 267–303 and pp 374–91 (repr. 2 vols, Felinfach, 1993), s. a. 697, 3; W.M. Hennessy (ed. and trans.), *Chronicum Scotorum: a chronicle of Irish affairs from the earliest times to AD 1135, with a supplement containing events from 1141–1156*

The law came to be known as *Cáin Adomnáin*. It is also referred to as *Lex Innocentium*, the 'Law of the Innocents' (henceforth *LxI*), a term that is found in the earliest contemporary annal reference, just cited. The text of the law is known from two surviving manuscripts: a fifteenth-/sixteenth-century manuscript in the Bodleian Library, Oxford (Rawlinson MS B 512, ff 48r–51v) and a copy made by Mícheál Ó Cléirigh in 1627, now held in the Bibliothèque Royale, Brussels (O'Clery MS 2324–40, ff 76r–82v).[3] Both copies can be traced to the same exemplar, a now lost dossier known as the 'Old Book of Raphoe', that, itself, cannot date from before the late tenth or early eleventh centuries, at a considerable remove from Adomnán's own time.[4] This law was unusual in that it attempted to limit the effects of warfare rather than to prohibit it or, indeed, to justify a particular war or wars. The purpose of this study is to place or situate *LxI* in the history of warfare and, more particularly, in the history of attitudes to non-combatant involvement in warfare and the laws giving expression to those attitudes,[5] and will be confined to the Western Christian world and to the early medieval period, as this is when *LxI* had its origin. It will be concerned with the concept that rules of proper behaviour apply to the conduct of war and, in particular, with the view that wars should be fought by the military on either side, and that non-combatants should not be involved and should have an immunity from the effects of war. This concept is integral to *LxI*.

THE CONCEPT

A distinction is made between the right to go to war, on the one hand, and right behaviour during the course of war, on the other.[6] This distinction is modern, and it is only in relatively recent times that it has been clearly made and articu-

(London, 1866), s. a. 697,1. For the Chronicle of Ireland see Chapter 3. **3** For copies of the texts see: Meyer, *Cáin Adamnáin*; M. Ní Dhonnchadha, 'The Law of Adomnán: a translation' in O'Loughlin (ed.), *Adomnán at Birr*, pp 53–68; P.P. Ó Néill and D.N. Dumville (eds and trans.), *Cáin Adomnáin and Canones Adomnani II* (Cambridge, 2003); Márkus, *Adomnán's 'Law of the Innocents'*, pp 10–25. **4** M. Ní Dhonnchadha, 'Birr and the Law of the Innocents' in O'Loughlin (ed.), *Adomnán at Birr*, pp 15–16; eadem, 'An edition of *Cáin Adomnáin*', pp 59–60. See Chapter 5 below for discussion. **5** Surprisingly little scholarship has been directed specifically at the position of the non-combatant. Works of relevance include: R.S. Hartigan, *The forgotten victim: a history of the civilian* (Chicago, 1982), this work has been republished, without amendment under the title *Civilian victims in war: a political history* (Piscataway, NJ, 2010); A. Gillespie, *A history of the laws of war* (3 vols, Oxford, 2011), ii (this volume is entitled *The customs and laws of war with regards to civilians in times of conflict*); C. Allmand, 'War and the non-combatant in the Middle Ages' in M. Keen (ed.), *Medieval warfare: a history* (Oxford, 1999). See also the following works that address the issue in a late medieval context: T. Russell Smith, 'Willing body, willing mind: non-combatant culpability according to English combatant writers, 1327–77' and A.J. Macdonald, 'Two kinds of war? Brutality and atrocity in later medieval Scotland', both in J. Rogge (ed.), *Killing and being killed: bodies in battle: perspectives on fighters in the Middle Ages* (Bielefeld, 2017), pp 79–107 and 199–230 respectively. **6** See M.M.N. Shaw QC, *International law* (6th ed., Cambridge, 2008), pp 1118–1203.

lated. *Jus ad bellum* is the term applied to the former and *jus in bello* to the latter.[7] *Lex Innocentium* was not an *ad bellum* law. That it was an *in bello* law is central to this study, as are its credentials as such a law. It may be surprising to learn that the terms *jus ad bellum* and *jus in bello* have only recently been coined. The International Committee of the Red Cross informs that the clear distinction between the two concepts has been made only recently, with the terms not becoming common in debates and writings about the law of war until after the Second World War. The concepts that the terms cover did feature in legal debate before then, but without the clear distinction the adoption of the terms has enabled.[8] Robert Kolb, in an article for the *International Review of the Red Cross*, gives an outline of the development of the use of this terminology to describe and to distinguish the concepts involved. The terminology first appeared in 1934.[9]

According to modern jurists, *jus ad bellum* or *jus contra bellum* proscribes the use or threat of force by a state against the territorial integrity or political independence of another state (UN Charter, Art. 2, para. 4).[10] Exceptions are provided in the case of self-defence or following a decision adopted by the UN Security Council under Article 51 of the UN Charter. *Jus in bello* governs the way in which warfare is conducted; it is purely humanitarian, seeking to limit the suffering caused. It is independent from questions about the justification or reasons for war, or its prevention, seeking to protect and assist the victims of war as far as possible. In a manner of speaking, *jus in bello* accepts the reality of a conflict without considering the reasons for, or legality of, resorting to force. It is not concerned with the justness of the cause of one side or the other. To attempt to make judgments between warring parties as to who is right and who is wrong would lead to controversy and, in some cases, paralyse implementation of the law. Each party would claim that the other was the aggressor.[11] A determination as to who is the aggressor is a separate and different process. *Jus in bello*, on the other hand, applies to both sides. Where it is clear that one of the parties had no right to go to war, the aggrieved party is, nevertheless, bound by *in bello* obligations. Even if it is defending itself against unjust aggression it is bound by *in bello* law. As the Red Cross have put it: '*In bello* must remain independent of *ad bellum*'.[12]

It is in international law that we find our current concept of non-combatant immunity.[13] *Ad bellum* laws are today the concern of the United Nations and are

---

7 R. Kolb, 'Origin of the twin terms *jus ad bellum/jus in bello*', *International Review of the Red Cross*, 320 (1997), p. 1. **8** *IHL and other legal regimes – jus ad bellum and jus in bello* (2010) (www.icrc.org/eng/war-and-law). Downloaded from ICRC website on 16 February 2011. **9** Kolb, 'Twin terms'. **10** Article 2(4) reads: 'All members shall refrain from the threat or use of force against the territorial integrity or political independence of any state, or in any other manner inconsistent with the purposes of the United Nations'. **11** *IHL and other legal regimes*, p. 1. **12** Ibid., p. 1. See also C. Greenwood, 'The relationships between *ius ad bellum* and *ius in bello*', *Internatinal Studies* 9:4 (October 1983), pp 221–34. **13** Modern international law covers a wide area: human rights, the law of the sea, environmental law, the law of treaties, the use of force by states, humanitarian law, and it governs the working of the United Nations including the International Court of Justice. See Shaw, *International law* for a comprehensive

found in international law under the heading of the Use of Force by States. *Jus in bello* is now called International Humanitarian Law (IHL) and it is under this heading that the various *in bello* laws are found. Among the *in bello* laws are those covering the treatment of prisoners of war, sick and wounded personnel, human rights at time of conflict, prohibited methods of warfare, and, of course, our concept, the rights of non-combatants.[14] These laws were sometimes referred to as the laws of war or the laws of armed conflict. While some of these still represent rules of customary international law, they are primarily derived from a number of international conventions. Indeed, IHL is one of the most codified parts of international law.[15] The most relevant international conventions, for our purposes, are the Four Geneva 'Red Cross' Conventions of 1949.[16] It is in the fourth of these conventions, and the protocols subsequently added to it, that the concept under discussion is enshrined in modern international law. While complex issues are dealt with within these laws, such as the defining of terms like civilians, belligerents, occupied territory, and many others, the underlying principle is that persons not actively engaged in warfare should be treated humanely. In an advisory opinion of the International Court of Justice dating from 1996 the principles underlying IHL are set out as follows:

> The cardinal principles contained in the texts constituting the fabric of humanitarian law are the following. The first is aimed at the protection of the civilian population and civilian objects and establishes the distinction between combatants and non-combatants; States must never make civilians the objective of attack and must consequently never use weapons that are incapable of distinguishing between civilian and military targets. According to the second principle, it is prohibited to cause unnecessary suffering to combatants.[17]

The first cardinal principle of IHL is, therefore, the distinction between combatants and non-combatants and that non-combatants should be protected, a distinction that is arguably central to Adomnán's thought. The International Court of Justice clearly enunciates the distinction between combatants and non-combatants and the latter's protection from violence at time of war. This is a striking parallel to what Adomnán did in his law in 697.[18]

---

coverage of modern international law. Also: M.D. Evans (ed.), *International law* (Oxford, 2003); A. Abass, *Complete international law* (Oxford, 2012); M. Dixon, *Textbook on international law* (Oxford, 2013); J. Klabbers, *International law* (Cambridge, 2013). **14** C. de Than and E. Shorts, *International criminal law and human rights* (London, 2003), p. 117. **15** Shaw, *International law*, pp 1167–8. **16** Ibid., p. 1169 and pp 1177–8. These dealt respectively with the wounded and sick in armed forces in the field, wounded, sick and ship wrecked members of armed forces at sea, the treatment of prisoners of war and, fourthly, the protection of civilians in time of war. The texts of the Geneva Conventions and Additional Protocols are available in booklet form from the International Committee of the Red Cross, Geneva, email shop@icrc.org. **17** de Than, *International criminal law*, p. 118. **18** Chapter 5 below.

HISTORICAL CONTEXTS

The attitudes underlying these principles evolved over time, with *ad bellum* predominating over *in bello* for many centuries. In fact, Aristotle is sometimes credited with coining the term 'just war'. He applied it to wars waged by Greeks against non-Greeks, who were considered barbarians.[19] War could be just when waged by virtuous men against less worthy men. Such virtuous men were entitled to extend their rule and to enslave others. Their virtue equated to justice and their wars were just wars. It is easy to see this thinking underlying many expansionary wars during the course of history. War was just when its purpose was to prevent one's own enslavement or to extend one's own rule over lesser people for their own benefit, over people who deserved slavery. War was not an end in itself. The just war had as its objective peace and justice.[20]

The Hellenic Greek approach to just war was somewhat abstract, with its emphasis on moral ends. The Roman approach was more juridical. They developed the concept of just causes, based on contractual obligation.[21] When a wrong was done by one city-state to another or to its citizens, the wronged state was entitled to seek redress. If redress was not forthcoming, it was entitled to go to war to obtain compensation and to punish the offending state for the wrong it had done. A denial of justice provided the just cause, that underpinned the just war. In the Republic, before a war commenced, a college of priests, the *fetiales*, had to determine whether the required conditions for going to war existed. If they did exist, the war is *justum*, in other words legally correct.[22] As in Roman private law, an injured party was entitled to damages, the recovery of which the state could ensure if not voluntarily forthcoming, so, in a dispute between states, the injured state, by a quasi extra-judicial procedure, namely war, could obtain redress. When states were not at war, in other words when they were at peace, they were considered to have made a pact wherein the obligations of both parties were defined. This is reflected in the word *pax*, the etymology of which comes from *pangere*, to make a pact or contract.[23]

---

19 Aristotle, *Politics*, I, 7, I255a, 3–I255b, 3; I255b, 37–40; I, 9, II256b, 23–6; VII, I4, I333a, 30, 35; I333b, 37–II334a, 3, I5; idem, *De Rhetorica ad Alexandrum*, 2, I425a, Io–I6; idem, *Nicomachean ethics*, X, 7, II77b, 9–II. See also Joachim von Elbe, 'The evolution of the concept of the just war in international law', *American Journal of International Law*, 33:4 (October 1939), pp 665–88, in which he writes 'Aristotle speaks of the "art of war" which ought to be practised "against men, who, though intended by nature to be governed, will not submit; for war of such kind is naturally just". (*Politics*, I, 3, 8)'. **20** See F.H. Russell, *The just war in the Middle Ages* (Cambridge, 1975), pp 3–4. **21** C. Philippson, *The international law and customs of ancient Greece and Rome* (2 vols, London, 1911), i, 376; Russell, *Just war*, p. 4. **22** Russell, *Just war*, pp 4–5; von Elbe, 'Concept of the just war', p. 666. **23** Philippson, *International law*, ii, 200, 233 and 337; Russell, *Just war*, pp 4–5. See also M. Ní Dhonnchadha's comments on this in 'The *Lex Innocentium:* Adomnán's law for women, clerics and youths, 697 AD' in M. O'Dowd and S. Wichert (eds), *Chattel, servant or citizen: women's status in church, state and society* (Belfast, 1995), pp 58–69 and p. 64; eadem, 'Birr and the Law of the Innocents', p. 20, in which she compares the etymology of *pax* to the etymology of *cáin* and *síocháin*, the Irish word

Cicero developed the Roman concept of just war further. A war was not just unless it was declared.[24] Just cause included the recovery not only of lost goods but also lost honour.[25] As war was occasioned by a wrong or injustice on the part of the enemy, its pursuit was a pious duty.[26] In that context, Cicero did stipulate that it had to be waged honourably. For him there were some *in bello* considerations. Virtue and courage were admired rather than base means or treachery. After a siege, only those who resisted were to be punished. Those who did not were to be spared.[27] However, the declaration of war abrogated the enemies' rights and there was no obligation to respect them. Civilians could be killed or enslaved and their land forfeited to the Roman state.[28] In the case of barbarians, with whom Rome had no legal relations, no legal protection existed; so also with pirates. For instance, Ulpian (d. AD 228) defined *hostes* as those against whom Rome publically declared war or who had declared war on the Romans. Other enemies were classified as *latrunculi* and *praedones*, robbers and brigands, who were not accorded the rights of public enemies and were beyond the pale of Roman law.[29] As Frederick H. Russell points out, 'The lumping together in Roman minds of two dissimilar legal categories of brigands and barbarians served as a model for later Christian hostility to pagans, infidels, rebels and heretics'.[30]

Chapter 2 below considers attitudes to violence and warfare in the late antique and early medieval periods, in an effort to understand the attitudes that would have informed Adomnán's thinking in late seventh-century Ireland. However, a few points are necessary at this juncture in order to contextualize this broader discussion. It will be clear that a certain tension existed between the pacifist traditions of the early church as exemplified by Origen (c.185–253/5) and Tertullian (c.150–c.240),[31] on the one hand, and the attempt made by later writers such as Ambrose of Milan (337–97) and Augustine of Hippo (354–430) to accommodate Christian

---

for peace. **24** Cicero, *De Officiis*, I, II, 36: '*Nullum bellum esse iustum nisi quod aut rebus repetitis geratur aut denunciatum ante sit et interdictum*'. **25** A. Nussbaum, 'Just war – a legal concept?', *Michigan Law Review*, 42 (1943), p. 454. **26** A. Heuss, 'Die völkerrechtlichen Grundlagen der römischen Aussenpolitik in republikanisher Zeit', *Klio*, supplement 31 (1933), pp 19–21; Russell, *Just war*, p. 5. **27** Cicero, *De Officiis*, I, II, 35; 1, 24, 82. **28** Philippson, *International law*, ii, 243; Russell, *Just war*, p. 7. **29** Ulpian expanded this definition from that of Pomponius; both were enshrined in Justinian's *Digest*, 49, 15, 24; 50, 16, 118 and 234. In general, see J. Gaudemet, 'L'étrangers au bas empire', *Recueils Bodin*, 9 (1958), pp 207–35. **30** Russell, *Just war*, p. 8. E.g., canon 27 of the Third Lattern Council of 1179. **31** Works on attitudes in the early church include: R.H. Bainton, 'The early church and war', *Harvard Theological Review*, 39 (1946), pp 189–213; idem, *Christian attitudes to war and peace* (Nashville, TN, 1960), pp 67–81; A. Harnack, *Militia Christi: die Christliche Religion und der Soldatenstand in den ersten drei Jahrhunderten* (Tübingen, 1905); C.J. Cadoux, *The early Christian attitude to war* (London, 1919); E.A. Ryan, 'The rejection of military service by the early Christians', *Theological Studies*, 13 (1952), pp 1–32; S. Windass and J. Newman, 'The early Christian attitude to war', *Irish Theological Quarterly*, 29 (1962), pp 235–47; S. Windass, *Christianity versus violence: a social and historical study of war and Christianity* (London, 1964), ch. 1. See also: Origen, *Contra Celsum*, VII, 26; idem, *Homilia in Jesu Nave*, XV, 1; idem, *Patrologia Graeca*, 12, p. 897; Tertullian, *Adversus Marcionem*, IV, 16.

teaching with the realities of Roman citizenship in the post-Constantinian Roman world. Ambrose saw the orthodox Roman emperor as the bulwark of the *Pax Romana*, standing steadfast against, not only the pagan and the barbarian, but also the heretic. Subsequent to the Edict of Thessalonica in 381, to be a heretic was to be a traitor to Rome.[32] Clearly a war against any of these categories would be a just war. For Augustine, as we will see, war was just when it restrained sinners from evil, even against their will, provided there was no malice or love of revenge or taking pleasure in suffering in the heart of the Christian soldier.[33] While Augustine's writings are complex and open to differing interpretations, it will be clear, in Chapter 2, that he widened the circumstances in which a war could be considered just by including among the wrongs that could be avenged not only illegal acts but also immoral and sacrilegious acts. In Russell's view Augustine argued that the subjective guilt of the enemy merited punishment of the enemy population without regard to the distinction between soldiers and civilians.[34] Augustine's just war thinking found an expression, having been tempered, developed and revived over the centuries, in Pope Urban II's preaching of the First Crusade at Clermont in 1095. A Christian knight was urged to abandon war at home and to fight a righteous war against the infidel. In return for this he was assured of a spiritual reward in heaven. This was the ultimate 'just war'.[35] Almost perversely, it was, also, an expression of the pacifist Christian tradition of which the Truce of God movement, a century or so earlier, was a manifestation.[36] That movement sought to limit warfare between Christians, as did Urban at Clermont by directing the fighting men away from violence among themselves at home and towards the infidel in Jerusalem.[37]

32 Russell, *Just war*, pp 13–15. See J.P. Migne (ed.), *Patrologia Latina* (221 vols, Paris, 1844–65), xiv, 816f.; xv, 1898f.; xvi, 686, 880, 87–90, 119, 170 and 173f. F.H. Dudden, *Life and times of Saint Ambrose* (2 vols, Oxford, 1935); N.B. McLynn, *Ambrose of Milan: church and court in a Christian capital* (Berkeley and Los Angeles, 1994). **33** For an excellent introduction to Augustine see P.R.L. Brown, *Augustine of Hippo* (London, 1967). Augustine and just war have been the subject of considerable scholarly attention: R. Regout, *La Doctrine de la Guerre Juste de Saint Augustin à nos jours, d'après les Théologiens et les Canonistes Catholiques* (Paris, 1935); H. Deane, *The political and social ideas of St Augustine* (New York, 1963), ch. 5; Windass, *Christianity versus violence*, ch. 2; R.S. Hartigan, 'Saint Augustine on war and killing: the problem of the innocent', *Journal of the History of Ideas*, 27:2 (1966), pp 195–204; P.R.L. Brown, *Religion and society in the age of Saint Augustine* (New York and London, 1972); Russell, *Just war*, pp 16–39; R.A. Markus, 'Saint Augustine's views on the "just war"', *Studies in Church History*, 20 (1983), pp 1–13; J. Langan, 'The elements of St Augustine's just war theory', *Journal of Religious Ethics*, 12:1 (1984), pp 19–38; J.M. Matthox, *Saint Augustine and the theory of just war* (London, 2006). **34** Russell, *Just war*, p. 19. **35** Ibid., p. 36. **36** T. Head and R. Landes (eds), *The peace of god: social violence and response in France around the year 1000* (New York, 1992). For a discussion of the Christian pacifist tradition see Chapter 2 below, and for Peace and Truce of God see Chapter 7. **37** For instance, Fulcher of Chartres quotes Urban as follows, 'Let those who have been accustomed to wage unjust private warfare against the faithful now go against the infidels and end with victory this war … Let those who have been fighting agint their brothers and relatives now fight in a proper way against the barbarians.' A.C. Krey

It is worth recalling what happened when the fighters of the First Crusade took Jerusalem. On 15 July 1099 they entered the city after a long siege. The garrison continued to resist but was eventually overcome with great slaughter. It is not possible to be precise as to the exact extent of the slaughter, but both Christian and Muslim sources attest that the numbers involved were substantial and that women and children were killed indiscriminately.[38] Fulcher of Chartres, not himself an eye-witness, reports that:

> Nearly ten thousand were beheaded in this temple (Temple of Solomon). If you had been there your feet would have been stained to the ankles in the blood of the slain. What shall I say? None of them were left alive. Neither women nor children were spared.[39]

No hint of regret or remorse at the slaughter is found. On the contrary Raymond of Aguilers, in his eye-witness account, exults in the Christian victory mentioning:

> wonderful sights were to be seen ... Piles of heads, hands and feet ... men rode in blood up to their knees and bridle reins. Indeed, it was a just and splendid judgment of God that this place should be filled with the blood of the unbelievers, since it had suffered so long from their blasphemies.[40]

The Jerusalem massacre can be seen as the ultimate expression of the medieval just war theory, which saw the justness of the cause as the essential ingredient to the exclusion of all others. As Jonathan Riley-Smith has pointed out, crusade propagandists ensured that their arguments conformed to the criteria of Christian violence that had been laid down, including the need for a just cause and a right intention on the part of the fighters. In the case of the crusades, there could be no argument with the justness of the cause, as it had been 'at Christ's command, mediated by the pope as his agent on earth'.[41] Furthermore, participation in the

---

(trans.), *The First Crusade: the accounts of eye-witnesses and participants* (Princeton, 1921), pp 33–40. **38** A. Jotischky, *Crusading and the Crusader States* (Harlow, 2004), p. 60. **39** Fulcher of Chartres, *A history of the expedition to Jerusalem, 1095–1127*, ed. H.S. Fink and trans. F.R. Ryan (Tennessee, 1969), pp 121–2. **40** Raymond of Aguilers, 'On the fall of Jerusalem' in Krey, *The First Crusade*, p. 279. **41** J. Riley-Smith, 'Religious warriors, reinterpreting the Crusades', *The Economist* (23 December 1995), pp 4–5. See idem, *Crusades: idea and reality 1095–1274. Documents of Medieval History*, 4 (London, 1981); *The First Crusade and the idea of crusading* (Philadelphia, 1991); *The Oxford illustrated history of the Crusades* (New York, Oxford, 1995); *The First Crusaders, 1095–1131* (Cambridge, 1997); *The Crusades: a history* (New Haven, 2005). Augustine, of course, was not the only influence on Christian thinking underpinning the Crusades: C. Erdmann, *The origin of the idea of the Crusade* (Princeton, [1935] 1977); N. Housley, *Contesting the Crusades* (Malden, 2006); idem, *Fighting for the Cross: crusading in the Holy Land* (Yale, 2008). C. Tyerman, *God's war: a new history of the Crusades* (Cambridge, MA, 2006). For a medieval viewpoint see *The Historia Ierosolimitana of Baldric of Bourgueil*, ed. S. Biddlecombe (Woodbridge, 2014). For a concise analysis and a full historiography and bibliog-

crusades was seen as a penance, with a substantial spiritual dividend. Fighting was put on the same plane in order of merit as prayer, works of mercy and fasting. From a situation where the early church had struggled to justify fighting, it now became a duty that should be undertaken as a penance to expiate sin.[42] This, it must be suggested, was a manifestation of the primacy of *ad bellum* considerations over *in bello* at its most extreme.

The Western mindset, therefore, was dominated from antiquity, into early and medieval Christian times, by the concept *jus ad bellum*, to the virtual exclusion of *jus in bello*.[43] Hugo Grotius (1583–1645), the Dutch jurist often credited as being one of the original international lawyers, as late as the seventeenth century, argued for four justifications for war: defence, recovery of property, recovery of debts and punishment.[44] In short, the subjective notion of the right to wage war in pursuit of certain causes *precluded* the emergence of an independent *jus in bello*.[45]

But this changed. Tentative moves towards change appeared in the writings of Francisco Vitoria (1492–1546),[46] Ayala (1548–84),[47] and Francisco Suarez (1548–1617).[48] These jurists questioned methods of warfare that were excessively disproportionate relative to military necessity. They, along with Piero Belli (1502–75)[49] and Alberico Gentili (1552–1608),[50] made the distinction between combatants and non-combatants and recognized the ideal that the latter should enjoy a measure of protection. Grotius himself wrote:

> Though there may be circumstances, in which absolute justice will not condemn the sacrifice of lives in war, humanity will require that the greatest precaution should be used against involving the innocent in danger, except in cases of extreme urgency ... it behoves all Christian Princes to prohibit all unnecessary effusion of blood ... Age [i.e., the old and children] and sex [i.e., women] are equally spared ... the same rule may be laid down with respect to males whose modes of life ... are remote from the use of arms.[51]

raphy see A.A. Latham, 'Theorizing the Crusades: identity, institutions, and religious war in medieval Latin Christendom', *International Studies Quarterly*, 55 (2011), pp 223–43. **42** J. Riley-Smith, 'Religious warriors', p. 5; Tyerman, *God's war*, p. 72. **43** Kolb, 'Twin terms', p. 1. See also P. Haggenmacher, *Grotius et la Doctrine de la Guerre Juste* (Paris, 1983); idem, 'Mutations du concept de guerre juste de Grotius à Kant', *Cahiers de Philosophie Politique et Juridique*, 10 (1986), pp 107–22. For a fuller treatment of this see Houlihan, 'Jurisprudence', pp 10–12. **44** Kolb, 'Twin terms', p. 1. See H. Bull, B. Kingsbury and A. Roberts (eds), *Hugo Grotius and international relations* (Oxford, 1990). **45** Kolb, 'Twin terms', p. 2. **46** F. de Vitoria, *De Iure Belli Relectiones*, ed. A. Pagden, *Vitoria: political writings* (Cambridge, 2012), nos. 15ff (lawful motives of war) and nos. 34ff. See Haggenmacher, *Grotius*, pp 607–8. **47** B. Ayala (1582), *Three books on the laws of war* (Washington, 1912), p. 107 and Book 1: V: 25, cited in Gillespie, *Laws of war*, ii, 134. **48** F. Suarez, 'De bello' in J.B. Scott, *Selections from three works of Francisco Suarez: original Latin text* (Oxford, 1944), i, 7, 15, 16 and section VII: 6, cited in Gillespie, *Laws of war*, ii, 134. **49** P. Belli (1563), *A treatise on military matters and warfare*, trans. H.C. Nutting (Oxford, 1936), pp 15 and 63, cited in Gillespie, *Laws of war*, ii, 134. **50** G. Van-der-Melen, *Alberico Gentili and the development of international law* (Amsterdam, 1930), pp 142–50. **51** Grotius, *De*

Real change, however, was largely the product of the eighteenth-century Enlightenment. Christian Wolff (1679–1754) was the first to see rights and duties *durante bello* as being independent of underlying causes of war.[52] Emerich de Vattel (1714–67) proposed a series of rules setting legal restrictions on means of warfare.[53] Furthermore, Immanuel Kant (1724–1804) made an explicit and modern distinction between the two branches of law (*Recht zum Krieg* and *Recht im Kriege*).[54]

Gradually just war theories gave way to the view that it was the sovereign's inherent right to wage war. States had discretionary powers to wage war and those powers could be used as a means of pursuing national policies. This was the era of *raison d'état*.[55] The foremost exponent of this view was Carl von Clausewitz (1780–1831), a Prussian veteran of the Napoleonic wars raised in the spirit of the Enlightenment. He spent his years of retirement composing what was destined to become the most famous book on war ever written, called *On war*. For him war was the continuation of politics by other means.[56] His work (not totally unlike Machiavelli's *The art of war*)[57] was hugely influential in the nineteenth century. However, a by-product of this thinking, which saw war as a *de facto* and morally neutral situation, was to shift the legal emphasis from the subjective lawfulness of resorting to war to the rights and duties relating to hostilities as such, in other words to rights and duties during war.[58] What now became important was the formal regulation of war, including both the opening of hostilities and the effects of war. Because of the indifference to the moral causes of war, space was opened for attention to be paid to the conduct of hostilities. Once causes, motives and ends were disregarded, armed violence came to be seen, first and foremost, as a process to be regulated in itself.[59] This acceptance of the fact of warfare and of the king's or sovereign's right to wage it echoes attitudes in seventh-century Ireland, as will be apparent in Chapters 3 and 4.

In 1859, Henry Dunant (1828–1910) was present to experience the aftermath of the battle of Solferino, one of the bloodiest battles of the nineteenth century.[60] He subsequently wrote his book, *A memory of Solferino*, and went on to found what was to become the International Committee of the Red Cross (ICRC) in 1863, the organization that is, in many ways, to this day the custodian of IHL.[61] The same year saw the first attempt (in modern times) to lay down specific

---

Jure, trans. W. Whewell (London, 1913), pp 360–3, cited in Gillespie, *Laws of war*, ii, 135. **52** C. Wolff, *Jus Gentium Methodo Scientifica Pertractatum* (1749), trans. T. James (Oxford, 1934), paras 888ff. See Haggenmacher, *Grotius*, pp 607–8. **53** E. de Vattel, *Le Droit des Gens* (1758), trans. J.B. Scott (Oxford, 1916), iii, ch. 8. See Haggenmacher, *Grotius*, pp 609–10 and idem, 'Mutations', p. 119. **54** I. Kant, *Metaphysek der Sitten, Rechtslehre*, trans. M.J. Gregor (Cambridge, 1991), paragraph 53. **55** Kolb, 'Twin terms', p. 2. **56** J. Keegan, *A history of warfare* (London, 1994), p. 324; C. von Clausewitz, *On war*, trans. J.J. Graham (London, 1908); A. Holmes, *Carl von Clausewitz's 'On war': a modern day interpretation of a strategy Classic* (Oxford, 2010); U. Hartmann, *Carl von Clausewitz and the making of modern strategy* (Potsdam, 2002). **57** Keegan, *Warfare*, p. 353. **58** Haggenmacher, *Grotius*, p. 599 and p. 605; idem, 'Mutations', p. 117. **59** Haggenmacher, *Grotius*, p. 599. **60** Gillespie, *Laws of war*, i, 155–6. **61** de Than, *International criminal law*, p. 117; A. Cassese, *International law* (Oxford, 2005), p. 428.

humanitarian rules to apply in time of war. This was the *Lieber Code*, drafted by Professor Francis Lieber and, after revision by a board of officers, promulgated as General Orders no. 100 of the Union Army, in the American Civil War.[62] Section II of the Code, containing Articles 31 to 47, provided for the 'protection of persons and especially of women, of religion, the arts and sciences. Punishment of crimes against the inhabitants of hostile countries'. There were also provisions requiring the humane treatment of prisoners of war.[63] While this Code was, of course, a national provision not applicable to other countries, it served as one of the sources of the international actions that were to follow. A conference in Geneva, again in 1863,[64] a convention there in 1864,[65] with additions in 1868,[66] addressed issues involving the treatment of wounded in armies in the field. In 1874, an international conference called by the Russian government met in Brussels and adopted the International Declaration Concerning the Laws and Customs of War,[67] a document that contained many provisions intended to make land warfare more humane. It did not become effective because of lack of ratifications.[68] However, it served as one of the sources for the Regulations attached to the 1899 convention (II) with Respect to the Laws and Customs of War on Land, drafted by the (first) International Peace Conference in The Hague. The Second International Peace Conference followed in 1907 in The Hague.[69] Provisions for wounded and sick in armies and protection of prisoners of war were made in 1929,[70] culminating, as we have seen, in the Four Geneva 'Red Cross' Conventions of 1949.[71] These *in bello* enactments were given impetus by the founding of the League of Nations. After the First World War support for the absolute sovereign right to go to war lost ground to *ad bellum* rules. The problem of recourse to force was at the centre of legal concerns, juxtaposed with *in bello* considerations. The distinction between laws aimed at preventing war and laws and customs of conduct in the course of warfare was thus clearly established.[72] Subsequently, in 1968, a resolution of the General Assembly of the United Nations,[73] inter alia, prohibited attacks against civilian populations as such and required that a distinction must be made at all times between persons taking part in the hostilities and members of the civilian population to the effect that the latter be spared as much as possible. In 1977, with difficulty, agree-

---

62 H.S. Levie, 'History of the law of war on land', *International Review of the Red Cross*, 838 (2000), p. 2. See reprint of the code in D. Schindler and J. Toman, *The laws of armed conflicts* (Geneva, 1988), p. 3. **63** Lieber Code, section 111, articles 49 to 80. **64** Schindler and Toman, *Laws*, p. 275. **65** Ibid., p. 279. **66** Ibid., p. 285. **67** Ibid., p. 25. **68** In 1880, the Institute of International Law completed the drafting of the *Oxford manual on the laws of war on land* (Schindler and Toman, *Laws*, p. 35). This was an unofficial document, but, like the unratified Brussels project, its importance in the drafting of subsequent conventions on the law of war cannot be overestimated. **69** Schindler and Toman, *Laws*, p. 63. **70** Ibid., p 325. This Convention was in force during the Second World War, but a number of the belligerents were not parties to it. **71** Schindler and Toman, *Laws*, p. 373. **72** Kolb, 'Twin terms', p. 3. **73** U.N. General Assembly resolution 2444 (XXIII) of 19 December 1968, reprinted in Schindler and Toman, *Laws*, p. 263.

ment was reached on a number of protocols to the 1949 Conventions, one of which provided for protection of victims of non-international armed conflicts.[74] Indeed, since the conflict in former Yugoslavia, IHL is tending to include internal armed conflict to an increasing extent.[75]

THE CONCEPT IN A MODERN CONTEXT

There is something nebulous about international law; it does not have the means of enforcement that we are used to in our own national laws.[76] It is, and it always will be, somewhat aspirational. There is much truth in the observation of Sir Herach Lauterpacht in 1952 when he said that 'if international law, is, in some ways, at the vanishing point of law, the law of war, is, perhaps even more conspicuously, at the vanishing point of international law'.[77] In a sense all law conducts a battle with force. In domestic law this is true and law generally has the upper hand; so too, in most areas of international law. In war, however, law loses ground to force. Here the best that can be achieved is a mitigation of some of the awful effects of war, which is what the rules of warfare endeavour to do.[78] The relevant word here is 'endeavour', because there are different, and conflicting, attitudes to IHL. Some are positively disposed, others are not, with many nuanced views in between. To complete our legal contextualization of *LxI*, some of these attitudes will now be considered. On the one hand, for instance, there are the views of Michael Walzer and on the other, for example, those expressed by people involved in, and others commenting on, the My Lai massacre (1968).

Walzer sees the *in bello* concept as emanating from universal attitudes of right and wrong.[79] He examines how people have reacted in practice and concludes that they naturally make the distinction between *jus ad bellum* and *jus in bello* to the extent that even enemy combatants, in some circumstances, command our respect.[80] He instances the First World War, where the common soldier tended to look on his counterparts in the opposing army as 'poor sods, just like me'. He can try to kill them, and they can try to kill him. But it is wrong to cut the throats of their wounded or to shoot them down when they are trying to surrender. The enemy soldier, though his war may be criminal, is nevertheless as blameless as oneself. Contrasting this to the Second World War, Walzer recounts how General Dwight Eisenhower refused to meet the captured German General von Arnim – as would have been the normal custom of war – because, in his view, his opponents were 'a completely evil conspiracy'. It did not matter whether von Arnim had fought well; his crime was to have fought at all. By the

---

74 Shindler/Toman, *Laws*, p. 689.   **75** Shaw, *International law*, p. 1192.   **76** In national legal systems there is, inevitably, a procedure for enforcing court judgments laid down in national law and the means, through the police and prison system, for implementing these procedures. Not so in international law.   **77** H. Lauterpacht, 'The problem of the revision of the law of war', *British Yearbook of International Law*, 29 (1952), art. 382, pp 1–46.   **78** Cassese, *International law*, p. 399.   **79** M. Walzer, *Just and unjust wars* (4th ed., New York, 2006), p. 47.   **80** Ibid., p. 38.

same token, it may not matter how Eisenhower fights. Against an evil conspiracy, what is crucial is to win. But, Walzer asks, what of General Erwin Rommel, a man, to this day, held by many in high regard. He never colluded with the iniquities of Nazism and disregarded Hitler's orders to kill all enemy soldiers found behind German lines. He fought a bad war well, both militarily and morally. Yet was he not part of the evil conspiracy? To quote the chief British prosecutor at Nuremberg:

> The killing of combatants is justifiable ... only where the war itself is legal. But where the war is illegal ... there is nothing to justify the killing and these murders are not to be distinguished from those of any other lawless robber bands.[81]

However, as Walzer claims, we do not regard Rommel as a bad man. Walzer argues that the explanation for this is that we make a distinction between the justness of the cause and the justness of the behaviour, between *ad bellum* and *in bello*. We view Rommel more benignly because of what Waltzer considers natural universal notions of right and wrong, although, as we will see, these are dependent on context and not always easily transposed to an early medieval setting.

In her work, *An intimate history of killing*, Joanna Bourke describes the My Lai massacre of 1968.[82] Of the many available, this is just one modern massacre of non-combatants, taken as an example.[83] What is primarily relevant is the attitude of mind of the perpetrators and the general public to the *ad bellum* and *in bello* issues involved. Just after 8 a.m. on 16 March 1968, 105 American soldiers of Charlie Company, 11 Brigade of the American Division, entered the village of My Lai, on the north-eastern coast of South Vietnam near the South China Sea.[84] They thought that the village was the base of the 48 Viet Cong Local Forces Battalion. By lunch time they had rounded up and slaughtered around 500 civilians. In that time troops had 'fooled around' and laughed as they sodomized and raped women, ripped vaginas open with knives, bayoneted civilians, scalped corpses and carved 'C Company' or the ace of spades on to their chests. Other soldiers had wept openly as they opened fire on crowds of unresisting old men, women, children and babies. At no stage did these soldiers receive any enemy fire or encounter any form of resistance. After the massacre, they burned their way through a few more villages, reached the sea shore, stripped off and had a swim. 'Rusty' Calley, the leader of the group, felt no remorse: after all, 'what the hell *else* is war than killing people?'. He was incredulous when first accused of mass murder:

---

[81] Quoted in R.W. Tucker, *The law of war and neutrality at sea* (Washington, 1957), p. 6. [82] J. Bourke, *An intimate history of killing* (London, 1999), pp 171–214. [83] See Gillespie, *Laws of war*, ii, 198ff for an account of massacres of civilians in recent years (since 1977) including those occurring in Cambodia, Lebanon, Iraq, the former Yugoslavia, Rwanda and to which must be added, Syria and Yemen. [84] Bourke, *Killing*, p. 172.

> I couldn't understand it. I kept thinking, though. I thought, *Could it be I did something wrong?* I knew that war's wrong. Killing's wrong: I realized that. I had gone to a war, though. I had killed, but I knew *So did a million others*. I sat there, and I couldn't find the key. I pictured the people of My Lai: the bodies, and they didn't bother me. I had found, I had closed with, I had destroyed the VC: the mission that day. I thought, it couldn't be wrong or I'd have remorse about it.[85]

In his autobiographical account of the massacre, *Body count* (1971), Calley recalls that during the morning he came across a colleague Dennis Conti forcing a young mother to give him oral sex. He ordered Conti to 'get on your goddam pants' but wondered 'why I was so damn saintly about it. Rape: in Vietnam it's a very common thing'. It is very revealing how he continues:

> I guess lots of girls would rather be raped than killed any-time. So why was I being saintly about it? Because: If a GI is getting a blow job, he isn't doing his job. He isn't destroying communism ... Our mission in My Lai wasn't perverted, though. It was simply 'Go and destroy it'. Remember the Bible: The Amalekites? God said to Saul, 'Now go ... and utterly destroy all that they have, and spare them not; but slay both man and woman, infant and suckling; ox and sheep, camel and ass. But the people took the spoil' – and God punished them. No difference now: if a GI is getting gain, he isn't doing what we are paying him for. He isn't combat-effective.[86]

Calley omitted to say that he immediately murdered the mother and her child: he was obeying orders, he was destroying communism.[87] He was also, as he saw it, following a tradition that had biblical roots. Calley's thought processes were not unusual,[88] even though he and all army personnel had been issued with cards that 'stressed humanitarian treatment and respect for the Vietnamese people' and stipulated that each individual had to comply with the Geneva Conventions of 1949.[89]

Calley was tried by a military court and sentenced to confinement with hard labour for life for premeditated murder.[90] A *Time* poll in 1970, before Calley's conviction, found that two-thirds of people questioned denied being upset when they heard the details of My Lai: 'incidents such as this are bound to happen in a war', most of them reasoned.[91] Within twenty-four hours of the announcement of Calley's conviction, President Nixon received over 100,000 letters and telegrams, practically all demanding Calley's release. When he was released by

---

85 Ibid., p. 171. 86 W.L. Calley, *Body count* (London, 1971), pp 108–9. 87 Bourke, *Killing*, p. 173. 88 Drill Sergeant Kenneth Hodges, who trained Charlie Company quoted in M. Bilton and K. Sims, *Four hours in My Lai: a war crime and its aftermath* (London, 1992), p. 55, declared Calley and his men to be good soldiers who carried out orders. 89 J. Goldstein, B. Marshall and J. Schwarth (eds), *The Peers Commission Report* (New York, 1976), p. 211. 90 Bourke, *Killing*, p. 172. 91 1,608 people were questioned: 'The war: new support for Nixon', *Time*, 12 January 1970, pp 10–11.

Lex Innocentium: *the concept and its contexts*

presidential order into house arrest, the House of Representatives applauded.[92] As with the crusades, the perceived justness of the cause, fortified by, if not largely motivated by, religious conviction dominated to the exclusion of all other considerations. It has been argued that modern war is directed primarily against civilians,[93] and, indeed, an extensive survey carried out by ICRC and published in December 2016 shows that while there is broad support world-wide for the belief that wars should have limits, only fifty per cent of those interviewed in the permanent member countries of the United Nations Security Council believe that it is wrong to attack enemy combatants in populated areas, knowing that many civilians would be killed.[94] This is the modern context, the starting point or, in a sense, the finishing point, from which Adomnán's ideas can be viewed.

HISTORIOGRAPHY

There is not a substantial body of existing work that addresses the central issue with which this study is concerned: the place of *LxI* in the medieval history of the laws of war. There are, however, a number of short contributions that are directly relevant and others indirectly. In an early commentary on *LxI*, John Ryan concluded that *LxI* was a law for the protection of those who did not bear arms in self-defence, clerics, women and innocent children.[95] He considered that it seems to have been conceived in large part as a law for the protection of non-combatants.[96] Gilbert Márkus developed the concept of innocents, to an extent. Under a heading 'War and peace', he stated the law did not seek to stop war altogether but rather to attempt to enforce *jus in bello*. He goes on to describe the Geneva Convention as the successor of Adomnán's Law.[97]

Two lawyers have published a paper entitled 'Cáin Adomnáin and the laws of war',[98] which, quite rightly, seeks recognition for *LxI* as part of the heritage of international humanitarian law. The paper provides an introduction to seventh-/eighth-century Ireland, to Adomnán and to the vernacular Irish legal system. It discusses the meeting in Birr and the introductory paragraphs in the text of the law. It goes on to consider implementation and offences and liability. Of its nature it is a superficial treatment, written from a modern legal perspective rather than from that of a trained historian. That said, it is a useful short

---

92 Bourke, *Killing*, p. 194. For an up-to-date view of US professional military ethics education, and by way of balance, see R. Wertheimer (ed.), *Empowering our military conscience: transforming just war theory and military moral education* (Farnham, 2010). **93** C. Hedges, *War is a force that gives us meaning* (New York, 2002), p. 28. See also C. Coker, *Humane warfare* (London, 2001), p. 83. **94** 17,000 people were interviewed from conflict-affected areas, UN Security Council member countries (permanent) and Switzerland, and the findings were published in a report entitled *People on war: perspectives from 16 countries* on 5 December 2016. The report is available online from ICRC (forum@icrc.org). **95** J. Ryan, 'The Cáin Adomnáin' in R. Thurneysen et al. (eds), *Studies in early Irish law* (Dublin, 1936), pp 269–76. **96** Ibid., p. 273. **97** Márkus, *Adomnán's 'Law of the Innocents'*, p. 2, n. 4 and p. 8. **98** C. Smith and J. Gallen, 'Cáin Adomnáin and the laws of war', *JHIL*, 16 (2014), pp 63–81.

introduction to *LxI* for the modern international humanitarian lawyer, although caution is required in relation to some of the historical detail.[99] One might quibble with the authors' slight reticence in pressing their case, perhaps because of perceived failure to meet modern legal definitions.[100] Nevertheless, this is a most welcome article, for according recognition to *LxI* as a *jus in bello*.

Of the eighteen papers included in 2010 in Wooding (ed.), *Adomnán of Iona*, arising out of the conference in Iona in 2004, marking the thirteenth centenary of Adomnán's death, only one is devoted exclusively to *LxI*.[101] James E. Fraser writes on 'Adomnán and the morality of war'. It is surprising that *LxI* attracted only one contribution. Fraser's essay is, however, extremely useful. In his view Adomnán accepted the fact of war. He was concerned to limit its effects. Fraser considers that it is far from a hyperbolic exaggeration to liken the law to the Geneva Conventions.[102] Even in a war that Adomnán would consider as just, men must not take it upon themselves to punish innocents. This is to be left to God. It is ironic that we find in this paper the same quotation from the Old Testament as used by 'Rusty' Calley of My Lai fame: we are referred to the Amalekites again.[103] Fraser examines Irish attitudes to warfare and violence, as revealed in Adomnán's writings.

While not addressing directly, in any substantial way, the question of *LxI*'s place in the history of the laws of war, the pioneering contributions of Máirín Ní Dhonnchadha to *LxI* studies must be acknowledged, and in particular her analysis of the guarantor-list contained in the text of *LxI* and the detailed scholarly examination in her PhD thesis.[104] As will be apparent, this study relies heavily on all of her works.

Among historians of the laws of war and of violence generally in the late antique and early medieval West, many of whose works we will encounter in the next chapter, *LxI* is not known.[105] There appears to be only one exception. Mathew Strickland cites *LxI* as the first attempt by the Christian church to protect non-combatants.[106] He states that the Council of Birr anticipated the Peace of God Councils of the later tenth and eleventh centuries. 'Before then, however, Adomnán's law stands in virtual isolation ...'[107] It is very regrettable, however, that he is under the mistaken impression that the text of *LxI* has not survived.[108]

---

99 Ibid., p. 66, where, for instance, Loingsech mac Óengusa is called Loingsech mac Uisnech and is described as sending Adomnán on several diplomatic missions to the king of Northumbria, whereas Finsnechtae Fledach was probably the king in question. **100** Ibid., p. 77. **101** Fraser, 'Adomnán and the morality of war', pp 95–111. **102** Ibid., p. 96. **103** Ibid., pp 105–6. **104** Her works include 'Guarantor-List', 'An edition of *Cáin Adomnáin*', 'The Law of Adomnán: a translation', 'Birr and the Law of the Innocents' and '*Lex Innocentium*'. **105** For a more detailed and comprehensive historiography see Houlihan, 'Jurisprudence', pp 19–30. **106** M. Strickland, 'Rules of war or war without rules? – some reflections on conduct and the treatment of non-combatants in medieval transcultural wars' in H.-H. Kortüm (ed.), *Transcultural wars from the Middle Ages to the 21st century* (Berlin, 2006), pp 114–15. **107** Ibid., p. 115. **108** Ibid., p. 117.

CHAPTER 2

Attitudes to warfare and violence in the early medieval West

When Adomnán enacted his law in 697 he would have been informed by a certain received wisdom with regard to violence and its proper use, common to Western Christianity in general. Any Christian legislator in the Western world, either lay or ecclesiastical, including Adomnán, would have been influenced by inherent attitudes to violence, to killing, to warfare and to the non-combatant. In this chapter, an attempt will be made to identify these attitudes.

Inherent and deeply ingrained in the psyche of the Christian of late antiquity and the early medieval period, and particularly among the Christian leadership, was an antipathy towards the taking of human life, as evidenced by decisions of episcopal councils during the fifth, sixth and seventh centuries.[1] It will be seen how the development of repeatable penance from the earlier position where penance was widely regarded as a once-in-a-lifetime institution, facilitated a nuanced approach to the taking of human life, that had a profound effect on warfare in the Christian West and on attitudes towards the taking of life in battle.[2]

With regard to *LxI* specifically, Máirín Ní Dhonnchadha has speculated that Adomnán's views may have been influenced by Augustine's just war theories, even to the extent of crediting Augustine with having inspired *in bello* considerations.[3] Gilbert Márkus seems to endorse this view.[4] It is proposed, therefore, to examine Augustine's just war theories and have particular regard to what he did and did not say on the question of non-combatants, and indeed, how he may have been interpreted in subsequent years.

It is often possible to obtain some insight into the preoccupations and attitudes of a people by looking at their laws. The period from the sixth to the ninth centuries saw the promulgation of an abundance of written laws in the

---

1 D.S. Bachrach, *Religion and the conduct of war* (Woodbridge, 2003), p. 24. For the relevant church councils and a detailed treatment of this, see pp 28–37 below. 2 Bachrach, *Religion and war* p. 31. See pp 28–37 below, where it will be seen that scholars do not agree on the public versus private penance issue, with some holding that forms of penance other than public once-in-a-lifetime penance were common outside the Insular world. However it is not contested that penitential tariff books were an Insular phenomenon which subsequently spread to the Continent. 3 Ní Dhonnchadha, '*Lex Innocentium*', p. 59; eadem, 'An edition of *Cáin Adomnáin*, pp 210–12. 4 Márkus, *Adomnán's 'Law of the Innocents'*, p. 2, n. 4.

Western world. With the laws of Salic Francia, followed immediately by the Burgundian laws, in the early part of the sixth century, the Germanic peoples continued to make laws through the seventh, eighth and ninth centuries, up to the end of that century, when the laws of Wessex were promulgated under King Alfred.[5] This chapter will look at some of these laws in an attempt to ascertain attitudes to violence towards weaker members of society. It will examine the extent to which the concept of the non-combatant is recognized, and investigate whether there is any provision for protection in time of warfare. It may be of interest also to look briefly at some of these laws that are more or less contemporaneous with *LxI*, for comparison purposes, such as the Saxon Laws of Ine (*c.* 694) and of Wihtred and the Visigothic Laws of Ervig, dating from around the same time.[6]

Finally, some of the contemporary accounts of battle and warfare will be examined to see what they yield up by way of information on what actually happened during the course of conflict, with a view to making a judgment on contemporary attitudes to violence towards non-combatants.[7]

BIBLICAL TRADITION: THE CHRISTIAN AND KILLING

It is not unreasonable to assume that Adomnán was influenced, in his attitudes to warfare and violence, primarily by his Christian faith.[8] What then was the church's attitude to war, to violence and killing in the course of war and, in particular, to the non-combatant, the innocent, at time of war?

---

5 The amount of scholarship directed at these laws is considerable. Works of a general nature include: J. Grimm, *Deutche Rechtsalterthümer* (Göttingen, 1828, repr. Darmstadt, 1983); H. Brunner, *Deutche Rechtsgeschichte: Systematisches Handbuch der deutchen Rechtwissenshaft* (Leipzig, 1882–92); more recently: K. Drew, *Law and society in early medieval Europe: studies in legal history* (London, 1988); M. Lupoi, *Alle Radici del Mondo Giuridico Europeo* (1994), with trans. by A. Belton as *The origins of the European legal order* (Cambridge, 2000). For more specifically directed work see, for example: S. Falk Moore, *Law as process: an anthropological approach* (London and Boston, 1978); S. Roberts, *Order and dispute: an introduction to legal anthropology* (New York, 1979); W. Davies and P. Fouracre (eds), *The settlements of disputes in early medieval Europe* (Cambridge, 1986); W. Brown, *Unjust seizure: conflict, interest and authority in early medieval society* (Ithaca, 2001); P. Wormald, *The making of English law: King Alfred to the twelfth century* (Oxford, 1999); M. Costambeys, *Power and patronage in early medieval Italy: local society, Italian politics and the abbey of Farfa, 700–900* (Stuttgart, 1982); C. Fell, *Women in Anglo Saxon England and the impact of 1066* (Bloomington, 1984); M. Elsakkers, 'Raptus ultra Rhenum: early ninth-century Saxon laws on abduction and rape', *Amsterdamer Beiträge zur Älteren Germanistik*, 52 (1999), pp 27–53; C. Hough, 'Two Kentish laws concerning women: a new reading of Aethelberht 73 and 74', *Anglia*, 119:4 (2001), pp 554–78. Where reference is made to a specific provision of a specific law the relevant original source is noted in part 4 of this chapter. For a comprehensive list of the primary sources in the form of edited translations of the laws see bibliography in L. Oliver, *The body legal in barbarian law* (Toronto, 2011), pp 263–9.   **6** G. Halsall, *Warfare and society in the barbarian West 450–900* (Abingdon, 2003), pp 57–8.   **7** See pp 55–8 below for the original sources in question.   **8** See Chapter 4 hereunder.

What did Jesus teach? The New Testament is sparse in its references to war and related matters. On the one hand, Jesus said that he came to bring not peace but the sword.[9] He seemed to teach that government should be left to the civil authorities, 'render unto Caesar the things that are Caesars'[10] and Paul preached submission to government authority as it encouraged right conduct.[11] Luke saw Rome and Christianity co-operating.[12] When soldiers sought the advice of John the Baptist, he did not condemn their profession, merely cautioning them to do violence to no one, to be content with their wages and refrain from false accusations.[13] On the other hand, Jesus taught his followers, in the Sermon on the Mount, to turn the other cheek and not to physically resist evil. He taught them to love their enemies and not judge one another.[14] Peter was commanded to sheath his sword, as those who lived by the sword died by it.[15] As we shall see below when considering Augustine, an attempt was made by him to accommodate the wars of the Old Testament in his synthesis of Christian teaching, but the New Testament gave no clear message to the early Christian.

How did early Christians interpret Christ's teaching with regard to violence and war? This can best be answered by looking at how they responded to the problem of military service in the armies of the Roman Empire. Did they willingly serve, reluctantly serve or refuse to serve? This question has been comprehensively addressed by E.A. Ryan and others.[16] Initially the problem did not arise to any significant extent. In the early days most Christians were converts from Judaism and were still regarded as Jews by the authorities. They consequently benefited from the exemption of the Jews from military service.[17] Later they did not participate with the Jews in the rebellion of 66–70, in keeping with their tradition of loyalty to established authority. The same applied to the Jewish revolt of 132–5. Both Ryan and Bainton are agreed that very few Christians, apart from some converted soldiers and their sons, participated in the army up to the period 170–80.[18] This did not cause problems with the authorities because the Roman armies, during this period, were massed on the far-flung corners of the empire, where there was an adequate supply of recruits and where, generally speaking, the Christian population was small. This was a time of relative peace and 'The Roman military formations could be filled without recourse to the Christian minority'.[19] Apart from this, Christians would not subject themselves to participating in the normal military practices of emperor-worship and sacrifice to the

9 Matthew 10:34. **10** Mark 12:17. **11** Romans 13:1–4. **12** Luke 2:1; 22:24–8. **13** Luke 3:14. **14** Matthew 5:39; 7:1; cf. Luke 6:27–9; Romans 14:13. **15** Matthew 26:52. **16** E.A. Ryan, 'The rejection of military service by the early Christians', *Theological Studies*, 13 (1952), pp 1–32. See also: Harnack, *Militia Christi*; C.J. Cadoux, *The early Christian attitude to war* (London, 1919); R.H. Bainton, 'The early church and war', *Harvard Theological Review*, 39 (1946), pp 189–213; idem, *Christian attitudes toward war and peace* (Nashville, 1960); S. Windass and J. Newman, 'The early Christian attitude to war', *Irish Theological Quarterly*, 29 (1962), pp 235–47; S. Windass, *Christianity versus violence: a social and historical study of war and Christianity* (London, 1964). **17** Ryan, 'Military service', p. 7. **18** Bainton, 'Church and war', p. 190; Ryan, 'Military service', p. 9. **19** Ryan, 'Military service', p. 10.

Gods. In any event, from the time of Nero (54–68) the practice of Christianity was a crime in the empire, carrying severe punishment. It was far easier to keep a low profile in the civilian world than in the military. In these relatively early days, therefore, the problem of military service was not a major immediate issue. The taking of a definitive position on it could be postponed. The involvement of Christians in the army was, as a matter of practice, limited.

By c.180 this was changing. The numbers of Christians in the empire was increasing, and gradually, their numbers in the army. The church now had to face the questions as to whether convert soldiers should remain in the army and how should Christians react if conscripted. Was it permitted for a Christian to volunteer? Rome was now fighting defensive wars in the West and against the Persian threat in the East. Many Christians saw that they had a vested interest in defending the empire. Nevertheless, the pagan practices of the army and the danger of discovery were seen as problems; not to mention any doctrinal difficulties about participating in killing and violence.[20]

There is no doubt that pure pacifism was an important part of the early church.[21] Two writers best exemplify this: Tertullian (c.160–220) and Origen (185–254). Tertullian was outspokenly hostile to military service, and that for 'reasons which derive in part from what he considered to be the nature of Christianity, rather than from the difficulties in which life in the Roman camps involved a Christian soldier'.[22] He believed that loyalty to God and the military oath were mutually exclusive; a Christian cannot serve two masters, God and Satan; a soldier must have a sword and a Christian cannot because Christ disarmed Peter. In his *De idolatria* Tertullian developed his pacifist thinking and articulated it even more positively in his *De corona*: the Christian who has taken the oath to Christ in baptism cannot take a second one.[23] For Origen, Christians must keep their hands free from blood. This does not preclude them from interceding with God for the righteous cause, but they must not themselves participate in violence.[24]

There were others, apart from Tertullian and Origen. For instance, Hippolytus (c.170–235) says:

> A soldier of the government must be told not to execute men, if he should be ordered to do it. He must be told not to take the military oath. If he will not agree, let him be rejected. If a catechumen, or a baptized Christian wishes to become a soldier, let him be cast out. For he has despised God[25]

---

20 Ibid., pp 13–14. On early Christian hostility to military service see also Russell, *Just war*, pp 10–12; C.J. Cadoux, *The early Christian attitude to war: a contribution to the history of Christian ethics* (New York, 1982). **21** Ryan, 'Military service', p. 17. See Bainton, *War and peace*, pp 66–84. **22** Ryan, 'Military service', p. 17. **23** Ibid., p. 18; Tertullian, *De idolatria* 19 in *CSEL* 20, ed. A. Rieffersheid and G. Wissowa (Vienna, 1890), p. 53; idem, *De idolatria*, ed. and trans. J.H. Waszink and J.C.M. Van Winden (Leiden, 1987); idem, *De corona* 11 in *CSEL* 70, ed. E. Kroymann (Vienna, 1942), pp 175–8. **24** Origen, *Contra Celsum* VIII, 73 in *GCS*, *Origenes* II, ed. P. Koetschau (Berlin, 1899); Ryan, 'Military service', p. 20. **25** Hippolytus,

Very often these strictures were ignored and many Christians joined the army of the empire and participated in its activities, to a lesser or greater extent. But there were those who did not and some of them, like Maximilianus (d. 295), died for their beliefs.[26]

During the last quarter of the third century and before the final persecution under Diocletian, Christians were allowed considerable latitude in the empire. They were entrusted with the government of provinces and allowed dispense with offering sacrifice.[27] In the army they were often tacitly exempted from pagan ritual. More and more Christians joined the ranks. As Ryan comments, 'The Church authorities accepted the situation in silence'.[28] Between 303 and 311 this was drastically, but temporarily, reversed. Many Christians were persecuted during these years; those in the army were particularly targeted because it was felt that the presence of Christians in the army weakened it.[29]

But fundamental and far-reaching change was at hand. In 306, Constantius Chlorus, father of Constantine the Great, died in Britain, and Constantine was acclaimed by the army. By 313, Constantine, having made himself sole ruler in the West, introduced a policy of toleration towards all cults, including Christianity, and persuaded Licinius, the pagan Eastern emperor, to do likewise. After the civil war (323–4) and the defeat of Licinius, Constantine became sole ruler of the entire empire and the position of Christians within it was assured.[30] In the army, Christian soldiers were free to practise their faith.[31] In fact, gradually, army practices were subtly changed by adding to the army oath a clause by which soldiers swore, not only to be faithful to the emperor, never to desert and to be willing to die for the good of the Roman state, but also to carry out their duties by God, Christ, and the Holy Spirit.[32] Changes were made in the traditional military standards by replacing them with the Chi-Rho symbol of the new faith. These changes were gradual and pagan practices continued in some instances into the fifth century.[33]

How did the church authorities react to the new dispensation for their members in the imperial army? Did they encourage participation or did they still hold reservations? Ryan is unequivocal in his response to this question. He states that the church spoke its mind on the licity of military service. He argues from the apparent absence of any conciliar decree against military service, and from a decree of the Council of Arles (314) excommunicating deserters even in time of peace, that there can be no doubt as to the attitude of the church.[34]

Apostolic tradition, ed. G. Dix (London, 1937); Ryan, 'Military service', p. 20. **26** Ryan, 'Military service', p. 1. **27** Ibid., p. 25. **28** Ibid., p. 26. **29** Ibid., p. 27. See W.H.C. Frend, *Martyrdom and persecution in the early church* (Oxford, 1965). **30** H. Chadwick, 'The early Christian community' in J. McManners (ed.), *The Oxford illustrated history of Christianity* (Oxford, 1990), pp 55–6. **31** Ryan, 'Military service', p. 27. **32** Bachrach, *Religion and war*, p. 9. See Eusebius, *Vita Constantini*, ed. F. Winkelman (*GCS*, 1975). **33** Bachrach, *Religion and war*, pp 9–10. See also M. McCormick, *Eternal victory: triumphal rulership in late antiquity, Byzantium, and the early medieval West* (Cambridge, 1986) for a study of the gradual nature of Constantine's efforts at Christianization and the enduring role of traditional imperial symbolism. **34** Ryan, 'Military service', p. 28.

While the church may not have opposed military service, its position on killing, during the course of that service, is far less clear-cut. Christian authorities, in the centuries following the acceptance of Christianity in the Roman Empire, and into the early Middle Ages, consistently condemned the taking of human life, even in a war that was considered just.

> Whoever takes a human life is to be excluded from the communion of the Church until cleansed through penance. (Canon I of the Concilium Veneticum, c.465).[35]

This clear condemnation of the taking of human life made it impossible for Christian legislators to have a nuanced approach to killing, such as would view violence towards innocents as more reprehensible than towards, for instance, enemy soldiers. In many cases bishops refused to distinguish between types of killing, grouping together all forms of taking a human life, including killing in the course of war, under the rubric of *homicidio*.[36]

Bishops continued to take an exceptionally rigid view towards the sinfulness of taking human life, but, gradually, they began to view *homicidio* in a more nuanced way. In the Council of Arles in 541 the bishops, while continuing to maintain that *homicidio* still meant the taking of a human life, distinguished, at least implicitly, between killing those who were innocent and those who were not innocent. Those who killed an innocent person were said to commit homicide *voluntarily*.[37] A similar distinction was made at the Council of Clichy (626–7), although this was from a later period.[38]

The church's strictures on killing, even in the course of a just war, had, of course, serious implications for a soldier in the service of the empire or of the successor kingdoms. Not only was his life in danger when he went to battle, but also his soul. The situation was made much more difficult because the Christian soldier did not have a means of cleansing his soul, either before going into battle or after it. The sacrament of penance was not acceptable. It was a once-in-a-lifetime sacrament. Furthermore it involved fasting, abstinence and prayer for the remainder of the penitent's life.[39] If the penitent fell back into sin, his position

---

35 *Concilium Veneticum*, ed. J.P. Mansi in *Sacrorum Conciliorum Nova et Amplissima Collectio* 7 (Florence, 1762), col. 953, '… *a communione ecclesiastica submovendos, nisi poenitentia satisfactione crimina admissa diluerint'*. See Bachrach, *Religion and war*, p. 1 and p. 24. **36** Bachrach, *Religion and war*, p. 24. See also R. Kottje, *Die Tötung im Kriege: Ein moralisches und rechtliches Problem im frühen Mittelalter* (Barsbüttel, 1991); J.A. Brundage, 'The hierarchy of violence in twelfth- and thirteenth-century canonists', *International History Review*, 17 (November 1995), pp 678–9; G.I.A.D. Draper, 'Penitential discipline and public wars in the Middle Ages. A medieval contribution to the development of humanitarian law', *International Review of the Red Cross* (1961), p. 16. **37** F. Maassen (ed.), *Concilium Aurelianense* in *MGH, Concilia Aevi Merovingici* (Hanover, 1893), p. 93, *quisquis homicidium voluntatecommiserit*. **38** *Concilium Clippiacense* in *Concilia Aevi Merovingici*, p. 198. **39** Bachrach, *Religion and war*, p. 25. See also: P. Cramer, *Baptism and change in the early Middle Ages, c.200–c.1400* (Cambridge, 1993); B. Poschman,

was irredeemable. Indeed, many aspiring Christians postponed baptism until the end of their lives. Constantine the Great was not baptized until he was on his deathbed in 337.[40] There was, therefore, an inherent contradiction between Christian practice and military service.[41] The church persisted in its stance against repeatable penance, the decree to that effect in Nicea in 325 being endorsed by the Council of Arles in 538, when it decreed that anyone who accepted penance, and subsequently returned to secular life and military service, was excommunicated until the end of his life.[42] The relapsed penitent who returned to secular life was described as a 'dog returning to his vomit' in the Council of Tours in 461 and he was to be excluded from the communion of the church and, indeed, from any association with the faithful.[43] A similar position was taken by the Council of Yenne in 517.[44]

The church's attitude to killing combined with its rejection of repeatable penance created major difficulties for laypeople, including soldiers and their pastors. It is suspected that the normative position differed considerably from what happened in reality. By the mid-fifth century, bishops and priests sought to develop strategies by which the strictures of the church could be circumvented. Bishop Rusticus of Narbonne (427–61) wrote to Pope Leo I (440–61) seeking advice on, inter alia, the position of a member of his congregation who, as a soldier, had to choose between penance, and thereby the end of his career, and death in battle in a state of sin. Leo replied that 'it is completely contrary to all the rules of the church for a soldier to return to duty after receiving penance'.[45] While Leo was repeating the church's long-held position, the fact of the correspondence shows that the issue was current and that solutions outside the strict letter of the law were being sought. In a letter to Bishop Salonius of Geneva, Salvian of Marseilles (d. c.480) refers to the less onerous gifts and works of mercy that were available to laypeople ill-equipped to undergo the full rigor of penitential life.[46] Caesarius of Arles (502–42) refers to a sermon by Bishop Faustus of Riez (d. c.500) in which the preacher refers to a query from a young married man, in the context of a call to everyone to the penitential life, as to the efficacy of such good deeds as almsgiving, fasting and prayer.[47] Caesarius stopped short from saying that these repeatable rites could replace sacramental penance. Pope

---

Penance and the annointing of the sick, trans. and rev. F. Courtney (New York, 1964), pp 81–116; C. Vogel, *Le Pécheur et la Pénitence dans l'Eglise Ancienne* (Paris, 1966), pp 27–54; P. Rouillard, *Histoire de la Pénitence des Origins à Nos Jours* (Paris, 1996), pp 27–33. **40** Chadwick, 'The early Christian community', p. 59. **41** Bachrach, *Religion and war*, p. 25. **42** *Concilium Aurelianense* in *Concilia Aevi Merovingici*, p. 81, *Si quis paenetentiae benedictione suscepta ad saeculare habitum miliciamque reverti praesumpserit, viatico concesso usque ad exitum excummunicatione plectatur*. **43** *Concilium Turonicum* in Mansi, *Sacrorum* 7, col. 946. **44** *Concilium Epaonense* in *Concilia Aevi Merovingici*, p. 24. **45** Bachrach, *Religion and war*, p. 26. See Pope Leo I, *Epistolae* in PL 54, cols 1199–1200. **46** Bachrach, *Religion and war*, p. 27. See Salvian of Marseilles, *Oeuvres*, ed. G. Lagarrigue in *Sources Chrétiennes*, 176 (Paris, 1971), p. 124. **47** Bachrach, *Religion and war*, p. 27. See Caesarius of Arles, *Sermones*, ed. G. Morin in *CCSL*, 103 (2 vols, Turnhoult, 1953), i, 250.

Gregory the Great (590–604), in an address to the people of Rome, urged them to confess their sins and to enhance their prayers with the merit of their good works, pointing to the people of Nineveh, who had obtained mercy for their long-standing sins after a penance of just three days.[48] In fact, the clear-cut distinction between canonical penance (public) and private penance has not been universally accepted by scholars. Rob Meens has argued for a more complex view on the position of penance in the early medieval period.[49] He suggests that canonical penance was not the only means by which forgiveness of sins could be obtained. Other methods included the giving of alms, fasting and caring for the sick. Significantly, however, it appears that public penance continued to be required for serious sins of a public nature, such as murder, adultery and honouring pagan cults. For instance, he points to the sermons of Caesarius of Arles in this regard.[50] Indeed, the preference for public penance for public sins seems to have persisted into the Carolingian period.[51]

Ultimately the predicament posed by the twin doctrines of the sinfulness of taking human life in all circumstances and once-in-a-lifetime penance was resolved, not by taking the sin out of killing, which was retained in modified form, but by the introduction of repeatable penance. This was done by way of the penitentials.[52] These were manuals that were initially popularized in the Insular world, containing lists of sins and provided a corresponding penalty for each sin. Once the sinner had completed the appropriate penance, the sin was expiated and he or she was reconciled with God and the church. This could be repeated if he or she sinned again.[53] All manner of sins were included in the penitentials, which can be categorized into idolatrous practices, sexual irregularities and violence in many forms.[54] It was possible, therefore, indeed necessary, to dif-

---

48 Bachrach, *Religion and war*, p. 28. For this address, preserved by Gregory of Tours, see his *Historia Francorum*, ed. W. Arndt and B. Krusch in *MGH SRM*, 10:1. See also idem, *Histories*, trans. L. Thorpe in *Gregory of Tours: The history of the Franks* (London, 1974).   **49** R. Meens, *Penance in medieval Europe, 600–1200* (Cambridge, 2014); idem, 'The Irish contribution to the penitential tradition' in R. Flechner and S. Meeder (eds), *The Irish in early medieval Europe* (London, 2016), pp 131–45. See also S. Hamilton, *The practice of penance, 900–1050* (London, 2001).   **50** Meens, *Penance*, pp 34–6.   **51** Meens, 'Irish contribution', pp 141–2.   **52** Bachrach, *Religion and war*, p. 28; see also: O.D. Watkins, *A history of penance* (2 vols, London, 1920), ii, 632–62; B. Poschmann, *Die abendländische Kirchenbue im frühen Mittelalter* (Breslau, 1930), pp 73–91; R. Pierce (McKitterick), 'The "Frankish" penitentials' in D. Baker (ed.), *Studies in Church History*, 11 (Oxford, 1975), pp 31–9; P. Rouillard, *Histoire de la Penitence des Origins à Nos Jours* (Paris, 1996), pp 43–8; A. Frantzen, *The literature of penance in Anglo-Saxon England* (New Brunswick, 1983); Hamilton, *The practice*; Meens, *Penance*. For the Irish penitentials see L. Bieler (ed. and trans.), *The Irish penitentials* (Dublin, 1963); J.F. Kenney, *The sources for early history of Ireland: ecclesiastical* (New York, 1929, repr. with corrections, Dublin, 1978 and 1993), pp 235–44; E. Pereira Farrell, 'Taboos and penitence: Christian conversion and popular religion in early medieval Ireland' (PhD, University College, Dublin, 2012); Meens, 'Irish contribution'; Chapter 3 below.   **53** Bachrach, *Religion and war*, pp 28–9. See also C. Stancliffe, 'Religion and society in Ireland' in P. Fouracre (ed.), *The new Cambridge medieval history, c.500–c.700* (7 vols, Cambridge, 2005), i, 406–7.   **54** Draper, 'Penitential discipline', p. 10.

ferentiate between violence of varying gravity and, indeed, between homicides of varying scales of gravity. Thus, for example, one penitential provided, in the case of killing a monk or other cleric, a penance of seven years, the laying down of arms and the dedication of the remainder of the penitent's life to the service of God. In the case of the killing of a layman, the same penitential provided for a penalty of four years' penance.[55] Many penitentials distinguished between homicide occurring during publicly sanctioned warfare or warfare conducted by the king and killing in other situations.[56] Very often – and in this regard there is an unusual consistency – the penalty provided for killing in public wars is a mere forty days.[57] In fact, Draper can conclude: 'Among the many vagaries and inconsistencies to be found in the penitential literature this rule [forty days' penance] was recurrent, persistent and substantially invariable'.[58]

The penitentials spread eastwards from Ireland, having been introduced there probably from western Britain or, possibly, Brittany.[59] From Ireland they appeared in the Anglo-Saxon world and in Francia and beyond, indeed spreading to most of Western Christendom.[60] The Penitential of Columbanus would have been introduced to Francia and Italy as early as the beginning of the seventh century. Kenney states of this penitential: 'Historically, it is a piece of religious legislation of remarkable significance: it marks the introduction of frequent private confession and of the Latin system of church-penance into the early Gallic Church'.[61] Their adoption was gradual. By the late seventh century they were in use in Saxon England, and by the mid-eighth they were being produced in Francia and Italy.[62] Canonical penance (once-in-a-lifetime) was not eclipsed. In 680, Wamba, the Visigothic king of Spain, fell seriously ill and thought he was going to die. He undertook penance and was tonsured. He recovered his health but was prevented recovering his kingdom by the twelfth council of Toledo, which ruled that the penitence and tonsuring must hold and that the penitential state was irrecoverable.[63] Over time attempts were made to adapt and further

---

55 Bachrach, *Religion and war*, p. 29. See F.H.W. Wasserschleben, *Die Bu ordnungen der abendländischen Kirche* (Leipzig, 1851, repr. Graz, 1958), pp 224–5, 294–5. For some discussion regarding the differences in approach to moral questions of killing in the early Middle Ages, see R. Kottje, 'Tötung im Krieg als rechtliches und moralisches Problem im früheren und hohen Mittelalter' in H. Hecker, *Krieg im Mittelalter und Renaissance* (Düsseldorf, 2005), pp 17–39. See Chapter 3 below for a detailed analysis of penalties for killing and other acts of violence in the Irish penitentials.   56 Bachrach, *Religion and war*, pp 29–30. For a detailed treatment of penances imposed on soldiers in the early Middle Ages see Kottje, *Die Tötung im Kriege*. He argues (pp 3–4) against C. Erdmann's assertion in *The origin of the idea of Crusade* (p. 17, n. 32) [orig. *Die Entstehung des Kreuzzugsgedankens* (Stuttgart, 1933)], trans. M.W. Baldwin and W. Goffart (Princeton, 1977) that the penitent soldier was obliged to forego arms and further involvement in war.   57 See Draper, 'Penitential discipline', pp 10–16 for list of relevant penitentals.   58 Draper, 'Penitential discipline', p. 18. See also Halsall, *Warfare*, p. 17.   59 Draper, 'Penitential discipline', pp 6–7; Kenney, *Sources*, p. 239; Bieler, *Irish penitentials*, pp 3–4; Pereira Farrell, 'Taboos and penitence', p. 4; Meens, 'Irish contribution', pp 131–3.   60 Draper, 'Penitential discipline', p. 7.   61 Kenney, *Sources*, p. 200.   62 Bachrach, *Religion and war*, p. 30; Meens, *Penance*, pp 79–149.   63 R. Collins, 'Julian of Toledo and the royal

refine the penitentials, such as in the case of the Pseudo-Roman Penitential of Hatligar of Cambrai (c.830).[64] In the light of contemporary canonistic discussion of killing, a distinction was made between killing in warfare generally, meriting a three-week fast, and killing in battle to defend oneself and one's close kin, not a sin and hence entailing only voluntary penance.[65] In any event, the penitentials flourished and remained a significant part of Christian life in the West up to the beginning of the thirteenth century, a span of seven hundred years.[66]

It is clear from the foregoing that there remained, in the Christian West, an attitude towards killing in warfare, which saw it as sinful and that this attitude was sufficiently ingrained in Christian thinking from earliest times to see it doggedly maintained into the late Middle Ages.[67] Those who had blood on their hands required cleansing. At first, this inhibited the making of distinctions between different types of killing and gave rise to a theoretical, doctrinal contradiction between the practice of the Christian faith and a soldier's involvement in war, even a war in pursuit of a righteous cause. Repeatable penance, as articulated in the penitentials, provided a mechanism for resolving the contradiction.[68] In the Insular world, where once-in-a-lifetime public penance 'never established itself',[69] nuanced thinking about taking human life was not blocked and the penitentials facilitated and demanded distinctions. Over time, after their initial introduction from Ireland, the penitentials were availed of in the rest of Western Europe as a practical expedient. As Draper says, 'The whole system of penitentials and private penance was in a sense one vast compromise with an all too wicked world that simply would not be yoked by public penance'.[70] It now became possible for Christianity to distinguish attitudinally between different types of killing. The penitentials facilitated and required distinctions. Thus distinctions were made in the case of some categories of people: clerics, Jews and pagans. It is not possible, however, to discern an attitude that specifically and clearly deplored the killing of women and children. There is no evidence of explicit concern for non-combatants as a group, 'no distinction is made between soldier and laic ...'.[71] While the penitentials facilitated nuanced laws on killing, the plight of the non-combatant does not appear to have been recognized in any

succession in late seventh-century Spain' in P. Sawyer and I. Wood (eds), *Early medieval kingship* (Leeds, 1977), p. 38; C. Wickham, *The inheritance of Rome: a history of Europe from 400 to 1000* (London, 2009), p. 130. See Julian of Toledo, *Historia Wambae Regis*, ed. and trans. J. Martinez Pizarro (Washington, 2005). **64** Draper, 'Penitential discipline', p. 8. **65** J.L. Nelson, 'Violence in the Carolingian world and the ritualization of ninth-century warfare' in G. Halsall (ed.), *Violence and society in the early medieval West* (Woodbridge, 1998), p. 101. **66** Draper, 'Penitential discipline', p. 9. **67** Ibid., pp 63–78, as applied to the battles of Soissons (923) and Hastings (1066). **68** Bachrach, *Religion and war*, p. 190. **69** K. Hughes, *Early Christian Ireland: introduction to the sources* (Cambridge, 1972), p. 88; Stancliffe, 'Religion and society', pp 406–7. See also Meens, *Penance*, pp 102–3, citing *Paenitentiale Theodori, Discipulus Umbrensium (U)*, ed. P.W. Finsterwalder in *Die Canones Theodori Cantuariensis* (Weimar, 1929), p. 306, from which it is clear that canonical penance was uncommon in Anglo-Saxon England. **70** Draper, 'Penitential discipline', p. 16. **71** Ibid., p. 11.

such laws outside Ireland, until the Peace of God movement towards the end of the tenth century.[72]

AUGUSTINE

Augustine of Hippo (354–430) is widely regarded as the father of Christian just war theories.[73] As R.A. Markus clearly put it, 'Augustine is the fountain-head of a tradition almost ubiquitous in medieval thought'.[74] Furthermore, he has been mentioned as a possible source of the thinking behind Adomnán's law.[75] It is appropriate, therefore, to examine Augustine's just war theories, with particular regard to how he dealt with *in bello* issues.

Peter Brown in discussing Augustine's attitude to religious coercion, cautions against searching Augustine's writings for a 'doctrine' in a state of rest. There is always movement and change. This, he states, is typical of the general quality of his thought, which 'is marked by a painful and protracted attempt to embrace and resolve tensions'. As a result, Augustine has, over the centuries, been regarded with ambivalence.[76] For this reason Brown abandons the word 'doctrine' and uses instead the word 'attitude'. So too, we must abandon the word 'theory', when applied to Augustine's just war thinking and replace it with 'attitude'. What was the attitude of this 'notoriously complex man' to violence in the context of warfare?[77]

In answering this question it is particularly important to attempt to do so by reference to Augustine's own intellectual and historical background, rather than in the perspective of tradition.[78] Our present question is: what was Augustine's attitude; what were his views? What did he say, write, teach? As R.A. Markus so succinctly puts it, we must, for once, 'turn the telescope the right way round and ... look at Augustine's thinking not in the long perspective of the tradition that his ideas inaugurated, but in the immediate context of his own intellectual biography'.[79]

Augustine's attitudes to warfare are not clearly set out in any one of his writings. Furthermore, no one individual episode during his career prompted his thinking. It is necessary to trawl through forty years of his writings to isolate his attitude to Christian warfare and this must be done, at all times, against the current historical and intellectual background. During his career he was constantly grappling with the complexities of Christian life; he often changed his mind.

---

72 See Chapter 7 below for fuller consideration of the Peace of God movement. **73** F.H. Russell, 'Love and hate in medieval warfare: the contribution of Saint Augustine', *Nottingham Medieval Studies*, 31 (1987), pp 108–24; Hartigan, 'Augustine on war and killing', p. 195. For historiography on Augustine and just war see Chapter 1, n. 33. **74** Markus, 'Saint Augustine's views on "just war"', p. 1. **75** Ní Dhonnchadha, '*Lex Innocentium*', p. 59; eadem, ' An edition of *Cáin Adomnáin*', pp 210–12; Márkus, *Adomnán's 'Law of the Innocents'*, p. 2, n. 4. **76** P.R.L. Brown, 'St Augustine's attitude to religious coercion', *Journal of Roman Studies*, 54 (1964), p. 107. **77** Ibid., p. 109. **78** Markus, 'Saint Augustine's views on "just war"', p. 1. **79** Ibid..

While this presents a difficulty for the historian of his ideas, it is the backdrop of the shifts in his perspective against which these changes are made, or indeed, sometimes, not made, that must be grasped in order fully to understand Augustine's thinking.[80]

Markus discerns three fundamentally different perspectives, providing three different backgrounds against which Augustine's pronouncements on war must be viewed. Augustine's first discussion on the morality of war appears in one of his early philosophical dialogues, *De libero arbitrio*,[81] written in or about 388.[82] Augustine had made up his mind to return to Africa. His 'conversion' had taken place in 386 and he had been baptized in April 387. Later that year his mother Monica had died in Ostia, where Augustine's party had been detained as a result of the blockade of the Roman ports by the usurper Maximus in his civil war with Emperor Theodosius. Intellectually Augustine had rejected the Manichaean explanation for the existence of evil in the world, which denied that God could have created a world in which evil exists. Mani (d. AD 274) taught that God was good, totally innocent. Evil came from a hostile force – the 'Kingdom of Darkness'. The Manichees were dualists: God was untainted by evil, which was the creation of an evil deity.[83] This explanation for the existence of evil Augustine now saw as far too easy.[84] He had turned to the writings of neo-Platonists such as Plotinus (d. AD 270) and Porphyry (d. c.AD 305) who, although pagans, had greatly influenced the Western Christian church and, in particular, such Christian leaders as Ambrose, bishop of Milan. Augustine lived and worked in Milan from 384. Whereas for a Manichee, the individual was entirely merged with the 'substance' of a good God, and everything that could not be identified with this perfection was split off as absolutely and irredeemably evil, the neo-Platonists believed in the existence of eternal principles. Everything in the world of the senses, the changing 'here', is contrasted with the changeless 'there'. The spiritual world was fundamental to the world of place and time, while still remaining distinct from it. In the minds of the avant-garde intellectuals of Milan in the 380s there was a certain synthesis between pagan Platonism and Christianity.[85] Augustine came to see the world as a Christian Platonist. Markus puts it thus:

> The step from the intellectual universe of 'the Platonists' to that of Saint Paul and the Fourth Gospel, as Augustine describes it in the seventh and eighth books of his *Confessions*, was a short one. The two sets of concepts fused into a single image in his mind.[86]

---

80 Ibid., pp 2–3. **81** Ibid., p. 3; *De libero arbitrio*, 1.5, 11–13 (*PL* 44). See trans. T. Williams (Indianapolis, 1993). **82** Markus, 'Saint Augustine's views on "just war"', p. 3; Brown, *Augustine of Hippo*, p. 64. **83** Brown, *Augustine of Hippo*, pp 35–49 for an outline of Manichaean thought. **84** Markus, 'Saint Augustine's views on "just war"', p. 3. **85** Brown, *Augustine of Hippo*, pp 79–92. **86** R.A. Markus, *The end of ancient Christianity* (Cambridge, 1990), p. 48.

This way of thinking represented a dramatic change of perspective for Augustine. He was no longer identified with God, no longer part of the substance of God. God stood outside him, separate and transcendent. Similarly, evil could no longer be viewed as something outside his existence. It had to be accommodated within his thinking. In *De libero arbitrio* Augustine was looking at the role of human freedom within 'the over-arching order he had come to see running through the *cosmos*'.[87] An intelligent well-educated mind could access this order. Evil was a breach in God's order, good was following it. Temporal law must follow an eternal law. In some circumstances killing can be a duty made necessary for a well-ordered society to conform to God's eternal order, such as in the case of the public hangman.[88] So too, war may be necessary to ensure compliance with God's order, and so may be sanctioned by law. This then is what Augustine wrote, at a relatively early stage in his career, about the circumstances in which war was just for a Christian.

The work in which Augustine considers warfare in most detail is *Against Faustus the Manichee (Contra Faustum)*. This dates from about 398, ten years after his first treatment of the subject. A full discussion of the theme of warfare appears in Book XXII. The purpose of *Contra Faustum* is to refute the Manichaean rejection of the Old Testament. Augustine defends Moses, who waged war on God's command. Thus, if God can command it, warfare cannot be morally wrong. There must be circumstances where warfare can be just and right. These circumstances are where it is waged on proper authority, without love of violence or other subjective sinful dispositions on the part of the person waging the war.[89] While *De libero arbitrio* and *Contra Faustum* both argue against the Manichees and both envisage circumstances where warfare can be justified, Augustine's perspective against the background of which the latter work was written had altered considerably. Warfare's place in the over-arching order of the *cosmos* was no longer its justification. Its legitimacy was now seen to derive from its place in the Old Testament and the unity of the Old Testament with the New Testament and of God's work to save mankind. Augustine, in the ten intervening years, had ceased to believe in a rationally ordered universe. He no longer had confidence that man could achieve salvation, unaided, by his own intellectual resources, by progressing through the ordered world, step by step, towards a distant goal. In short, man's propensity to sin was too strong, he needed God's grace to overcome it and could not do it alone. In the same way, Augustine's confidence in the link between the eternal law and temporal law vanished. His justification for warfare had been underpinned by his concept of the ordered world operating to an eternal law that was reflected in the temporal law under the authority of which a just war could be waged. Now he needed to rethink his attitude to war.[90]

---

[87] Markus, 'Saint Augustine's views on "just war"', p. 3. [88] Ibid., p. 3, citing *De Ordine*, 11.8.25 (*CCSL* 29). See trans. R.P. Russell (Whitefish, MT, 2010). [89] *Contra Faustum*, XXII.74–8 (*CSEL* 25). See P. Schaff (ed.), *Nicene and post-Nicene Fathers* (Grand Rapids, MN, 1956). [90] Markus, 'Saint Augustine's views on "just war"', pp 5–9; idem, *Ancient Christianity*,

Once again his attitude fits into a closely integrated set of ideas, this time based on his concept of the unity of the Old and New Testaments. The prophecies of the Old Testament were fulfilled in the New Testament and, crucially, were still being fulfilled in the Roman world of the late fourth and early fifth centuries. In common with most educated Christians of the period, Augustine interpreted contemporary history as a fulfilment of Old Testament prophecies. The Theodosian epoch corresponded to 'Christian times' when God's purposes were being worked out visibly in the history of the Roman Empire of his own day. In 399–400 Augustine wrote:

> The few pagans that remain fail to realize the wonder of what is happening ... Now the God of Israel is himself destroying the idols of the heathen ... Through Christ the king he has subjugated the Roman Empire to the worship of his name; and he has converted it to the defence and service of the Christian faith, so that the idols, on account of whose cult his sacred mysteries had previously been rejected, should now be destroyed.[91]

The Theodosian regime was enforcing Christian orthodoxy. Augustine could write in *Contra Faustum* that the prophetic promises of the Old Testament are always being fulfilled, even now, notably in the conversion of the rulers of the earth and the imposition of Christ's yoke on the nations through the agency of kings.[92]

This, therefore, was the context in which Augustine argued that Moses' wars were a just and righteous retribution. Punishment of unwilling souls could be compared to punishment of a child by a loving father.[93] War was just when the motivation was love rather than revenge or taking pleasure in suffering. Augustine condemned private violence. However, rulers and officials acting on their authority could kill because they could so do without hatred or other sinful passions.[94] It is a matter of motivation and authority. The wars of the Old Testament can be justified in this way and so also, because of the inherent integration of Old, New and contemporary worlds, can war generally. Augustine asks Faustus:

> What is the evil in War? Is it the death of some who will soon die in any case, that others may live in peaceful subjection? This is mere cowardly dislike, not any religious feeling. The real evils in war are love of violence (*nocendi cupiditas*), revengeful cruelty (*ulciscendi crudelitas*), fierce and implacable enmity, wild resistance, and the lust of power (*libido dominandi*) and such like.[95]

p. 50; Brown, 'Religious coercion', p. 114; idem, *Augustine of Hippo*, pp 139–50. **91** Markus, 'Saint Augustine's views on "just war"', p. 8; *De consensu evangelistarum*, 1.14.21 (CSEL 43). **92** *Contra Faustum*, XIII.79; XXII.76. **93** Ibid., XXII.74, 78; Russell, *Just war*, p.17. **94** *Contra Faustum*, XXII.76, 79. **95** Ibid., XXII.74; Hartigan, 'Augustine on war and killing',

The objective horrors of war are subordinated to the subjective spiritual inner disposition of the participant.

The need for such a just war arises, not merely to right a wrong, but to punish. In *Contra Faustum* Augustine writes: 'It is generally to punish these things, when force is required to inflict the punishment, that, in obedience to God, or some lawful authority, good men undertake wars.'[96] A just war is a positive effort initiated by lawful authority. Furthermore, it is not for the individual to question that authority. Augustine sees a passivity on the part of the individual. When there is authorization, even from an 'ungodly king' or involving an 'unrighteous command', the soldier is innocent 'because his position makes obedience a duty'.[97]

In the years between 413 and 426/7 Augustine wrote his great work *City of God (De Civitate Dei)*. War is a recurring theme but receives its fullest treatment in two chapters, XV.4 and XIX.7. Once again Augustine's perspective had changed radically. Gone was confidence that the Christian Roman Empire, the embodiment of the prophecies of the Old Testament, with an assured historical destiny, was the divinely ordained framework for mankind. What concerns him now is the precariousness of human order. The essential role of sovereign power, with its political institutions and judicial authority, was to provide a minimal barrier against the forces of disintegration.[98] On 24 August 410, the inconceivable had happened when Alaric's Goths entered Rome. Refugees were arriving in Africa. While this was but a step in the long road to the final fall of the Roman Empire, and Augustine took its survival for granted, a mood of panic had developed. There was now a sense of fragility in the minds of his contemporaries, a sense shared by Augustine.[99] It is now more necessary than ever to stand firm. War is seen as, what we might term today, a necessary evil.[100] It is a necessity that the just man may not avoid, but will pray to God to be delivered from,[101] because Augustine says of war:

> Let one of them who thinks with pain on all these great evils, so horrible, so ruthless, acknowledge that this is misery. And if any one either endures or thinks of them without mental pains, this is a more miserable plight still, for he thinks himself happy because he has lost human feeling.[102]

It is clear, therefore, that Augustine is cognisant of the pain of wars. But, unfortunately they are necessary. He refers to them as 'stern and lasting necessities ...

---

p. 198; Langan, 'The elements of St Augustine's just war theory', p. 21. **96** *Contra Faustum*, XXII.74; Langan, 'The elements of St Augustine's just war theory', p. 22; Russell, *Just war*, pp 18–19. **97** *Contra Faustum*, XXII.75; Langan, 'The elements of St Augustine's just war theory', p. 23. **98** Markus, 'Saint Augustine's views on "just war"', pp 9–10. **99** Brown, *Augustine of Hippo*, pp 285–96. **100** Markus, 'Saint Augustine's views on "just war"', pp 10–11. **101** *Epp.* 189.6; 220.10; 229.2; cf. 138.14–15. See W. Parsons (trans.), *The Fathers of the church* (New York, 1951), pp ix–xiii; Markus, 'Saint Augustine's views on "just war"', p. 11. **102** Hartigan, 'Augustine on war and killing', p. 198; *De Civitate Dei*, XIX.7 (*CCSL* 47–8). See trans. M. Dodds (New York, 1950).

the wise man will wage just wars,' though he laments 'the necessity of just wars ... for it is the wrong doing of the opposing party that compels the wise man to wage just wars'.[103]

Elsewhere, Augustine accepts that wars fought for the sake of peace, even earthly peace, for the sake of enjoying earthly goods, are just wars.

> This peace is purchased by toilsome wars; it is obtained by what they style a glorious victory. Now when victory remains with the party which had the juster cause, who hesitates to congratulate the victor, and style it a desirable peace? These things, then, are good things, and without doubt the gifts of God.[104]

This is an almost grudging concession to earthly goods as distinct from the ultimate peace of the heavenly city.[105]

In spite of the changing historical circumstances and radically changing intellectual perspectives which prompted and underpinned his ideas, there was a constancy to Augustine's observations on war over the forty-year span of his adult life.[106] Langan has attempted to isolate the essential elements of his thinking on war, drawn from all his writings.[107] These can be paraphrased as follows: (a) a conception of war as positive rather than defensive; (b) a conception of the evil of war in terms of the moral evil of certain attitudes and desires rather than in terms of actions wrong in themselves or in their evil consequences; (c) a search for appropriate authorization, either divine or human, for the use of violence; (d) the holding of spiritual considerations to be pre-eminently important relative to mere temporal considerations; (e) the interpretation of evangelical norms in terms of inner attitudes rather than overt actions; (f) an assumption of general social passivity and quiescence in the decisions and moral judgment of authority; (g) the appeal to specific New Testament texts to legitimate military service and participation in war, and we might expand this by mentioning his insistence on the unity of the Old and New Testament; (h) his notion of peace, which he sees as a harmonious ordering of rights and duties among men, and between men and God.[108] These attitudes underlie the oft-quoted bald, short statement of Augustine's just war thinking: 'Just wars avenge injuries'.[109] However, for Augustine, as we have seen, 'injuries' include moral injuries. A just war seeks to restore a violated moral order and to punish.

It is clear from the foregoing that Augustine did not directly address *in bello* issues. Both Hartigan and Langan are agreed that *in bello* issues do not form part of what is loosely referred to as Augustine's just war theory.[110] Some may find

---

103 *De Civitate Dei*, XIX,7. **104** Ibid., XV.4. **105** Langan, 'The elements of St Augustine's just war theory', p. 29. **106** Ibid., p. 27; Markus, 'Saint Augustine's views on "just war"', p. 11. **107** Langan, 'The elements of St Augustine's just war theory', p. 24. **108** Hartigan, 'Augustine on war and killing', p. 199. **109** Ibid., p. 199; idem, *Civilian*, p. 29, citing Augustine's *Quaestiones in Heptateuchum*, 6, 10 (*CSEL* 28); Russell, *Just war*, p. 18. **110** Hartigan,

this surprising. Hartigan puts forward two explanations for Augustine's lack of concern for *in bello* issues.[111] First, because of the intimate relationship between individual and social morality, Augustine would not consider it likely that there would be many innocent individuals in an unjust nation, particularly having regard to Augustine's concept of guilt and innocence as being a matter of interior disposition. Second, and, perhaps, more to the point, his view that physical death is a relatively minor evil by comparison with the evil of those who kill with the wrong motivation. For Augustine, what was really important was the inner state of mind of the soldier and the authority under which he was acting and not the mere physical death of an individual, whether innocent or not.

Langan suggests two explanations, also, for Augustine's failure to deal with *in bello* issues.[112] In the first place, it is clear that, if God authorized the wars of Moses and did not require the sparing of non-combatants, it is not for Augustine to disagree. Having considered Augustine's writings and attitudes, it is clear that he would not have felt it necessary to include a concept of immunity for innocents, as an essential element in the carrying on of a just war, when particuarily, God did not do so. In the second place, it has been argued by Langan that there is something in Augustine's attitudes that implied a support for such immunity; something that might ultimately have influenced Adomnán's attitudes at the end of the seventh century. While it can clearly be argued that a virtually exclusive reliance on proper inner motivation on the part of the soldier excludes considerations of the impact on the enemy, Langan draws the opposite conclusion. This continuous warning against base human passions on the part of the soldier, he claims, points 'the way to a limitation of the horrors of war by focusing on the virtues and attitudes of warriors'.[113] He goes on to say that, while this does not eliminate the need for a rule on non-combatant immunity, it does encourage merciful behaviour and inculcates values that *jus in bello* seeks to protect. It is submitted, however, that, while this may be a subordinate by-product of Augustine's thinking, it can hardly be advanced as an explanation for his failure to consider the position of the non-combatant. Markus makes a somewhat similar point to Langan when he argues that in his 'measured, if unsystematic statements' Augustine offered later generations a means of restricting warfare by insisting that war was not a law unto itself but that it must be amenable to *ad bellum* criteria if it was to be considered just.[114] Hartigan makes the same point when he claims that 'it is doubtful that without his (Augustine's) synthetic structuring of war's permissibility within a Christian commonwealth an eventual concern for *debitus modus* would have occurred at all'.[115]

From the point of view of a historian of *in bello* issues, and with all due respect to these eminent scholars, they are grasping at straws. In any event, our present

---

'Augustine on war and killing', p. 195; Langan, 'The elements of St Augustine's just war theory', pp 31–2. **111** Hartigan, 'Augustine on war and killing', pp 202–3; idem, *Civilian*, p. 32. **112** Langan, 'The elements of St Augustine's just war theory', p. 32. **113** Ibid., p. 32. **114** Markus, 'Saint Augustine's views on "just war"', pp 12–13. **115** Hartigan, *Civilian*, p. 33.

concern is with what Augustine actually said, not his legacy. As a matter of fact, Augustine actually poses the question himself and goes on to answer it. As already quoted above, from *Contra Faustum*, Augustine asks 'What is the evil in War? Is it the death of someone who will soon die in any case ... The real evils in war are love of violence ...'[116] Essentially Augustine is not concerned with the physical effects of war. He does write sympathetically of the horrors of war and while, as Russell puts it, 'His own justifications of violence were balanced by his sheer condemnation of the evils of warfare',[117] he sees them as being of less importance than the subjective state of mind of the warrior. This attitude, and only this attitude, is consistent with Langan's distillation of the elements of Augustine's just war thinking already listed.[118] As Hartigan points out, the only factors that constrain an attacker are the subjective ones of his own intent.[119] The requirement to vindicate justice obviates all other considerations.[120] Augustine's attitudes are revealed, when, in a different context (punishment for original sin), Julian of Eclanum (c.386–454) asks Augustine how his God could inflict punishment on innocent creatures, who sends tiny babies to eternal flames, and Augustine replies 'you must distinguish the justice of God from human ideas of justice'.[121] As Brown puts it, 'The justice of God was as inscrutable as any other aspect of his nature, and human ideas of equity as frail as "dew in the desert"'.[122] Augustine's just war theory, therefore, did not deal with *in bello* issues either explicitly or implicitly. He saw them as subordinate and relatively insignificant, nor is it reasonable to see in his attitudes any implied serious concern for them.

INTERPRETATIONS OF AUGUSTINE

Virtually all scholars considering Augustine's just war thinking are concerned primarily with his legacy,[123] and its impact, for instance on the wars of the Carolingians, or the Crusades,[124] or, indeed, the effect of his legacy up to the present day.[125] What R.A. Markus calls 'a quarry of authoritative texts to quote according to need'[126] was available to medieval canonists and theologians, and indeed, is available to their modern equivalents. Our concern is with its impact, if any, on Adomnán's thinking.

---

116 *Contra Faustum*, XXII.74.   **117** Russell, 'Love and hate', p. 116.   **118** Langan, 'The elements of St Augustine's just war theory', p. 32.   **119** Hartigan, 'Augustine on war and killing', p. 203.   **120** Ibid., p. 202.   **121** *Opus imperfectum contra Julianum*, III.27 (*PL* 45); Brown, *Augustine of Hippo*, p. 395.   **122** Brown, *Augustine of Hippo*, p. 396.   **123** See, for example, J.L. Nelson, 'The church's military service in the ninth century: a contemporary view', *Studies in Church History*, 20 (1983), p. 29; M.E. Moore, 'The ancient Fathers: Christian antiquity, patristics and Frankish canon law', *Millennium Yearbook/ Millennium Jahrbuch*, 7 (2010), pp 293–342.   **124** See Chapter 1, pp 17–19.   **125** For instance, Hartigan, *Civilian*, is in part an examination of the relevance of Augustine's thinking for the Cold War world, as is Langan, 'The elements of St Augustine's just war theory'. Markus, 'Saint Augustine's views on "just war"', seems to have been prompted by the Falklands war.   **126** Markus, 'Saint Augustine's views on "just war"', p. 12.

With regard to just war thinking, there are two significant stepping-stones between the death of Augustine in 430 and the end of the seventh century. These are the writings of Pope Gregory the Great (540–604) and Isidore of Seville (c.560–636). It is possible to see a development of attitudes to warring and violence in their writings. Before them, Augustine's influence inspired a forged letter *Gravi de pugna*, which went a little further than he did by assuring Christians that God was on their side and would grant them victory in a just battle.[127] Augustine had declared that Providence determined victory but did not necessarily grant it to the just party. But now the tendency was to consider success in war as an indication of divine favour. In fact, Russell considers that this pseudo-Augustinian view reinforced the Germanic legal practice of ordeal, whereby the victor was judged to have justice on his side.[128]

In the face of Lombard onslaughts, Gregory, who fully accepted that divine aid was available to rulers who waged war at clerical behest, also believed – and in this he went further than Augustine – that wars waged for the purpose of converting heretics were just.[129] This is what C. Erdmann called 'indirect missionary war'; that is, the subjugation of pagans so as to enable subsequent missionary activity.[130] Attitudes had shifted to include a wider view of what was considered acceptable. Indeed, as Russell puts it, 'The program of repression of barbarians and heretics adumbrated by Ambrose and Augustine had now found a papal executor'.[131]

Isidore, on the other hand, did not so much develop just war thinking as summarize it. He can be described as a chronological stepping-stone in that he brings us closer in time, his life overlapping by some few years with that of Adomnán, but his thinking does not represent a progression.

> Now there are four kinds of war: just, unjust, civil, and more than civil. A just war is that which is waged in accordance with a formal declaration and is waged for the sake of recovering property seized or of driving off the enemy. An unjust war is one that is begun out of rage, and not for a lawful reason.[132]

Russell argues that 'genuine Augustinian opinions in all their complexity were neglected' in the early Middle Ages.[133] In an analysis of Latin culture in the West in the seventh century, J.N. Hillgarth has shown that literary production had all but ceased in erstwhile prolific North Africa. In Italy only a trickle was produced in the period of 150 years after the death of Gregory the Great, one of the notable exceptions being the writings of Jonas of Bobbio, an Italian member of

---

127 Russell, *Just war*, p. 26; Pseudo-Augustine, *Epist* 13 (*PL* 33). **128** Russell, *Just war*, p. 26. **129** Ibid., p. 28; Gregory I, *Registrum Epistolarum* in *MGH Epp*, ed. P. Ewald and M. Hartmann (2 vols, Berlin, 1891–9). **130** Latham, 'Theorizing the Crusades', p. 234; Erdmann, *Origin*, pp 9–10. **131** Russell, *Just war*, p. 28. **132** Isidore, *Etymologies*, XVIII.i, ed. and trans. S.A. Barney et al. (Cambridge, 2006), p. 359. See idem, *Isidori Hispalensis Episcopi Etymologiarum sive Originum Libri XX*, ed. W.M. Lindsay (Oxford, 1911). **133** Russell, *Just war*, p. 27.

an Irish foundation. Francia, in the seventh century, produced very little more, although there has been some positive reassessment of this view.[134] One scholar has commented that 'if any of the (bishops) wanted to study the scriptures they went to Ireland, and while this might be exaggerated it is a reflection of Irish interests in this area'.[135] Moreover, in Spain and in Ireland production was quite extensive. More specifically, on the question of patristic scholarship, which would of course include Augustine, M.E. Moore, in a comprehensive survey, has demonstrated that evidence of its use in the church councils of Merovingian Francia is rare.[136] For reasons of considerable interest to historians of the Carolingian period, it was revived particularly in the Council of Frankfurt (794) and became a feature in law-making thenceforth.[137] It was only in this later period that patristic literature became a source of law in the Frankish kingdoms and 'The writings of Augustine, Isidore and other authorities of the past were thus newly situated in an imperial-conciliar expression of power'.[138]

To a remarkable extent this development had Irish roots. The use of patristic literature was a particular feature of the *Collectio Canonum Hibernensis* (*c.*700),[139] that provided a methodology for the *Admonitio Generalis*, promulgated at the Council of Aachen (789). The *Admonitio* has been regarded by scholars as providing a particular insight into the cultural and ecclesiastical agendas of the Carolingian Empire in the context of the historical importance of early medieval canonical collections.[140] Furthermore, it was often in the libraries of the monasteries in Francia with an Irish connection, such as Luxeuil, where patristic literature was available.[141] Indeed, Luxeuil had a flourishing scriptorium from the second half of the seventh century until its sack in 732.[142] Many of the books that the Carolingians later recuperated and which became of major importance in the later Middle Ages barely survived the sixth and seventh centuries, such as the *Confessions* of St Augustine.[143]

The seventh-century prolific output of Latin texts from Spain is reflected by the equally prolific references to them by Irish scholars of the seventh century.[144]

---

134 I. Wood, 'The Irish in England and on the Continent in the seventh century', *Peritia*, 26 and 27 (2015/16), pp 171–98 and 189–216. See also Flechner and Meeder (eds), *The Irish in early medieval Europe*. **135** See J.N. Hillgarth, 'Ireland and Spain in the seventh century', *Peritia*, 3 (1984), pp 1–16. Here (on p. 3) he is quoting P. Riché, 'Columbanus, his followers and the Merovingian church' in H.B. Clarke and M. Brennan (eds), *Columbanus and Merovingian monasticism* (Oxford, 1981), pp 59–72, esp. 61, 63. **136** Moore, 'The ancient Fathers', pp 294–9. **137** Ibid., p. 341. **138** Ibid., p. 336; R. McKitterick, *History and memory in the Carolingian world* (Cambridge, 2004), p. 220. **139** The *Hibernensis* is considered in some detail in Chapter 3. **140** Moore, 'The ancient Fathers', p. 330; R. McKitterick, 'Knowledge of canon law in the Frankish kingdoms before 789: the manuscript evidence', *Journal of Theological Studies*, 36 (1985), pp 140–68; E. Magnou-Northier, 'La tentative de subversion de l'état sous Louis le Pieux et l'oeuvre des falsificateurs', *Moyen âge*, 105 (1999), pp 331–65 and 615–41. **141** Moore, 'The ancient Fathers', p. 309, p. 313. **142** R. McKitterick, *The Frankish kingdoms under the Carolingians* (Harlow, 1983), p. 142. **143** Moore, 'The ancient Fathers', p. 304. **144** Hillgarth, 'Ireland and Spain', p. 8 for an extensive list of the works of

This applies primarily, but by no means exclusively, to Isidore's *Etymologies*. References to him in Francia in this period are minimal. One of the few is a reference to his *Etymologies* by Theofrid, the first abbot of Corbie (a monk from Luxeuil), who died after 683. In the main, references to Isidore in Italy begin only after 700. It has been suggested that this should be associated with the arrival of exiles fleeing from Spain after the Islamic invasion of 711. In Anglo-Saxon Britain the first writers to cite Isidore are Aldhelm (c.670s) and Bede (c.702). Ireland was entirely different. As Hillgarth put it, 'Nowhere else, outside Isidore's own Spain, can one find anything approaching either the range of works used or the range of writers using them'.[145]

It is clear, therefore, that Russell was right when he stated that Augustine was neglected during this period in Continental Europe, with the possible exception of Spain. In fact, there is no evidence to suggest that Augustine's thinking on war was developed in any way during the seventh century, particularly in Francia, where his thinking was to be taken up again in the Carolingian period.

Augustine's attitudes to warfare appear to have had little or no affect on Adomnán's thinking. That Adomnán had the wherewithal to know them is reasonable to posit. The relative state of knowledge in Ireland of the patristic writers has been demonstrated. More specifically, it has been shown that many of Augustine's, Isidore's and Gregory the Great's works were available in the library in Iona.[146] In any event, whatever about the influence of Augustine's attitudes, knowledge of them is very likely.

But having the wherewithal to know them is not sufficient to establish their influence. In one important respect, Adomnán's and Augustine's attitude to war coincide. Both accept the reality and inevitability of war.[147] But while Adomnán is concerned with the victims of war, the innocents, Augustine considers their interests of relatively lesser importance than the inner disposition of the warrior. Adomnán legislated for the non-combatant; Augustine felt this unnecessary. Why should he interfere where the God of the Old Testament did not? Augustine's war was punitive, whereas Adomnán was prepared to leave the punishment to God.[148] If Augustine did limit the evils of war it was by urging the soldier to banish all evil passions from his heart. Adomnán did this by proscribing the killing of a category of person, the non-combatant. In short, Augustine was concerned with *ad bellum*; Adomnán with *in bello*. Augustine's attitudes to warfare

---

Isidore quoted and of the authors who quote them. **145** Ibid., pp 7–9. Hillgarth mentions such scholars as Laicend, Virgilius Maro, Pseudo-Jerome, Pseudo-Cyprianus and the authors of computistical texts, some dating from the first half of the seventh century. **146** T. O'Loughlin, *Adomnán and the holy places: the perceptions of an Insular monk on the location of the biblical drama* (London, 2007), pp 246–9. For more on this see Houlihan, 'Jurisprudence', pp 57–8. **147** See Fraser, 'Adomnán and the morality of war', pp 108–10. **148** Ibid., p. 106. Somewhat singularly, this view was also held by Pope Nicholas I (d. 867). See Russell, *Just war*, p. 33; Nicholas I, *Responsa ad Consulta Bulgarorum*, 41 and 102, ed. E. Perels in *MGH Epistolae*, VI (Berlin, 1925), p. 582f., p. 599.

did not significantly influence Adomnán. In fact, Augustine's ideas were a force running counter to any move to consider *in bello* issues, and their dissemination in Carolingian times postponed such a consideration until the Peace of God movement at the end of the tenth century, and inhibited a development of *in bello* thinking for many centuries thereafter.

THE BARBARIAN LAWS

The laws of the Germanic peoples, written down between the sixth and ninth centuries, are generally referred to as the barbarian laws. While this term, to our ears, is somewhat pejorative, it is used in this study, without any judgmental connotations, for the sake of convenience.

Historians are careful to warn their readers that, as with the laws of today, the barbarian laws do not tell us how people behaved, rather, ideally, how they should behave.[149] What is important for us is that they do give an idea of what a people, or at least their legislators, considered important and even, by omission, what they considered unimportant or not sufficiently important. This is especially the case in the area of violence and, more particularly, violence towards the weaker members of society. We are, in fact, more concerned with attitudes than with what happened in reality, because *LxI* too was a law, disclosing attitudes and priorities and not necessarily actual behaviour. It can be said therefore that, in broad terms, we are comparing like with like. These laws may be accepted as expressions of normative principles widely held by the peoples of Western Europe in the early Middle Ages.[150]

They do not, of course, represent the only efforts being made in these societies to impose order. The church was also attempting to limit the extent of violence in time of war. There is evidence in the *Acta* of the Merovingian church councils of concern on the part of the bishops of the extent of violence in the civil wars of the sixth and seventh centuries and of its effects on society.[151] The *Acta* of the Council of Tours in 567 is a case in point where the seizure of ecclesiastical property, particularly in time of war, is forcefully and specifically condemned.[152] The practice of allowing followers, either explicitly or tacitly, as a means of attracting support in the interregnal wars, to appropriate church property had become common among the Merovingian kings.[153] Apart from the detrimental effects on the *Pax Ecclesiae*, the primary concern of the bishops seems

---

149 For example: Wickham, *The inheritance of Rome*, p. 14; McKitterick, *Frankish kingdoms*, p. 100. **150** McKitterick, *Frankish kingdoms*, pp 100–1. **151** For the Merovingian conciliar acts see C. de Clercq (ed.), *Conciliae Galliae A. 511– A. 695* in *CCSL* 148 A (Turnhout, 1963). For a useful overview of this topic see G.I. Halfond, 'War and peace in the *acta* of the Merovingian church councils' in idem (ed.), *The medieval way of war: studies in medieval history in honour of Bernard S. Bachrach* (Oxford, 2015), ch. 2. **152** *Conciliae Galliae*, Tours (567), Canon 25. **153** B. Rosenwein, *Negotiating space: power, restraint and privileges of immunity in early medieval Europe* (Ithaca, 1999), pp 42–7.

to have been the threat to church property and, incidentally, to the church's defenceless charges, such as captives and the poor being supported by the income derived from ecclesiastical property.[154] It is interesting to note that the *Acta* do not condemn war itself. Rather, as will be clear from the next chapter in the case of Irish attitudes, the canonical criticisms are concerned with the effects of violence.[155] However, the predicament of the non-combatant, as such, does not appear to have been a concern and does not feature among the *Acta* of the Merovingian councils.

Sometime between 507 and 511 the laws of Salic Francia were produced.[156] These were followed by the Burgundian laws in 517. Then came the laws of Kent (*c*.600), Alamannia (beginning of seventh century), Ripuarian Francia (*c*.623, as an extension and emendation of Salic Law), Lombardy (643), and Visigothic Spain in 654. The eighth century saw the Bavarian laws (*c*.745) and Saxon laws (*c*.785), followed by the laws of Frisia (*c*.785–803). From time to time, kings of these territories promulgated new laws to meet current exigencies, such as the laws of Ine in Saxon England,[157] and Ervig in Visogothic Spain.[158] The laws are preserved in manuscripts dating from the eighth century onwards, in a variety of forms, many containing collections of laws from several regions.[159]

The barbarian law codes filled the legal vacuum created when the Germanic peoples settled within the borders of the former Roman Empire, by providing legal structures which drew on both local tradition of the provinces and the imperial constitution, and absorbing much vulgar law.[160] The laws were not merely repositories of ancient Germanic legal traditions. With the exception of Saxon England, the laws were written in Latin and followed the Roman legal model.[161] On the other hand, as Oliver points out, they 'exhibit a distinctly Germanic remnant of earlier legislation in their personal injury tariffs',[162] or as Wormald puts it, in a reference to the laws generally, 'a great deal of the extant material can only be understood in terms of the customs imported by the West's new masters'.[163] In general they were a mixture, neither directly inherited nor

---

154 Halfond, 'War and peace', ch. 2. For the *Pax Ecclesiae* see R. Bonnaud-Delamare, *L'idée de Paix á l'époque Carolingienne* (Paris, 1939); E. Magnou-Nortier, 'The enemies of the peace: reflections on a vocabulary 500–1100' in Head and Landes, *Peace of God*, pp 60–3; M.E. Moore, *A sacred kingdom: bishops and the rise of Frankish kingship, 300–800* (Washington, DC, 2011), pp 281–2. **155** P. Fouracre, 'Attitudes towards violence in seventh- and eight-century Francia' in G. Halsall (ed.), *Violence and society in the early medieval West* (Woodbridge, 1998), pp 60–75; L. Sarti, *Perceiving war and the military in early Christian Gaul* (Leiden, 2013), pp 86–90 and 300–7. **156** Oliver, *Body legal*, p. 14 for a useful chronological summary. **157** Halsall, *Warfare*, p. 57. **158** Ibid., pp 60–2. **159** Oliver, *Body legal*, p. 20. **160** P. Amory, 'The meaning and purpose of ethnic terminology in the Burgundian laws', *Early Medieval Europe*, 2:1 (1993), pp 16–17. **161** Oliver, *Body legal*, p. 9. See E. Levy, *West Roman vulgar law: the law of property* (Philadelphia, 1951). **162** Oliver, *Body legal*, p. 10. **163** P. Wormald, 'The *Leges Barbarorum*: law and ethnicity in the medieval West' in H.-W. Goetz, J. Jarnut and W. Pohl (eds), *Regna and Gentes: the relationship between late antique and early medieval peoples and kingdoms in the transformation of the Roman world* (Leiden and Boston, 2003), p. 23.

directly mimicked. It is important to note also that the laws were not as exclusively ethnic as is often thought. While ethnicity mattered, the law codes were generally regional codes.[164]

Many barbarian law codes contain provisions that are designed to give women, per se, special protection. This applies to both sexually related assaults on women and to assaults of a non-sexual nature. For instance, with regard to the latter, both the laws of Alamannia and Bavaria provide for a fine that is double the value of the fine prescribed for injury to a freeman.[165] The Bavarian laws are quite explicit as to the thinking behind this provision.

> If any of these acts happen to the women of those freemen, let all be compensated for twofold. Since a woman cannot defend herself with weapons, let her obtain a double compensation. If however, she wishes to fight through boldness of heart, just as a man does, her compensation will not be twofold.[166]

Clearly the woman's non-combatant status is recognized and she is afforded the protection of a double fine because of it. Similar thinking is evident in a provision of the Burgundian code, which stipulates a fine for cutting off the hair of a native freewoman in her courtyard but requires no fine if the hair is cut off after the woman leaves her courtyard to fight,[167] because, in that case, she has lost her status as a non-combatant. The same applies, under Lombard law, to a woman who is injured while participating in a brawl. For penalty purposes she is to be treated 'as if the deed had been done to a brother of that woman.' The clause goes on to stipulate that the normal penalty of 900 *solidi* is not required 'since she had participated in a struggle in a manner dishonourable to women'.[168] In some regions, on the other hand, increased fines for non-sexually related injuries to women do not apply. The Kentish laws, for instance, specifically stipulate that the compensation for a woman should be the same as for a freeman.[169] It is important to note, at this stage, that the rationale of women's status as non-combatants, evident in the examples mentioned above, which applies to laws relating to injury to women, is not replicated in laws concerned with the killing of women or sexually related offences; a different dynamic applied in these cases.

Invariably, laws dealing with the killing of women link the amount of the fine to their child-bearing ability. For instance, Salic law trebles the fine from 200 to 600 *solidi* for the killing of a woman when she reaches child-bearing age.

---

164 Idem, p. 28; Amory, 'The meaning and purpose', p. 6; Wickham, *The inheritance of Rome*, p. 149. **165** Oliver, *Body legal*, p. 181; *Lex Ala.*, 49.2 in J. Merkel (ed.), *Leges Alamannorum, MGH Legum* (Hanover, 1898), iii, 1–182. **166** *Lex Baiu.*, IV, 29 in J. Merkel (ed.), *Leges Baiuwariorum, MGH Legum* (Hanover, 1898), iii, 183–496. **167** *Lex Bur.*, XCII. See K. Fischer Drew (trans.), *The Burgundian code* (Philadelphia, 1972). **168** *Edict Roth.*, 378. See K. Fischer Drew (trans.), *The Lombard laws* (Philadelphia, 1973). **169** Oliver, *Body legal*, p. 181; *Kent*, 73. See P. Wormald (trans.), *The first code of English law* (Medway, Kent, 2005).

It reduces again after she has passed child-bearing.[170] Thuringia and Ripuarian Francia do likewise. The seriousness of attitudes towards killing potentially child-bearing women is clear. The fine for killing a free man is one third – 200 *solidi* as compared to 600.[171] Under the *Lex Saxonum*, however, killing a virgin attracts double the penalty applied to a woman after she has given birth. Here, it would appear, a woman's value as a marriage commodity is of more importance than as a producer of children.[172] Most codes deal comprehensively with the killing of pregnant women and with attacks on them which bring about the death of the foetus, and with intentional abortions.[173] The underlying rationale in these cases is the threat to the kin group, tribe, nation. Attitudes to women and to violence towards them are dominated by a preoccupation with the need to perpetuate and strengthen the population group.

Sexually related assaults against women, and in particular, rape, are dealt with extensively in all of the barbarian laws. Here there is a somewhat different dynamic at work. Heavier fines are stipulated for the rape of married women than for a single woman. For instance, Salic law provides for a fine of 200 *solidi* for the rape of a man's wife and only 62½ for the rape of a free girl. The 200 *solidi* fine is the same fine as is stipulated for the murder of a man's wife, and the 62½ is equivalent to the fine for striking out an eye or a foot.[174] The same distinction between married and unmarried is made in Thuringian,[175] and Alamannian laws.[176] It would appear that the higher fine applying to a married woman takes into account the insult to the husband.[177] Another feature of rape laws is the latitude often extended to a victim's husband or kin if he kills or otherwise exacts retribution on the culprit. Under Visigothic law the killing of a rapist is not considered criminal homicide because 'the act was committed in the defence of chastity'.[178] The laws of Frisia, and, later, Wessex echo this.[179] *Lex Ribuaria* provides:

> [If the father or husband] is unable to tie him up, and strikes him a blow and kills him, he should raise him up in a hurdle at the crossroads in the

---

170 Oliver, *Body legal*, p. 194; *Lex Sal.*, XXIV. See K. Fischer Drew (trans.), *The laws of the Salian Franks* (Philadelphia, 1991). See also, W.C. Brown, *Violence in medieval Europe* (Harlow, 2011), pp 47–52. **171** *Lex Thur.*, V, 46–7 in K.F. von Richthofen (ed.), *Lex Thuringorum*, *MGH Legum* (Hanover, 1875–89), v, 103–42; *Lex Rib.*, 41, 17 in R. Sohm (ed.), *Lex Ribuaria*, *MGH Legum* (Hanover, 1875–89), v, 185–268. **172** Oliver, *Body legal*, p. 194; *Lex Sax.*, 15 in K. and K.F. Von Richthofen (eds), *Leges Saxonum*, *MGH Legum* (Hanover, 1875–89), v, 1–102. **173** Oliver, *Body legal*, p. 195. **174** Oliver, *Body legal*, p. 182; *Lex Sal.*, XIII, 4 and XV, 1, 2. Note, however, that a capitulary of Childebert II dating from 595 made rape a capital offence enforceable by a royal official. See Brown, *Violence*, pp 59–60. **175** *Lex Thur.*, IV, 56. **176** *Lex Ala.*, CVIII, 1. **177** Oliver, *Body legal*, p. 182. **178** Ibid., p. 184; *Forum Iud.*, III, 3, vi in S.P. Scott (trans.), *The Visigothic code (Forum Iudicum)* (Boston, 1910). Available at the *Library of Iberian Sources Online*, http://libro.uca.edu/vcode/. **179** *Lex Fris.*, V, 1 in K. von Richthofen (ed.), *Lex Frisionum*, *MGH Legum* (Hanover, 1898), v, 631–711; *Wessex*, XCII, 7. See F.L. Attenborough (ed. and trans.), *The laws of the earliest English kings* (Cambridge, 1922), pp 62–93.

presence of witnesses and safeguard [the corpse] forty or fourteen nights. And then let him swear at the sanctuary [*harapus*] before the judge that the man he killed had forfeited his life. But if he does not do this, let him be held guilty of homicide.[180]

It is clear, therefore, that the rape of a woman was seen as a crime against the kin and not merely an offence against a defenceless person. It is interesting to note how the law, while recognizing the right to private justice, required a public element – the exposition of the corpse at the crossroads in the presence of witnesses.[181] This was part of moves towards privatization of justice culminating in the necessity, centuries later, for the Peace of God movement as a defence against the excess of private justice.[182]

Many codes provided for less serious sexually related offences. The fines increased as the inherently sexual nature of the act increased. Salic law stipulated a fine of 15 *solidi* for touching a woman's hand or finger, 30 her arm, 35 her elbow and 45 her breast.[183] Under Bavarian law the fine for lifting a woman's garments above her knee is 12 *solidi*. The law does not specify to whom the fine is to be paid.[184] In Burgundy the uncovering of a woman's hair, or slandering her, attracts a fine of 12 *solidi*, a woman's loose hair being seen as indicating a loose character. The payment is to be made to the woman herself.[185] These provisions are clearly for the protection of women from unwanted male attention and would appear, at least in part, to have her interests at heart.

In considering attitudes to the weaker sections of society and, in particular, to people who do not fight or carry arms, it is of interest to consider how the barbarian laws provided for children. In general the rank of a person, and therefore their value for the purpose of determining fines or compensation, is decided at birth. The rank of the father determines the position of the child.[186] The Salic law, somewhat singularly, makes provision for an increased fine of 600 *solidi* for killing a child before s/he reaches the age of majority.[187] There is also provision for a fine of 45 *solidi* for cutting a male child's hair without the consent of his relatives. Katherine Fischer Drew suggests that by cutting the hair, his majority is indicated, thereby making him liable for fines for criminal actions or competent to control his own property.[188] She points out that the child's inheritance could not be challenged until he was twelve years and therefore of legal age. In her view, the same probably applies to girls. Apart from any concern for children,

---

180 Oliver, *Body legal*, p. 184; *Lex Rib.*, LXXVII. See also T.J. Rivers (ed. and trans.), *Laws of the Salian and Ripuarian Franks* (New York, 1986), pp 39–112. **181** G. Halsall (ed.), *Violence and society in the early medieval West* (Woodbridge, 1998), pp 16–17. **182** See Chapter 7 below. **183** Oliver, *Body legal*, p. 199; Brown, *Violence*, p. 51; *Lex Sal.*, XX. **184** *Lex Baiu.*, VIII, 4. **185** Oliver, *Body legal*, p. 200; *Lex Burg.*, XCII, 1. **186** Oliver, *Body legal*, p. 225. **187** Lex Sal., XXIV, 1. This is somewhat similar to the provision made in Irish vernacular law for the protection of children under seven years. See next chapter. **188** K. Fischer Drew, *Salian Franks*, p. 38.

there were, therefore, economic and social reasons for this special provision. It is, however, noteworthy that children are included with women in the same section of the law, which is entitled: 'Concerning the killing of little children and women'.[189] At first glance this would appear to be a recognition of a category of persons who didn't carry arms. However, the intention of the section, taken as a whole, seems to be primarily concerned with the safeguarding of the younger generation of Franks, whether as young children, potential children in the form of child-bearing women, or unborn children in the form of pregnant women.

The other category of person who did not normally bear arms was the cleric, both male and female. Many of the codes addressed the question of violence towards clerics. In most cases higher penalties were prescribed than in cases of violence towards non-clerics.[190] In general, the higher the rank of cleric, the higher the penalty. The underlying rationale appears to be religious. For instance, Bavarian law requires twice the fine for abducting a nun as for abducting a betrothed woman, on the basis that 'we know that the abduction of another's betrothed is a punishable crime; how much more punishable is a crime that usurps the betrothed of Christ'.[191]

Of the barbarian laws enacted by their kings there are laws dating from approximately the same time as *LxI*. The point has to be made, of course, that laws must be viewed in their immediate context rather than, as Halsall puts it, 'seen as passively reflecting age old situations'.[192] For no other reason than its contemporaneity, and keeping Halsall foremost in mind, it might be of some interest to consider Ine's laws of *c*.694.[193] Ine, West-Saxon king of Wessex, sets out fines for non-performance of military service. This was done against a background of a recently terminated lengthy war with Kent, and concerns that attempts might be made to seize the kingships as, indeed, Ine's father had earlier seized it. Ine wanted to ensure that a call to arms from him would be heard and acted upon. Like *LxI*, this is a law for war. It does concern itself with combatants and non-combatants, in that it stipulates who is expected to serve in the king's army. For instance, young men, on obtaining fourteen or fifteen years, are expected to play a military role. Unlike *LxI*, which sought to limit who were the legitimate targets of war, Ine's code stipulated who was obliged to participate. Wihtred of Kent in 695 introduced similar laws.[194] As Halsall has pointed out, Visigothic laws of Wamba and the almost exactly contemporary Ervig also address the question of who is expected to participate in the king's army.[195]

---

189 *Lex Sal.*, XXIV. **190** Oliver, *Body legal*, p. 223. **191** Ibid., p. 224; *Lex Baiu.*, I,11. **192** Halsall, *Warfare*, p. 62. **193** Ibid., p. 57. For discussion of Ine's code see Wormald, '"Boni genti suae": law-making and peace-keeping in the earliest English kingdoms' in idem, *Legal culture in the early medieval West: law as text, image and experience* (London, 1999), pp 179–99. **194** Halsall, *Warfare*, p. 58; idem, *Violence*, p. 8; Wormald, *Leges*, p. 42; Oliver, *Body legal*, p. 35. **195** Halsall, *Warfare*, p. 60; *Leges Visigothorum*, 9.2.8–9. See P.D. King, *Law and society in the Visigothic kingdom* (Oxford, 1972); C.H. Lynch, *St Braulio of Saragossa (631–651), his life and writings* (Washington, DC, 1938).

While the similarities between these laws and *LxI* are tenuous, they do reveal something of contemporary attitudes to the combatant and, therefore, by implication the non-combatant.

The above brief study of the barbarian laws does provide some insight into attitudes to violence towards the weaker sections of society among the peoples of Western Europe around the time of the enactment of *LxI*. The concept of non-combatant is reflected in the laws dealing with non-sexual assaults on women. As we have seen, increased penalties were provided, in recognition of the fact that women did not normally bear arms. This is legal protection afforded to women as non-combatants per se. Their non-combatant status entitled them to greater compensation for injuries suffered. It is clear, however, that their non-combatant status is not the basis of the protection afforded by the laws in the case of the killing of women and for serious sexual offences such as rape. Here the rationale is the birth-rate of the kin groups and the insult to the family of the victim.[196] One has the impression that a female's non-combatant status is all very well, but, when it comes to the most serious offences, there are more important considerations. In any event, the laws are concerned with violence arising during the course of private altercations and not at time of war. There is no law proscribing the killing or injuring of women during the course of wars, less still assaults on non-combatants or innocents as a category.

Chapter 7 below will address the question as to why an *in bello* law emerged from Ireland rather than from elsewhere in Western Europe. It is important to point out at this stage, however, that many of the barbarian laws were concerned with the limitation of violence.[197] They particularly condemned violence in certain places such as palaces, cities where the king was resident, or the place of assemblies. Illegitimate violence, threatening the king's peace and protection was often referred to as *seditio* or *preaesumptio*. Controlling armed gangs was a major concern. As time progressed, rather than exempting certain categories of people from violence in the civil wars of the period, the tendency was to consider actions against rebels to be without sin or blame.[198] The laws delegitimized violent actions carried out outside the ambit of the state's coercive powers.[199] In all regions civil wars were common. Feuding and its concomitant violence were a regular part of early medieval society. However, in societies that were primarily concerned with creating law codes for their people, that would help to regulate their relations with their king and among themselves, it is understandable that they considered these matters should be given priority and that, to refer back to Sir Herach Lauterpacht's comment in 1952, the law of war was at a vanishing point some considerable distance over the horizon. It is hard to imagine, how-

---

196 Halsall, *Violence*, p. 15.   **197** Ibid., pp 7–16.   **198** Ibid., p. 10. See, for example, F. Kurse (ed.), *Royal Frankish annals* in *MGH SRG* (Hanover, 1895), ch. 6, s. a. 787 where the Pope absolved Charlemagne and the Franks of all guilt for military action against Tassilo of Bavaria. **199** L.A. García Moreno, 'Legitimate and illegitimate violence in Visigotic law' in Halsall (ed.), *Violence*.

ever, that non-combatants would not need protection or that an *in bello* law would be unnecessary. What can we know of the actual conduct of war?

CONTEMPORARY ACCOUNTS

It will be of interest to know, when it came to the actual waging of war, how those who did not bear arms, the non-combatants, the innocents, were treated; to see, as a matter of actual practice, were they left unmolested or were they attacked indiscriminately. The first point that must be made is that, even if it were possible to establish that non-combatants were often slaughtered in the wars of the period, this does not mean that such actions were not abhorred by society. The normative position is no necessary indicator of what happens in fact, and *vice versa*. The second point that must be made – and this renders the first point somewhat redundant – it is not possible to know, to any full extent, how non-combatants were treated. In fact, it is very difficult to know what happened during the course of a war or during the course of any particular battle, to those actually participating, because the sources, generally, do not provide factual detail.[200] Halsall cites as an example Nithard's account of the battle of Fontenoy in 841, that, he suggests, is more detailed than most descriptions.[201] Later in his work he takes, as a further example, Asser's account of the battle of Ashdown in 871,[202] possibly the longest Latin description of a battle. While both of these are outside the period under discussion, they do illustrate the problems in ascertaining, from the sources, the detail of what actually happened during the course of, or immediately after, battle. Neither source tells us anything about whether the fighting was done on foot or on horseback, whether with swords, axes, spears, bows or javelins, or whether the fighting was hand-to-hand or from a distance using missiles. No manoeuvres are described.[203] It is not surprising, therefore, that no details are given of women, children, clerics or other non-participants that may have become involved and suffered death or injury. The writers of these accounts did not see their function as giving a factual account of what happened, rather than to offer an exegetical explanation in a learned manner common to the demands of the genre. Various explanations for the laconic nature of the reports, as compared to those of classical authors, have been suggested, from the effect of Christian attitudes to killing to the influence of the Bible, with its emphasis on the overriding role of divine intervention in determining *why* battles were won or lost, with a consequential lessening of interest in *how* victory or defeat came about. 'Ultimately, the question of why warfare was not written about in detail in the early medieval world remains utterly intractable'.[204]

200 Halsall, *Warfare*, pp 1–16. **201** Ibid., p. 1; Nithard, *Histories*, 2.10 in *Carolingian Chronicles*, trans. B.W. Scholz (Ann Arbour, 1972), pp 127–74. For Nithard himself see J.L. Nelson, 'Public *Histories* and private history in the work of Nithard' in *Politics and ritual in early medieval Europe* (London, 1986), pp 195–237. **202** Halsall, *Warfare*, pp 178–80; Asser, *Life of King Alfred*, trans. S.D. Keynes and M. Lapidge in *Alfred the Great* (London, 1983), pp 65–110. **203** Halsall, *Warfare*, p. 180. **204** Ibid., p. 6.

Notwithstanding the lack of detail in the sources, they do, here and there, provide snippets of information of military practices both on and off the battlefield, some demonstrating an awareness of combatant status, if not a concern for non-combatants, and others showing a pronounced disregard. The story of Imma in Bede is particularly noteworthy.[205] Imma was a young nobleman fighting in the army of the Northumbrians against the Mercians in a battle on the river Trent in 679. He was wounded and knocked unconscious and lay among the dead for some time. When he recovered consciousness he tried to flee but was apprehended by the Mercians and brought before their leader. He told him that he was a poor married peasant who had come with others of his kind with provisions for the army. On the basis that he was not a soldier, his life was spared and he was ultimately sold into slavery after his true identity had been discerned. Had the Mercian leader realized that he was a soldier in the aftermath of the battle, he would have been killed in revenge for the deaths of the leader's brothers and kinsmen in the battle. It would appear that his non-combatant status was recognized and his life was saved on account of it. The other side of this coin, however, is the account, dating from 859 Francia, of how noble Franks butchered poorer freemen for daring to take up arms against the Vikings. Although this occurred at a considerable remove both in time and in place, it does illustrate that there was a class element in the perception of combatant and non-combatant.[206]

Another determining factor was age. Military service was a male preserve,[207] which was reached in some societies on attaining about fourteen to fifteen.[208] The carrying of weapons symbolized the male's role as head of a household with a legal identity and dependants to defend.[209] Clearly, that status could change, as with King Sigbert of the East Angles, in the seventh century. He had retired to a monastery. His people insisted on him leaving the monastery and leading them into battle against the Mercians under Penda. However Sigbert refused to carry a weapon because of his new status as a tonsured cleric and, therefore, non-combatant. Without the means or the will to defend himself, he was killed in battle.[210]

While there appears to have been a reasonably clearly defined demarcation between combatant and non-combatant, there is evidence of violence towards

---

205 Ibid., p. 58; Bede, *Historia Ecclesiastica*, ed. and trans. B. Colgrave and R.A.B. Mynors in *Bede's Ecclesiastical history of the English people* (Oxford, 1969), 4.22. **206** Halsall, *Warfare*, p. 100; Nelson, 'Violence in the Carolingian world', pp 95–6; *Annals of St-Bertin*, s. a. 859, trans. J.L. Nelson in *The annals of St-Bertin. Ninth-century histories* (Manchester, 1991). **207** Halsall, *Warfare*, p. 33; R. Balzaretti, '"These are things that men do, not women": the social regulation of female violence in Langobard Italy' in Halsall (ed.), *Violence*, p. 175. **208** Halsall, *Warfare*, pp 35, 58; Eddius Stephanus, *Life of Wilfrid*, ch. 2 (fourteen), ed. and trans. B. Colgrave in *The life of Bishop Wilfrid by Eddius Stephanus* (Cambridge, 1927); Felix, *Life of Guthlac*, ch. 16 (fifteen), ed. and trans. B. Colgrave in *Felix's life of Guthlac* (Cambridge, 1956). **209** Halsall, *Warfare*, p. 33, on the evidence from furnished burials. **210** Ibid., p. 194; Bede, *HE* 3.18. See C. Stancliffe, 'Kings who opted out' in P. Wormald (ed.), *Ideal and reality in Frankish and Anglo-Saxon society* (Oxford, 1983), pp 154–6.

the latter. One of the more notorious accounts dates from the ninth century, where Notker the Stammerer tells us of how Eishere, with whom he was acquainted in childhood, 'spitted Bohemians and Wilzes and Avars on his spear as if they were little birds ... and carried them about ... squealing their incomprehensible lingo'.[211] Other notable accounts include that of Charlemagne's slaughter of 4,500 Saxons after they came to surrender,[212] and how, as described by Einhard, only those whose height did not exceed the height of a sword were spared, the remainder being 'shortened by a head'.[213] The sources do recount the killing of the Merovingian queen Brunichildis in 613. The seventy-year-old was torn to pieces by a horse in public. Her gender provided her with no protection, although she certainly was not an innocent.[214] Far from her killing, and the manner of it, provoking protest or horror on the part of the author, he saw it, to quote Paul Fouracre, as a 'manifestly vigorous execution of divine judgment'.[215] The reaction of another writer to the killing in 675 of Queen Bilichildis is also of interest. She was killed with her husband King Childeric II. The chronicler does not condemn the king's killing, but he regrets the fact that the queen was killed, particularly because she was pregnant.[216] Bede appears to approve of the action of a Saxon lord, who, in revenge for the killing of two English missionaries, 'slew all the villagers and burned down their village' of those responsible, in c.692.[217] Earlier, in c.603, Bede tells of how the Northumbrian pagan king, Aethelfrith, directed the killing of a large host of British Christian monks because, as the king said, 'If they are crying to their God against us, they are fighting against us even if they do not bear arms'. Bede goes on to say that about twelve hundred monks perished.[218] What is remarkable about this is not so much the fact that it happened but the reporting of it so uncritically. Elsewhere Bede writes of a terrible slaughter in Northumbria in c.633 by the Christian king

---

211 Halsall, *Warfare*, p. 3; Nelson, 'Violence in the Carolingian world', p. 90; Notker, *Deeds of Charlemagne*, 2.12, trans. L. Thorpe in *Einhard and Notker the Stammerer, Two lives of Charlemagne* (London, 1969). **212** Halsall, *Warfare*, p. 142. **213** Einhard, *Life of Charlemagne*, ed. and trans. A.J. Grant, *Early lives of Charlemagne by Eginhard and the Monk of St Gall* (London, 1922), pp 130–1. **214** Fouracre, 'Attitudes towards violence', p. 63; Wickham, *The inheritance of Rome*, p. 116; *Fredegar*, IV.42, ed. B. Krusch in *Chronicle, MGH SRM* (Hanover, 1888), ii, 1–193; Jonah, *Vita Columbani*, I.27, ed. B. Krusch in *MGH SRM* (Hanover, 1902), iv, 61–152. **215** Fouracre, 'Attitudes towards violence', p. 63; Brown, *Violence*, pp 42–7. **216** Fouracre, 'Attitudes towards violence', p. 64; B. Krusch (ed.), *Liber Historiae Francorum*, 41, 45–8 in *MGH SRM*, ii, 213–328 and trans. in P. Fouracre and R. Gerberding, *Late Merovingian France: history and hagiography, 640–720* (Manchester, 1996); J.M. Wallace-Hadrill, 'The bloodfeud of the Franks' in idem, *Long haired kings and other studies in Frankish history* (London, 1962), pp 459–87. See Fouracre's account in 'Attitudes towards violence' of the speculation among scholars that the author of *LHF* and, indeed, the *Annals of Metz* and *Passio Praejecti*, were women. He concludes by commenting that if they were, their attitudes towards violence does not differ from their male counterparts (p. 64, n. 3). **217** Halsall, *Warfare*, p. 66; Bede, *HE* 5.10. **218** Strickland, 'Rules of war', p. 119; Bede, *HE* 2.2. See also *HE* 4.14 [16], where Bede seems to have had no difficulty with Bishop Wilfrid being gifted a quarter of the land and spoils of the Isle of Wight after its native inhabitants had been exterminated.

Cadwallon, 'a barbarian more savage than any pagan'. Bede says of him that 'He was set upon exterminating the entire English race in Britain, and spared neither women nor innocent children, putting them all to horrible deaths with ruthless savagery ...'[219] Clearly, there was an awareness of the non-combatant, but his or her immunity from violence in warfare varied according to the perceived justness of the cause.

It is reasonable to conclude, therefore, that attacks on non-arms-bearing people, whether women, children, clerics, the aged or others, did take place, to a lesser or greater degree, in the frequent warring, raiding, feuding and pillaging of the early Middle Ages in Western Europe. It would be naive to think otherwise. Steps were taken by leaders to impose discipline on their troops. Clovis attempted to restrict pillaging by his troops when on campaign against the Visigoths in Aquitaine.[220] Gregory of Tours expressed concerns about Merovingian Frankish soldiers pillaging their own territory.[221] In 547, Sigibert stoned to death a number of auxiliaries for plundering and in 583 Chilperic beheaded the count of Rouen for pillaging.[222] Wamba was concerned by the looting and rape carried out by his troops on the march which he felt, according to Julian of Toledo, might incur divine disfavour.[223] Whatever action leaders took falls short of legally forbidding the killing of innocents, because no such proscriptions can be found in the sources. Sometimes these wars concluded in the opposing parties entering into a peace treaty, as, it has been suggested, was the case in the making of the Laws of Wessex and Kent by their respective kings, Ine and Wihtred, after the conclusion of a war between them in 694, almost exactly contemporaneous with the promulgation of *LxI*.[224] It would appear that, for one reason or another, the opportunity to make a law for innocents was not taken.

---

219 Strickland, 'Rules of war', p. 120; Bede, *HE* 2.20. See Strickland's comment that Adomnán had promulgated his *lex innocentium* precisely to counter such behaviour among the warring tribes of Ireland and Dalriada.   **220** Halsall, *Warfare*, p. 152; Gregory of Tours, *Histories*, 2.37, trans. L. Thorpe.   **221** E.g. Gregory of Tours, *Histories*, 6.31, 8.30, 10,3.   **222** Ibid., 4.49, 6.31.   **223** Halsall, *Warfare*, p. 152; Julian of Toledo, *History of King Wamba*, 10, ed. W. Levison in *MGH SRM* (Hanover, 1910), v, 501–26.   **224** Halsall, *Warfare*, p. 229.

CHAPTER 3

Irish attitudes to violence

LATE SEVENTH-CENTURY IRELAND

By the seventh century a characteristic of church organization in Ireland was the model based on monastic (broadly defined) institutions.[1] Tomás Ó Carragáin, drawing on archaeological evidence, prefers to refer to their centres as 'episcopal-monastic',[2] in order not to minimize the importance of bishops in the early Irish church. Indeed Colmán Etchingham has argued for the existence of territorial bishoprics and an episcopal hierarchy.[3] That said, Ireland was never formally part of the Roman Empire and this fact alone made it different in many respects, although it was not totally isolated from the rest of the Western world.[4] It was a rural society. There were no cities, at least initially. The process by which bishops filled the gaps left by the declining imperial bureaucracy in the cities of late antique and early medieval continental Europe did not occur. As Ireland had not been governed by Romans there was not the 'impetus to appropriate their highly bureaucratic institutions directly'.[5] Church power structures developed in the form of ecclesiastical federations or *paruchiae* or *familiae*, with overall authority resting with the abbot of the mother house.[6] The most powerful *paruchiae* included Armagh, Clonmacnoise, Kildare and Iona. Iona was founded by St Columba in or about 563, and Adomnán was its abbot from 679 to 704. By Columba's death he had been responsible for the establishment of a number of monastic foundations both in Ireland and in northern Britain. As a

---

[1] The nature of church organization in early medieval Ireland has been the subject of debate. See K. Hughes, *The church in early Irish society* (London, 1966); eadem, 'The church in Irish society, 400–800' in D. Ó Cróinín (ed.), *NHI*, i, with updated notes; C. Etchingham, *Church organization in Ireland AD 650 to 1000* (Naas, 1999); Charles-Edwards, *Early Christian Ireland*, pp 241–81; idem, 'Introduction: prehistoric and early Ireland' in Ó Cróinín (ed.), *NHI*, i, pp lxix–lxxv; Johnston, *Literacy*, p. 61; T. Ó Carragáin, *Churches in early medieval Ireland: architecture, ritual and memory* (New Haven and London, 2010), pp 8–10 and pp 215–21; Stancliffe, 'Religion and society', pp 417–25. [2] Ó Carragáin, *Churches*, p. 9 and p. 217. [3] Etchingham, *Church organization*, pp 177–94, esp. 194. [4] Charles-Edwards, *Early Christian Ireland*, pp 145–81; E. Bhreathnach, *Ireland in the medieval world, AD 400–1000: landscape, kingship and religion* (Dublin, 2014), p. 68 and pp 152–9; E. Johnston, 'Literacy and conversion on Ireland's Roman frontier: from emulation to assimilation?' in N. Edwards, M. Ní Mhaonaigh and R. Flechner (eds), *Transforming landscapes of belief in the early medieval Insular world and beyond: converting the Isles II* (Turnhout, 2017), pp 35–51. [5] Johnston, *Literacy and identity in early medieval Ireland* (Woodbridge, 2013), p. 61. [6] Ó Cróinín, *Early medieval Ireland*, pp 165–8. See Etchingham,

consequence, there existed a network of authority and communication linking these monasteries on both sides of the Irish Sea. Columba organized the government of his monastic foundations on the basis of established secular concepts of overlordship, kinship and inheritance with potential for mutual benefit out of co-operation between the church and the Uí Néill dynasty.[7] During the course of the following century Iona was responsible for the conversion to Christianity of much of northern England.[8] It is only a slight over-statement, therefore, to describe the Irish Sea as a 'great Celtic lake' and there is no exaggeration at all in the assertion that 'Lindisfarne [a Columban foundation] superseded Canterbury as the effective ecclesiastical centre of England for thirty years'.[9] At the same time the influence of Iona in Ireland expanded with the founding of daughter-houses in many locations, most notably, Durrow and Derry.[10] In his capacity as abbot of Iona Adomnán was, therefore, a powerful and influential figure in late seventh-century Ireland.[11] Indeed, Etchingham goes so far as to describe Iona as holding 'an island-wide, quasi-metropolitan or quasi-archiepiscopal jurisdictional prerogative'.[12] Gradually, many of the larger monasteries, of all *paruchiae* and of none, acquired the characterization of urban settlements. They were economic and population centres, sometimes being the sites of temporary or seasonal markets.[13] When Adomnán came to Birr in 697, to promulgate his law, he came to one such centre.[14]

The fundamental political division in seventh-century Ireland was the *tuath*. This term covers both the basic geographical entity, i.e., the block of land, and the people, or kindred, or tribe involved.[15] Apart from being a spatial division, the *tuatha* were central to the maintenance of social and genealogical relation-

---

Church organization, pp 105–94, p. 223 and pp 235–6 on *paruchiae* and *familiae*.   **7** M. Herbert, *Iona, Kells and Derry: the history and hagiography of the monastic* familia *of Columba* (Oxford, 1988), pp 31–5.   **8** Charles-Edwards, *Early Christian Ireland*, pp 309–19. H. Mayr-Harting, *The coming of Christianity to Anglo-Saxon England* (London, 1972), pp 94–102; J. Campbell, 'The debt of the English church to Ireland' in P. Ní Chatháin and M. Richter (eds), *Irland und Europa: Die Kirche im Frühmittelalter/Ireland and Europe: the early church* (Stuttgart, 1984), pp 332–46.   **9** For both quotes see Mayr-Harting, *The coming*, p. 34 and p. 94 respectively. The thirty years was, presumably, post 634.   **10** For a list see Charles-Edwards, *Early Christian Ireland*, p. 250. See also, B. Lacey, *Medieval and monastic Derry: sixth century to 1600* (Dublin, 2013).   **11** See the next chapter for a full treatment of Adomnán.   **12** Etchingham, *Church organization*, p. 222.   **13** Charles-Edwards, *Early Christian Ireland*, pp 119–21; Johnston, *Literacy*, p. 61.   **14** See Chapter 5; Bhreathnach, *Medieval world*, pp 183–92 relating to Clonmacnoise; C. Doherty, 'The monastic town in early medieval Ireland' in H. Clarke and A. Simms (eds), *The comparative history of urban origins in non-Roman Europe* (Oxford, 1985), pp 45–75; J. Bradley, 'Towards a definition of the Irish monastic town' in C. Karkov and H. Damico (eds), *Aedificia Nova: studies in honour of Rosemary Cramp* (Kalamazoo, 2008), pp 325–60; M. Valante, 'Reassesing the Irish "monastic town"', *Irish Historical Studies*, 31 (1998), pp 1–18; idem, *The Vikings in Ireland: settlement, trade and urbanization* (Dublin, 2008), p. 29 and p. 98.   **15** Ó Cróinín, *Early medieval Ireland*, pp 110–11; Charles-Edwards, *Early Christian Ireland*, pp 102–6; Johnston, *Literacy*, p. 72; Bhreathnach, *Medieval world*, p. 40. See also Wickham, *The inheritance of Rome*, p. 164.

ships.¹⁶ The laws defined rights and obligations by reference to an individual's, or category of individuals' place in the *tuath*. Within the *tuath* the king ruled and the various lesser members had clearly defined positions by reference to him. There were well over one hundred such petty kingdoms.¹⁷ These small lesser kingdoms were themselves part of a hierarchy of kingdoms comprising of larger *tuatha*, regional and sub-regional kingdoms and provincial kingdoms. The king of the *tuath* was classified in the laws as a *rí tuaithe* and the provincial king as a *rí cóicid* 'king of a province' or a *rí ruirech* 'king of kings', in other words an overking. There were five provinces, whose boundaries changed from time to time, but which were, in the late seventh century, Ulster (north, but then confined to the north-east) Munster (south), Leinster (east), Connacht (west) and Mide (midlands).¹⁸ The king of Tara, usually one of the Uí Néill, took precedence over the provincial kings, although this may have had limited application in reality.¹⁹ Tara, an ancient ceremonial centre, was situated in Mide, but the dominant king among the provincial kings, from wherever he came, claimed the title king of Tara.²⁰

One of the main features of the political landscape at the end of the seventh century was the dominant position of the Uí Néill in the northern half of the country. The Uí Néill appear to have originated in Connacht and from there expanded into the north and midlands where they rewrote the political history. They were a dynasty, rather than a tribe or a people.²¹ There were two main divisions. In the south, which comprised Brega, Mide and Tethbae, two powerful dynasties of the southern Uí Néill emerged: the Clann Cholmáin Máir of western Mide and the Sil nÁedo Sláine centred on Brega in the east and encompassing Tara itself.²² In the north also, over time, the Uí Néill became a powerful force, dominating the Airgialla and pushing the Ulaid to east of the Bann. Two major families emerged, the Cenél Conaill in the west and the Cenél nEógain in the middle of Ulster.²³ Thus the southern Uí Néill held most of the fertile lands in the midlands, while their cousins to the north straddled the strategic territories across the north-west to the sea. Very broadly speaking, most of the kings of Tara, so called, came from these four families and 'By the end of the seventh century, it is clear, the Uí Néill were the dominant power in the northern half of the country'.²⁴ They had, therefore, a near monopoly of the kingship of Tara, which they equated with the dominant kingship of Ireland.²⁵ By the sev-

---

16 Johnston, *Literacy*, p. 72. **17** Ibid., p. 72; P. MacCotter, *Medieval Ireland: territorial, political and economic divisions* (Dublin, 2008), p. 22 and pp 41–4. **18** Bhreathnach, *Medieval world*, p. 40. **19** Indeed, Congal Clóen of the Ulaid was claiming to be king of Tara well into the seventh century. See D. Ó Cróinín, 'Ireland, 400–800' in idem (ed.), *NHI*, p. 219. **20** See E. Bhreathnach (ed.), *The kingship and landscape of Tara* (Dublin, 2005) for a comprehensive consideration of Tara. **21** F.J. Byrne, *Irish kings and high-kings* (Dublin, 1973), p. 86. **22** Ó Cróinín, 'Ireland, 400–800', pp 201–11; Charles-Edwards, *Early Christian Ireland*, pp 441–68; Bhreathnach, *Medieval world*, p. 60. **23** For a different view which challenges this traditional view, see B. Lacey, *Cenél Conaill and the Donegal kingdoms, AD 500–800* (Dublin, 2006), p. 145. **24** Ó Cróinín, 'Ireland, 400–800', p. 210. **25** See Charles-Edwards, *Early Christian Ireland*, pp 469–521.

enth century they had established a pattern of alternation whereby the most powerful king of Southern Uí Néill would hold the kingship of Tara, followed by the most senior overlord of Northern Uí Néill and so on. This consolidation helped cement their political position. Indeed, their influence extended beyond the shores of Ireland. One of the Cenél nEógain high-kings is said to have been the maternal grandfather of the Northumbrian king Aldfrith,[26] who appears to have been placed on the Northumbrian throne with the help of the Uí Néill and who had links with Iona.[27] In 695, Loingsech mac Óengusso of the Cenél Conaill became the king of Tara, being referred to, both in the guarantor-list in the text of *LxI* and in the annals upon his death, as 'king of Ireland', which strongly suggests that he enjoyed a practically dominant position within the Irish political landscape.[28] Adomnán himself was of the Cenél Conaill, a fourth cousin of Loingsech. It has generally been accepted that most of the abbots of Iona after Columba were also of the Cenél Conaill. This may not be strictly correct, and Adomnán may have been the first truly Cenél Conaill abbot of Iona for over eighty years,[29] thus making the confluence of the political and ecclesiastical power all the more significant.

In the southern half of the country the various branches of the Eóganacht contended for supremacy. There appears to have been relatively little military interaction between the Munster kings and the Uí Néill in the period immediately before 700, the first Munster king to advance a serious claim to the high-kingship being Cathal mac Finguine (721–42). His efforts were ultimately unsuccessful and it was not until the next century, in the reign of Fedelmid mac Crimthainn, that a Munster king was able to mount a challenge for the high-kingship.[30] While it may have been militarily cut off, it would be wrong, however, to see Munster as being totally disengaged, as will be apparent from the involvement of their lay and ecclesiastical leaders as guarantors of *LxI* in 697.

As Edel Bhreathnach points out, while, in reality, power was fragmented, nevertheless, 'The Irish learned class emerged in the seventh century, asserting a sense of a united ethnicity among the island's people ... they constructed a centralizing authority around the kingship of Tara, a kingship that had been sacral and exceptional in prehistory'.[31] The regnal lists of those who were recognized as kings of Tara provided a chronological framework for Irish history and prehistory. With the arrival of Christianity it became immediately necessary to reconcile any existing traditions of the origin of the inhabitants of the island with the book of Genesis. In *Lebor Gabála* (the book of the taking of Ireland) the tra-

---

26 Byrne, *Kings*, p. 260; C. Ireland, 'Aldfrith of Northumbria and Irish genealogies', *Celtica*, 22 (1991), pp 64–67; idem, 'Alfrith of Northumbria and the learning of a *sapiens'* in K.A. Klar et al. (eds), *A Celtic florilegium: studies in memory of Brendan O Hehir* (Andover, MA, 1996), pp 63–77. **27** M. Richter, *Ireland and her neighbours in the seventh century* (Dublin, 1999), pp 89–108. **28** AU s. a. 703. **29** See Lacey, *Cenél Conaill*, pp 243–6, for a full treatment, and Chapter 4 below. **30** Ó Cróinín, 'Ireland, 400–800', pp 225–7; Byrne, *Kings*, pp 165–201. **31** Bhreathnach, *Medieval world*, pp 3–4. See also, eadem (ed.), *The kingship and landscape of Tara*.

dition of the invasion of Ireland by the sons of Míl was linked with the new, and incontrovertible, biblical history of the origin of the world. It is not clear when a specific work of this title came into being but the tradition of this 'origin tale' of the Irish is thought to have existed in the seventh century or earlier.[32] The text, although not in its original form, has survived in a large number of medieval manuscript copies.[33] This sense of shared descent was, of course, greatly facilitated by the fact that the inhabitants of the island of Ireland shared the same language. 'The spread of a single language throughout Ireland before Rome fell to the Goths gave a unity to the history of the island that geography alone could not confer'.[34] In fact, 'the Irish were apparently the first Western European people to develop a full-scale vernacular written literature expressed in a range of literary genres'.[35] From this developed a strongly linguistic sense of identity as a people among the inhabitants. At a minimum there was a single literary language in use throughout the island of Ireland from at least the sixth century onwards. A dialect-free literary language was an unusual feature of Irish culture. This unity of language led to 'an awareness that the island of Ireland formed one unit and was perceived as such'.[36]

While it is important to acknowledge this sense of united origin and descent among the elite, particularly against the background of seemingly very fragmented political power structures, there is nothing unique about it. It will be apparent from our survey in the previous chapter of the laws of the Germanic peoples that they had a strong sense of their own individual identities. What was unique to Ireland, however, was its complex relationship with another language, Latin. While there was, presumably, some knowledge of Latin in pre-Christian Ireland, particularly for trade purposes, the introduction of Christianity in the fifth century brought with it, not just the language, Latin, but also its literature and intellectual tradition.[37] Writing in Irish, which by the end of the seventh century flourished, was a product of the introduction of the Latin alphabet, although there was a pre-existing limited vernacular literacy, as evidenced by the ogam inscriptions.[38] But writing in Latin also flourished, during the course of the seventh century, as did the intellectual training it necessitated.[39] The result was a high level of scholarship in such subjects as exegesis, grammar and computus.[40] What was different about the Irish was that they learned Latin as a foreign, albeit

---

32 J. Carney, 'Language and literature to 1169' in Ó Cróinín (ed.), *NHI*, p. 460. 33 Ibid., p. 461. 34 Charles-Edwards, 'Prehistoric and early Ireland', pp lxv–lxvi. 35 Johnston, *Literacy*, p. 15. 36 Richter, *Neighbours*, p. 41. 37 Johnston, *Literacy*, p. 14; D. Ó Cróinín, 'Hiberno-Latin literature to 1169' in *NHI*, pp 371–404. 38 Johnston, *Literacy*, pp 11–12; eadem, 'Literacy and conversion', pp 23–46. On ogam see A. Harvey, 'Problems in dating the origins of the ogham script' in J. Higgitt et al. (eds), *Roman, runes and Ogham: medieval inscriptions in the Insular world and on the Continent* (Donnington, 2001), pp 37–50; D. McManus, *A guide to Ogam* (Maynooth, 1991). See also T.M. Charles-Edwards, 'The contexts and uses of literacy in early Christian Ireland' in H. Pryce (ed.), *Literacy in medieval Celtic societies* (Cambridge, 1998), pp 62–82; idem, *Early Christian Ireland*, pp 163–76. 39 Johnston, *Literacy*, pp 14–15. 40 Ó Cróinín, *Early medieval Ireland*, p. 211.

specifically Christian, language rather than as a spoken form of Latin, gradually evolving into one or other of the Romance languages.[41] This relationship with Latin, it is suggested, was fundamental to and a major defining factor in producing the Ireland of the late seventh century of which Bede could write, in a reference to foreign students coming to Ireland for learning,

> *Quos omnes Scotti libentissime suscipientes, victum et cotidianum sine pretio, libros quoque ad legendum et magisterium gratuitum praebere curabant.*
>
> The Irish welcomed them all gladly, gave them their daily food, and also provided them with books to read and with instruction, without asking for any payment.[42]

It is fair to say, therefore, that the Ireland of the late seventh century was, in terms of learning, relatively advanced. Clearly this type of comparative assertion may not be true of other periods, such as the late fifth century, or even the late eighth or ninth centuries. It is true, however, of Adomnán's Ireland that produced *LxI* in 697.[43]

Any outline of the nature of Irish society in the late seventh century must include a recognition that it was a violent society. What might be considered low-level violence, in medieval terms, was endemic.[44] It is very difficult to say whether Irish society was more or less violent than contemporary neighbouring societies. One of the main problems in comparing societies stems from the fact that the sources differ so much. In looking to seventh-century Francia, for instance, there is nothing similar to the laconic, almost detached, account of the Irish chronicles. Gregory of Tours, Fredegar and the *Liber Historiae Francorum* had different agendas, both from the Irish annals and, as well pointed out by Paul Fouracre, from each other.[45] Fouracre demonstrates that the widely-held view that Merovingian Francia was, relatively, a more violent society than the later Carolingian, is not necessarily correct. The later sources, such as the *Continuations of the Chronicle of Fredegar* and the *Annals of Metz*, had different agendas and purposes from the earlier, and the result was 'to make the eighth-century Franks look more stable and less endemically violent than their counterparts of the sev-

---

41 Johnston, *Literacy*, p. 15; R. Wright, *Late Latin and Early Romance in Spain and Carolingian France* (Liverpool, 1982), pp 105–18. **42** *HE* 3, 27; Ó Cróinín, *Early medieval Ireland*, pp 196–232; Charles-Edwards, *Early Christian Ireland*, pp 8–9. **43** To gain an appreciation of the depth and breadth of learning in early medieval Ireland see M. Lapidge and R. Sharpe (eds), *A bibliography of Celtic-Latin literature, 400–1200* (Dublin, 1985); R. Sharpe, *A handlist of Latin writers of Great Britain and Ireland before 1540* (Turnhout, 1997); D. Ó Corráin (ed.), *Clavis Litterarum Hibernensium: medieval Irish books and texts (c.400–c.1600)* (3 vols, Turnhout, 2017). For a useful comparative study of the state of learning in Western Europe in the sixth and seventh centuries see J. Fontaine, 'Education and learning' in idem (ed.), *The new Cambridge medieval history*, i (Cambridge, 2005), pp 735–59. **44** Bhreathnach, *Medieval world*, p. 122. **45** Fouracre, 'Attitudes towards violence', pp 68–74. See references to these sources in Chapter 2.

enth century'.[46] With regard to Britain also, while the sources are scant, it appears that, there too, violence was endemic. The Anglo Saxons 'fought each other, indeed, rather more than they fought the Welsh',[47] with persistent rivalries between, by 700 or so, Northumbria, Mercia, Wessex and East Anglia.[48] Meaningful comparisons are extremely difficult, if not impossible.

The lack of a central authority in Ireland to compel observance of the law is sometimes seen as a source of violence because petty kings were required to take it upon themselves to ensure that the terms of judgments were implemented and acted as enforcing sureties on behalf of clients, thus leading to raiding, feuding and low-level warfare. This is partly true, but not unique to Ireland, and not entirely a source of disorder and violence. As Fouracre points out, in Francia, as in every early medieval kingdom, the ruler exercised authority over a limited range of issues.[49] Most were settled locally by violent action or the threat of it. In fact, violence, as a self-regulating system, could have positive rather than negative effects on social order.[50] Thomas Charles-Edwards refers to it as 'the law of self-help'.[51] F.J. Byrne describes the same process: 'The armed posse of such a lord would recover debts or damages by distraining after due legal form upon the chattels of the defaulting party …'[52] Robin Chapman Stacey illustrates the operation of the self-help system in the areas of distraint, *tellach* (land claims), sick-maintenance and the giving of gages, pointing to the elaborate performance of numerous steps, in public, that was involved.[53]

While the frequency of this type of violence might be a concern, it was even more imperative to regulate it on an agreed basis among participants, and to lay down accepted parameters, such as the non-involvement of innocents.

EMPIRICAL EVIDENCE

The chronicles
Consideration will first be given to those sources that might offer observable evidence of violence, including the chronicles and archaeology. The former are our obvious initial port of call, being 'the principal narrative source for early Irish history'.[54] It is now widely accepted by scholars that a parent-text lay behind the extant chronicles up to 911.[55] This text, which no longer exists, has been recon-

46 Fouracre, 'Attitudes towards violence', p. 69. 47 Wickham, *The inheritance of Rome*, p. 158. 48 Ibid., p. 159. On early England see F.M. Stenton, *Anglo-Saxon England* (Oxford, 1971); J. Campbell (ed.), *The Anglo-Saxons* (Oxford, 1982); B. Yorke, *Kings and kingdoms of early Anglo-Saxon England* (London, 1990). 49 Fouracre, 'Attitudes towards violence', p. 71; Charles-Edwards, 'Early Irish law', p. 368. 50 Fouracre, 'Attitudes towards violence', p. 71; Brown, *Violence*, pp 16–17 and pp 57–8. 51 Charles-Edwards, 'Early Irish law', p. 341. See also, idem, *Early Irish and Welsh kinship* (Oxford, 1993), pp 259–61, p. 265 and pp 272–3. 52 Byrne, *Kings*, p. 31. 53 R. Chapman Stacey, *Dark speech: the performance of law in early Ireland* (Philadelphia, 2007), pp 15–52. 54 T.M. Charles-Edwards (ed. and trans.), *The chronicle of Ireland* (2 vols, Liverpool, 2006), i, 1. 55 Charles-Edwards, *Early Christian Ireland*, p. xix; idem, *Chronicle*, p. 1; R. Flechner, 'The Chronicle of Ireland: then and now', *Early Medieval Europe*,

structed by Thomas Charles-Edwards,[56] and is utilized here as our standard work of reference. It was dubbed 'The Chronicle of Ireland' by Kathleen Hughes in 1972.[57] It covers the period 432 to 911, with the first contemporary recording commencing, in Iona, shortly after the foundation of the monastery there by Columba in c.563.[58] It continued to be compiled there until c.740 when the compilation moved to Brega where it remained until 911.[59] The main basis for the acceptance of the existence of the Chronicle is the fact that so many entries under individual years occur in the same sequence and in the same wording in many of the daughter-texts, including both the Annals of Ulster and the annals comprising the Clonmacnoise group of annals.[60] This, needless to say, is a simplified and abbreviated summary of something complex and controversial.[61] In any event, it appears to be generally accepted that the annal content up to c.740 was compiled in Iona where Adomnán presided as abbot from 679 to 704.[62] It has been suggested that he would have taken an active interest in the content of the Chronicle.[63]

An analysis of the chronicles for the hundred-year period up to and including 697 reveals a recording of 187 acts of violence, including killings, battles, sieges, burnings, laying waste, storming, slaughters, engagements and skirmishes.[64] It is interesting to note that there is no record of violence towards innocents, apart from one, the killing of Lóchéne Menn, abbot of Kildare, in 696. Violence towards women and children is simply not reported. Ironically the single year recording the most incidents of violence, six, is 697, the year of the enactment of *LxI*.[65] As the Chronicle of Ireland in this period tends to concentrate on the northern half of Ireland and northern Britain, it is reasonable to assume that there were many incidents of violence in the southern half not recorded in the Chronicle.[66] Apart from the violence generated by Uí Néill expansion and their internal squabbles,[67] much of the violence related to raiding, collection of tribute and institutional violence, recognized as legitimate under the laws.[68] There are no entries recording the killing of innocents in the course of the many vio-

---

21:4 (2013), p. 422. McCarthy takes a different view: D. McCarthy, *The Irish annals: their genesis, evolution and history* (Dublin, 2008), pp 96–117; idem, 'Review of Charles-Edwards' *The Chronicle of Ireland*', *Peritia*, 20 (2008), pp 379–87. See also N. Evans, *The present and the past in medieval Irish chronicles* (Woodbridge, 2010). **56** Charles-Edwards, *Chronicle*. **57** K. Hughes, *Early Christian Ireland: introduction to the sources* (London, 1972), p. 118. **58** Charles-Edwards, *Chronicle*, pp 8–9. **59** Ibid., p. 9; A.P. Smyth, 'The earliest Irish annals: their first contemporary entries, and the earliest centres of recording', *PRIA*, 72C (1972), pp 1–48; G. Mac Niocaill, *The medieval Irish annals* (Dublin, 1975), pp 21–3. **60** Charles-Edwards, *Chronicle*, p 1. **61** For more on the controversy see Flechner, 'Chronicle', pp 426–7; D. McCarthy, 'The genesis and evolution of the Irish annals', *Frühmittelalterliche Studien*, 52 (2018), pp 119–55. **62** Charles-Edwards, *Chronicle*, p. 9; McCarthy, *Annals*, pp 166–7. **63** Hughes, *Sources*, p. 118. **64** This statistic is extracted from Charles-Edwards, *Chronicle*, pp 119–73. **65** AU s. a. 697. **66** See Ó Cróinín, 'Ireland, 400–800', pp 221–34. **67** For instance the battle of Imlech Pich in 688. See Ó Cróinín, 'Ireland, 400–800', p. 218. **68** Byrne, *Kings*, p. 31, p. 45 and p. 49; Bhreathnach, *Medieval world*, p. 122.

lent incidents that are mentioned. Either, there were no innocents harmed or the chronicles did not record such incidents, because they were outside its scope and/or contrary to its desired style. The latter explanation is the more credible, given human propensities as we know them. Furthermore, it is extremely unlikely that Adomnán would have initiated a law for the protection of innocents if there was no need, nor would he have won the support he did. The chronicles' entries are 'descriptive, concise and laconic'.[69] There is no effort to give the cause of an event or make causal connections between different events.[70] The chronicles, although very selective, are, to a quite remarkable degree, non-partisan. They have been described as demonstrating a 'dispassionate objectivity' from which they very rarely deviated,[71] and on the rare occasions when they did, it was not always in favour of the party one would expect. This form and style, including its concise entries, absence of causality and objectivity, which was maintained over three-and-a-half centuries, might, of themselves, go some of the way to explaining the lack of references to the fate of innocents in the chronicles. To this must be added the fact that there is a remarkable consistency, also, in the genre of topics covered. Deaths and battles predominate, whereas other events, such as Irish church councils or marriage alliances, do not feature. There appears to have been a convention as to what should be covered and what not. The point has been made that the uniformity of approach over the centuries might be due to editing by a scribe who, it is suggested, copied the entire text c.911, or due to retrospective chronicling.[72] In any event, some form of intervention may explain the uniformity over such a long time and explain the absence of references to innocents. The killing of clerics is mentioned regularly.[73] Also, in the years subsequent to 697, both with reference to Viking violence and inter-Irish violence, there is occasional reference to violence which included 'common people'.[74] An unusually explicit reference to innocents is an entry for 814, 'Muirgus and Forcellach summoned a hosting against the Uí Maini south of the Socc, where very many innocent people were killed'.[75] There is only one reference to women as such. It is recorded for the year 821, 'The plundering of Étar by *gennti*; from there they carried off a great number of women.'[76] In the final analysis the annalists were concerned with the elite and did not record the fate of people of lesser value. This, of itself, reveals an attitude towards people's relative worth, making Adomnán's concern all the more remarkable.

It is possible, nevertheless, to discern a nuanced attitude to death and killing from the language used to describe these events. Thomas Charles-Edwards maintains that the primary concern of the chronicles is death, and, more particularly,

---

69 Flechner, 'Chronicle', p. 242. **70** Charles-Edwards, *Chronicle*, p. 4; Evans, *Present and past*, p. 226. **71** Charles-Edwards, *Chronicle*, p. 13; Flechner, 'Chronicle', p. 425. **72** Flechner, 'Chronicle', pp 432–3, 441; Evans, *Present and past*, pp 89–90. **73** For example, two separate such killings are recorded for the year 744. AU s. a. 744. See Charles-Edwards, *Chronicle*, pp 215–16. **74** AU s. a. 780, 816, 836, 850 and 895. **75** AU s. a. 814. See Charles-Edwards, *Chronicle*, p. 279. **76** AU s. a. 821.

with the spiritual quality of each individual's death.[77] This is determined by the manner in which death is met. For a layman the most admired death was death by natural cause. There was no admiration for heroic death by combat. The worst death for a layman was to be slain in an individual act of violence, particularly by one's own kinsman, or, if a king, by his own retinue. For a king to die peacefully in his own bed was seen as a sign of God's favour. For him to die in battle was a spiritually inferior death because he died in a process that was dominated by demons. War, sometimes, was a necessary evil, but, for the annalist, 'most battles were great evils and were not necessary'. Peace was inherently spiritually superior to violence. The word used for those dying in battle was *ceciderunt*, for death in a single killing, *iugulatio*. A distinction was also made in recording the deaths of clerics, with *quies* being used for the death of an admirable churchman and *mors* as a neutral description.[78] While the significance of this can be debated by scholars, what cannot be disputed is that the annalist and those generally responsible for The Chronicle of Ireland graded death and, while accepting violence as a fact of life, deprecated it. It is important to remember that it was produced in a church for a readership also based in churches, and its concerns were primarily ecclesiastical.[79] It may not reflect the views of society at large but only a section, albeit an influential section of it. That said, and this is fundamental, it probably reflects Adomnán's views.

Archaeology
There is 'an apparent lack of solid archaeological evidence' for violence in early medieval Ireland.[80] Analyses of bones from recent archaeologically excavated cemeteries are beginning to fill the gap, however. About 140 early medieval burial-sites have been excavated in Ireland to date and thirteen per cent of these have been found to contain skeletal evidence of weapon trauma.[81] Beheading is prevalent and there have been some cases of extreme violence.[82] A number of

---

77 Charles-Edwards, *Chronicle*, pp 24–35.   **78** Ibid., pp 27–9, 32; see also N.B. Aitcheson, 'Regicide in early medieval Ireland' in Halsall (ed.), *Violence*, pp 111–15. Charles-Edwards goes on to argue that the purpose of grading deaths was to guide the clerical readers of the chronicles as to who required prayers for their souls and who did not. Evans takes a different view, *Past and present*, p. 227. Flechner suggests that the chronicles had an eschatological agenda which demanded a deliberate suspension of judgment about the events described, leaving it to future readers who might have an exegetical instinct which would enable them to look beyond the wording of the text and see patterns and connections not apparent to modern readers, with our limited understanding of causality, 'Chronicle', pp 440–9.   **79** Charles-Edwards, *Chronicle*, p. 6 and p. 24.   **80** J. Geber, 'Human remains from Owenbristy' in G. Delaney and J. Tierney (eds), *In the lowlands of south Galway: archaeological excavations on the N18 Oranmore to Gort National Road Scheme* (Dublin, 2011), p. 90.   **81** J.Geber, 'Comparative study of perimortem weapon trauma in two early medieval skeletal populations (AD 400–1200) from Ireland', *International Journal of Osteoarchaeology*, 25:3 (May/June 2015), p. 253 (first published on line 6 November 2012, Wiley online library); www.mappingdeathdb.ie, final report, p. 18.   **82** Geber, 'Comparative study', p. 258.

sites have produced evidence of violence towards women. In an excavation of a cemetery in Corbally, Co. Kildare, a female skeleton showed evidence of stabbing by a double-edged sharp blade that involved the sixth and seventh ribs, piercing the left lung and heart and was almost certainly fatal.[83] Excavation of an early medieval site in Parknahown 5, Co. Laois, yielded up evidence of trauma suffered by an adult female. She had thirteen sharp-force wounds on the cervical vertebrae, indicating a number of blows to the throat that would certainly have caused death.[84] In an excavation in Owenbristy, Co. Galway, two female adults were found to have been brutally killed and decapitated. One, aged between thirty-five and forty-five, was beheaded between the fourth and fifth cervical vertebrae with, what appears to be, one blow from the right. The other, aged between twenty-five and thirty-five, suffered a horrible death. She had six stab wounds around her eyes. Stab wounds on the left and right side of her skull suggest that she was lying on the ground desperately moving her head from side to side. It appears that all the stab wounds were caused by the same knife. She was also struck by a sword or an axe through the stomach and eventually decapitated.[85]

It is worth noting that, while all of the female trauma cases mentioned date from the early medieval period,[86] the last mentioned remains have been specifically radiocarbon dated to before 697.[87] Incidentally, Owenbristy also produced evidence of violence towards adolescents. One, aged between thirteen and sixteen, had been stabbed three times in the neck, three times in the back, two times in the chest and at least once in the throat. The body had been decapitated after death. The second individual displayed a cranial blunt force wound and sharp force trauma through the posterior portions of the parietal bones, indicating use of a sword.[88]

It is difficult to interpret these findings. While they do not conclusively establish that violence towards women and children in warfare-like situations was common, they do establish that it existed. Of the 140 or so early medieval burial-sites that have been excavated, approximately 18 have yielded evidence of deaths due to violence. Of that 18, the above 3 sites, Corbally, Parknahown 5 and Owenbristy, include women among the victims. Assuming the 140 sites are a representative sample – and this is a major assumption – roughly seventeen per cent of battle or skirmish sites included women victims. This, it is suggested, would be a considerable percentage, warranting legislative intervention. It must be stressed that the foregoing analysis is anything but scientific. The archaeological evidence, however, when taken with the fact that a law for the protection of innocents was enacted, is compelling.[89]

---

83 F. Coyne (with a contribution by L.G. Lynch), 'Corbally, Co. Kildare: the results of the 2003–4 excavations of a secular cemetery' in C. Corlett and M. Potterton (eds), *Death and burial in early medieval Ireland in the light of recent archaeological excavations* (Bray, 2010), p. 86. **84** T. O'Neill, 'The changing character of early medieval burial at Parknahown 5, Co. Laois, AD 400–1200' in Corlett and Potterton (eds), *Death and burial*, p. 256. **85** Geber, 'Context and content', p. 94. **86** Coyne, 'Corbally', p. 88; O'Neill, 'Parknahown', p. 252; Geber, 'Context and content', p. 88. **87** Geber, 'Comparative study', p. 260. **88** Ibid., p. 260. **89** mappingdeathdb.ie

NORMATIVE TEXTS

Vernacular law
A brief study of vernacular law, canon law and the penitentials will be helpful in identifying attitudes towards violence.[90] Irish society, in the seventh century, was regulated by a long-established, detailed and comprehensive set of vernacular laws.[91] These laws covered all the normal concerns of society. Fergus Kelly categorizes the laws: law of persons, property, offences, contracts, distraint, procedure, punishment and so on, not unlike the categorization in law books in Ireland today.[92] He lists seventy-nine surviving law texts and seven surviving wisdom texts that contain these laws.[93] They constitute what has been described as early-medieval Europe's largest corpus of vernacular laws.[94]

Society was hierarchical and inegalitarian.[95] Central to the operation of the legal system was the concept of honour-price. The king, lord, cleric and poet were of the higher rank and had higher honour-prices as a result. Lesser ranks included the free man and the unfree. Offences against a high-ranking person attracted a higher penalty, for the same offence, than against a person of lower rank. Dependants, including a man's wife, son or daughter, had an honour-price of normally half the man's honour-price. They did not have an honour-price in their own right. The oath of a person of high rank automatically outweighed that of a person of lower rank. Evidence from a female was not acceptable except in exceptional circumstances.[96] The concept in Roman law that all (Roman citizens) were equal before the law did not apply in Ireland, as it did not in most other legal systems of that time.[97] It is important to always remember, therefore, that, in early Irish society, some people were more valuable than others.

(accessed 18/12/17) appears to throw up somewhat different figures: total sites 183, total trauma 22 (12%), of which 14 (63%) include females, of which only 3 (Corbally 2, Owenbristy and Parknahown 5) include females who suffered violent trauma. **90** For vernacular Irish law see D.A. Binchy (ed.), *Corpus Iuris Hibernici* (6 vols, Dublin, 1978) (*CIH*); Fergus Kelly, *A guide to early Irish law* (Dublin, 1988). For canon law, H. Wasserschleben (ed.), *Die irische Kanonensammlung* (Leipzig, 1885, repr. Aachen, 1966); R. Flechner (ed.), *A study, edition and translation of the Hibernensis, with commentary* (Dublin, forthcoming). For the Irish penitentials, Bieler, *Irish penitentials*; Kenney, *Sources*; Pereira Farrell, 'Taboos and penitence'; Meens, 'Irish contribution'. Note the brief mention of Irish canon law and the Irish penitentials in the previous chapter. **91** These tracts are collected in *CIH*; while many are later than the seventh century it has been argued by Liam Breatnach, *The early Irish law text Senchas Már and the question of its date*, E.G. Quiggin Memorial Lectures, 13 (Cambridge, 2011) that the core of the collection of tracts, known as the Senchas Már, had reached written form by the second half of the seventh century. For list of texts see Ó Corráin, *Clavis*, pp 863–924. **92** Kelly, *Guide*. **93** Ibid., pp 264–86. **94** Flechner, *A study*, ch. 1. **95** Kelly, *Guide*, pp 7–11 for a concise summary of rank in early Irish society including citation of the original sources. **96** Ibid., p. 207. **97** See, for example, in relation to the position of women in marriage in Ireland, relative to their position under Roman and Germanic laws, B. Jaski, 'Marriage laws in Ireland and on the Continent in the early Middle Ages' in C.E. Meek and M.K. Simms (eds), *'The fragility of her sex': medieval Irish women in their European context* (Dublin, 1996), pp 16–42.

On the other hand, while a system which is based on a division of rights according to social standing cannot, to the modern mind, be considered equitable, Fergus Kelly is correct when he says that the 'approach (of the early Irish lawyer) to legal problems is – within the limits set by the strictly hierarchical structure of the society – fair and humane'.[98] The law texts lay down basic principles of what was considered fair-dealing between neighbours. *Bechbretha* states that 'no-one is obliged to give something to another for nothing'.[99] *Bretha Crólige* stipulates that 'the misdeed of the guilty should not affect the innocent'.[100] Heptad 49 excludes as a witness anyone who stands to gain by the outcome on the grounds that 'greed distracts from honesty'.[101] Furthermore, there are many provisions aimed at protecting the weaker members of the community, such as those protecting their clients against lords, those seeking to prevent exploitation of persons of unsound mind and those attempting to provide legal support for the destitute.[102]

To a large extent, much of the vernacular law was committed to writing around the second half of the seventh century, the same time as *LxI* was being enacted.[103] There is considerable debate as to who wrote the law texts; D.A. Binchy took the view that the texts were composed by professional lay jurists.[104] Others, including Donnchadh Ó Corráin, argue that they were written by clerics and influenced by canon law.[105] Fergus Kelly very succinctly summarizes the arguments on both sides, and Roy Flechner, more recently, makes useful observations on the issue.[106] Clearly the two traditions, early Irish and Christian, became enmeshed to some degree. But in general 'the native law, therefore, remained a distinct legal tradition from that of the canonist, and the two were maintained by distinct, though overlapping, groups of men'.[107]

Apart from the law contained in the law texts and wisdom texts, there was a second type of law known as *cáin* law. This was enacted law as distinct from customary law.[108] The *cáin* originated from the laws enacted at the *óenach* by the king for his *tuath*. *Críth Gablach* (*c*.700) gives us a considerable amount of information about the *cáin*.[109] It could be a law for just one *tuath* or several.[110] It cites a range of *rechtgi* (enacted law) covering a wide spectrum, from special edicts for emer-

---

98 Kelly, *Guide*, p. 236. **99** *CIH* 445. 3; Kelly, *Guide*, p. 274. **100** *CIH* 2300. 31–2. See D.A. Binchy (ed. and trans.), '*Bretha Crólige*', *Ériu*, 12 (1938), pp 1–77, discussed in Kelly, *Guide*, p. 236. **101** *CIH* 45.4. **102** For example: clients, *CIH* 1778.34–1804.11, 479.23–502.6 = W.N. Hancock et al. (eds), *AL* (6 vols, Dublin, 1865–1901), ii, 223–341= *ZCP* (Halle, Tübingen, 1897), 14 (1923) 338–94 and *CIH* 432.21–436.32; unsound mind, *CIH* 372.21 = *AL* i, 124.9–10; destitute, *CIH* 2193.26–27 = *ZCP* 15 (1925) 317. See Kelly, *Guide*, pp 236–7. **103** See observations on date of compilation of *Senchas Már* below, p. 75. **104** Introduction to *CIH*, pp ix–x. **105** D. Ó Corráin, L. Breatnach and A. Breen, 'The laws of the Irish', *Peritia*, 3 (1984), pp 382–438. **106** Kelly, *Guide*, pp 232–6; Flechner, *A study*, ch. 1. See also Ó Cróinín, *Early medieval Ireland*, pp 123–5. **107** Charles-Edwards, 'Early Irish law', p. 366. **108** Ó Cróinín, *Early medieval Ireland*, pp 78–84; Charles-Edwards, *Early Christian Ireland*, pp 559–69; idem., 'Early Irish law', pp 334–7. **109** *CIH* 777.6–783.38; 563.1–570.32; Kelly, *Guide*, p. 267; Charles-Edwards, *Early Christian Ireland*, pp 560–1. **110** Charles-Edwards, *Early Christian Ireland*, p. 560. See also, Grigg, 'Aspects'.

gencies to edicts designed to reinforce rules of native law. Many *cána* were never written down. They applied to a single *tuath* and had authority only within the territory of that king. *Críth Gablach* mentions *LxI* explicitly, perceiving it as *recht Adomnáin*, the Law of Adomnán and an example of *Recthtge ríg*, royal edict. It, therefore, was an unusually important law in that it enacted a law for all of Ireland and Dál Riata but was a *cáin*, in the traditions of the existing legal system nevertheless. It will be clear from the foregoing that Ireland was, to an extent, a law conscious society.[111]

The position of women, under the law, was woven into the legal system via the honour-price concept. Their honour-price was normally half that of their husband, father or son as the case may be.[112] The laws deal with the legal capacity of women and with such issues as inheritance, marriage, divorce and separation.[113] However, as far as the killing of a woman is concerned, or the causing of injury to her, compensation for it is greater or less, depending on the rank of the man on whom she is dependent.[114] A female dependant of a king or high ranking man who suffers an injury commands higher compensation than that payable to a dependant of a lower ranked man who suffers the same injury. The compensation is payable to the man. There are no special provisions for the protection of a woman per se; she is part of the general honour-price system. As will be clear in Chapter 5, the provisions of *LxI* differ from these vernacular law provisions. While the latter came to be written down around the same time as *LxI* was enacted, it is probable that they reflect the position before *LxI*,[115] which sought to strengthen the legal protection of women.

The laws refer to two types of rape: *forcor* and *sleth*. *Forcor* is forcible rape and *sleth* any other situation where a woman is subjected to sexual intercourse without her consent, for instance, where a woman is taken advantage of while intoxicated.[116] Again the penalty is determined by the honour-price of the male on whom the victim is dependent. However, an extra fine, known as the *éraic* or full body fine, has to be paid for the rape of a young woman of marriageable age, a chief wife or a nun who has not renounced the veil. In the case of a rape of a concubine, referred to in the laws as an *adaltrach*, only half the body fine is payable. If the victim becomes pregnant, the rapist is responsible for rearing the child.[117] Clearly, the laws reflect a concern for the loss caused to the kin of the victim and, in particular, loss of honour.

The legal position of children is known from two texts that survive in fragmentary form, *Cáin Íarraith* and *Maccshlechta*, as well as from scattered references in other law texts.[118] Matters covered include legal capacity, from birth to age of

---

111 Bhreathnach, *Medieval world*, p. 102; Chapman Stacey, *Dark speech*, p. 54 and p. 153. **112** Kelly, *Guide*, p. 11. **113** Ibid., pp 68–77 and p. 104; Bhreathnach, *Medieval world*, pp 82–7. **114** Kelly, *Guide*, p. 79. **115** See discussion on which came first, see below, p. 75. **116** Kelly, *Guide*, p. 135. **117** Ibid., p. 135. **118** Ibid., p. 81; *Cáin Íarraith*, *CIH* 1759.6–1770.14; *Maccshlechta*, *CIH* 1296.17–1301–16, 1546.26–1550.14. On children in early Ireland, see B. Ní Chonaill, 'Child-centred law in medieval Ireland' in R. Davis and T. Dunne (eds), *The empty*

seven, from seven to fourteen and from fourteen to seventeen and then to twenty, responsibility for the rearing of children, fosterage and even liability for injury to children while playing games.[119] It has been remarked that, in the laws, 'the treatment and safety of the child remained central'.[120] This is underlined by the unusual provision of *Bretha Crólige,* which stipulates that the honour-price of a child between baptism and the age of seven is the same as that of a cleric, and consequently, as Kelly points out, 'any injury inflicted on a young child entails a heavy penalty no matter what social class he or she belongs to'.[121] The text reads: *id comdíre mac ríg agus mac aithig co cenn .vii. mblíadnae* 'The son of a king and the son of a commoner have the same honour-price up to seven years'.[122] An unusual level of protection is, therefore, accorded to very young children, perhaps the most innocent of the innocents.

The third major category of innocents – clerics – was, as far as the higher clergy are concerned, well protected by vernacular law; the lesser clergy not so well. Unlike women and children over the age of seven, they had the protection of an honour-price in their own right. *Uraicecht Becc* lists the honour-price of clerics: lector –7 *séts*, usher –10 *séts*, exorcist –15 *séts*, sub deacon –20 *séts*, deacon –30 *séts*, priest –3½ *cumals*, bishop – 7 *cumals*.[123] A bishop, therefore, had an honour-price equivalent to a king. Indeed, according to *Crith Gablach,* a bishop was nobler than a king.[124] *Uraicecht Becc* places an archbishop, along with an abbot of a major monastery such as Cork or Emly, on the same level as a provincial king, with an honour-price of fourteen *cumals*.[125] By way of further protection for clerics the law provided an extra penalty (*pennait*) on anybody who committed a serious offence against them in addition to the victim's honour-price.[126] This high level of protection seems to stem, more from the perceived contractual relationships between society and the church, by which the clergy provided high-value services in exchange, rather than from the clerics' non-combatant status. *Bretha Nemed toísech* makes it clear that the church must give good 'considerations' by way of religious services in return for its privileges.[127]

It would appear, therefore, that there was a deficit of protection provided by vernacular law, which affected the three classes of innocents. Women of marriageable age, chief wives and nuns were protected against rape by the *éraic*. However, they, as victims of any other offence, and all other women in respect

---

throne: childhood and the crisis of modernity (www.eprints.gla.ac.uk/3812/). **119** Kelly, *Guide,* pp 81–91 and p. 150. **120** Bhreathnach, *Medieval world,* p. 88; B. Ní Chonaill, 'Child-centred law'. **121** Kelly, *Guide,* p. 83; *CIH* 2288.1–2 = *Ériu,* 12 (1938) 8.7. **122** *CIH* 923.3–4. **123** *CIH* 1594.37–1595.14 = *AL* v 22.1–2 and *CIH* 2212.24–6 for clerics in orders. *CIH* 2101.1–7 and *CIH* 586.1–2 for clerics not in orders. See Kelly, *Guide,* p. 39, n. 1; L. Breatnach (ed. and trans.), *Uraicecht na Ríar: the poetic grades in early Irish law* (Dublin, 1987). **124** *CIH* 570.31–2 = *CG* 604–5; Kelly, *Guide,* p. 41. **125** *CIH* 1618.5 = *AL* v 112.1; *CIH* 1618.7; 2282.27; 2334.35–6 = *AL* v 112.1–3; Kelly, *Guide,* p. 41. **126** For example, *CIH* 1602.38–1603.2 = *AL* v 52.23–5; *CIH* 2287.17–18 = *Ériu,* 12 (1938), 6.4; Kelly, *Guide,* p. 43. **127** *CIH* 2211.4–14; Kelly, *Guide,* pp 41–2. See P. Brown, *The rise of Western Christendom: triumph and diversity, AD 200–1000* (2nd ed., Oxford, 2003), pp 332–3.

of all offences against them, were valued less than the men on whom they were dependent. Children under seven were well protected, but older children were relatively under-protected. The higher clergy, likewise, were well protected by their high honour-price, but the lesser clergy were left exposed by their relatively low value. It is easy to imagine how a marauding band of warriors might calculate that they could raid with impunity in the knowledge that death or injury caused to women of lower rank, youths and lesser clergy would not be unduly expensive if they were ultimately held accountable. *LxI* fills these lacunae in the law. Adomnán had to win acceptance for the increased penalties provided for in *LxI*. This would surely have been difficult, as it would be necessary to win acceptance for the underlying change of attitude that demanded an acceptance that, in certain situations such as in time of warfare, women, children and lesser clerics were of equal value to high-ranking men.[128]

With the exception of the provision of *Bretha Crólige* relating to children under seven, no awareness of the vulnerability of the innocent has been disclosed in vernacular law. Nor is there any recognition of the concept of non-combatants or their immunity from violence in warfare. There is one curious exception to this. Irish vernacular law has many provisions stipulating that a person who witnessed an offence and does nothing to prevent it, is himself guilty of an offence, for 'everyone who looks on at an offence consents to it'.[129] The term used is *aircsiu* meaning 'looking on'. The offence of *aircsiu* can arise in many situations, often involving trespass and land law.[130] The text dealing with this offence is known as the *sellach* (onlooker) text. It grades the offence from the most serious, where the onlooker is an instigator, to the least serious, where he merely looks on without making an attempt to stop the crime. The text contains a clause that specifically exempts from liability certain onlookers described in the text as follows:

> (6) There are also other exempt onlookers, i.e., clerics and women and boys and those who are not able to wound or protect or forbid and senseless persons and senile persons.
>
> (6) *Bit sellaig slana and chena -.i. cleirig agus mná agus mec agus aes nad meisi gona na anacal na urgair agus eccuind agus escunid [escuind]*.[131]

What is significant about this is that it groups together women, children and clerics (and persons of unsound mind) and exempts them because they are non-combative. This clause clearly recognizes the concept of non-combatants and exempts them, as a group, as a category on that account. The *sellach* text affords those who qualify as non-combatants special protection under the law. While its

---

128 Issue must be taken with J.E. Fraser, 'Adomnán and the morality of war', p. 110 when he implies that Adomnán would have had little difficulty in winning acceptance for his law. **129** *CIH* 1315.15–18; Kelly, *Guide*, p. 155. **130** Kelly, *Guide*, pp 154–5. **131** Ibid., pp 352–3; *CIH* 404.7–405.12 = *AL* i 240–2.

provisions do not specifically apply in time of war, they do apply in a situation where the use of force and physical violence is envisaged. In articulating the concept of non-combatant and in defining those who qualify as non-combatants, the *sellach* text mixes together clerics, who have an honour-price in their own right, and women and children, who do not. It recognizes a distinct category of person, outside the honour-price system, i.e., the innocent or non-combatant. It will be clear in Chapter 5 that *LxI* also provided substantial protection by way of enhanced penalties over and above those provided under the honour-price system for this distinct category.

It is likely that there will not be academic agreement on whether *LxI* influenced the *sellach* provisions or vice versa; on which came first. We know that *LxI* was enacted in 697, when it was given to the people by Adomnán.[132] Scholars differ on the date of *Senchas Már*, of which the *sellach* text forms a part.[133] A date has been authoritatively argued, more recently, by Liam Breatnach, at between 660 and 680.[134] Furthermore, he rejects the idea that the component tracts of *Senchas Már* were composed at different times, considering it to have been 'conceived of and transmitted as a unitary whole'.[135] Following Breatnach therefore, one must conclude that all of *Senchas Már*, including the *sellach* text, was compiled within the time-span 660 to 680, and therefore before *LxI*. Bearing in mind that *Senchas Már* is a compilation, it is reasonable to assume that the laws and concepts that it contains predated the compilation, making it even more likely that they existed and were current in Irish society before the promulgation of *LxI* in 697. Even if *LxI* had never been enacted and looking at the *sellach* provisions entirely on their own merits, it is only to be expected that unarmed members of society would not be obliged to intervene when they were onlookers at a crime, and that a provision granting them exemption would be essential. It is not argued by scholars that the *Senchas Már* represents new law, although it may have included new elements. It was largely a compilation of existing customary law,[136] including existing onlooker law, with its necessary exemption for the unarmed. In a society in which the bulk of the laws were self-regulated, i.e., the injured party was entitled under law, and expected, to enforce any judgments in his favour by his own force of arms or threat of force,[137] with or without the aid of his lord, it is self-evident that the laws should make it clear who was expected to participate and who was not. It was a matter of practical necessity that people incapable of effective intervention as onlookers on a crime should be excluded from any obligation to intervene. That would appear to be the motivation behind this clause in the *sellach* text. It is reasonable to conclude, nevertheless, that the *sellach* text, or the customs underlying it, would have been available to Adomnán as a precedent or template and was one with which the guarantors would have been familiar.

---

132 AU s. a. 697. **133** See Kelly, *Guide*, pp 242–6; Charles-Edwards, 'Early Irish law', pp 337–50. **134** Breatnach, 'The early Irish law text *Senchas Már*'. **135** Idem., p. 42. **136** '... the written expression of an oral tradition'. See Charles-Edwards, 'Early Irish law', p. 344. **137** Kelly, *Guide*, p. 214.

Canon law

The next body of law to be considered is Irish canon law, which, fortunately for the modern scholar, was codified at an early date. The *Collectio Canonum Hibernensis* was compiled in Ireland, between 716 and 747 by Ruben of Dairinis (d. 725) *scriba* of Munster and Cú Chuimne (d. 747) *sapiens* of Iona.[138] It was the first canon law text in the Latin West to attempt to codify laws for a Christian society generally and not only for the church. It also was the first to consider questions of jurisprudence, such as the concepts of law and its purpose, and the first systematically to extract from the Old and New Testaments, sources for legislation. Without precedent in canonical texts of comparable size, the *Hibernensis* divided its subject-matter systematically. Its preface states that it was compiled with a view to bringing order and harmony to a forest of synodical rulings. By the second half of the eighth century it was circulating widely in continental Europe, copies and derivations being made in Brittany, Tours, Cambrai, Freising, Salzburg, Reichenau, St Gallen, Würzburg and Bobbio. Its appeal was due to its systematic structure, which facilitated its adaptation for the drafting of continental ecclesiastical legislation, and its extensive use of written sources which could be conveniently mined for citations.[139] Its popularity was primarily due, however, to its objective to be a comprehensive Christian law code that legislated for Christian society at large and was not restricted to matters of ecclesiastical jurisdiction and administration. It was, as Thomas Charles-Edwards puts it, 'an attempt to create a Christian law for a Christian society',[140] or as he goes on to say, 'the substance of much of the *Hibernensis* is thus the application of biblical text to Christian living'.[141] Non-ecclesiastical areas covered include kingship, theft, inheritance, contract law, treason and fair wages for workmen.[142] It is not unreasonable, therefore, to seek among its provisions indications of attitudes to violence and, more particularly, attitudes to violence towards the weaker sections of society.

Before examining the provisions of the *Hibernensis*, one must, however, in the light of Breatnach's dating of the compilation of *Senchas Már,* question some fundamental thinking on their positions with respect to each other. It is generally believed that *Hibernensis* pre-dates *Senchas Már* and that the latter was a response to the former, that the *Hibernensis* stimulated the compilers of *Senchas Már* into action. Charles Edwards is of this view, and much of his opinion as expressed in 'Early Irish law' is predicated upon it.[143] Likewise, Flechner approaches his consideration of the *Hibernensis* and native law from the perspec-

---

138 Wasserschleben, *Die irische Kanonensammlung;* Flechner, *A study,* ch. 1. See also, idem, 'An insular tradition of ecclesiastical law: fifth to eighth century', *Proceedings of the British Academy,* 157 (2009), p. 24; M. Gorman, 'Patristic and pseudo-Patristic citations in the *Collectio Hibernensis*', *Revue Bénédictine,* 121:1 (2011), pp 18–93. **139** See Flechner, *A study,* ch. 1; Charles-Edwards, 'Early Irish law', p. 353. **140** Charles-Edwards, 'Early Irish law', p. 353. **141** Ibid., p. 363. **142** Ibid., p. 353; Flechner, *A study,* ch.1. **143** Charles-Edwards, 'Early Irish law', p. 343, p. 346, p. 348 and p. 362.

tive of the former pre-dating the written expression of the latter, which may not be correct. One way or the other, he goes on to list many instances of where the *Hibernensis* is clearly following and adapting and accommodating native law.[144] Indeed, he sees native law as posing a great challenge to Christian jurists, to which they responded in the *Hibernensis*. It is, of course, important to remember that canon law existed before the compilation of the *Hibernensis*, as did native law exist before the compilation of the legal tracts. They were influencing each other in a process of cross-fertilization, presumably from the time of the earliest Christian impact in Ireland. Whether the *Hibernensis* was, in any way, a response to *Senchas Már* or not, it used, as its sources, synodal material, the Bible and the Fathers of the church. Its authorities were, thus, firmly grounded. The use of the Bible and the Fathers was an innovation. In one of the recensions (A) of the *Hibernensis* there are approximately 500 citations from the Bible, two-thirds of which were derived from the Old Testament. With regard to the Fathers, Augustine is cited by name at least 149 times and Jerome 238 times.[145] As mentioned in the previous chapter the influence of the *Hibernensis* on the Continent was considerable, not least 'for introducing the Bible and the Fathers to a continental canonical framework that previously drew solely upon synodal decrees and papal decretals'.[146] What is relevant for us is that, both in Ireland and on the Continent, the effect of this would tend to limit Christian thinking to these authorities. While initially expanding sources it would also have the effect of confining them. We have seen in the previous chapter that the Old Testament is positively unhelpful on our *in bello* concept. The New Testament is ambivalent and the Fathers, particularly Augustine, by and large, unconcerned. Drawing on these sources would not inspire interest in *in bello* concerns. In so far as the *Hibernensis* was intended to be a Christian law for a Christian people, underpinned by the most authoritative of Christian sources, and responding, at least in part, to native law, it was a definitive statement to which little more needed to be added. If the Christian authorities did not proclaim on *in bello* issues, why should it? There were no obvious authorities on these issues from which to draw. Of course, it must also be remembered that *LxI*, which did legislate for the protection of innocents, had been promulgated only a short time before and the compilers of the *Hibernensis* may have felt that there was no need for them to be concerned about these issues.

It is not surprising, therefore, that even the hopefully captioned section of the *Hibernensis* 'On matters concerning women' (44) yields nothing by way of concerns for their vulnerability in society by virtue of their non-combatant status. The section covers issues such as virginity, the killing by women of their unborn children, regulations regarding widows, on the wearing of the veil and on the proper behaviour of women.[147] Likewise, the section captioned 'On crimes and their punishment' (26) is concerned with justifying punishment in many cases.

144 Flechner, *A study*, ch. 1.   **145** Flechner, 'Insular tradition', p. 25. See Gorman, 'Patristic' for a negative view.   **146** Flechner, 'Insular tradition', p. 26.   **147** *Hib* 44.

Augustine is much quoted throughout, a particular example being 26.9, where his emphasis on the attitude of mind of the dispenser of punishment is evident. Provided one does not have hatred in one's heart, to punish a wrongdoer can be an act of mercy because pain and even death caused to the body in this life is relatively unimportant compared to the saving of his or her soul and the achievement of life everlasting in the next. Following Augustine and others, the *Hibernensis* is concerned with what it sees as the major issues, rather than with what, one might speculate, it sees as a relatively minor issue, or at least an issue with which it need not be concerned, the protection of innocents in time of conflict. In the section dealing with *Ius* (11.6) Isidore is followed, almost word-for-word.[148] There are three types of law, natural, civil and the law of nations. It is interesting to note that among the rights that are considered natural is the right to repulse violence by force. Clearly, and not surprisingly, the use of force in such circumstances was regarded as acceptable in late seventh-century and early eighth-century Ireland. The same section goes on to list among its examples of the law of nations 'the pledge not to molest embassies'.[149] This is a type of provision, which, today, is part of international law and the regulation of conflict. The *Hibernensis* differs from Isidore in two interesting respects: the *Hibernensis* reads 'wars, captives, enslavement beyond borders, treaties of peace' whereas Isidore reads 'wars, captives, enslavements, the right of return, treaties of peace'. It is difficult to say whether the inclusion of 'beyond borders' and the exclusion of 'the right of return' in the *Hibernensis* are significant. The return of the captives from Britain in 687 at Adomnán's instigation (see next chapter) comes to mind as does the incident, described in *VC* II.33, of Broichan's reluctant release of a female captive. In any event, it must be concluded that the *Hibernensis*, as one of the normative texts to be consulted in seeking out attitudes to violence in the Ireland of Adomnán's time, is not fertile ground. Its relevance lies more in what it does not say, and in the reasons for its silence, than in what it does say.

The penitentials

The Irish penitentials have been briefly introduced above.[150] Essentially, they list 'sins' and assign penances for each 'sin'.[151] They were written between the sixth and eighth centuries, generally but not always, by identified notable ecclesiastics. Bieler lists some eleven or so texts,[152] but our consideration will be limited to the seven texts known as: First synod of St Patrick, Penitential of Finnian, Penitential

---

148 Isidore, *Etymologies*, V (p. 117 Barney). **149** *Hib* 16.6; Isidore, *Etymologies*, V. vi (pp 117–18 Barney). **150** Chapter 2, pp 34–7. **151** See references in Chapter 2, p. 34. See also P.J. Payer, 'Confession and the study of sex in the Middle Ages' in V.L. Bullough and J.A. Brundage (eds), *Handbook of medieval sexuality* (New York, 1996), pp 3–4; A. Breen, 'Hiberno-Latin literature' in S. Duffy (ed.), *Medieval Ireland: an encyclopedia* (New York and London, 2005), p. 216; A.J. Frantzen, 'Penitentials' in M. Lapidge et al. (eds), *The Blackwell encyclopaedia of Anglo-Saxon England*, p. 362. **152** Bieler, *Penitentials*, pp 1–50. For a comprehensive list see Ó Corráin, *Clavis*, pp 754–68.

of Cummean, Welsh Canons, Irish Canons, Bigotian Penitential and the Old Irish Penitential, purely on the basis that whatever these may yield in our search for the *in bello* concept, the remaining are in no way relevant. Our interest will be confined to sins involving violence, which, in fact, do not constitute a major part of penitential literature.[153] As mentioned in the previous chapter, the penitential system appears to have originated in western Britain or Brittany, coming at an early stage to Ireland, where it developed before spreading to Anglo-Saxon England and Continental Europe.[154] Elaine Pereira Farrell has considered the dating of each of the texts, concluding after careful examination of all the most recent scholarly opinion that these texts date from the end of the sixth century (First synod of St Patrick) to the eighth century (Bigotian Penitential), thus offering potential insights into Adomnán's contexts.[155]

It was envisaged that the confessor would play an active role in the penitential process. He was seen as the penitent's soul friend (*anmchara*) who often would have an intimate knowledge of the penitent and his or her circumstances.[156] He was a doctor of souls (*spiritualis medicus*) who would use his informed discretion to prescribe 'cures' for the penitent's soul. Thomas Charles-Edwards sees the penitentials and canon law working in close harmony, with the former very often providing the penalty, by way of penance, for infringements of both, and the roles of the *anmchara* and the *iudex* or *scriba* sometimes overlapping 'The *Canones* and *leges penitentiae* are two parts of a single system of law and moral instruction'.[157]

It is clear that the penitentials represent a source of information about attitudes spanning a period of around 200 years before *LxI* and approximately fifty years after. They tell us something of what was being 'persecuted, tolerated, accepted, obeyed and disobeyed by the church and Christians between the sixth and eighth century in Ireland'.[158] It has been argued, as a result of a comparative study of the texts, that the list of 'sins' varied from place to place, with varying penances, suggesting that the compilers differed in their ideas of what needed to be included, possibly based on the individual compilers' experiences as a confessor.[159] While the penitentials are, without doubt, a rich source, the drawing of conclusions needs to be approached with caution. If a particular 'sin' appears very frequently over a large number of the penitentials – for instance fornication – does this indicate that fornication was particularly prevalent in society, or that its curtailment was a particular priority for the ecclesiastical authors, or both? Is the frequent mention of homosexuality an indication that it was common?[160] The drawing of conclusions about such matters in the modern world, with all the

---

153 Pereira Farrell, 'Taboos and penitence', appendix. **154** Ibid., p. 4; Bieler, *Penitentials*, p.3; Kenny, *Sources*, p. 239. **155** Pereira Farrell, 'Taboos and penitance', pp 43–81. **156** Bieler, *Penitentials*, pp 98–9; Pereira Farrell, 'Taboos and penitance', p. 21. **157** Charles-Edwards, 'Early Irish law', p. 366. **158** Pereira Farrell, 'Taboos and penitance', p. 8. **159** Frantzen, *Literature of penance*, pp 56–7 and p. 200; idem, 'Spirituality and devotion in the Anglo-Saxon penitentials', *Essays in Medieval Studies*, 22 (2005), p. 121; Pereira Farrell, 'Taboos and penitance', p. 8. **160** Pereira Farrell, 'Taboos and penitance', p. 205.

available data, is difficult. How much more difficult at a remove of 1300 years? Furthermore, there is a fundamental difference between the law's response to problems arising in society and the church preparing its pastors for the battle with sin. As in a medical general practitioner's guide or hand-book, which has to cover all eventualities, even the most rare, so too the confessor must be prepared for all manner of 'sins', even the most bizarre.

The penitentials do not, however, provide protection for innocents, by imposing stricter penances on those who use violence towards them than the penances imposed for 'sins' of violence towards people who are not innocents. This can best be illustrated in the context of an imaginary hypothetical scenario. An abbot, say a fictional Colmán of Leamanaghan, is *anmchara* to the king of his local *tuath*, say a fictional Áed mac Taidc. Áed approaches Colmán seeking to confess his sins and cure his soul. He tells Colmán that he has recently returned from raiding a nearby *tuath* where he was seeking to enforce a judgment. On his way back, while still in the territory of the neighbouring *tuath*, he and his men came across a dwelling with a mother and her three children outside. In the heat of the moment the woman and children were killed by Áed and his men. He feels that he has committed a grave sin, for which he is very repentant and he wishes to cleanse his soul. Colmán tells him that he, Colmán, first needs to consult his penitential books before forgiving the sin and imposing an appropriate penance. Colmán possesses the seven texts mentioned above. He searches them for a provision that takes into account the fact that the victims of the murder were defenceless, never bore arms and were not involved in the strife or conflict in any way. Colmán can find nothing in the First synod of St Patrick other than paragraph 14, dealing with a Christian who commits murder, whether it be of man, woman or child.[161] The Penitential of Finnian deals with a cleric committing murder (paragraph 23) but not a layman, never mind the killing of an innocent.[162] Paragraph 5 of the Penitential of Cummean, like the First synod of St Patrick, covers murder in general but makes no provision for the killing of innocents.[163] Colmán will find the Welsh Canons frustrating. Homicide as a result of strife is covered (paragraph 1), as are homicide out of envy (2), slave killing a free man (5), free man killing another's slave (7), slave killing slave (33), bearing arms at church (46), cleric striking a layman (56) and layman striking a cleric (57).[164] There is nothing, however, to meet his situation. Similarly, the Irish Canons do not meet the case.[165] The Bigotian Penitential deals with the slaying of a bishop and suicide. It deals with violence in the course of strife and distinguishes, in diminishing grades of severity, between killing with premeditation out of hatred after vows of perfection, through anger and quarrels but not with premeditation out of hatred, and unintentional accidental killing.[166] Finally, the Old Irish

---

161 Bieler, *Penitentials*, p. 57. **162** Idem, p. 75. For a review of the content of Finnian see R. Meens, 'The Penitential of Finnian and the textual witness of the Penitentiale Vindobonense "B"', *Medieval Studies*, 55 (1993), pp 243–55. **163** Bieler, *Penitentials*, p. 119. **164** Idem, pp 137–59. **165** Idem, p. 171. **166** Idem, p. 229.

Penitential concentrates on the most severely punished violence, kin-slaying. It does provide seven years' penance for all other homicides, except where the offender is a bishop or priest, where the penalty will be more severe. It goes on to stipulate for 'Anyone who kills a man in battle or a brawl or by lying in wait for him, a year and a half or forty nights, provided he does not pursue the slaughter after a fight is won'.[167]

It is quite clear, therefore, that the penitentials do not offer innocents any special protection, and this is not for a want of capacity to distinguish between violence of varying degrees, because they envisage innumerable scenarios. As we know from the fact that Colmán consulted eighth-century penitentials that *LxI* was part of existing law, he would therefore refer Áed to the community of Iona and its *familia*. It is to them, by proclamation of the kings and high ecclesiastics of Ireland, that he would be answerable for his crime against the mother and her children. Once again, it is apparent that there was a lacuna in existing legal provisions, whether secular, ecclesiastical or mixed, a lacuna which Adomnán recognized, filled and, indeed, exploited.

LITERARY TEXTS

Quasi-legal texts
Before examining the more obviously literary texts, such as the hagiographies and the sagas, there are two contemporary literary texts of a quasi-legal nature that merit some consideration as sources of information on values and attitudes, at least among certain sections of society, at the end of the seventh century. *Audacht Morainn* is a seventh- century text in which the mythical judge Morann advises, through his pupil Néire, the mythical young king Feradach Finn Fechtnach on the ideals of kingship.[168] Fundamental to a good king's rule is the concept of *fír flathemon* the 'Ruler's Truth'.[169] He is to be just and merciful and to care for his people. A consequence of his justice will be avoidance of plagues, wars and successful enemy incursions into his territory, and nature will respond by providing fertile land and animals and plentiful fish. He is to respect old men and exalt good judges, avoid unnecessary violence, care for the weak and not be too interested in rich gifts.[170] He is told 'not to redden many fore-courts, for bloodshed is a vain destruction of all rule and of protection from the kin for the

167 Bieler, *Penitentials*, p. 271. **168** F. Kelly (ed. and trans.), *Audacht Morainn* (Dublin, 1976); Kelly, *Guide*, p. 284; Bhreathnach, *Medieval world*, p. 49; Charles-Edwards, *Early Christian Ireland*, p. 138; Aitchison, 'Regicide', p. 118; Fraser, 'Morality of war', p. 101; M. Ní Bhrolcháin, *An introduction to early Irish literature* (Dublin, 2009), p. 93; Pereira Farrell, 'Taboos and penitence', pp 188–9; A. Ahlqvist, 'Le Testament de Morann', *Études Celtiques*, 21 (1984), pp 151–70. **169** Ó Cróinín, *Early medieval Ireland*, pp 77–8; Bhreathnach, *Medieval world*, p. 50; M. Dillon, 'The Hindu act of truth in Celtic tradition', *Modern Philology*, 44 (1947), pp 137–40; C. Watkins, '*Is tre fhír flathemon*: marginalia to *Audacht Morainn*', *Ériu*, 30 (1979), pp 181–98. **170** Kelly, *Audacht*, paragraph 51.

ruler'.[171] It is important to keep in mind that these strictures represent the views of one order, the learned order, and seek to promote their interests.[172] They may not reflect the attitudes of the lay nobility. In any event, while excessive violence is discouraged, the virtuous ruler is urged to 'remove the shame of his cheeks by arms in battle against other territories', and so, necessary and judiciously used violence is not.[173] There are no explicit strictures here on violence towards non-combatants as such. It is fair to say, though, that the attitudes expressed in *Audacht Morainn*, would have been known to all those who subscribed to *LxI*, and accepted by many.

Another text of whose attitudes they would have been aware is a Latin text, *De duodecim abusivis saeculi* (On the twelve evils of the world).[174] This is a mid-seventh-century text in which an unjust king is listed as the ninth abuse.[175] This, like *Audacht Morainn*, is in the *tecosc*, *admonitio* or *speculum principum* genre, involving advice to kings, and it echoes it, in many ways. The just king, as opposed to the *rex iniquus*, has a duty 'not to oppress anyone unjustly by force; to judge people without regard for the reputation of a person; to be the defender of strangers, orphans and widows'.[176] This text, which is now accepted to be of Irish provenance, circulated widely in Britain and on the Continent and it has been described as 'one of the most profoundly influential formulations of Christian political obligation in the entire Middle Ages'.[177] While it does not recognize the non-combatant as such, in requiring the just king to protect strangers, orphans and widows, it shows concern for people who may be without a legal protector under existing law. This is not too far away from seeking to protect those who, because they do not bear arms, cannot protect themselves.

Hagiography
In the one-hundred-year period between *c*.650 and *c*.750 hagiography emerged as a new genre in Ireland with a number of saints' lives being written. Apart from Adomnán's life of Columba, *VC* (which will be considered in the next chapter), two independent lives of Patrick appeared and two of Brigit. At first sight, one might be inclined to dismiss these as 'mere collections of pious fantasies which overtax one's credulity'.[178] However, on closer examination, scholars point out,

---

171 Ibid., paragraph 29. **172** Charles-Edwards, *Early Christian Ireland*, pp 139–40. **173** Kelly, *Audacht*, paragraph 30; Fraser, 'Morality of war', p. 102. **174** S. Hellmann (ed.), *Ps.-Cyprianus. De xxii abusiuis saeculi* (Leipzig, 1909); A. Breen, 'The evidence of antique Irish exegesis in Pseudo-Cyprian, *De duodecim abusivis saeculi*', *PRIA*, 87C (1987), pp 71–101; idem, 'Towards a critical edition of *De xii abusivis*: introductory essays with a provisional edition of the text and accompanied by an English translation' (PhD, Trinity College, Dublin, 1988), pp 219–28; J. Grigg, 'The just king and *De duodecim abusiuis saeculi*', *Parergon*, 27:1 (2010), pp 27–52; Bhreathnach, *Medieval world*, p. 51; Ó Cróinín, *Early medieval Ireland*, p. 78; Pereira Farrell, 'Taboos and penitence', pp 190–3. **175** Grigg, 'Just king', p. 29. **176** Breen, 'Critical edition', pp 401–5; Bhreathnach, *Medieval world*, p. 51. **177** P. Wormald, 'Celtic and Anglo-Saxon kingship: some further thoughts' in P.E. Szarmach (ed.), *Sources of Anglo-Saxon culture* (Kalamazoo, 1986), p. 160. See Kenney, *Sources*, pp 281–2 (no. 109). **178** S. Connolly (ed.

they can prove to be useful contemporary sources that tell us much about the times when they were written and the priorities and concerns of society.[179] As Kathleen Hughes says of the saints' lives, 'their incidental information, properly criticized, will yield much that is of value'.[180] 'Since some saints' Lives often mirrored the moral and social concerns of certain sections of society',[181] do they mirror a concern for *in bello* issues?

Consideration will first be given to the two early lives of Brigit, Cogitosus' 'Life of St Brigit' and the *Vita Prima Sanctae Brigitae*,[182] the former believed to date from *c*.650 to 675,[183] and the latter, possibly earlier, but certainly from no later than the middle of the eighth century.[184] From the point of view, therefore, of reflecting underlying attitudes, both are reasonably contemporary with *LxI*. In Cogitosus, the section of society for whom most concern is evident is the poor. Approximately one-third of the thirty-two paragraphs relate, directly or indirectly, to them. Lepers also are of concern.[185] The text essentially consists of a list of miracles performed by Brigit. Water is turned into ale in paragraph 8 and stone into salt in paragraph 10. She has a rapport with nature: she hangs her cloak on a sunbeam (paragraph 6), she tells a story about the king's pet fox (20), pigs are herded by wolves (19). While the miracles have at their core a strong Christian message such as the power of God and of faith, and extol Christian virtues such as virginity, they often appear, to the modern reader, simple and innocent. Only one paragraph (22) relates to violence. It tells of how Brigit dealt with a band of brigands (*díbergaig*) who were planning slaughter and murder. The theme of brigandage occurs in many early medieval Irish sources and is discussed in some detail below. In any event Brigit, having failed to dissuade them from their diabolical resolve, rendered a miracle by which they were made to think

and trans.), '*Vita Prima Sanctae Brigitae*: background and historical value', *JRSAI*, 119 (1989), p. 7. **179** Kenney, *Sources*, p. 293 and p. 297; Hughes, *Sources*, p. 219 and p. 246; Bhreathnach, *Medieval World*, p. 68 and p. 83; Brown, *Violence*, p. 42. **180** Hughes, *Sources*, p. 246. **181** Bhreathnach, *Medieval world*, p. 68. **182** For Cogitosus see S. Connolly and J.-M. Picard (eds and trans.), 'Cogitosus's Life of Brigit: content and value', *JRSAI*, 117 (1987), pp 5–27. For the *Vita Prima* see Connolly, '*Vita Prima*'. See also N. Kissane, *Saint Brigid of Kildare: life, legend and cult* (Dublin, 2017); Kenney, *Sources*, p. 359; Hughes, *Sources*, pp 226–9; Ó Cróinín, 'Hiberno-Latin literature', p. 384; Charles-Edwards, *Early Christian Ireland*, p. 438; Johnston, *Literacy*, p. 84. **183** Connolly and Picard, 'Cogitosus', p. 1; Charles-Edwards, *Early Christian Ireland*, pp 438–40. **184** Connolly, '*Vita Prima*', p. 6. There is some controversy as to whether *Vita Prima* pre- or post-dates Cogitosus. For an early date see M. Esposito, 'Notes on Latin learning and literature in medieval Ireland, IV: on the early Lives of St Brigid of Kildare', *Hermathena*, 49 (1935), pp 120–65; R. Sharpe, '*Vitae S Brigitae*: the oldest texts', *Peritia*, 1 (1982), pp 81–106; D. Howlett, '*Vita I Sanctae Brigitae*', *Peritia*, 12 (1998), pp 1–23; T. Charles-Edwards, 'Brigit [St Brigit, Brigid] (439/452–524/526), patron saint of Kildare', http://www.oxforddnb.com/view/article/3427, accessed 19 Oct 2015. For a later date, apart from Connolly, see F. Ó Briain, 'Brigitana', *ZCP*, 36 (1977), pp 112–37; D. Ó hAodha (ed. and trans.), *Bethu Brigte* (Dublin, 1978); K. McCone, 'Brigit in the seventh century: a saint with three lives?', *Peritia*, 1 (1982), pp 107–15. **185** For example, paragraphs 1, 8, 14, 15, 27, 26, 28.

that they had carried out their designs, even being provided with 'blood and gore' on their weapons, whereas it was, in fact, an apparition that they had killed and not the real man. With an absence of vindictiveness on the part of Brigit and her biographer, on becoming aware of the truth, the *díbergaig* 'were converted to the Lord through repentance'.

The *Vita Prima* is similar to Cogitosus in many respects. In fact Seán Connolly calculates that they share over thirty episodes.[186] There are, however, a number of paragraphs with distinctly violent content. Paragraphs 65 and 67 deal with *díbergaig* and are considered below. Paragraph 88 is of some interest. Brigit asks a favour of the king of the Laigin that he is prepared to grant only in return for a favour from her. She offers him eternal life and that his descendants will be kings for ever. The king rejects this replying, 'A life I can't see I've no desire for. About the sons who will come I've no concern'.[187] He asks instead for the gift of a long life and an assurance of victory in all his battles. This was granted to him and we are told that he went on to fight thirty victorious battles and conduct nine successful campaigns. In fact, because he was known to be assured of victory, he was able to sell his services to other kings. While this tells us nothing about attitudes to innocents, it does illustrate attitudes to wars waged by kings, that they were common and legitimate when employed against traditional enemies and that Augustine's concept of just cause was relatively unimportant, so as not to merit mention.[188] While Edel Bhreathnach sees paragraph 75 of this text as, possibly, reflecting a concern for hostages and prisoners,[189] paragraph 88 discloses an acceptance of the fact of war and unconcern for the fate of innocents.

Tírechán's Life of Patrick,[190] which was written c.688–93, and thus a contemporary source,[191] is of little assistance. It is an account of a supposed journey by Patrick around the northern half of Ireland indicating the locations where he founded churches and won the loyalty of local leaders, a loyalty to which, by implication, his successor in the person of the bishop of Armagh was now entitled.[192] Violence does not feature, except in paragraph 32, where Patrick intervenes in a sword-fight between two brothers 'since', as he is quoted saying to them, 'you are brothers'.[193] This concern is echoed subsequently in paragraph 64 of the *Vita Prima*, where Brigit renders a miracle making two brothers, Conall and Cairpre, invisible to one another on the road, thereby avoiding the brothers 'murder[ing] each other'.[194] Clearly, violence among members of the same family

---

186 Connolly, '*Vita Prima*', p. 7. **187** Paragraph 88.4. **188** For legitimacy of attacks on traditional enemies see paragraphs 88.5 and 65.3. **189** Bhreathnach, *Medieval world*, p. 68. **190** L. Bieler (ed. and trans.), 'Tírechán, *Collectanea*' in *The Patrician texts in the Book of Armagh* (Dublin, 1979), pp 122–62. **191** Charles-Edwards, *Early Christian Ireland*, p. 440. **192** Ibid., pp 9–11. In fact Charles-Edwards constructs his first chapter describing Ireland in the seventh century (pp 8–67) around Tírechán's account of Patrick's travels. See also, Ó Cróinín, *Early medieval Ireland*, pp 154–61; C. Swift, 'Tírechán's motives in compiling the *Collectanea*: an alternative interpretation', *Ériu*, 45 (1994), pp 53–82, in which she argues that Tírechán was a Patrician propagandist but not an Armagh one. **193** The other instance of violence is in paragraph 42, where Patrick kills the chief druid. **194** Paragraph 64.2.

was considered particularly abhorrent. The laws stipulated very severe penalties for kin-slaying, known as *fingal*, although, as Fergus Kelly points out, some kings who acquired their titles through *fingal* reigned successfully for many years.[195]

In Muirchú's Life of Patrick we have a work virtually contemporaneous (*c.*695) with *LxI*.[196] Furthermore, he is listed among the guarantors of the law.[197] Unfortunately, it does not disclose anything of value regarding current attitudes towards violence. Patrick does deal violently with the druids who oppose him, one of whom is caused to 'hit his brain against a stone, and smashed to pieces, and died ...'[198] This is not particularly remarkable, merely a case of God smiting his enemies through the agency of Patrick. Is it surprising that neither Cogitosus, Tírechán, Muirchú nor the anonymous author of the *Vita Prima* chose to show any concern for the plight of innocents at the very time, or thereabouts, that Adomnán was preparing a law for their protection? In some ways it is, particularly if it was a matter of major concern in society. However, these authors had very specific agendas; their motivation was largely political. Rival monastic *paruchiae* sought to advance their respective positions by what Dáibhí Ó Cróinín refers to as a 'propaganda war':[199] Cogitosus, Kildare, Tírechán and Muirchú, Armagh and the cult of Patrick and the *Vita Prima*, Kildare, with emerging Uí Néill influence.[200] Nevertheless, no miracles or incidents of help for innocents are recorded in these works. Perhaps it is because no such traditions existed in the cases of Brigit and Patrick, upon which miracles could be based, or was it that the authors felt that violence towards innocents was not an issue that would inspire their audience? If the latter is the case, why did Adomnán espouse their cause?

Díbergaig

If it is difficult to find in our sources any explicit reference to innocents, or indeed implied concern for them, there is one form of violence of which the opposite is true. The sources from the seventh century and earlier abound with descriptions, and prescriptions, of *díbergaig*. They appear with such prevalence, in both hagiography and the sagas, as to be a ubiquitous feature of the written output of early medieval Ireland. They were brigands engaged in brigandage or *díberg*.[201] In his Life of Brigit, Cogitosus describes them as being diabolical,

195 Kelly, *Guide*, pp 127–8. A king who is guilty of *fingal* loses his honour-price – *CIH* 15.4 = *AL* v 172.19. **196** For Muirchú see *Muirchú Moccu Machthéni 'Vita Sancti Patricii': Life of Saint Patrick*, ed. and trans. D. Howlett (Dublin, 2006) and for dating see pp 180–6; Charles-Edwards, *Early Christian Ireland*, p. 440. **197** *LxI*, paragraph 28, guarantor number 36; Ní Dhonnchadha, 'The law of Adomnán: a translation', p. 58. **198** Paragraph 1.17. **199** Ó Cróinín, 'Hiberno-Latin literature', p. 385. **200** Connolly, '*Vita Prima*', p. 7. **201** R. Sharpe, 'Hiberno-Latin *laicus*, Irish *láech* and the Devil's men', *Ériu*, 30 (1979), pp 75–92; K. McCone, 'Werewolves, cyclopes, *díberga* and *fianna*: juvenile delinquency in early Ireland', *Cambridge Medieval Celtic Studies*, 12 (1986), pp 1–22; idem, *Pagan past and Christian present in early Irish literature* (Maynooth, 1990), p. 206; Kelly, *Guide*, pp 222–4; Ní Dhonnchadha, '*Lex Innocentium*, pp 60–1; Etchingham, *Church organization*, pp 298–306; Breathnach, *Medieval world*, pp 140–3; Pereira Farrell, 'Taboos and penitence', pp 195–202. C. Doherty, 'Warrior

although Brigit is able to overcome them through her saintly power.²⁰² As Richard Sharpe has demonstrated, *díbergaig* were groups of marauders intent on robbery and murder.²⁰³ Their characteristics included paganism and ritual, diabolical vows and the wearing of *signa* that could not be removed until the vows had been fulfilled.²⁰⁴ A member of this group is sometimes referred to as a *mac báis* (son of death) or *mac mallachtan* (son of malediction).²⁰⁵ Scholars have identified *díbergaig* with groups of young men who had undergone rites of passage and who were indulging in wanton destruction and murder prior to them settling down to a normal family life in the *tuath* with its concomitant rights and duties.²⁰⁶ The similarity with the widely attested phenomenon of the *Männerbund*, the wild young warrior-hunters, has been noted.²⁰⁷

It seems unlikely, however, that *díbergaig* were confined to young men between the ages of fourteen and twenty. The sense of alienation from conventional society that is apparent in the sources would suggest a more permanent membership. Sharpe seems to support this when he speculates on the causes of the phenomenon: the price the church and society had to pay for driving overt paganism into outlawry, the only option for dynastic groups displaced in the political changes of the seventh century, a conscious and deliberate espousal of old cult practices by those who lost out and felt ill-served by the Christian God.²⁰⁸ In fact, it has been suggested that these bands probably comprised both young men as temporary members and the disaffected as older permanent members.²⁰⁹ Vernacular Irish law provided for banishment from the *tuath* for a variety of crimes.²¹⁰ Where was the *élúdach* (banished criminal) to go? He was cut off from his *tuath* and all the security and support it provided. The law even proscribed the harbouring of an *élúdach*.²¹¹ The sense of alienation and of grievance must have been considerable. He was a man 'without fixed nation'.²¹² Clearly, the penalty of banishment facilitated the formation of groups of *díbergaig*, who were, thenceforth, outside the system and, being outside, presented a problem for it.

The extent of that problem, and of society's concern about it, are attested to by the frequency and vehemence of its treatment in the sources. *Díbergaig* feature in all of the saints' lives already considered. Apart from Cogitosus, quoted above, the author of the *Vita Prima Sanctae Brigitae* tells how 'worthless and superstitious men came to Brigit with diabolical amulets on their heads'.²¹³

---

and king in early Ireland' in J.E. Rekdal and C. Doherty (eds), *Kings and warriors in early northwest Europe* (Dublin, 2016), pp 110–17; K. Murray, *The early Finn cycle* (Dublin, 2017), pp 57–63. **202** Paragraph 22. Connolly and Picard, 'Cogitosus', p. 20. **203** Sharpe, *Laicus*, p. 81. **204** Ibid., pp 82, 84. **205** Ní Dhonnchadha, '*Lex Innocentium*', p. 61. **206** Bhreathnach, *Medieval world*, p. 140; J.F. Nagy, *Conversing with angels and ancients: the literary myth of medieval Ireland* (Dublin, 1997), pp 293–9; McCone, *Pagan past*, pp 203–10. **207** McCone, 'Werewolves', p. 22; Ní Dhonnchadha, '*Lex Innocentium*', p. 61; Charles-Edwards, *Early Christian Ireland*, p. 464. **208** Sharpe, *Laicus*, p. 92. **209** Murray, *Finn cycle*, pp 60–2. **210** *CIH* 55.1–6 = *AL* v 318.12–19; *CIH* 451.23–27; Kelly, *Guide*, p. 222. **211** *CIH* 15.7–8 = *AL* v 174.17–18; Kelly, *Guide*, p. 223. **212** Sharpe, *Laicus*, p. 91. **213** Paragraph 67. Connolly, *Vita*, p. 33.

Muirchú describes Mac Cuil maccu Greccae, a savage and pagan tyrant with l *signa*, a word glossed in the Book of Armagh as *diberca*,[214] and Tírechán also refers to a *díbergach*.[215] At least two of the penitentials, both from the seventh century, are concerned with *díbergaig* and the extent of their concern can be gauged by the severity of penance. The Irish Canons stipulate a penance of seven years on bread and water for 'one who has vowed himself to evil'.[216] It has been argued that the Penitential of Cummean also, in its reference to furnishing 'guidance to barbarians', relates to *díbergaig*,[217] and the Old Irish Table of Commutations specifically lists brigandage among the serious sins for which a remission of penalty can never be allowed.[218]

The sagas, which are considered further below, also provide an insight into attitudes to *díbergaig* in our period. They are central to the early Irish saga *Togail Bruidne Da Derga* (The destruction of Da Derga's hostel), which has been dated to the ninth century.[219] The mythological king Conaire was bound by nine taboos, one of which was not to allow brigandage during his reign. However, he broke this taboo when he gave a judgment on a number of *díbergaig*, including his foster-brothers, which discriminated in their favour. Ultimately he breaks all nine taboos and is killed in Da Derga's hostel by a band of brigands that included his foster-brothers, whom he had unjustly spared.[220] All of these references illustrate the importance of *díberg* in the early medieval Irish mindset. It was abhorred and feared, to the extent that it was essential for the hagiographer to demonstrate that his saint could provide protection,[221] and for the teller of the saga tales to rank its perpetrators high among his villains. It is important to note, however, that the majority of sources considered have a clerical provenance. While all of the foregoing is true, it must be pointed out – and this is a timely reminder that there is nothing straightforward about early medieval Irish society – vernacular Irish law does recognize, in certain instances, a legitimate role for *díbergaig*.[222]

On the question of violence towards innocents, our sources are virtually silent. On brigandage they are shouting at us. The contrast is quite stark. *Díberg* is seen in those sources as totally illegitimate violence, outside the system and, as such, uncontrollable and completely unacceptable. The corollary to this is that, what Sharpe calls 'honourable warfare',[223] is seen as legitimate violence, part of

---

214 Sharpe, *Laicus*, p. 82; W. Stokes (ed. and trans.), *The tripartite life of Patrick with other documents related to the saint* (2 vols, London, 1887), ii, p. 286. See L. de Paor, 'St Maccreiche of Liscannor', *Ériu*, 30 (1979), pp 93–121, esp. 100–1. 215 Sharpe, *Laicus*, p. 86; Stokes, *Tripartite Life*, ii, pp 324–5. 216 Bieler, *Penitentials*, pp 160–1; Pereira Farrell, 'Taboos and penitence', p. 197. 217 Pereira Farrell, 'Taboos and penitence', p. 198. 218 Ibid., p. 197. Bieler, *Penitentials*, pp 126–7. 219 E. Knott (ed.), *Togail Bruidne Da Derga* (Dublin, 1936); J. Gantz (trans.), *Early Irish myths and sagas* (London, 1981), pp 67–8 and pp 72–3; Carney, 'Language', p. 483; Pereira Farrell, 'Taboos and penitence', p. 195; Charles-Edwards, *Early Christian Ireland*, p. 229; Kelly, *Guide*, p. 20 ; Sharpe, *Laicus*, p. 85; R. O'Connor, *The destruction of Da Derga's hostel: kingship and narrative artistry in a medieval Irish saga* (Oxford, 2013). 220 Kelly, *Guide*, p. 21. 221 Sharpe, *Laicus*, p. 92. 222 See Murray, *Finn cycle*, pp 59–60 for a number of examples. 223 Sharpe, *Laicus*, p. 86.

the system, controllable and not completely unacceptable. Apart from honourable warfare, violence arising in the course of executing a lawful judgment, for example a cattle raid, would be seen as a legitimate exercise of the system and, therefore, acceptable. The crucial difference is that *díberg* is not amenable to normal regulation within the system, whereas violence occurring in honourable warfare and under the self-regulation system, 'the law of self-help',[224] is. An example of the latter was *Cáin Fhuithirbe*, dating from *c*.680.[225] This is the earliest of the *cána* known to have been enacted and is of Munster origin. It aims at prohibiting the person seeking to enforce a lawful judgment from continuing his incursion after he has been adequately compensated. It is clearly a refinement or elaboration of the existing 'law of self-help'. *Cáin Fhuithirbe* also deals with the conduct of Sharpe's honourable warfare, with references to such matters as 'intentional wounding on a battlefield' and 'violent taking of hostages', demonstrating that the distinction between warfare and law enforcement could become blurred. Issue must be taken with Sharpe, however, when he suggests that there was a 'falling together of war and brigandage'.[226] Bands of warriors wearing diabolical *signa* and bound by heathen oaths were clearly distinguishable from the warrior operating under the accepted system. It was the conduct of the latter that *LxI* sought to regulate, with, what might be called today, all-party consent. *Díberg* was abhorred; by contrast, honourable warfare was tolerated as a reality.

Paragraph 65 of the *Vita Prima Sanctae Brigitae* neatly illustrates the two different attitudes.[227] It tells us of Conall, a *díbergach*, wearing 'sinister amulets', who asks for Brigit's protection while he is on a violent escapade with the purpose of fulfilling his diabolical vows by killing and slaughter. Brigit prays to God that Conall and his companions lay aside their amulets and not harm anyone and not be harmed themselves. However, they proceeded and stormed a certain fort, as it seemed to them, and 'killed and beheaded many people'. But the next day they were dumfounded because they 'did not see any heads or blood, nor was any gore to be seen on either their clothes or their weapons'. Having sent emissaries to check, they discovered that, by Brigit's miracle, nobody had been harmed. This sufficiently impressed them that they laid aside their amulets 'and did not go against God or Brigit'. It did not stop them, however, from going against their enemies. Within a year, with the blessing and protection of Brigit, who was gratified by the fact that they had laid aside their amulets for her sake, 'Conall marched with a large army into the territory of his enemies and there inflicted great slaughter'. The account goes on to relate how Brigit continued to help Conall, even to the extent of making his enemies confuse the heads that he had taken for books!

It is quite apparent from the above that the reality of violence was accepted. A king, in the normal course, had enemies and he waged war against them. A

---

224 See p. 65 above. **225** Ní Dhonnchadha, '*Lex Innocentium*', pp 61–2. For text, translation and discussion see L. Breatnach, 'The ecclesiastical element in the Old-Irish legal tract *Cáin fhuithirbe*', *Peritia*, 5 (1986), pp 36–52; Kelly, *Guide*, p. 246 and p. 273. **226** Sharpe, *Laicus*, p. 87. **227** Connolly, *Vita*, p. 33.

study of the phenomenon of *díberg*, as described in the sources, has helped to reveal the attitude of mind of the seventh- and eighth-century Irish to conventional violence and warfare. It is reasonable to conclude that this was the attitude, to a greater or lesser degree, of many if not all of those setting out for Birr in the early summer of 697. While the sources reveal little of attitudes to the involvement of innocents in warfare, they do show that warfare was accepted as the norm and this was the mindset in which Adomnán was operating. Just as the self-regulatory system of law-enforcement needed to be controlled by *Cáin Fhuithirbe*, so too did the broadly accepted system of internecine warfare need to be refined by *LxI*, the quintessential *jus in bello*.

The sagas
There are substantial difficulties in using the sagas as a source of information about attitudes to violence.[228] In the first place, they are essentially unreal. It is a little like a historian, centuries hence, using current Batman stories as a source for a study of twenty-first century attitudes to violence. True, with judicious discretion, something might be gleaned, but the danger of faulty conclusions would be great. Muireann Ní Bhrolcháin, in the introduction to her study, inserts a quote by way of timely caveat 'we should never assume too serious a purpose in this literature … Perhaps we should stop wasting our time asking what it's for and just enjoy the stories as literature'.[229] A further and substantial difficulty lies in the fact that our inquiries are time-specific and the sagas, as they have come down to us, are generally not. We need to know the content, and role in society, of the sagas in the period up to c.700. This is not possible because the sagas changed, not only over the centuries, but from performance to performance depending on the audience, the current political context, the whims of the teller of the tale and many other factors.[230] As Elva Johnston has pointed out, these saga narratives cannot be treated as fixed texts. She instances that the first recension of the *Táin*, probably dating from the ninth century, contains narrative doublets, thus facilitating a choice of alternative texts.[231] It has been suggested that each scribal 'copy' is itself an individual performance, and the multiformity of the texts mirrors the multiformity of oral performance.[232] This 'flexibility … within the

---

228 For translation of the sagas see Gantz, *Myths and sagas*. See also, P. Mac Cana and T. Ó Floinn, *Scéalaíocht na Ríthe* (Baile Átha Cliath, 1956); T. Kinsella (trans.), *The Táin* (Oxford, 1969); J.T. Koch and J. Carey, *The Celtic heroic age* (3rd ed., Andhover, MA, and Aberystwyth, 2000); M.B. Ó Mainnin and G. Toner (eds), *Ulidia 4: Proceedings of the Fourth International Conference on the Ulster cycle tales* (Dublin, 2017). **229** Ní Bhrolcháin, *Literature*, p. 1, citing A. Bruford, 'Why an Ulster cycle?' in J.P. Mallory and G. Stockman (eds), *Ulidia* (Belfast, 1994), p. 30. **230** Johnston, *Literacy*, pp 169–76. **231** Ibid., pp 173–4. She gives as an example: C. O'Rahilly (ed. and trans.), *Táin Bó Cúailnge: Recension I* (Dublin, 1976), p. 18 (lines 575–87) and p. 141 (translation), which incorporates two differing accounts into its famous tale of how Cú Chulainn got his name. **232** E.M. Slotkin, 'Medieval Irish scribes and fixed texts', *Éigse*, 17 (1979), pp 437–56. He further suggests that this casts doubt on the notion of a single archetype. See also T. Ó Cathasaigh and S. Ó Coileáin, 'Oral or literary: some strands of the argu-

Irish *scél* tradition'[233] makes the sagas a difficult source of information for attitudes in early medieval Ireland generally, and an almost useless source for our time-specific investigation. Notwithstanding these serious reservations, it may be of some assistance to look briefly at some of the sagas that are thought to be early.

Scholars are of the view that *some* of the Otherworld sagas, including the *echtrai* (adventures) and *immrama* (voyages), and the Heroic or Ulster Cycle sagas, date from the seventh century.[234] Even among those that do, because of accretions and rewritten episodes, and in spite of a great deal of linguistic analysis, it is not possible to know the content as it would have appeared initially, and we are still left with many tales made up of multiple strata.[235] Subject to this reservation, however, they are contemporary sources and our discussion will be limited to these sagas of possible early origin. It is not unreasonable to presume that Adomnán and those appearing in the list of guarantors contained in the text of *LxI* would have been aware of them or of some version of them. Adomnán in his *VC* recounts a meeting between Columba and the poet Crónán when Columba is asked by his companions why he did not ask the poet to perform for them 'as custom allows'.[236] It would have been normal for a group in Columba's time, and presumably Adomnán's, to enjoy listening to a tale or a poem. It is worth noting also Adomnán's awareness of the motif of the threefold death.[237]

Violence is a prominent, indeed almost predominant, feature. Proinsias Mac Cana lists approximately 185 story-titles appearing in the sagas.[238] Muireann Ní Bhrolcháin summarizes these as mainly: destructions, cattle-raids, wooings, battles, terrors, voyages, deaths, feasts, sieges, adventures, elopements, plunderings, eruptions, visions, love stories, hostings and migrations.[239] It is clear from this list that there is a violent element in the majority of themes. The beheading of enemies is a common feature, with the heads subsequently being displayed as trophies.[240] In general, the question of violence towards innocents does not feature in the accounts of wars and battles. Although, at one point in the *Táin*, Cú Chulainn spares Queen Medb because he did not kill women;[241] this appears to be a statement of principle. On the other hand, we are told of how Cú Chulainn, on his return journey from the Otherworld, meets and kills an old woman, blind in her left eye, who tries to throw him off a narrow road over which he must pass.[242] Elsewhere, he kills 150 queens at a place subsequently called the Ford of

---

ment', *Studia Hibernica*, 17–18 (1977), pp 16–19; T. Ó Cathasaigh, 'Pagan survivals: the evidence of early Irish narrative' in P. Ní Chatháin and M. Richter (eds), *Irland und Europa: Die Kirche im Frühmittelalter* (Stuttgart, 1987), p. 293. **233** Johnston, *Literacy*, p. 174. **234** Ní Bhrolcháin, *Literature*, p. 1, p. 8 and pp 53–4; J. Carney, 'Language and literature to 1169' in *NHI*, p. 469, p. 477 and p. 503. **235** Carney, 'Language', p. 469. **236** *VC* 1.42. **237** Idem, 1.36. See J.-M. Picard, 'The strange death of Guaire mac Áedáin' in D. Ó Corráin et al. (eds), *Sages, saints and storytellers: Celtic studies in honour of Professor James Carney* (Maynooth, 1989), pp 367–75. **238** P. Mac Cana, *The learned tales of medieval Ireland* (Dublin, 1980), pp 41–9. **239** Ní Bhrolcháin, *Literature*, p. 6. **240** Kinsella, *The Táin*, pp 88–9; Ní Bhrolcháin, *Literature*, p. 43. For the practice of beheading generally, see Doherty, 'Warrior and king', pp 139–41. **241** Ní Bhrolcháin, *Literature*, p. 52; Kinsella, *The Táin*, pp 51–3. **242** Kinsella, *The Táin*, pp

Woman-Slaughter, in revenge for the torture and killing of Derbforgaill. Clearly these ladies are not the most innocent of innocents though.[243]

It is of some interest to learn the author's description of the ideal woman. In *The wooing of Emer*, Cú Chulainn sets out his requirements in a wife. She is to be his equal in age and form and 'the best handiworker of the girls of Ireland', and these are said to be Emer's six gifts: beauty, voice, sweet speech, needlework, wisdom and charity.[244] It is important to stress, however, that early medieval Irish literature was primarily concerned with men and masculinity.[245] It was concerned with proper manly behaviour as constructed by the learned classes, associated with the concept *fír* (truth), exemplified by the most masculine of men, warriors and kings.[246] The corollary to this extreme laddishness (to use a modern term) can be found in two stories involving expeditions or voyages to the Otherworld, *Echtrae Chondlai* ('The expedition of Connlae the Fair') and *Immram Brain maic Febail* ('The voyage of Bran son of Febal'), where an idealized picture of a world akin to the Garden of Eden before the Fall is envisioned; the name given to the ideal land, in each case, is the Land of Women. The stories describe a land where there is no violence and everybody lives in harmony, 'where there is neither death nor sin nor transgression, where all live in peace and consume everlasting feasts',[247] and 'where there is no race ... but women and maidens',[248] in the case of *Echtrae Chondlai*, and 'many thousands of variegated [Otherworld] women'[249] in the case of *Immram Brain*. Both of these texts are thought to date from the seventh century.[250]

25–39; Ní Bhrolcháin, *Literature*, p. 128. **243** C. Marstrander (ed.), 'The deaths of Lugaid and Derbhforgaill', *Ériu*, 5 (1911), pp 201–18; Ní Bhrolcháin, *Literature*, p. 136. **244** Kinsella, *The Táin*, pp 25–39; Ní Bhrolcháin, *Literature*, p. 124. **245** E. Johnston, 'Kingship made real? Power and the public world in *Longes mac nUislenn*' in F. Edmonds and P. Russell (eds), *Tome: studies in medieval Celtic history and law in honour of Thomas Charles-Edwards* (Woodbridge, 2011), pp 193–206, esp. 196–8. **246** For treatments of the concept of *fír* see, for example, D.A. Binchy, *Celtic and Anglo-Saxon kingship* (Oxford, 1970); Watkins, '*Is tre fhír flathemon*', pp 181–98; T. Ó Cathasaigh, 'The concept of the hero in Irish mythology' in R. Kearney (ed.), *The Irish mind* (Dublin, 1985), pp 79–90; P. O'Leary, '*Fír Fer:* an internalized ethical concept in early Irish literature?', *Éigse*, 22 (1987), pp 1–14; C. Doherty, 'Kingship in early Ireland' in E. Bhreathnach (ed.), *The kingship and landscape of Tara* (Dublin, 2005), pp 3–31, esp. 25–7. For literacy's role in fashioning identities see Johnston, *Literacy*, p. 175. **247** H.P.A. Oskamp (ed.), '*Echtra Condla*', *Études Celtiques*, 14 (1974/5), pp 207–28; K. McCone (ed.), *Echtrae Connlai and the beginnings of vernacular narrative writing in Ireland* (Maynooth, 2000); Carney, 'Language', p. 500. **248** Carney, 'Language', p. 501. **249** Ibid., p. 503. See also: K. Meyer and A. Nutt (ed. and trans.), *The voyage of Bran son of Febal* (London, 1895); S. Mac Mathúna (ed. and trans.), *Immram Brain: The voyage of Bran to the Land of Women* (Tübingen, 1985). **250** Carney, 'Language', p. 500 and p. 503. See also E. Johnson, '*Immacallam Choluim Chille 7 ind Óclaig*: language and authority in an early-medieval Irish tale' in E. Purcell et al. (eds), *Clerics, kings and vikings: essays on medieval Ireland in honour of Donnchadh Ó Corráin* (Dublin, 2015), pp 418–28, in which she considers the dating of these texts in relation to *Immacallam Choluim Chille 7 ind Óclaig*, p. 420 and p. 423, citing J. Carey, 'On the interrelationships of some *Cín Dromma Snechtai* texts', *Ériu*, 46 (1995), pp 71–92 at 77–83.

In the law text *Bretha Crólige* reference is made to 'a woman who turns back the streams of war'.[251] While D.A. Binchy suggests that this may refer to a woman such as the abbess of Kildare whose prayers alleviate the effects of the sins of war, it could be interpreted to mean the intercessions of womenkind generally on behalf of peace. Clearly, in the society of late seventh-century Ireland, women, as a class of person, although inferior legally, were identified with peace and the absence of violence. The ideal community, as imagined by the authors of the sagas, where hurt was not caused (*innocere*), was their domain. This, it must be argued, was part of the mindset of those men who subscribed to the Law of the Innocents in Birr in 697.

* * *

It is possible, now, to come to two broad conclusions about late seventh-century Ireland. First, with regard to attitudes to violence in general, while the chronicles disclose a value system that deprecated violent death, even in battle, many of the other sources show an acceptance of violence, not just as a necessary evil, but as a normal fact of life. This is particularly apparent from how *díbergach* violence is juxtaposed with so-called honourable warfare in so many of the sources. This acceptance is the context in which *LxI* emerged. Second, with regard to violence towards innocents specifically, some may find it surprising that there is no evidence in any of the religious literature, such as canon law, the penitentials and hagiography, of any concern for their predicament. In fact, it is in vernacular law, in the *sellach* text, that a template for *LxI* is to be found. In this text the innocent is recognized and defined and he or she per se is exempted, in a situation involving violence, by a specific clause in the law, from obligations imposed on others.

---

251 Binchy, *Bretha Crólige*, 32.

CHAPTER 4

Adomnán

INTRODUCTION

Scholars have studied Adomnán the theologian, the diplomat, the lawyer.[1] They have pointed to his intellectual attainments, have contrasted him with Bede, particularly on the Easter question, have seen him as a man with an international outlook, and praised the quality of his Latin.[2] Adomnán's attitude to violence has rarely been considered,[3] and in doing so now it is hoped to learn something of what motivated him, his objectives and thought processes. As Thomas O'Loughlin has pointed out, trying to have an insight into the motivations of someone alive today whom we know can be extremely difficult. It is even more difficult in the case of a figure in history such as Napoleon, even though we can draw on a vast quantity of public and private records. It is even harder 'when the person lived over a millennium ago, where all we have are a few formal documents that were not intended as autobiographical, and where many of the dates and details are deductions or shrewd guesses'.[4] Unlike many other figures of seventh-century Ireland, however, whether kings, churchmen or poets, there is sufficient in the sources to disclose a real figure of history, and it is possible to conjecture in an informed way about Adomnán's career, his abilities, his concerns and the reasons behind his doings and writings, whatever about knowing his personality.[5] An attempt will be

---

[1] Many of the contributions to Wooding (ed.), *Adomnán of Iona*, are concerned with Adomnán as a theologian. Clare Stancliffe's essay, '"Charity with peace": Adomnán and the Easter question' is of particular interest, underlining as it does Adomnán's subtlety of mind as a theologian and exegete. See pp 62–8 in particular; O'Loughlin, *Holy places*, pp 111–42. As a diplomat see Adomnán, *VC*, trans. R. Sharpe, *Adomnán of Iona: Life of St Columba* (London, 1995), pp 46–7; B. Yorke, 'Adomnán at the court of King Aldfrith' in Wooding (ed.), *Adomnán of Iona*, pp 36–50 at p. 36; T. O'Loughlin, 'Adomnán: a man of many parts' in idem (ed.), *Adomnán at Birr*, p. 44. As a lawyer see O'Loughlin, 'Adomnán: a man of many parts', p. 42; Sharpe, *Adomnán of Iona*, pp 56–7. For instance also the contribution of Pamela O'Neill to a recent meeting of the Irish Conference of Medievalists in University College Dublin, and I am grateful to her for her confirmation of my recollection of the content. [2] Herbert, *Iona, Kells and Derry*, pp 12–13. J.-M. Picard, 'Bede, Adomnán and the writing of history', *Peritia*, 3 (1984), pp 50–70; Charles-Edwards, *Early Christian Ireland*, pp 436–7; O'Loughlin, *Holy places*, pp 188–97. On international outlook see, for instance, Johnston, *Literacy*, p. 59. On Latin see Richter, *Neighbours*, pp 84–5. [3] Fraser, 'Adomnán and the morality of war' being the exception. [4] T. O'Loughlin, 'Adomnán: a man of many parts', pp 50–1.

made, therefore, to know and understand Adomnán, with particular focus on his attitudes to violence and innocents.

Adomnán, like most of his contemporaries, firmly believed in the comprehensive Christian world-view.[6] Exegesis was the most important branch of study and Irish authors contributed to it.[7] Similarly, Bede saw the interpretation of the Bible, verse by verse, as the most fundamental of all intellectual activities.[8] It followed from this that the training of a young cleric taught him to seek the spiritual significance that lay behind any occurrence, rather than, as we do today, to seek the material relation of cause and effect. To do the latter would have been seen as superficial. Adomnán, therefore, believed, as did Bede, in miracles.[9] This was not due to credulity on the part of these two men, two of the most learned of their time, but because their focus of attention was completely different from our own. Events happened or did not happen because of God's intervention and it was believed that saints could influence that intervention.[10] Thus Adomnán believed that Columba had an *entrée* to God and he expresses this in *VC*.[11] Even in late seventh-century Ireland, and more so in Britain, Christianity had to prove itself vis-à-vis the remaining non-Christians, and the power and influence of its saints were a major weapon in that struggle.[12] Allied to this is the belief that 'observance of true Christianity brought worldly success in its train'.[13] An understanding of this mindset, of what Máire Herbert refers to as Adomnán's 'thought-world',[14] is fundamentally crucial for a knowledge and understanding of the man. For instance, we can conclude that the success of Adomnán's kinsmen the Cenél Conaill and the accession of his cousin to the kingship of Tara in 695 would be seen by him as having been willed by God through the intercession of the Cenél Conaill saint, Columba. He would have viewed it as, not only a God-given power and opportunity, but also a God-given responsibility. It is hoped that, following this chapter, it will be possible to know and understand, to some degree,

---

5 Sharpe, *Adomnán of Iona*, pp 43–4.   **6** For an interesting, step-by-step analysis of how this evolved in the Christian West see Markus, *Ancient Christianity*.   **7** Sharpe, *Adomnán of Iona*, p. 45. For instance: important early exegetical experts included Laidcenn mac Baíth Bannaig (d. 661), whose work is considered in M. Herren, 'The authorship, date of composition and provenance of the so-called *Lorica Gildae*', *Ériu*, 24 (1973), pp 35–51. Also see Lapidge and Sharpe, *Bibliography*, to have a sense of the volume of work in general, including exegetical works. To that end see Sharpe, *A handlist*, and in particular Ó Corráin, *Clavis*, especially pp 81–229 (*Biblica*) and pp 711–51 (Hiberno-Latin writers and texts).   **8** For general context see, Mayr-Harting, *The coming*, p. 210. For instance, Bede's own work shows this in operation. His contribution to biblical commentary was extensive. See, for instance, S. DeGregorio (trans.), *Bede: On Ezra and Nehemiah* (Liverpool, 2006). C. O'Brien, *Bede's Temple: an image and its interpretation* (Oxford, 2015), shows the depth of exegetical thinking in Bede's approach. **9** Picard, 'Bede, Adomnán', pp 54–5.   **10** See the works of Benedicta Ward, e.g., *Miracles and the medieval mind: theory, record and event, 1000–1215* (Aldershot, 1982), *Signs and wonders: saints, miracles and prayers from the fourth century to the fourteenth* (Aldershot, 1992).   **11** Herbert, *Iona, Kells and Derry*, p. 137.   **12** Richter, *Neighbours*, p. 31.   **13** Mayr-Harting, *The coming*, p. 256. **14** Herbert, *Iona, Kells and Derry*, p. 140.

this man who has been described as 'one of the most interesting figures in early Irish history',[15] the author of *LxI*.

BIOGRAPHY AND WORKS

Biography
Adomnán's birth is recorded in the annals in the year 624, although this is very likely to be retrospective.[16] His death is recorded in 704, where he is said to be in his seventy-seventh year at time of death.[17] Clearly both entries cannot be correct. Scholars consider that the entry of his death is more reliable, because it is likely that the annalist in Iona had an accurate knowledge of his abbot's age. Therefore it can be tentatively concluded that Adomnán was born between 24 September 627 and 23 September 628.[18] His place of birth is generally accepted as Donegal on the basis that he mentions Ireland in *VC* as being 'our own Ireland',[19] and that he was of the Cenél Conaill, whose homeland was in modern Co. Donegal. There is no agreement as to the exact location in Donegal. Reeves suggested somewhere in the vicinity of Druim Tuama (Drumhome),[20] relying on the fact that Adomnán mentions in *VC* that he was told a story in his youth about Columba's death by the monk Ernéne, who is buried there.[21] Both Máirín Ní Dhonnchadha and Richard Sharpe express doubts about this conclusion,[22] and Brian Lacey, in a detailed analysis of the territorial expansion of the Cenél Conaill within Donegal in the century or so before Adomnán's birth, has suggested an alternative location, the area close to Raphoe.[23] He is, however, at pains to stress that this is not connected with the later tradition associating Adomnán with the church there, which may not have existed until about a century after his death.

Little is known of Adomnán's father, Rónán, but it is accepted that he was of the Cenél Conaill, being descended from Sétna, a grandson of the eponymous Conall Gulban. Loingsech mac Óengusso, king of Tara and described as king of Ireland in *LxI*'s guarantor-list as well as the Annals of Ulster,[24] was also descended

---

15 Sharpe, *Adomnán of Iona*, p. 43. **16** AU s. a. 624. **17** Ibid., s. a. 704. **18** Sharpe, *Adomnán of Iona*, p. 44; B. Lacey, *Cenél Conaill and the Donegal kingdoms, AD 500–800* (Dublin, 2006), p. 243. **19** *VC* III.23 (henceforth, when reference is being made to *VC* or paragraphs from it, Sharpe, *Adomnán of Iona*, will be utilized unless otherwise stated. Coincidently, the page number in which this appears is the same in Sharpe and Adomnán, *VC*, ed. and trans. A.O. Anderson and M.O. Anderson, *Adomnán's Life of Columba* (Edinburgh, 1961; 2nd ed. Oxford, 1991), p. 233 in both). See also: Sharpe, *Adomnán of Iona*, pp 43–4; B. Lacey, 'Adomnán and Donegal' in Wooding (ed.), *Adomnán of Iona*, p. 20; idem, *Kingdoms*, p. 243. **20** Adomnán, *VC*, ed. and trans. W. Reeves, *The Life of St Columba, founder of Hy: written by Adamnán, ninth abbot of that monastery* (Dublin, 1857, 2nd 1874), p. 238. See also Sharpe, *Adomnán of Iona*, p. 376, n. 416. **21** *VC* III.23. **22** Ní Dhonnchadha, 'An edition of *Cáin Adomnáin*', p. 6; Sharpe, *Adomnán of Iona*, p. 44. **23** Lacey, *Kingdoms*, p. 245; idem, 'Adomnán and Donegal', p. 35. **24** AU s. a. 703. *LxI*, paragraph 28, number 41.

from Sétna. In fact, Adomnán and Loingsech are both at a remove of five generations from Sétna making them fourth cousins. Columba, the founder of Iona and the subject of Adomnán's great work, *VC*, was a son of Fedelmid, who was a brother of Sétna. Adomnán's mother was also of the Cenél Conaill, a separate branch, the Cenél nÉndai.[25] It has been widely accepted that most of the successors of Columba as abbots of Iona were also of the Cenél Conaill and in some way related to the founder and to each other. The exceptions are Fergna (Virgno), who died in 623, and Suibne moccu Urthri (d. 657). Baíthéne (d. *c.*600),[26] Columba's successor, was his first cousin. Laisrén (d. 605) was first cousin once removed of both Columba and Baíthéne; Ségéne (d. 652) was a nephew of Laisrén; Cumméne (d. 669) was a nephew of Ségéne and Faílbe (d. 679), Adomnán's immediate predecessor, Cumméne's third cousin.[27] Brian Lacey casts some doubt on the Cenél Conaill credentials of Laisrén, Ségéne, Cumméne and Faílbe, although not on their interrelationship, suggesting that they belonged to an independent people, the Cenél Duach. This people, he suggests, were incorporated into the Cenél Conaill genealogies at a later date.[28] This being so means that Adomnán was the first truly Cenél Conaill abbot of Iona since Baíthéne, and thus the first true kin of Columba to hold that position for almost eighty years. This may have been seen as providential, and a link back to Columba. Taken in conjunction with his kinsman's commencement of his reign as king of Tara in 695, a mere two years before the centenary anniversary of Columba's death,[29] there may have been no doubting the hand of God.

The contemporary sources tell us nothing of Adomnán's life from the date of his birth until his appointment as abbot of Iona in 679, when he would have been over fifty. It is reasonable to assume that he became a monk in a Columban monastery and spent much of his early monastic life studying the Bible and the Fathers,[30] which would have been necessary to qualify him as a candidate for the abbacy of Iona, and the results of which are manifest in the conscientious scholarly standards evident in his works.[31] In *VC*, when referring to his predecessor abbots, Adomnán mentions personal contact with his immediate predecessor Faílbe only. This may indicate that he never met any of the earlier abbots. On this rather tenuous basis,[32] some scholars have argued that it is unlikely that Adomnán was in Iona before the commencement of Faílbe's abbacy in 669.

25 For a full discussion see Lacey, *Kingdoms*, p. 244; idem, 'Adomnán and Donegal', pp 24–31.   **26** See discussion in Herbert, *Iona, Kells and Derry*, pp 38–9.   **27** Ibid., pp 36–46; P. Ó Riain (ed.), *Corpus Genealogiarum Sanctorum Hiberniae* (Dublin, 1985), nos. 8, 327, 336–48, Genealogical Table I.   **28** Lacey, 'Adomnán and Donegal', pp 31–2.   **29** Anderson and Anderson, *Columba*, pp xxxv–xxxvi. Lacey, following McCarthy, differs on the date of death, see Lacey, *Kingdoms*, p. 253.   **30** Sharpe, *Adomnán of Iona*, p. 45.   **31** Herbert, *Iona, Kells and Derry*, p. 12; eadem, 'The world of Adomnán' in O'Loughlin (ed.), *Adomnán at Birr*, p. 36. His work *DLS* demonstrates this. See T. O'Loughlin, 'The library of Iona in the late seventh century: the evidence of Adomnán's *De Locis Sanctis*', *Ériu*, 45 (1994), pp 33–44, which helps reconstruct the texts at Adomnán's disposal.   **32** *VC* I.1 (Sharpe, p. 111). See Ní Dhonnchadha, 'An edition of *Cáin Adomnáin*', p. 7 for a different view.

Indeed, it has been suggested that Adomnán may have been recruited by Faílbe as his successor on the latter's visit to Ireland between 673 and 676.[33] Other speculation has linked Adomnán with Columban monasteries in Durrow, and Druim Tuama, and, indeed, the case has been made for a much earlier association with Iona.[34] It is difficult to believe, however, that a man of Adomnán's ability, initiative and prominent family background would have lived in relative obscurity, however scholarly and pious, for his first fifty years. There is, however, insufficient evidence in contemporary sources to enable a reasonable picture to emerge without entering into pure speculation.[35]

Adomnán succeeded Faílbe as abbot of Iona and head of the Columban *familia* in 679.[36] The first record in the sources of his activities thereafter is an entry in the annals for the year 687: 'Adomnán brought back sixty captives to Ireland'.[37] In *VC* Adomnán tells us that he made two visits to Northumbria, to 'my friend King Aldfrith'.[38] He states that his first visit took place 'after Ecgfrith's battle' and the second two years later.[39] We do not know the full extent of the friendship between Adomnán and Aldfrith. At a minimum, we know from the Anonymous Life of St Cuthbert that, immediately before he became king in 685 or 686, Aldfrith was on Iona, where Adomnán was abbot since 679.[40] It has been suggested, however, that Aldfrith (or Flann Fína as he came to be known by the Irish) may have spent a considerable part of his youth in Ireland and Iona pursuing studies with a view to a life in religion.[41] Aldfrith was the son of the Northumbrian king Oswiu (642–70) by an Irish mother of the Cenél nÉogain, and appears to have remained in Ireland with his mother's family when Oswiu returned to Northumbria after a period of exile in Ireland. It is likely, therefore, that the two men knew one another well, moved in the same circles, had had similar educations and were close friends, as suggested by Adomnán's language.

Aldfrith came to the throne in 685/6 after Ecgfrith's death at the battle of Nechtanesmere on 20 May 685 and he may well have had Uí Néill support.[42] The

---

33 Anderson and Anderson, *Columba*, p. xl; Herbert, *Iona, Kells and Derry*, p. 47; eadem, 'The world of Adomnán', p. 36; Sharpe, *Adomnán of Iona*, pp 45–6. **34** A.P. Smyth, *Celtic Leinster: towards an historical geography of early Irish civilization, AD 500–1600* (Dublin, 1982), pp 118–20; Sharpe, *Adomnán of Iona*, pp 45–6; Lacey, *Kingdoms*, p. 246. Sharpe, *Adomnán of Iona*, p. 44. Ní Dhonnchadha, 'An edition of *Cáin Adomnáin*', pp 7–9. **35** Lacey, *Kingdoms*, p. 251. **36** Herbert, *Iona, Kells and Derry*, p. 47. **37** AU s. a. 687. See Charles-Edwards, *Chronicle*, p. 167 and n. 6. In his opinion the correct year is, in fact, 686. **38** B. Yorke, *Kings and kingdoms of early Saxon England* (London, 1990); eadem, *Rex Doctissimus: Bede and King Aldfrith of Northumbria*, Jarrow Lectures (Jarrow, 2009). For Aldfrith and Ireland see Ireland, 'Alfrith of Northumbria and the Irish genealogies'; idem (ed. and trans.), *Old Irish wisdom attributed to Aldfrith of Northumbria* (Tempe, AR, 1999); Yorke, 'Adomnán at the court of King Aldfrith'. **39** *VC* II.46. **40** *Vita S. Cuthberti Auctore Anonymo* III.6 in B. Colgrave (ed. and trans.), *Two lives of Saint Cuthbert: a life by an anonymous monk of Lindisfarne and Bede's prose life* (Cambridge, 1940). See Yorke, 'Adomnán at the court of King Aldfrith', p. 36. **41** Yorke, 'Adomnán at the court of King Aldfrith', pp 36–7; Richter, *Neighbours*, pp 94–7; Ní Dhonnchadha, 'An edition of *Cáin Adomnáin*', p. 9; Ireland, 'Aldfrith of Northumbria and the Irish genealogies'. **42** Herbert, *Iona,*

point has been made that a raid ordered by Ecgfrith in 684 on the Southern Uí Néill territory of Brega was intended as a pre-emptive strike to discourage just such support.[43] The raid was particularly violent and unexpected. Bede describes how Ecgfrith's commander 'brutally harassed an inoffensive people … sparing neither churches nor monasteries from the ravages of war'.[44] Adomnán's friendship with Aldfrith made him the obvious ambassador to seek the return of the captives and it is unlikely he encountered any difficulties in securing their release. The question must be asked, however, is this friendship, of itself, sufficient to explain how a Southern Uí Néill king of Tara, Finsnechtae Fledach, predecessor of Loingsech mac Óengusso, Adomnán's Cenél Conaill kinsman, might have asked for the assistance of the abbot of Iona in retrieving prisoners taken from Brega, his own backyard? It is possible that this unusual friendship was enough, particularly if Adomnán was perceived as a powerful figure. Contemporary sources are insufficient to supply any other explanation. A later source, the Middle Irish *Fragmentary annals of Ireland*, however, although unreliable, does claim a special relationship between Adomnán and Finsnechtae Fledach, established in the years before Adomnán's abbacy of Iona.[45] Adomnán and Finsnechtae were, of course, related; the latter was at a remove of four generations from Cerrbél, a brother of Sétna, Adomnán's and Loingsech's common ancestor.[46] There may be evidence here of a moment of cohesion between the Southern and Northern Uí Néill, which resulted in the unusual description of Loingsech as king of Ireland in both *LxI* and the Annals of Ulster. Another explanation is suggested by a second Middle Irish source, the prologue to *LxI*, and, in particular, paragraphs 6 to 15, that describe the circumstances which impel Adomnán to introduce his law.[47] Adomnán and his mother Rónnat are described as arriving at the aftermath of a battle in Brega where scenes of the most awful violence are encountered.

> Of all they saw on the battlefield, they saw nothing which they found more touching or more wretched than the head of a woman lying in one place and her body in another, and her infant on the breast of her corpse. There was a stream of milk on one of its cheeks and a stream of blood on the other cheek.[48]

Kells and Derry, p. 48; Richter, *Neighbours*, pp 94–7; H. Moisl, 'The Bernician royal dynasty and the Irish in the seventh century', *Peritia*, 2 (1983), pp 103–26.   **43** Yorke, 'Adomnán at the court of King Aldfrith', p. 37; Moisl, 'The Bernician royal dynasty and the Irish', pp 120–4; Smyth, *Celtic Leinster*, pp 120–1.   **44** Bede, *HE* IV.26; Sharpe, *Adomnán of Iona*, p. 351. For Ecgfrith see: N. Hyams, *Ecgfrith: king of the Northumbrians, high-king of Britain* (Donington, 2015).   **45** J.N. Radner (ed. and trans.), *Fragmentary annals of Ireland* (Dublin, 1978), p. 25; Lacey, *Kingdoms*, pp 250–2; Ní Dhonnchadha, 'An edition of *Cáin Adomnáin*', pp 8–11.   **46** A. Mac Shamhráin and P. Byrne, 'Prosopography I: kings named in *Baile Chuinn Chétchathaig* and *The Airgíalla Charter Poem*' in E. Bhreathnach (ed.), *The kingship and landscape of Tara* (Dublin, 2005), p. 190 and pp 344–50.   **47** For an English translation of these paragraphs see Márkus, *Adomnán's 'Law of the Innocents'*, pp 11–13; Ní Dhonnchadha, 'An edition of *Cáin Adomnáin*', p. 11 and p. 33.   **48** Márkus, *Adomnán's 'Law of the Innocents'*, p. 11.

It has been suggested that this reflects a tradition that Adomnán was inspired by the Northumbrian raid on Brega to introduce his law for the protection of innocents.[49] If there is any truth in this, it would not be inconceivable that he might have, of his own initiative, offered his services to the king of Tara, to act as an ambassador to the court of his close friend Aldfrith. We know that churchmen frequently acted as political envoys.[50] While it is tempting to see this as Adomnán's Solferino moment, it is unlikely that Adomnán, then abbot of Iona, attended at the scene of Brega's aftermath, as did Henry Dunant attend the aftermath of the battle of Solferino.[51] On the other hand, Adomnán's concern for innocents was singular and not evident in any of the contemporary sources. Adomnán is unusual in the concerns expressed by him. Was this difference caused by a traumatic personal experience?

In any event, we know, from Adomnán's own words in *VC*, that he made a second visit to Northumbria two years after his first, in 688. On one of his visits, we do not know which, Adomnán gave a copy of his recent work on the holy places, *De locis sanctis* (*DLS*), to King Aldfrith.[52] It appears that Adomnán may have spent some time there. Bede, who is our principle source for what happened on these visits, conflates them and the annals do not mention the second.[53] While the vexed question of Adomnán, Bede and the date of Easter is outside the scope of this work and has been extensively considered by scholars,[54] from the point of view of this biographical outline one issue arising out of Bede's account must be mentioned. He creates the impression that Adomnán was converted to the Roman orthodox method for the calculation of the date of Easter, as distinct from the Irish method, while in Northumbria, and that he returned to Iona where he failed to persuade his community to change and became alienated from them; that he returned to Ireland, where he spent the rest of his life preaching the Roman view, successfully except in Iona, and that he returned to Iona shortly before his death in 704, still at odds with his *familia*.[55] This truncated account of Adomnán's life is not supported by the Irish sources and has been hotly contested by scholars.[56] The annals inform us that Adomnán journeyed to

---

49 Ní Dhonnchadha, 'An edition of *Cáin Adomnáin*', p. 33. This point is considered further in Chapter 7, p. 188.   **50** See, for instance, A. Gillett, *Envoys and political communication in the late antique West, 411–533* (Cambridge, 2003), which, while dealing with an earlier period, shows how this operated in practice.   **51** Smith and Gallen, 'Laws of war', pp 71–2; H. Dunant, *Un Souvenir de Solferino* (Geneva, 1862).   **52** The text is edited by D. Meehan, *De Locis Sanctis* (Dublin, 1958). For a radically different view of its composition, see D. Woods, 'On the circumstances of Adomnán's composition of *De locis sanctis*' in Wooding (ed.), *Adomnán of Iona*, pp 193–204.   **53** Sharpe, *Adomnán of Iona*, p. 47.   **54** Picard, 'Bede, Adomnán'; Charles-Edwards, *Early Christian Ireland*, pp 391–415; Stancliffe, 'Charity with peace'; Woods, 'On the circumstances'. See Jonathan Wooding's comments in his Introduction in Wooding (ed.), *Adomnán of Iona*, pp 14–15.   **55** Sharpe, *Adomnán of Iona*, p. 49.   **56** Ibid., pp 49–51; Picard, 'Bede, Adomnán, pp 63–70; Herbert, *Iona, Kells and Derry*, pp 48–53; eadem, 'The world of Adomnán, pp 36–7. For the opposing view see Ní Dhonachadha, 'The guarantor-list', pp 183–4; eadem, 'An edition of *Cáin Adomnáin*', pp 15–

Ireland in 692, probably as part of his obligations as abbot of Iona to visit the churches under his jurisdiction.[57] He presumably returned to Iona, because the next entry in the annals tells of his return in 697, 'Adamnán proceeded to Ireland and gave the Lex Innocentium to the peoples'.[58] We are told by Adomnán himself that he returned to Iona in the summer, after he had attended 'the meeting of the Irish synod'.[59] It seems clear that this refers to Birr.[60] On the basis that he refers to *LxI* in *VC*, it is likely that Adomnán would have spent some time in the period after 697 writing *VC* or, at least, putting the finishing touches to it, up to his death, on Iona in 704, 'in the 77th year of his age'.[61] Indeed, it has been argued that our earliest witness to *VC*, Dorbbéne's copy, was written under Adomnán's direction.[62]

Works

Apart from *LxI*, the main works for which Adomnán is remembered today are *De locis sanctis (DLS)* and *VC*. *De locis sanctis* is a short text divided into three books with twenty-nine concise chapters in the first, thirty in the second and six in the third.[63] At the beginning of the text Adomnán explains that a bishop from Gaul, who had spent nine months in Jerusalem, dictated to him, Adomnán, in response to careful inquiries, a 'faithful and accurate record of all his experiences', which Adomnán first caused to be written down on tablets and which were then written succinctly on parchment.[64] Bede tells us that Arculf's ship was driven by a storm onto the coast of Britain and that, after many vicissitudes, he came into contact with Adomnán.[65] The first book describes Jerusalem in the early Islamic period, more specifically during the caliphate of the Umayyad, Mu'awiya (658–80), giving details of the site of Jerusalem, many of its churches and many of the locations featuring in the Bible.[66] In the second book Arculf moves further afield, describing significant sites of Galilee and concluding with a lengthy account of Alexandria, its lighthouse and the Nile crocodiles.[67] The third book deals with the city of Constantinople and Sicily. There is scholarly dispute on Arculf, with Thomas O'Loughlin seeing him as a literary device,[68] and Rodney Aist taking issue, pointing to Arculf's descriptions of specific features which, when properly interrogated, establish him 'as a distinct and trustworthy witness of seventh-century Jerusalem'.[69]

18; A.A.M. Duncan, 'Bede, Iona and the Picts' in R.H.C. Davis and J.M. Wallace-Hadrill (eds), *The writing of history in the Middle Ages* (Oxford, 1981), pp 1–42. **57** AU s. a. 692; Herbert, 'The world of Adomnán', p. 37; Sharpe, *Adomnán of Iona*, p. 50. **58** AU s. a. 697. **59** *VC* II.45. **60** Sharpe, *Adomnán of Iona*, p. 50; Anderson and Anderson, *Columba*, p. 177, n. 203. **61** AU s. a. 704. **62** M. Stansbury, 'The composition of Adomnán's *Vita Columbae*', *Peritia*, 17–18 (2003–4), pp 154–13 in which he posits that Dorbbéne finished *VC* from a draft compiled from Adomnán's notes. **63** Meehan, *DLS*; O'Loughlin, *Holy places*. **64** Meehan, *DLS*, p. 37. **65** Bede, *HE* V.15. **66** See R. Aist, 'Adomnán, Arculf and the source material of *De locis sanctis*' in Wooding (ed.), *Adomnán of Iona*, p. 168. **67** Meehan, *DLS* II.30. **68** O'Loughlin, *Holy places*, pp 61–6. **69** Aist, 'Adomnán, Arculf', p. 170. See also comments in Woods, 'On the circumstances', pp 201–3.

Adomnán's purpose in writing *DLS* is clear. Although, as he states at the end of the third book, he is 'daily beset by laborious and almost insupportable ecclesiastical business from every quarter',[70] it is hard to imagine a more important task. On the assumption that he met Arculf, he must have seen it as God's will that he bring to a wider audience all of the information about the holy places that Arculf imparted to him. In a world where biblical studies were the very essence of education and Ireland and the areas of northern Britain under Iona influence seen as a centre of such learning, to do so would be imperative. *DLS* would be of considerable assistance in understanding and appreciating the scriptures. For instance, as has been pointed out, the Psalms, so central to monastic prayer, mention Jerusalem/Zion fifty-seven times.[71] Arculf's descriptions of Jerusalem would help Christians envisage biblical scenes. Thomas O'Loughlin argues that this is even more crucial in a world, such as the early medieval one, which saw the liturgy as something immediate and real, not symbolic, and not separate in time and space from the events recalled.[72] In any event, it is to be expected, and not confined to Christianity, that adherents want to know about the places mentioned in their scriptures. An example is the famous journey to the west, to India, of the Chinese Buddhist monk, Xuanzang (c.602–64), some forty years before Arculf's journey, so that he might experience the places where the Buddha flourished,[73] which later formed the basis of one of China's best-loved novels, *Journey to the West*.[74]

As already mentioned, Adomnán presented Aldfrith with a copy of *DLS* on one of his visits to Northumbria. The annal entry recording Aldfrith's death refers to him as a *sapiens*.[75] This had a special meaning in the Irish context over and above excellence in learning. It signified a distinct grade in the Irish church,[76] with attainments that included special skill in biblical exegesis. Adomnán's gift, therefore, was no nominal gesture, but a present of essential importance. That it was so regarded is clear from the favourable references to it in Bede's *Historia Ecclesiastica* and to the fact that Bede subsequently produced his own version.[77] *DLS* 'was copied extensively throughout medieval Europe, was excerpted, translated, and used as a basis for other works'.[78] As a result Adomnán was known, down to the sixteenth century, as an 'illustrious teacher' and as one who had 'instructed many in wisdom'.[79]

However, the work for which Adomnán is best known today is *Vita Columbae* (*VC*), his life of Columba, not only for what it tells us about Columba, but also

---

70 Meehan, *DLS* III.6.   **71** O'Loughlin, 'Adomnán: a man of many parts', p. 49.   **72** T. O'Loughlin, 'The *De locis sanctis* as a liturgical text' in Wooding, *Adomnán of Iona*, pp 183–6.   **73** R. Bernstein, *Ultimate journey: retracing the path of an ancient Buddhist monk (Xuanzang) who crossed Asia in search of enlightenment* (New York, 2001).   **74** Wu Cheng'en (trans. W.J.F. Jenner), *Journey to the West* (Beijing, 1982).   **75** AU s. a. 704.   **76** For a comprehensive treatment of this topic, with specific mention of Aldfrith, see Johnston, *Literacy*, esp. 102–12. See also: Charles-Edwards, *Early Christian Ireland*, pp 264–71; Yorke, 'Adomnán at the court of King Aldfrith', p. 43.   **77** Bede, *HE* V.16–17; Yorke, 'Adomnán at the court of King Aldfrith', p. 47.   **78** O'Loughlin, 'Adomnán: a man of many parts', p. 48.   **79** Ibid., p. 48; idem, *Holy places*, pp 198–203.

as one of the most valuable sources for the study of early medieval Ireland generally.[80] It is a narrative of Columba's life, in three books, detailing his prophecies, miracles and angelic visitations. While clearly in the hagiographical genre, it is a subtle and spiritual work, biblical and international in its approach in depicting Columba as a saint in the mould of St Anthony, St Martin and St Benedict.[81] It demonstrates a remarkable absence of rancour and rivalry in its descriptions of contact between Columba and other monastic founders such as Comgall of Bangor and Ciarán of Clonmacnoise.[82] Indeed, harmony between the various Irish churches is what is being advocated.[83] As mentioned above, it is likely that Adomnán did not complete the writing of VC until after his return to Iona from Birr in the summer of 697. He died in 704 and the earliest surviving manuscript was copied by the scribe Dorbbéne, whose death is recorded in the annals for the year 713.[84] Dorbbéne's manuscript is preserved in the public library in Schaffhausen, Switzerland. It has an immediacy with events in Birr in 697.[85]

Adomnán was convinced that Columba was a saint and that he was in a position to influence the outcome of events by interceding with God.[86] He cites occasions in his own lifetime when Columba, in response to Adomnán's prayers, preserved him from plague or provided him with favourable winds.[87] Given his thought-world, he had no reason to disbelieve accounts of miraculous deeds from reliable sources. For him these accounts were inherently probable.[88] This is not to say that he could not envisage some doubters and he appears to have concerns in that regard.[89] However, he naturally would feel impelled to communicate these miraculous happenings, in which he believed implicitly, especially to his own community. He needed to do this all the more because his community may have felt that he had rejected Columba if he now accepted the Roman method of calculating the date of Easter and had turned his back on the old method followed by Columba.[90] Adomnán advocated co-existence in spite of differences. The subtlety with which this is done in the final chapter of VC,

---

80 Among the many works availing fully of this source are: Herbert, *Iona, Kells and Derry*; D. Brown and T.O. Clancy (eds), *Spes Scotorum, hope of Scots: Saint Columba, Iona and Scotland* (Edinburgh, 1999) and virtually all scholars of early medieval Ireland and Northern Britain including all of the contributors to Wooding, *Adomnán of Iona*. **81** Sharpe, *Adomnán of Iona*, p. 63. See J.-M. Picard, 'Structural patterns in early Hiberno-Latin hagiography', *Peritia*, 4 (1985), pp 67–82, for an analysis of the influences on early Irish hagiography and of underlying structures. **82** For example: *VC* III.13 and 17; *VC* I.3. See Ó Cróinín, *Early medieval Ireland*, pp 208–9; Idem, 'Hiberno- Latin literature to 1169', p. 386. **83** Herbert, *Iona, Kells and Derry*, p. 54. **84** AU s. a. 713; Herbert, *Iona, Kells and Derry*, p. 58. **85** This sense of connection can be enjoyed in a special way through the magnificent facsimile of Dorbbéne's manuscript now available: D. Bracken and E. Graff (eds), *The Schaffhausen Adomnán, Schaffhausen Stadtbibliothek, MS Generalia 1* (2 vols, Cork, 2015). See reviews of this work by Elva Johnston in *Irish Literary Supplement*, spring 2017 and by D. Ó Cróinín in *Peritia*, 28 (2017), pp 227–36, esp. 229–32. See also Sharpe, *Adomnán of Iona*, pp 235–8. **86** Herbert, *Iona, Kells and Derry*, p. 137. **87** *VC* II.45 and 46. **88** Herbert, *Iona, Kells and Derry*, p. 141. **89** Sharpe, *Adomnán of Iona*, pp 55–6. **90** Herbert, *Iona, Kells and Derry*, pp 142–3.

woven into the moving account of Columba's last hours on earth, attests, not only to Adomnán's fine mind and exegetical command, but also to his instinct to ameliorate, to compromise when faced with immovable forces.[91]

His intended audience extended further than the Iona community. The first preface contains literary allusions and devices which are suggestive of the composition style of the classics of hagiography that would be apparent to a wider learned audience and that would place Columba among the saints venerated throughout Christendom.[92] Adomnán goes on to address, directly, a Northumbrian audience. He reminds them that Oswald, their king, acknowledged the intercession of Columba in his victory over the British in 634, from which ensued their conversion to Christianity. It behoved them, therefore, to render him due acknowledgment for delivering them from 'the darkness of heathenism and ignorance'.[93] That an even wider audience was envisioned has also been suggested, although this is not universally accepted.[94] The point has also been made that part of the purpose of *VC* was to counteract the advance of Armagh and its propaganda.[95] Máire Herbert argues strongly that this is not the case both because Iona and its influence was exceptionally strong at that time, as evidenced by the synod of Birr, relative to Armagh, whose rise was still aspirational, and the absence of polemics and the conciliatory tone of *VC*.[96] Adomnán emerges, therefore, as a Christian leader confident in his own strongly-held views, which he saw as being best promoted by non-confrontational means. He had the capacity to distinguish between the essential and the not so essential and in the latter case was prepared to compromise.

There are two other extant works attributed to Adomnán. *Canones Adomnani* is a list of twenty canons, eighteen of which relate to when it is permissible, and when not, to eat the flesh of animals and fish when found dead. One deals with the remarriage of a man whose wife has become a prostitute and one prohibits a Christian receiving stolen cattle.[97] Some question has been raised on Adomnán's authorship, but this now seems settled beyond reasonable doubt.[98] The text is in the nature of a penitential, although penances are not prescribed. While many of the provisions may seem obvious to the modern mind from a health point of view, such as the stricture against eating land-animals that have died in water 'since their blood remains in them',[99] others are less so, not having

---

91 *VC* III.23. See Herbert, *Iona, Kells and Derry*, pp 143–4; Stancliffe, '"Charity with peace"', pp 62–8. **92** Herbert, *Iona, Kells and Derry*, pp 144–5. **93** Ibid., p. 145; *VC* I.1. **94** Herbert, *Iona, Kells and Derry*, p. 145; J.-M. Picard, 'The purpose of Adomnán's *Vita Columbae*', *Peritia*, 1 (1982), pp 175; Sharpe, *Adomnán of Iona*, pp 63–4. **95** Picard, 'The purpose', pp 167–9; Ó Cróinín, *Early medieval Ireland*, pp 209–10. **96** Herbert, *Iona, Kells and Derry*, p. 146. **97** Ó Néill/Dumville, *Cáin Adomnáin and Canones Adomnani*; Kenney, *Sources*, p. 245; Lapidge and Sharpe, *Bibliography*, p. 155; O'Loughlin, 'Adomnán: a man of many parts', pp 45–6; Bieler, *Irish penitentials*, pp 176–180; Pereira Farrell, 'Taboos and penitence', p. 74; Ó Corráin, *Clavis*, pp 800–1 (621). **98** See Pereira Farrell, 'Taboos and penitence', p. 74ff for a summary of relevant scholarship. **99** Ó Néill/Dumville, *Cáin Adomnáin and Canones Adomnani*, Canon 3, p. 2.

been fully understood until more recent times, such as the advice to clean out a well in which is found the remains of a man or animal, and 'the mud in it, which the water has moistened',[100] before treating it as clean. To regard this, however, as a simple tract dealing with culinary hygiene would be mistaken. There are elements of spiritual pollution and contagion involving anomalies of nature and the transgression of cosmological laws, as perceived by early medieval societies.[101] Some of these strictures attempt to define the boundaries between man and animal. They also define the Christian as distinct from the non-Christian, with contact between them having a polluting influence. Paragraph 4 stipulates that 'Animals seized by beasts and half alive are to be taken for food by bestial men', and paragraph 18 states that 'A beast which has only been seized with a deadly bite and not quite killed is to be eaten by beasts and bestial men ...' Rob Meens suggests that non-Christians are the 'bestial men'.[102] It seems likely, however, that Adomnán is here referring to díbergaig and it is apparent that he regarded them with the same abhorrence with which they were regarded in the many contemporary sources considered in the last chapter. In any event, it stretches to its fullest limit, and maybe beyond, the capacity of the modern mind to understand the underlying full significance of *Canones Adomnani*. It does demonstrate that Adomnán felt the need to lay down the boundaries, as expressed by eating practices, for his Christian community and to preserve that community from spiritual pollution.

The other text with which Adomnán is associated is very different. It is possible that he was the author of a commentary on Virgil.[103] James F. Kenney explains that it is evident from the extant manuscripts of this commentary, which he lists, that some Irish scholar towards the end of the seventh century edited a collection of scholia on the Bucolics and Georgics which was copied, maybe modified, and transmitted to the Continent in the ninth century. There may have been numerous copies all deriving ultimately from the original. All of the extant copies, and this establishes their Irish provenance, contain many very old glosses in the Irish language which Thurneysen, from a study of the glosses on two of the manuscripts, can date to the end of the seventh century or not much later, in spite of the fact that the glosses are very corrupt, having been copied in the ninth and tenth centuries by continental scribes who did not know Irish, from copies made on the continent by scribes who themselves did not know Irish. The name of the original author is preserved in one manuscript as Adananus and as Adannanus in another. While this name is not unique to the ninth abbot of Iona,[104] having regard to similarities of the names to our

---

100 Ibid., Canon 9, p. 6. **101** R. Meens, 'Pollution in the early Middle Ages: the case of the food regulations in penitentials', *Early Medieval Europe*, 4:1 (1995), pp 3–19; M. Douglas, *Purity and danger: an analysis of the concepts of pollution and taboo* (London and New York, 1980). **102** Meens, 'Pollution', p. 13 and p. 16. **103** Kenney, *Sources*, pp 286–7; Hughes, *Sources*, p. 195; Wooding, *Adomnán of Iona*, p. 17; D. Daintree, 'Virgil and Virgil scholia in early medieval Ireland', *Romanobarbarica*, 16 (1999), pp 347–61. **104** Examples of others bearing this name

Adomnanus, the late seventh-century date and Adomnán's familiarity with Virgil,[105] Kenney concludes, 'The supposition is not far fetched that the two men were identical'.[106] Ó Corráin appears to agree, postulating that Adomnán 'may have been one of the teachers-compilers of these texts'.[107] It would be wrong, of course, to think of Adomnán's interest in Virgil as a foray into the profane as distinct from the sacred, separate from his normal spiritual interests. Virgil and the classical authors had long since been assimilated into the life of the elite in the late antique Christian West.[108] It is not possible to know with any certainty whether Kenney and Ó Corráin are correct, but if they are, this does demonstrate the breadth of Adomnán's Christianity and extent of his learning.

ADOMNÁN AND VIOLENCE

It is clear, therefore, from the brief outline of his life and from his surviving works that Adomnán was a man of considerable influence and learning. From our study in the last chapter, of attitudes to violence in early medieval Ireland, it is reasonable to assume that Adomnán would have shared the views disclosed in the annals. He would have considered peace to be spiritually superior to violence. He would not have admired heroic death in combat, seeing the death of a king in his own bed as a sign of God's favour. It is clear also, from the *Canones Adomnani*, if we accept that they are of his authorship, that he shared the general abhorrence of *díbergaig* that is so evident in the sources. In fact, this strange phenomenon features in three chapters of *VC* and this will be considered further below.[109]

Kingship

Much, although not all, of the incidents of violence to which reference will be made involve kings and Columba's interaction with them. Because of this, and because the perceived legitimacy or illegitimacy of any particular act of violence often reflects Adomnán's attitude to kingship, it is important to consider his attitude. The nature of Irish kingship in the pre-Christian and early Christian periods has received considerable attention from scholars.[110] It has been argued that in the earlier period the king was sacred. His role was to act as a mediator between his people and the gods, thereby ensuring their safety and welfare.[111] It has been pointed out that the bond between the king and his people was one of

are Adamnan of Coldingham mentioned by Bede (*HE* 4.25) and Adamnán, bishop of Ráith Maige Oínaig, who died in 731 (see Chapter 6, p. 156). **105** O'Loughlin, *Holy Places*, p. 249. **106** Kenney, *Sources*, p. 287. **107** Ó Corráin, *Clavis*, pp 730–1 (569). **108** Markus, *Ancient Christianity*, pp 27–43, p. 35; Johnston, *Literacy*, pp 4–5. **109** *VC* I.1, II.22 and II.24. See Sharpe, *Adomnán of Iona*, p. 253, n. 45. **110** For instance Byrne, *Kings*, pp 7–27; Ó Cróinín, *Early medieval Ireland*, pp 63–84; Charles-Edwards, *Early Christian Ireland*, pp 469–520; Bhreathnach, *Tara*, especially Doherty, 'Kingship in early Ireland', pp 3–31; Bhreathnach, *Medieval world*, pp 40–129. See also, J.E. Rekdal and C. Doherty (eds), *Kings and warriors in early north-west Europe* (Dublin, 2016). **111** Doherty, 'Kingship in early Ireland', p. 13.

the two fundamental bonds in early medieval Irish society (the other being familial kinship).[112] Having regard to its pagan sacred nature and its fundamental importance, it was imperative that kingship be Christianized. The early church had gone about changing the landscape of early medieval Ireland from a pagan one to a Christian. Places of sacred importance to the people, such as wells and ancestral burial-sites, were given a Christian significance. The inauguration-sites of kings were high on the church's list of priorities.[113] This was, however, but a stepping-stone to the much more important objective, the Christianization of kingship itself. The church replaced the old inauguration rituals, involving the mating of the new king with the land as represented by a female figure, with the Christian God, as the source and justification of kingship.[114] The king would not be successful unless blessed by God, as interceded by the church.

In promoting this concept Adomnán was to the fore and, indeed, goes further. In VC he makes it clear that kings hold office by divine providence.[115] Thus the English king, Oswald, owed his victory over the British king, Cadwallon, to the intercession of Columba, as a result of which he 'was afterwards ordained by God as emperor of all Britain'.[116] So too Columba, as God's instrument, chose from among the sons of Áedán mac Gabráin, Eochaid Buide to be the one who would succeed him as king of Scottish Dalriada,[117] and, indeed, further reference is made to Áedán mac Gabráin below. It was God's will that Domnall mac Áedo become a 'famous king. He will never be handed over to his enemies but will die at home in his bed, in a peaceful old age, in the friendly presence of his household', as foretold by Columba when Domnall was brought as a child to receive the saint's blessing.[118] The annals record that this Cenél Conaill king died, as king of Ireland, in 642 in the fourteenth year of his reign.[119] Even lesser kings required, and prospered because of, the Christian God's favour. Óengus mac Áedo Commáin, known as Óengus Bronbachal, a minor king of the Cenél Coirpri Gabra centered on Granard, Co. Longford, owed his accession and his long and successful reign to the fact that he sought God's favour and was granted it through Columba's intercession.[120] Likewise, the British king, Rhydderch ap Tudwal, prospered and ultimately died 'at home on his own pillow'.[121] Columba had predicted this, having first satisfied himself of the merit of the king, his kingdom and his people. Clearly, in all these cases, Adomnán was making the point that it was the will of God that determined the success or otherwise of a king's reign, and God's will favoured the church and its adherents. In a special way, Columba had an insight into and a rapport with the will of God, although, as

---

112 Bhreathnach, *Medieval world*, p. 48. **113** Doherty, 'Kingship in early Ireland', pp 9–11. **114** Bhreathnach, *Medieval world*, pp 48–56. **115** Sharpe, *Adomnán of Iona*, p. 61. M.J. Enright, *Iona, Tara and Soissons: the origin of the royal anointing ritual* (Berlin and New York, 1985). **116** VC I.1. The ordination of kings is treated in this chapter below. **117** VC I.9. See Sharpe, *Adomnán of Iona*, pp 270–1, notes 84 and 85. **118** VC I.10. **119** AU s. a. 642. **120** VC I.13. See Sharpe, *Adomnán of Iona*, p. 275, n. 94; Doherty, 'Kingship in early Ireland', p. 26. **121** VC I.15.

seen in the case of Áedán mac Gabráin, divine will was paramount. It behoved kings and aspiring kings to heed the church and, in particular, Columba and his successors.[122] In support of this Adomnán could point to prophecies made by Columba during his lifetime concerning kings which, viewed from Adomnán's time, could be seen to have happened as predicted. The fact that, from the perspective of c.700, these were *ex post facto* prophecies did not matter. What did matter was that, on the evidence of the best of authorities, Columba had made them and they happened as predicted.

In Christianizing kingship by making success dependent on God's blessing and inauguration a function of his will, the church, as pointed out by Charles Doherty, was redefining existing concepts in Christian terms, similar to the manner in which Buddhist ideas of kingship adapted older ones in India and Sri Lanka and, also in late eighth-, early ninth-century Japan.[123] Indeed, the same can be said of the replacement of the Merovingian 'pagan sacral dynasty of war-kings with a new Christian sacral dynasty of war-kings. The essential nature of Frankish kingship remained unchanged; what changed was the religious definition of the sacred character of that kingship'.[124] In pursuing the Christianization of kingship in the Irish context, Adomnán was ahead of his time and takes his place among those throughout the world who sought to adapt ancient concepts to suit new beliefs.[125]

There is a further dimension to Adomnán's thinking on kingship. In the reference above to King Oswald, it will be noted that Adomnán uses the expression 'ordained by God'.[126] Later he refers to King Diarmait mac Cerbaill as having been 'ordained by God's will as king of all Ireland',[127] and subsequently, referring to his killer, Áed Dub, 'who was ordained unfittingly [to the priesthood], will return as a dog to his vomit; he will again be a bloody murderer'. Ultimately, Columba prophesizes that Áed will die ignominiously 'for having killed the king of all Ireland'.[128] A later chapter relates how an angel appeared to Columba and ordered him to ordain Áedán mac Gabráin as king of Scottish Dalriada. Columba was reluctant to do so because he considered Áedán's brother Éoganán a more suitable candidate. However, the angel struck Columba with a whip and directed him, in the most stern terms, to obey the word of the Lord. After three nightly visitations Columba agreed. Adomnán tells us, 'As he was performing the ordination, St Columba also prophesied the future of Áedán's sons and grandsons and great-grandsons, then he laid his hand on Áedán's head

---

122 Sharpe, *Adomnán of Iona*, p. 62. **123** Doherty, 'Kingship in early Ireland', pp 29–30, citing J.S. Duncan, *The city as text: the politics of landscape interpretation in the Kandyan kingdom* (Cambridge, 1990), pp 38–9 and R. Abé, *The weaving of Mantra: Kukai and the construction of esoteric Buddhist discourse* (New York, 1999), p. 15 and pp 330–2, 352–3, 359–67. **124** D.H. Miller, 'Sacral kingship, biblical kingship, and the elevation of Pepin the Short' in T.F.X. Noble and J.J. Contreni (eds), *Religion, culture and society in the early Middle Ages: studies in honour of Richard E. Sullivan* (Michigan, 1987), p. 131; Doherty, 'Kingship in early Ireland', pp 30–1. **125** Doherty, 'Kingship in early Ireland', p. 31. **126** *VC* I.1. **127** *VC* I.36. **128** *VC* I.36.

in ordination and blessed him'.[129] These extracts have given rise to much scholarly debate.[130] M.J. Enright considers that Adomnán, in the term *ordinatio*, specifically means anointing and Adomnán is presenting a new theory of 'clerically mediated kingship based upon the unction created covenant of the Old Testament'.[131] For our purposes it is sufficient to concentrate on the two concepts that emerge: the concept of a high-king of all Ireland and the concept of the ordination of kings by God through his agents on earth. With regard to the latter, it seems clear that Adomnán was inspired by the Old Testament where kings were the Lord's anointed and to kill such a king was sacrilege.[132] Richard Sharpe finds Adomnán's words as 'most extraordinary', in an AD 700 context and 'a remarkable innovation in the idea of kingship'.[133]

It is clear also that Adomnán was a strong proponent of the concept of the kingship of all Ireland.[134] Not only that, but he believed, having regard to the rise in Uí Néill fortunes over the previous century or so, that their claim to the kingship of Ireland must represent the will of God. As Máire Herbert has pointed out, this belief may have originated in the work of an earlier abbot of Iona, Cumméne, and echo the acclamation in the annals in 642 of an earlier Cenél Conaill king, Domnall mac Áedo.[135] However, its re-iteration in *VC* clearly indicates Adomnán's agreement. Máire Herbert concludes, 'His [Adomnán's] ideal model for Irish society would seem to have been a Christian kingship held by Uí Néill rulers, with the successors of Colum Cille, their kinsmen and allies, exercising a beneficent influence over them'.[136] This, then, is an essential context for any approach to a study of Adomnán's attitudes to violence as disclosed in his writings, and, ultimately, to an understanding of his mindset as he set out for Birr in 697.

Violence in VC
Once again it is to *Vita Columbae*, the inexhaustible quarry, that one must turn to gain a deeper understanding of Adomnán's attitudes to violence. Approximately 22 of its 119 chapters contain accounts of violence, excluding divine and angelic violence.[137] For convenience, these accounts can be divided

---

129 *VC* III.5. **130** Enright, *Iona, Tara and Soissons*; idem, 'Further reflection on royal ordinations in the *Vita Columbae*' in M. Richter and J.-M. Picard (eds), *Ogma: essays in Celtic studies in honour of Próinséas Ní Chatháin* (Dublin, 2002), pp 20–35; Sharpe, *Adomnán of Iona*, pp 60–1 and n. 157, n. 358; D. Woods, 'Four notes on Adomnán's *Vita Columbae*', *Peritia*, 16 (2002), pp 40–67; Doherty, 'Kingship in early Ireland', p. 28; D. Broun, *Scottish independence and the idea of Britain from the Picts to Alexander III* (Edinburgh, 2007). See also, J. Prelog, 'Sind die Weihesalbungen insularen Ursprungs?', *Frümittelalterliche Studien*, 13 (1979), pp 303–56. **131** Enright, 'Further reflection', p. 35. **132** Sharpe, *Adomnán of Iona*, pp 296–7, n. 157; Doherty, 'Kingship in early Ireland', p. 28. **133** Sharpe, *Adomnán of Iona*, p. 297, n. 157 and p. 355, n. 358. **134** See Doherty, 'Warrior and king', p. 115. **135** Mac Shamhráin and Byrne, 'Prosopography I: Kings named', p. 197. **136** Herbert, *Iona, Kells and Derry*, p. 52; Byrne, *Kings*, pp 255–9. **137** *VC* I.1, 7, 8, 9, 10, 11, 12, 13, 14, 15, 20, 36, 39, 42, 43, 46, 47, 49 and II.22, 23, 24, 25.

into two categories: those that contain no explicit condemnation of a protagonist and those that do, with 13 in the first category and 9 in the second.[138] What immediately strikes the modern reader is the matter-of-factness with which Adomnán describes the first category. Columba does not condemn Cadwallon as an evil man deserving of defeat and death.[139] He merely tells Oswald that Cadwallon, his enemy, will be delivered into his hands. In his description of 'the crash of battles far away' there is no moral justification offered for the victors beyond the fact that the Lord gave them victory.[140] Columba prophesizes that three of the sons of King Áedán 'will all be slaughtered by enemies and fall in battle'.[141] Clearly, this was normal and there was no exhortation by Columba, on either compassionate grounds or moral grounds, to desist from warfare. No explanation is offered by Columba as to why the two kings Báetán mac Maic Ercae and Eochaid mac Domnaill 'were recently killed by their enemies, and their heads cut off', nor was any sought.[142] Likewise, the poet Crónán appears to have been murdered by his enemies within a very short time of meeting Columba, as if it was a normal occurrence, with no explanation offered.[143] Rhydderch ap Tudwal was concerned to know 'whether he should be slaughtered by his enemies or not, and 'at what hour he may be killed by his enemies?',[144] and Columba assures him that he will not be delivered to his enemies, as he does Guaire mac Áedáin, when asked how he would meet his death.[145]

The above accounts seem to suggest that for Adomnán violence, particularly among kings, was normal, if not entirely acceptable. It seemed to be part of the game of life, a working out of God's will. Columba, in response to kings' inquiries about whether they will survive or be delivered into the hands of their enemies, is never heard to advise them to avoid violence, make peace, love their enemies. In this, Adomnán seems to agree with *Audacht Morainn*, referred to in the last chapter, whereby it is a mark of a virtuous ruler that he should 'remove the shame of his cheeks by arms in battle against other territories'.[146] It was not unlawful under vernacular Irish law to kill in battle,[147] and the concept of honourable violence was recognized.[148] Indeed, it has been posited that Adomnán would have been among those churchmen who did not consider the taking of human life as being always sinful.[149] As was considered in Chapter 2, this would have facilitated a nuanced approach to killing, whereas the stricter traditional view, that all killing was sinful, would have inhibited such an approach. Having regard to Adomnán's belief in a kingship of all Ireland, which could only be realized by violent means, it is not surprising that he would have considered some violence acceptable. In this world of acceptable honourable violence there would

---

138 First category: *VC* I.1, 7, 8, 9, 10, 11, 12, 13, 15, 20, 42, 43, 47. Second category: I.14, 36, 39, 46, 49 and II.22, 23, 24, 25. **139** *VC* I.1. **140** *VC* I.7. **141** *VC* I.9. **142** *VC* I.12. **143** *VC* I.42. **144** *VC* I.15. **145** *VC* I.47. **146** Kelly, *Audacht*, paragraph 30; Fraser, 'Morality of war', p. 102. **147** *CIH* 779.19; Kelly, *Guide*, p. 129. **148** Kelly, *Guide*, pp 128–129; Fraser, 'Morality of war', p. 97. **149** Fraser, 'Morality of war', p. 102; Bachrach, *Religion and war*, pp 29–30.

always be the natural human tendency to 'push things too far'. What Adomnán considered 'too far' will be found in an examination of the second of the two categories, those nine incidents of violence described in *VC* where Columba condemns the perpetrators.

In these episodes Adomnán uses harsher language, with Columba being depicted as a stern man of God, thereby disclosing the issues that seriously concerned Adomnán. He warns Áed Sláine, son of Diarmait mac Cerbaill, against the sin of family murder, which was particularly abhorred in vernacular law.[150] In this case, because of it, Columba predicts that Áed Sláine will lose the prerogative of the kingship of Ireland that God had predestined for him. In this he may be following Cummeneus Albus, in whose *Liber uirtutibus sancti Columbae* a very similar anecdote appears.[151] Clearly Adomnán strongly disapproved of kin-slaying and one can detect a note of aggravation with Áed for having frustrated the divine plan for the kingship of Ireland. As we have seen, Adomnán is even stronger in his condemnation of Diarmait's killer, Áed Dub, for having killed the anointed king of all Ireland and is repulsed by his return to violent lay life after, supposedly, repenting and embracing the religious life.[152]

VC, like the sources studied in the last chapter, touches upon the phenomenon of *díbergaig*. They are described as savage marauders.[153] One of their number, Ioan mac Conaill maic Domnaill, is referred to 'as a man of evil who persecuted good men',[154] and another, Lám Dess, as being from a 'band of these men of evil'.[155] It is evident that Adomnán viewed *díbergaig* with the same distain as did his contemporaries. It is noteworthy, however, that Adomnán's anger, as expressed through Columba, seems to be caused more by the *díbergaig* contempt for Columba than by their devilish nature. In fact, in chapter I.1, some of their group were allowed to escape their enemies 'through flames and swords and spears' by singing songs 'in praise of St Columba and by the commemoration of his name'.[156] Those who scorned Columba and refused to sing, perished. Notwithstanding this, it is clear from the language used by Adomnán that he saw these evil men as a breed apart meriting special condemnation, a condemnation withheld from those involved in honourable warfare.

Whether a *díbergach* or not, and many of those condemned by Columba were not, anyone who shows contempt for Columba or who breaches his trust or violates his sanctuary, is the most reviled and merits the severest penalties, even eternal damnation. Neman mac Gruthriche, who, when reproached by Columba for his bad deeds, 'took no notice but laughed under his breath', suffered the prediction that his enemies would find him lying in bed with a whore and there he would be cut down and that devils would seize his soul and take him to the place of torments. This happened as predicted, with the added detail that his enemies

---

150 *VC* I.14; Kelly, *Guide*, p. 127. **151** See Kenney, *Sources*, pp 428–9; Herbert, *Iona, Kells and Derry*, pp 24–5; Sharpe, *Adomnán of Iona*, pp 56–7. **152** *VC* I.36. See Fraser, 'Morality of war', pp 100–1 for his comments on Adomnán's view of repeatable penance. **153** *VC* I.46. **154** *VC* II.22. **155** *VC* II.24. **156** *VC* I.1; Sharpe, *Adomnán of Iona*, p. 111.

cut off his head.[157] Likewise, the aforesaid Ioan mac Conaill maic Domnaill, when confronted by Columba, as he and his men were carrying away booty in their boat, stolen from Columba's charge, Colmán, 'looked with contempt at the saint' and 'scoffed at the saint and mocked him'.[158] Columba refers to him as 'This wretched fellow who has despised Christ in his servants',[159] and predicts that he will be overcome by a storm and he and his men will drown. This duly happened and the squall 'snatched them down to the depths of hell – a wretched end, but well deserved – all the sea round about remained perfectly calm'.[160] Taran, who had sought sanctuary with Columba, was entrusted by the saint to the care of a rich man called Feradach. However Feradach, in breach of that trust, ordered the murder of Taran. Columba reacted by predicting that in the following autumn, Feradach, before he had a chance to taste the meat of his pigs fattened on acorns, would die suddenly and be 'carried off to hell'.[161] This duly happened. Another, Lám Dess, mentioned above, described by Adomnán in the heading to the chapter as 'an attacker of churches', has one of his number attack Columba physically. However, the spear thrown at Columba is stopped by Columba's companion Findlugán who stepped forward between Columba and the spear. Findlugán was wearing Columba's cowl, which, because of its miraculous properties, was like an impenetrable breastplate. Neither the saint nor Findlugán was injured, although Lám Dess thought Columba had been pierced by the spear. Punishment for this physical attack was duly meted out when, exactly one year later, Columba was able to tell his companions in Iona, that at that moment, Lám Dess was being killed by a spear thrown in Columba's name.[162] The key to what sets these stories apart and distinguishes them from the first category is found in the quote from the account of Colmán and Ioan, where the latter is described as one 'who has despised Christ in his servants'.[163] The enormity of these offences is in the fact that the perpetrators, whether *díbergaig* or not, have snubbed their noses at the Christian God by despising his earthly representative.

Adomnán would have believed implicitly in Columba's special relationship with God. To act towards him, as these evil men are described as having acted, was shockingly unconscionable. To extend his protection and, by implication, Columba's, to a category of persons in Irish society, innocents, which, as was seen in the last chapter, lacked adequate protection under the law, would be to take acts of violence towards them out of the first category above described and into the much more serious second. As will be clear from the next chapter, *LxI* brought innocents under the protection of Columba and his community and to violate that sanctuary would be, similarly, to despise Christ in his servants.

That this was Adomnán's mindset is quite apparent from the chapter of *VC* which he has headed 'Again concerning another persecutor of innocents'.[164] This chapter recounts how when Columba was a young man, still a deacon and a stu-

---

157 *VC* I.39. **158** *VC* II.22. **159** '*Hic miserabilis homuncio qui Christum in suis dispexit seruis*'. (Anderson and Anderson, *Columba*, p. 124). **160** *VC* II.22. **161** *VC* II.23. **162** *VC* II.24. **163** *VC* II.22. **164** *VC* II.25.

dent, it happened that, one day, a young girl came running across the plain to where Gemmán, Columba's old teacher, was reading. She was being chased by 'a cruel man, a pitiless persecutor of innocent folk'. She made straight for Gemmán seeking his protection. He called to Columba, who was nearby, for his assistance. However, the pursuer 'showed no reverence to the clerics but at once drove his spear into the girl, even as she clutched at their habits, and left her dead at their feet'. Gemmán, in a state of distress asked Columba how long would 'this crime and our dishonour go unpunished?'[165] Columba replied that, as the soul of the girl ascends into heaven, at the same time the soul of her killer will descend to hell. Whereupon, Adomnán writes, 'that slaughterer of innocents fell dead on the spot'. In this chapter, Adomnán uses the term *innocents* three times.[166] Clearly he is, quite contemporaneously, deliberately linking it with his law. As we have seen, *LxI* is referred to in the annals as the Law of the Innocents, and Adomnán, probably, would have had an input into that nomenclature.[167]

It has been suggested that the stories relating to Colmán and Ioan, Taran and Feradach and Lám Dess, also relate to innocents and violence towards them.[168] As will be apparent, paragraph 34 of *LxI* not only includes clerics, women and children among the innocents to be protected, but also 'her [the church of God's] law-abiding laymen with their legitimate spouses who abide by the will of Adomnán and a proper, wise and holy confessor'. Were Colmán and Taran in this category? It is not too farfetched to think that they may have undergone sacramental penance, in which circumstance they would be under the protection of the church, being precluded by their vows to bear arms. Taran was certainly under Columba's protection and Colmán may well have been. Both appear to have been non-combatants, as there is no mention of either attempting to defend themselves by force of arms. Clearly, Lám Dess was an attacker of innocents, being so described in Adomnán's heading of chapter II.24 as 'another impious man, an attacker of churches'. In addition to this, the heading to the next chapter in the sequence, II.25, '*De alio itidem innocentium persequutore*', translated by the Andersons as 'Concerning yet another oppressor of innocents',[169] clearly suggests that more than one of the foregoing chapters relate to innocents.

It is reasonable to conclude, therefore, that Adomnán had a particular awareness of innocents and the concept of non-combatants, and a pronounced distaste for violence directed at them. Apart from the incidents already mentioned, he makes reference to innocents on two other occasions in *VC*. He refers to a hostile attack on Derry during which 'the lay population round about, including women and children, took refuge in the church there'.[170] Later, in referring to the Italian city consumed by fire, he tells us 'nigh on three thousand men have

---

165 See Sharpe, *Adomnán of Iona*, p. 329, n. 268. **166** See Anderson and Anderson, *Columba*, p. 130: '*De alio itidem innocentium persequutore*', '*innocuorum inmitis persequutor*', '*ille innocentium iugulator*'. **167** See comments on Adomnán's probable input into the annal content in the last chapter (p. 66). **168** Fraser, 'Morality of war', p. 98. **169** Anderson and Anderson, *Columba*, p. 131; Sharpe, *Adomnán of Iona*, p. 174. **170** *VC* I.20.

perished, not to mention women and children'.[171] Clearly, Adomnán had an acute awareness of non-combatants and their entitlement to special consideration. This might appear normal to some modern minds, but when contrasted with the absence of such awareness from all the contemporary sources examined in our two preceding chapters, both Continental and Irish, it is remarkable. This is an explicitly articulated awareness with little precedent, apart from the early Irish law tract, the *sellach* text, referred to in the last chapter. What is also remarkable is the vehemence with which Adomnán condemns violence towards innocents. Not only do the perpetrators suffer violent death, but in three of the four cases in Book II, Ioan mac Conaill maic Domnaill, Feradach and the unnamed 'slaughterer of innocents' in II.25, they are consigned to eternal damnation. There is no reference to his fate for Lám Dess, perhaps because he attacked Columba himself and for the saint to cause him to suffer an eternity in hell would appear vengeful. It is interesting to note that these stories are included in Book II, the implication being that they are examples of miracles wrought by Columba himself rather than mere predictions of the unfolding of God's will as appear in Book I. Furthermore, it is only in these tales of violation of innocents that Columba is seen consigning souls to hell, the ultimate penalty.[172]

* * *

This, therefore, is the mindset with which Adomnán travelled to Birr in 697. He wanted to ensure that, in the course of the broadly acceptable internecine warfare of the time, innocents would have an immunity. This was to be achieved, as agreed among those who would be participating in that warfare, by bringing them under the protection of Columba and the Iona *familia*. Violence towards innocents was to be moved into the second category as described above and would attract at least the same level of opprobrium as *díbergaig* violence. Those who engaged in it were to be seen, as Ioan mac Conaill maic Domnaill, who violated Columba's sanctuary, as 'one who despised Christ in his servants'.[173]

Adomnán's purpose was to ameliorate the effects of violence and his law was to be binding on all sides. This is not an expression, in any remote sense, of Augustine's just war theories and, it is submitted, it is misleading and unproductive to attempt to measure Adomnán against the just war yardstick.[174] Adomnán was operating in a different milieu from that for which Augustine's theories were designed, the crucial difference being that all Irish kings had a right to go to war.

---

171 *VC* I.28 '*triaque ferme milia uirorum excepto matrum puerorumque numero disperierunt*' (Anderson and Anderson, *Columba*, p. 54). **172** Both I.35 and I.39, while mentioning hell, are prophecies of how God punishes, not miracles wrought by Columba. **173** *VC* II.22. **174** Here issue is being taken with: Fraser, 'Morality of war', pp 108–9, A.P. Smyth, *Warlords and holy men: Scotland AD 80–1000* (London, 1984), pp 114–15, Ní Dhonnchadha, 'Birr and the Law of the Innocents', pp 18–20 and Márkus, *Adomnán's 'Law of the Innocents'*, p. 2, n. 4. See Chapter 2.

God's will determines who succeeds and who fails, but the right to wage war was not debated, *jus ad bellum* was not an issue. The evidence of *VC*, as presented in the episodes of category one violence mentioned above, bear this out. Adomnán does not condemn the losers. In category two there is one clear case where Adomnán does write most disparagingly of a defeated king, Áed Dub, who 'killed the king of all Ireland'. However, apart from frustrating his idea of a king of Ireland, Adomnán clearly had other issues with Áed, such as his false ordination to the priesthood, his return to a lay violent life thereafter, and his possible homosexuality.[175] It will be noted that notwithstanding all of this, he does not appear to have been consigned to hell in Columba's prophesy, as was the fate of the violators of innocents in Columba's miracles. In the course of war, Adomnán rated the gravity of sin according to the nature of the victims, Augustine according to the state of mind of the perpetrator. When innocents themselves deserved punishment, as appears to have been the case of the Italian city 'consumed by sulphurous fire',[176] it was done directly by God, not through the agency of man. Likewise, as we shall see, *LxI* provides that where a woman unlawfully kills, she is to be put to sea in a boat with one paddle and it will be a matter for God, not man, to determine her punishment, whether she will be blown to shore by the wind and be saved or out to sea and be lost.[177] It is clear from a study of *VC* that Adomnán's focus was to shield innocents from man's inevitable violence by having them designated as *hors de combat*. His instrument for so doing was *LxI*.

175 *VC* I.36. **176** *VC* I.28. See Fraser, 'Morality of war', pp 105–6. **177** *LxI*, paragraph 45.

CHAPTER 5

The Law

BIRR

And so to Birr, in the late spring or early summer of 697. In *Vita Columbae*, Adomnán tells us that he was delayed by contrary winds when he was returning to Iona 'during the summer, when I had been to the meeting of the Irish synod'.[1] It is reasonable to accept that this is a reference to the meeting in Birr.[2] Adomnán was concerned that the weather would prevent him from reaching Iona in time for the celebration of Columba's feast day on the 9 June. However, in answer to Adomnán's prayer, Columba changed the wind direction, thus enabling Adomnán to reach Iona in time to partake in the solemn Mass at the hour of Sext on Columba's feastday. Allowing for travel time, therefore, it is unlikely that Adomnán could have departed from Birr any later than the end of May. Máirín Ní Dhonnchadha points out also that St Moling, one of those listed among the guarantors of the law, was dead by 17 June 697.[3] One can reasonably conjecture, therefore, that the meeting took place in or about May. The annals do not specify where in Ireland the meeting took place. The surviving texts of the law contain this information, and reference is made to Kuno Meyer's Irish text along with Máirín Ní Dhonnchadha's translation contained in *Adomnán at Birr*,[4] copies of which can be found in the Appendix,[5] and which will be followed here unless otherwise indicated. Furthermore, the provenance of the surviving texts is treated fully later in this chapter. Paragraph 28, which lists the guarantors of the law, specifies Birr as the place of its enactment.[6] In addition the Middle Irish introduction refers to the 'plain of Birr at the confines of the Uí Néill and Munster'.[7] Why did Adomnán chose Birr as the place for the meeting that would promulgate his law?

---

1 *VC* II.45. '*cum nos aesteo tempore post euerniensis sinodi*', Anderson and Anderson, *Columba*, p. 176; Sharpe, *Adomnán of Iona*, p. 202. **2** Anderson and Anderson, *Columba*, p. 177, n. 203; Sharpe, *Adomnán of Iona*, p. 346, n. 341; Ní Dhonnchadha, 'Birr and the Law of the Innocents', p. 15. **3** Ní Dhonnchadha, 'An edition of *Cáin Adamnáin*', p. 188; eadem, 'Birr and the Law of the Innocents', pp 14–15. **4** Ní Dhonnchadha, 'The Law of Adomnán; a translation', pp 57–68. **5** I am grateful to Máirín Ní Dhonnchadha for her consent to the reproduction of her translation. **6** Ní Dhonnchadha, 'The Law of Adomnán; a translation', pp 57–9. **7** Meyer, *Cáin Adamnáin*, paragraph 15, p. 9; Márkus, *Adomnán's 'Law of the Innocents'*, pp 12–13 in which he translates as '… to the Plain of Birr, to the provincial boundary between the Uí Néill and the Men of Munster'.

Birr lies near the centre of the island of Ireland.[8] From a purely geographical point of view, it was a convenient central location for those attending, placing the minimum travel burden on the participants. St Brendan of Birr had founded a monastery there in the middle of the sixth century.[9] It was, presumably, an important monastic settlement in 697 and was to become more so in the ensuing couple of centuries. The deaths of many of its abbots in the eighth and ninth centuries are noted regularly in the annals.[10] It waged a war against Clonmacnoise in 760.[11] Birr clearly had a significant scriptorium, capable of producing the magnificent gospel book known as the Mac Regol Gospels or the Book of Birr.[12] The scribe's death is recorded in the annals at 822, 'Mac Riagoil descendant of Magléne, *scriba* and bishop, abbot of Birra, died'.[13] Its wealth, by the mid-ninth century, was sufficient to merit the attentions of the Vikings from Dublin, who, the annals inform us, raided in 842.[14] It is important to emphasize, however, that many of these characteristics, which were a phenomenon of a later period, may not have been present in the Birr of 697.[15] It is not possible to say to what extent St Brendan's monastery had grown and developed by the end of the seventh century, or to what extent it would have been capable of accommodating a large number of important personages and their retinues. The use of tents or temporary buildings may have been required.[16] On the other hand it was a significant centre and, in common with other monasteries in the Shannon basin, was probably a location for seasonal markets.[17]

It was its political location, however, that made Birr an obvious choice as the place of enactment of *LxI*. By the end of the seventh century a system of border monasteries had materialized on either side of the dividing line between the

---

8 A block of ancient limestone known as the Seefin stone stands as a monument in a prominent position in the town of Birr today, which is described in an adjoining notice as *Umbilicus Hiberniae*, the navel of Ireland. **9** His death is variously recorded in the annals at 565 and 573, AU s. a. 565, AT s. a. 573. **10** For instance, AU s. a. 750, 765, 785, 796, 804, 822. **11** AU s. a. 760. **12** The manuscript is held in the Bodleian, Oxford, MS Auct. D.2.19. See S. Hemphill, 'The Gospels of MacRegol of Birr: a study in Celtic illumination', *PRIA*, 29C (1911), pp 1–10; E.A. Lowe, *Codices Latini Antiquiores: a palaeographical guide to Latin manuscripts prior to the ninth century* (12 vols, Oxford, 1934–72), ii, 231; J.J.G. Alexander, *Insular manuscripts 6th to the 9th century* (London, 1978), no. 54; C. Farr, 'The incipit pages of the MacRegol Gospels' in R. Moss (ed.), *Making and meaning in Insular art* (Dublin, 2007), pp 275–87; M. Hogan, *The gospel book of Macregol of Birr* (Offaly, 2007). A magnificent facsimile of the manuscript is available for public viewing in Birr public library. **13** AU s. a. 822. **14** Ibid., s. a. 842. **15** See Sharpe, *Adomnán of Iona*, p. 81, regarding Durrow and how the nature of these midland monasteries changed in the eighth century. **16** Bhreathnach, *Medieval world*, pp 75–6; E. FitzPatrick, *Royal inauguration in Gaelic Ireland, c.1100–1600: a cultural landscape study* (Woodbridge, 2004), pp 81–97. **17** Johnston, *Literacy*, p. 61. See also: Bhreathnach, *Medieval world*, pp 26–30; C. Doherty, 'Some aspects of hagiography as a source for Irish economic history', *Peritia*, 1 (1982), pp 300–28; idem, 'The monastic town in early medieval Ireland' in H. Clarke and A. Simms (eds), *The comparative history of urban origins in non-Roman Europe: Ireland, Wales, Denmark, Germany, Poland and Russia from the ninth to the thirteenth century* (Oxford, 1985), pp 45–75.

Southern Uí Néill territory of the Cenél Fiachach and Munster.[18] On the northern side were Clonmacnoise, Durrow, Gallen, Rahan and Lynally among others. To the south were, for instance, Terryglass, Lorrha, Kinnitty, Clonfertmulloe and Roscrea. Birr was in the centre, on the border itself. So marginal was it that some historians put it in Munster, while others include it with the northern group in what was sometimes called Fir Chell (men of the churches), the territory of the Uí Néill Cenél Fiachach.[19] To the east also, Birr was in close proximity to Osraige, its border monastery of Seirkieran lying a mere 6km distant and the Leinster monastery of Killeigh within an easy day's journey by horseback. To the west, the Connacht Uí Maine territory, lying on the east bank of the Shannon and controlling the first crossing-points by foot above Killaloe, now approximating to the modern parish of Lusmagh in Co. Offaly, is also only 6km from Birr.[20] Its border location is today reflected in modern diocesan boundaries.[21] This uniquely central location meant that many of those attending the meeting could lodge in a monastery of their choice on their journey, within a day's travel from Birr. For the Munstermen, Lorrha and Terryglass were within a couple of hours on horseback and the same was the position of Clonfert and Clonmacnoise for the men of Connacht. What is more important, however, is that the extent to which the leaders attending were required to leave their own territories and journey into another territory was minimized. Meetings on the boundary suggest equality, while those within one territory suggest the superiority of the ruler of that region.[22] By choosing Birr, Adomnán was being diplomatic to the maximum possible extent and this would have been recognized by all concerned. In fact, Birr was the location of a meeting of kings (*rígdál*) in 827 between Conchobar mac Donnchada, king of Tara and Fedilmid mac Crimthainn, king of Munster.[23]

It is difficult to say who actually was present in Birr. Máirín Ní Dhonnchadha suggests that some, perhaps many, of the listed guarantors were present.[24] In *VC*, Adomnán describes the meeting as a synod.[25] It is not unreasonable to conclude

---

18 Charles-Edwards, 'Prehistoric and early Ireland', p. lxiv; Byrne, *Kings*, p. 170; Ní Dhonnchadha, 'Birr and the Law of the Innocents', pp 13–14. **19** Byrne, *Kings*, p. 169, Munster; Charles-Edwards, *Early Christian Ireland*, p. 554, Uí Néill. **20** R. Ó Floinn, 'The Shannon Shrine: a suggested provenance' in E. Purcell, P. MacCotter, J. Nyhan and J. Sheehan (eds), *Clerics, kings and vikings: essays on medieval Ireland in honour of Donnchadh Ó Corráin* (Dublin, 2015), p. 295 and pp 299–300. See also: D. Ó Corráin, *Ireland before the Normans* (Dublin, 1972), p. 12; Byrne, *Kings*, p. 218; E. FitzPatrick and C. O'Brien, *The medieval churches of County Offaly* (Dublin, 1998), pp 1–2. **21** Birr itself is in the diocese of Killaloe, in the ecclesiastical province of Cashel, three-hundred metres from Eglish parish, in the diocese of Meath and ecclesiastical province of Armagh. Clareen, otherwise Seirkieran, is an island parish in the diocese of Ossory and ecclesiastical province of Dublin, and Lusmagh is in the diocese of Clonfert and ecclesiastical province of Tuam. **22** Charles-Edwards, *Early Christian Ireland*, pp 279–80. Another example of a meeting on a boundry is the synod of Mag Léna in *c*.633, probably no more than three kilometres north of Birr. See Ó Cróinín, *Early medieval Ireland*, pp 152–4. **23** AU s. a. 827; Charles-Edwards, *Early Christian Ireland*, p. 280. **24** Ní Dhonnchadha, 'Birr and the Law of the Innocents', p. 13. **25** *VC* II.45. Sharpe, *Adomnán of Iona*, p. 202.

that many, if not all, of the forty ecclesiastics named in the list of guarantors were present. It was a synod of the Irish church, being so described by Adomnán in VC,[26] and it is likely that all the most important clerics would have wanted to be there. Of the fifty-one lay guarantors, the king of Tara, Loingsech mac Óengusso,[27] the most powerful king in Ireland and Adomnán's kinsman, would certainly have been present and playing a leading role. His presence, in the centre of Ireland, for the enactment of a law that was intended to be binding on all of 'the men of Ireland and Britain',[28] bore witness to his power and authority. As an all-Ireland gathering, under such ecclesiastical and temporal auspices, it would have been the place to be, and, it is suggested, an occasion where the major kingdoms of Ireland would want to be represented. Support for the proposition that the guarantor-list is a list of the names of those present is found in the fact that, as will be clear from our analysis of paragraph 28 later in this chapter, it originated as a list of names only, without mention of titles. If an individual had indicated his willingness to act as a guarantor by some means other than his personal attendance at the meeting, it is more likely that his title, and the kingdom which he represented, would have been recorded. Furthermore, the fact that so many of those listed appear to have been *táinisi*, that is, heirs-apparent,[29] or could have been (approximately twenty, e.g., nos. 42, 43, 44, 45, 46, 53, 55, 57, 58, 61, 62, 63, 70, 74, 76, 77, 79, 82, 84, 86),[30] suggests that they were there representing their kingdoms. Otherwise the name of the current king would have appeared. It is unlikely that the *táinisi*, as representatives of their kingdoms, would, themselves, be represented. It is much more likely that they attended in person. By the same token, where the name listed has been shown to be a living king at the date of the meeting in Birr, it is likely that he was there in person because, if he was not, the name of his representative would have been listed. In a 'face-to-face' society such as early Ireland, presence would have been important. While we cannot know with any certainty who was present in Birr, in the absence of any firm knowledge of an alternative method by which the listed guarantors could have pledged their support and participation, it is reasonable to conclude that most, if not all, of those listed were in attendance.

There is another reason why Adomnán would have favoured Birr. While it was an independent monastery and not part of the Iona *familia*, it had close links with the latter. St Brendan of Birr is the subject of two chapters of VC. In the first, Adomnán describes the proceedings at the synod of Teltown, where the clergy had wrongly excommunicated Columba for 'some trivial and quite excusable offences'.[31] On Columba's approach, only one of their number, Brendan,

---

26 VC II.45. '... *post euerniensis sinodi condictum*', Anderson and Anderson, *Columba*, p. 176. **27** See *Dictionary of Irish biography* (*DIB*) under Loingsech. **28** *LxI*, paragraph 28. **29** See Charles-Edwards, *Early Christian Ireland*, p. 567; idem, *Chronicle*, p. 175, n. 5; R. Chapman Stacey, *The road to judgment: from custom to court in medieval Ireland and Wales* (Philadelphia, 1994), p. 92; Kelly, *Guide*, p. 26 for his list of further references on succession to kingship. **30** Ní Dhonnchadha, 'Guarantor-list', pp 197–212. **31** VC III.3; Ní Dhonnchadha, 'Birr and

rose to greet him. The others remonstrated with Brendan for showing reverence to an excommunicate. Brendan told them that their judgment was wrong, as was apparent to him, because God had enabled him to see the 'bright column of fiery light' and the holy angels beside Columba as he approached, which God had caused as an indication of Columba's innocence. As a result, the sanctions were lifted and all honoured Columba. The second describes how Columba saw angels coming from heaven to greet the soul of Brendan on his death.[32] He saw this even though news of St Brendan's death had not yet reached Iona. We do not know whether these two chapters had been written by Adomnán before or after his visit to Birr, or, indeed, were inspired by his experience of this midland monastery, but we can be certain that he would have received a welcome and would have been very happy to spend some time in the foundation of Columba's friend.[33]

SURVIVING MANUSCRIPTS: PROVENANCE AND DESCRIPTION

Provenance

The content of Adomnán's law and the names of those who guaranteed it are known from two surviving manuscripts. These are a fifteenth-/sixteenth-century manuscript, now held in the Bodleian Library, Oxford (Rawlinson MS B 512, ff 48–51, henceforth R) and a copy made in 1627, now in the Bibliothèque Royale in Brussels (O'Clery MS 2324–40, ff 76–82, henceforth B). The latter copy was made by Mícheál Ó Cléirigh on the 31 March 1627 while, as he indicates in a colophon at the end of the manuscript, he was staying in the Franciscan convent in Bundrowse, Co. Donegal. The colophon explains that Mícheál's copy is from a manuscript, now lost, made by Cúmhumhan Ó Cléirigh, Mícheál's cousin. We are told, in an earlier colophon located at the beginning of the manuscript, that Cúmhumhan's copy derived ultimately from the 'Old Book of Raphoe'.[34] There is no indication in R as to its line of transmission, but scholars are agreed, from a study of its forms and orthography, that it too derives from the Old Book of Raphoe.[35] We saw in the last chapter that it is unlikely that Adomnán founded the church in Raphoe. However, in later years it became associated with him.[36] It has been suggested that Raphoe had a

the Law of the Innocents', p. 14; Sharpe, *Adomnán of Iona*, p. 207. **32** *VC* III.11. **33** There is a third story linking Brendan with Columba involving an intricate play on the name of Iona when Brendan is said to have been instrumental in choosing Iona as Columba's place of exile. The story is quoted by Ussher from a lost life of Brendan. See Sharpe, *Adomnán of Iona*, pp 352–4, n. 354, citing J. Ussher, *The whole works*, ed. C. Elrington (17 vols, Dublin, 1844–64), vi, 240. **34** The colophon at the beginning of B reads '*Incipit cain Adamnain ar slict sen libuir ratha bothae*' and the colophon at the end reads '*As na duilleoccaib do scrioph Cumumhan mac tuatail i clerig, do scribad an beccanso. Atigh na mbratur ag Drobaois 31 Marta 1627*'. See Ní Donnchadha, 'An edition of *Cáin Adomnáin*', p. 59; eadem, 'Birr and the Law of the Innocents', pp 15–16; Ó Néill/Dumville, *Cáin Adomnáin*, p. 51, n. 218. **35** Kenney, *Sources*, p. 245; Márkus, *Adomnán's 'Law of the Innocents'*, p. 4; Ní Dhonnchadha, 'Birr and the Law of the Innocents', p. 16. **36** M. Herbert and P. Ó Riain (eds), *Betha Adamnáin: the Irish Life*

dossier of Adomnán-related material. Ó Cléirigh made copies of a Middle Irish *Betha Adamnáin* and *Fís Adamnáin* and it is not surprising that material relating to Adomnán would be unearthed by Ó Cléirigh (himself a native of Donegal) in Donegal.[37] Perhaps the 'Old Book of Raphoe' was such a dossier.[38]

The text, as we have it today, is a compilation consisting of a number of layers dating from the seventh to the late tenth or early eleventh century.[39] It follows that the 'Old Book of Raphoe' itself cannot date before the late tenth century. Máirín Ní Dhonnchadha suggests that it was compiled in Raphoe from diverse sources, with the Middle Irish first twenty-seven paragraphs being, in parts, authored by the compiler, and the remainder originating in a number of older sources.[40] In this chapter it is proposed to isolate those sections of the text that can be known, with reasonable certainty, to post-date 697. Subsequently, the remaining sections, that appear to have emanated from Adomnán himself, will be examined in some detail.

Description
The earlier of the two manuscripts, R, is contained in a volume consisting of five parts, with *LxI* appearing in part two and running, in double columns from the top of folio 48r to folio 51v, line 9. It is preceded by a fragment of an Old Irish treatise on the Psalter and followed by the poem *Sreth a salmaib súad slán*. From a study of a colophon in the margin of folio 33r, which is earlier in the volume than where *LxI* appears, it has been suggested that parts 1, 2 (containing *LxI*) and 3 may have been written by members of the Ó Maoil Chonaire family in Cullentragh, Rathmolyon, Co. Meath.[41] Mícheál Ó Cléirigh's copy, B, was sent to his superiors in St Anthony's College in Leuven where it remained until 1793, when the college became the property of the French Republic.[42] It ultimately ended up in the Burgundian Library, now the Bibliothèque Royale in Brussels.[43] It is bound into a volume containing 356 quarto sized folios and consisting of

---

of Adamnán (London, 1988), pp 2–3. **37** For a discussion of these two texts see Chapter 6, p. 159 and p. 164 respectively. **38** Kenney, *Sources*, p. 245; Charles-Edwards, 'Early Irish law', p. 337; Ní Dhonnchadha, 'Birr and the Law of the Innocents', p. 16. **39** Ní Donnchadha, 'An edition of *Cáin Adomnáin*', p. 42 and pp 59–60; eadem, 'Birr and the Law of the Innocents', p. 16; Márkus, *Adomnán's 'Law of the Innocents'*, p. 2. **40** Ní Donnchadha, 'An edition of *Cáin Adomnáin*', pp 28–42. **41** The colophon reads, 'a mbaili na cuilindthrach dam ag scribenn na bethad sa naembrigte 7 ara faesad dom anmaim 7 dom churp 7 coromsoera ar duailchib 7 duinebad'. See Ní Donnchadha, 'An edition of *Cáin Adomnáin*', p. 59, in which she cites W. Stokes, *The Tripartite Life of Patrick* (London, 1887), pp xiv–xlv and R.I. Best, 'Notes on Rawlinson B.512', *Zeitschrift für celtishe Philologie*, 17 (Halle, 1896–1943), pp 389–402. See also B. Ó Cuív, *Catalogue of Irish manuscripts in the Bodleian Library at Oxford and Oxford College libraries, Part 1: description* (Dublin, 2001), B 512/1 (ff 101–2, 1–36, 45–52). **42** F. O Brien, 'Irish Franciscan College of St Anthony, Louvain' in N. Ó Muraíle (ed.), *Mícheál Ó Cléirigh, his associates and St Anthony's College, Louvain* (Dublin, 2008), p. 165. **43** Kenney, *Sources*, p. 119. See P.A. Breatnach, *The Four Masters and their manuscripts: studies in palaeography and text* (Dublin, 2013), pp 153–4.

two parts: 1, ff 1–106, and 2, ff 107–356.⁴⁴ *Lex Innocentium* commences on 76r and ends on folio 82v. The volume comprises, in its entirety, Ó Cléirigh manuscripts, but is in no particular order, either chronologically or in terms of the nature of manuscripts copied.

In neither of the manuscripts is the text of *LxI* divided into numbered paragraphs. However, capitals are employed in both manuscripts to mark most paragraphs.⁴⁵ Meyer divided his edition into numbered paragraphs and Máirín Ní Dhonnchadha has followed the same system, having found Meyer satisfactory, the paragraphs constituting units of sense. Her order of paragraphs follows B, however, unlike Meyer, who followed the order in R. Extra-large ornamental capitals appear in R at the beginning of paragraphs 1, 28, 33 and 34 and in B at the beginning of 1, 28 (somewhat smaller) and 34.⁴⁶ Significantly, paragraphs 50–3 appear only in B, with R terminating with 49. Paragraph 33 appears only in R; it is omitted from B.⁴⁷ Ní Dhonnchadha divides the text into three strata: A, comprising paragraphs 1–27 and subdivided into sub-strata, a, b, c, d, and e, B, comprising 28–32, 34–49 and 50–3, dubbed sub-strata f, h, i, and C, comprising paragraph 33 (g).⁴⁸

DATING

Before proceeding any further we need to investigate how much of the material that has come down to us, via R and B, can be known, with reasonable certainty, to have been in the law given 'to the peoples',⁴⁹ in Birr in 697, and thus emanating from the mind of Adomnán.

Paragraphs 1–27, 33 and 50–3
Scholars have considered this question and all are agreed that paragraphs 1–27 were not part of the law as originally drafted.⁵⁰ Máirín Ní Dhonnchadha, in particular, has conducted a comprehensive study from which it is clear, particularly on linguistic grounds, that these paragraphs date from no later than the late tenth or early eleventh century.⁵¹ Unlike the later paragraphs, 1–27 are written in Middle Irish. They will be considered in the next chapter, when developments post–697 are being treated. They relate to women exclusively, with no mention of the other categories, children, clerics, penitents and those under the care of the church, which constitute innocents. These paragraphs are not concerned with non-combatants per se and they did not form part of Adomnán's thinking. While these

---

44 Breatnach, *Four Masters*, p. 137, n. 9. **45** Ní Donnchadha, 'An edition of *Cáin Adomnáin*', p. 68. **46** Ibid. **47** Ibid., p. 38 and p. 42; Ó Néill/Dumville, *Cáin Adomnáin*, p. 35, n. 61 and p. 49, n. 216. See below for a detailed discussion. **48** Ní Donnchadha, 'An edition of *Cáin Adomnáin*', p. 28. **49** AU s. a. 697. **50** Ní Donnchadha, 'An edition of *Cáin Adomnáin*', p. 28; eadem, 'Birr and the Law of the Innocents', pp 16–17; Márkus, *Adomnán's 'Law of the Innocents'*, p. 4; Charles-Edwards, 'Early Irish law', p. 337. **51** Ní Donnchadha, 'An edition of *Cáin Adomnáin*', pp 28–37.

paragraphs are included in both Meyer's and Márkus' translations, they have been excluded by both Máirín Ní Dhonnchadha and Pádraig P. Ó Néill/David N. Dumville, who confine their translations to paragraphs 28–53. It can be concluded that they did not form part of Adomnán's law as originally drafted.

There is another paragraph that scholars consider to be a discrete paragraph not forming part of the original composition: 33.[52] There are a number of compelling reasons for this. In the first instance it is written in Latin, whereas the remainder of the text is in Old Irish, apart from parts of paragraph 32. It does not form part of a sequence, being isolated by itself without any reference to the preceding or subsequent paragraphs in terms of the sense of the text as a whole. It is omitted from B, although there is a space left for it in a somewhat peculiar fashion, which will be considered further in the next chapter.[53] In R it is marked out by being accorded an extra-large ornamental capital for its first letter, and the entire text of the paragraph is surrounded by a thin roughly-drawn red line, with a capital marking the first letter of paragraph 34, thereby emphasizing its separateness. More significantly, the penalties stipulated in 33 for the killing of a woman differ from the penalty provided in 41 and referred to in 42 for the same offence. The latter prescribes fines whereas 33 provides for mutilation, death and fines. It is very unlikely that such a divergence would occur if both paragraphs had been included in the law as originally drafted. It is more likely that one or other of the paragraphs was drafted independently of the other and added in subsequently. From a reading of the text, it is apparent that 41 and 42 sit naturally with the paragraphs preceding and succeeding them, whereas 33 is not part of any sequence. Máirín Ní Dhonnchadha considers that 33 was independent in point of composition from the remainder of the text and suggests that it may have been added to the text some years later, perhaps around the time the law was renewed in 727.[54] Gilbert Márkus refers to 33 as 'An angelic addition' and an 'obviously additional piece of material' and draws attention to the similarities with the Middle Irish paragraphs in the tone of its language relative to the more specific, complex, technical and nuanced terms of the core of the text.[55] Unfortunately, a study of the Hiberno-Latin of paragraph 33 has proved inconclusive, it not being possible to date the Latin one way or the other.[56] Crucially, however, like paragraphs 1–27, 33 is concerned with women only, making no reference to the other classes of persons who are included in the term 'innocents'. This is in stark contrast with paragraph 34 which, as well as appearing from its language to be the commencement of the law, so clearly and explicitly defines innocents as including women, children, clerics and penitents, and which echoes the title of the law, so singularly referred to in the annals as *LxI*. It is reasonable, therefore, to conclude that paragraph 33 forms no part of Adomnán's thinking and no part of the law promulgated in Birr in 697.

---

52 Ibid., pp 37–42; Márkus, *Adomnán's 'Law of the Innocents'*, p. 6; Richter, *Neighbours*, pp 43–4.   **53** Chapter 6, p. 163.   **54** Ní Dhonnchadha, 'Birr and the Law of the Innocents', p. 56.   **55** Márkus, *Adomnán's 'Law of the Innocents'*, p. 6.   **56** A most sincere thanks to Dr Anthony Harvey of RIA for his painstaking consideration of the text.

There is a group of further paragraphs that is unlikely to have formed part of the original *LxI*, paragraphs 50–3. Scholars have cast doubt on the dating of these paragraphs,[57] and there are a number of good reasons for their exclusion from consideration here. They only appear in manuscript B; they do not feature in R, which proceeds to a new and unconnected text after paragraph 49, without any evidence of a textual lacuna.[58] From a reading of the text, it is clear that there is a coherence to paragraphs 34–49. All of the necessary elements of *cáin* law are present, in a self-contained way, in these paragraphs.[59] Even a modern legal draughtsman would derive some satisfaction from how the law states its objectives (34), specifies its offences and the penalties for them (e.g., 35, 36, 41, 42, 44), specifies who are to be the judges of the law (37), deals with pledges and sureties (e.g., 38, 39) and addresses practical matters involved in the collection of fines (47, 48, 49). S/he would be confused and a little irritated by the manner in which this unity is upset by the incoherence of paragraphs 50–3 that have the appearance of being added on. For instance, paragraph 53, that makes provision for hostage-sureties,[60] duplicates and contradicts paragraph 39, which has already made this provision. It would appear that 53 was intended to apply to paragraphs 50–2 only and that these last four paragraphs are a discrete section and not originally linked to the main text. That this is the case is considerably reinforced by an examination of 51, which provides that fines for the offences against women mentioned in the paragraph are to be assessed according to rank. In the main body of the law, rank is not a factor in determining penalties. For instance, in 41, the same fine is payable for the killing of *any* woman, regardless of rank. Furthermore, in 51, it is the rank of the injured woman's husband that counts. She is not given protection, in her own right as is the case in the main body of the law.[61] Apart from the clear incompatibility of paragraphs 50–3 with the core of the text, this points to a different author, with a different mindset and agenda. Paragraph 52 is a hotchpotch of diverse matter, ranging from the making use of women in battle to domestic issues involving 'madder and woad and onion'. It has been suggested that some of this may have originally belonged to a text on marriage and separation.[62] It is to be noted that, apart from the Middle Irish section, this is the only mention in the text of women's involvement, either voluntarily or involuntarily, in military activity. Again, there is a divergence between this paragraph and paragraph 35

---

[57] Ní Donnchadha, 'An edition of *Cáin Adomnáin*', p. 30, p. 42 and p. 258; D. Stifter, 'Towards the linguistic dating of early Irish law texts' in A. Ahlqvist and P. O'Neill (eds), *Medieval Irish law: text and context* (Sydney, 2013), pp 163–208, esp. 199–204. [58] Ní Donnchadha, 'An edition of *Cáin Adomnáin*', p. 42; Stifter, 'Linguistic dating', p. 200. [59] See Charles-Edwards, *Early Christian Ireland*, pp 566–9 for analysis of the usual elements characteristic of *cáin* law. This will be considered in more detail later in this chapter. [60] On hostage-sureties see Kelly, *Guide*, p. 172; D.A. Binchy, 'Celtic suretyship, a fossilised Indo-European institution', *The Irish Jurist*, 7:2 (1972), pp 360–72, esp. 369–71. [61] Ní Donnchadha, 'An edition of *Cáin Adomnáin*', p. 42; Stifter, 'Linguistic dating', p. 203. [62] Ní Donnchadha, 'An edition of *Cáin Adomnáin*', p. 42.

in the method by which liability is to be divided among the perpetrators when a number are involved.⁶³ In addition to the foregoing, it has been pointed out that a strong case can be made, on linguistic grounds, that these paragraphs were written at a considerably later date than the main body of the text.⁶⁴ It is clear, therefore, that paragraphs 50–3 did not form part of Adomnán's original design and so must be excluded from our considerations. What is of the utmost relevance, however, is that these four paragraphs, also, are concerned only with women, to the total exclusion of the other categories constituting Adomnán's broader concept of innocents. The significance of this will be considered further below and an explanation will be offered.

Paragraphs 28 (incorporating the guarantor-list) and 29–32
Scholars are of the view that paragraphs 28–32 form a discrete stratum.⁶⁵ It is quite clear that this section of the text, as presented in the surviving manuscripts, based, as they are, on the 'Old Book of Raphoe', differs from how it might have appeared, if it appeared at all, in 697 and this will be pursued further below.

In the first instance, however, the exceptional list contained in paragraph 28, merits consideration.⁶⁶ It is a list of 91 names of those who are stated to have guaranteed the law: 40 clerical leaders and 51 lay. In her 1982 paper, Máirín Ní Dhonnchadha examined each of these names, seeking to find mention of them in other sources such as the annals and genealogies, and, where they are mentioned elsewhere, seeking to establish from obits whether they were alive, or could have been, in 697.⁶⁷ Having regard to the limited records available and to the vicissitudes of the centuries in terms of redactions and scribal caprice and errors, her results are remarkable. In general terms, no obits could be found for thirty-one of the names. Of these, nineteen (2, 8, 10, 11, 15, 16, 17, 27, 28, 30, 31, 32, 33, 34, 35, 37, 38, 39, 71) lack any data whatsoever. Of this nineteen, all are clerics except 71. For twelve (6, 19, 22, 36, 29, 50, 51, 57, 59, 67, 74, 87) there is circumstantial evidence that they were alive in 697 or could have been. Obits for 59 were found: 18 clerics and 41 laymen.⁶⁸ These annal entries independently corroborate the list by establishing that, at a minimum, approximately 65 per cent of the total, were alive at the time of promulgation of the law in Birr. It is not at all surprising that the deaths of many are not recorded in the annals. Indeed, it is quite remarkable that only one name throws up an obit which would make it impossible for that person to have been in attendance in 697. Number 63 in the list, Dúnchad Muirisce, is recorded as having died in 683. A

63 Ibid., p. 258. **64** Stifter, 'Linguistic dating', pp 200–3. **65** Ní Donnchadha, 'An edition of *Cáin Adomnáin*', pp 28–9, p. 37 and pp 55–8; eadem, 'The Law of Adomnán: a translation', pp 54–5; Márkus, *Adomnán's 'Law of the Innocents'*, p. 6. **66** Ní Dhonnchadha, 'Guarantor-list'; eadem, 'An edition of *Cáin Adomnáin*', pp 187–96; eadem, 'The Law of Adomnán: a translation', pp 54–5. **67** Ní Dhonnchadha, 'Guarantor-list'. **68** The numbers used in the text follow the numbers in the appended translation, which, in turn, follows the numbers in the 'Guarantor-list'. Máirín Ní Dhonnchadha calculates the total for which there are obits at fifty-eight, eighteen clerics and forty laymen, which appears to be incorrect.

possible explanation is offered for this, on the basis that the title given to Dúnchad was added incorrectly at a later date.[69]

Indeed, Máirín Ní Dhonnchadha's study of the titles given to the names on the list is most revealing. Many of the titles are wrong and, indeed, often hopelessly so. For instance, among the ecclesiastical guarantors, Cillíne mac Luibnén (6) was not abbot of Birr but of Lorrha, and was probably succeeded by the next guarantor, Colmán mac Sechnasaig (7), who is described as abbot of Lorrha in the text.[70] Oisíne mac Galluist (13) was not abbot of Clonfertulloe (Old Kyle) but of Clonmacnoise at the time of the synod of Birr.[71] Among the many inaccurate titles given to the lay guarantors, examples include Congal mac Fergusa (42) whose title, king of Cenél Conaill, would not have applied until some years after 697,[72] and Conchubur mac Maíle Dúin (44), who did not become king of the Cenél Coirpri until after the death of his brother, Muirges (64), in 698, the latter not being accorded his proper title in the list.[73] While the list is correct in its designation of the titles, as of 697, of kings of Leinster (56) and Ulster (54), it is incorrect for both Munster (45) and Connacht (61), among many others.[74]

From this it is clear that the author of the list, as it appears today, was working from an accurate and contemporary list of names, which, when drawn up, did not require titles because all concerned would have known the guarantors by their names alone. This supports the contemporaneity of the list of names.[75] This is also supported by the contrast between the accuracy of the names and the inaccuracy of the titles, in that an author writing at some distance in time from the event would not have compiled so accurate a list of names, unless he was working from a contemporary list, as evidenced by the inaccuracy of his titles. It is possible, of course, that he was not concerned to give titles that were applicable in 697, but only titles that subsequently became applicable. His task was complicated by his desire to give each a unique title.[76]

One way or the other, there is clear evidence that paragraph 28 was written, or, at least, amended, sometime after 697. From the point of view of one who is attempting to isolate the sections of the text that are contemporary to Adomnán, it is reasonable to conclude that paragraph 28 is not. The question arises as to when the titles were added and as to whether this happened at one specific time by one annotator or over a period by a number. Máirín Ní Dhonnchadha, who is the only scholar who has studied the list in detail, offers some suggestions.[77] What is important, however, is to have some guidance as to when paragraph 28 may have been finalized, regardless as to whether this was done by one annotator or a number over time. Our attention is drawn to

---

69 Ní Dhonnchadha, 'Guarantor-list', pp 214–15; eadem, 'An edition of *Cáin Adomnáin*', pp 187–8. **70** Ní Dhonnchadha, 'Guarantor-list', p. 187. **71** Ibid., p. 188. **72** Ibid., p. 197. **73** Ibid., p. 198. **74** Ibid., pp 198–9, p. 201, p. 202 and p. 204. **75** Ibid., p. 185; eadem, 'The Law of Adomnán: a translation', p. 55. **76** Ní Dhonnchadha, 'Guarantor-list', p. 185. **77** Ibid., p. 215; eadem, 'An edition of *Cáin Adomnáin*', p. 188 and p. 190; eadem, 'The Law of Adomnán: a translation', p. 55. See also Houlihan, 'Jurisprudence', pp 148–9.

number 90 in the list, Írgalach mac Conaing, who is given the title, king of Cíanachta. This title would not have been current until the eighth century, the first to receive the designation being Conaing mac Amalgada, whose death is recorded at 742.[78] Furthermore, on linguistic grounds, there is nothing in the forms of the titles to date them any later than the eighth century and they do not appear to have been tampered with much after that period. The last of the titles to become effective, which was not correct for 697, but correct for a later date, did so in 722. Number 62, Dlúthach mac Fithchellaig, became king of Uí Maine in that year, thus acquiring the title assigned to him subsequently in paragraph 28.[79] We can conclude, therefore, that this paragraph dates from sometime between 722 and the end of the century, based on a list of names contemporary with Birr 697. An approximate date and context for it, along with paragraphs 33 and 50–3, will be suggested below.

This leaves for consideration the remaining paragraphs of this discrete stratum, 29–32. That paragraphs 28–32 form a unit is argued from the fact that capital letters are used in both manuscripts at the commencement of 28, and capitals are used again to demarcate the paragraph following the stratum, 33 in the case of R and 34 in the case of B (33 being omitted from the latter). More importantly, it is clear, from reading them, that these paragraphs, while having a unity of meaning *inter se*, have no continuity with what goes before or follows. On the basis that paragraph 28 has been shown to post-date Birr 697, and the following four paragraphs are part of a unit with it, it can be argued that the entire segment was a later addition to the original *LxI*, and that Gilbert Márkus is correct in referring to it as 'later material'.[80] There are some clues in the four paragraphs, and particularly 29 and 32, which might support a later date. Paragraph 32 is of interest, in that it describes a procedure involving the ritual chanting of maledictive psalms or liturgical curses directed against malefactors with a view to coercing them into submission. In Europe it was a standard part of liturgy between the ninth and twelfth centuries.[81] It has been suggested that it may have originated in Ireland at the time of Adomnán.[82] Alternatively, it may point to a later provenance both for the practice in Ireland and for paragraph 32.[83] The fact that the practice was often associated with relics in continental practice and was conducted in churches may also be an indicator of a later provenance.[84]

78 AU s. a. 742; Ní Dhonnchadha, 'An edition of *Cáin Adomnáin*', p. 189. **79** Ní Dhonnchadha, 'An edition of *Cáin Adomnáin*', p. 190. **80** Márkus, *Adomnán's 'Law of the Innocents'*, p. 6. **81** Ní Dhonnchadha, 'An edition of *Cáin Adomnáin*', pp 201–5; eadem, 'The Law of Adomnán: a translation', pp 55–6. **82** Ní Dhonnchadha, 'The Law of Adomnán: a translation', p. 56. She deals at some length with the phenomenon in her unpublished PhD thesis (pp 198–205) drawing an analogy with the later post-Carolingian liturgical practice known as the Clamor. See also, D.M. Wiley, 'The maledictory psalms', *Peritia*, 15 (2001), pp 261–79. **83** See Ní Dhonnchadha's discussion of the word *escoine* which came to mean curse only by the late Old Irish period in her 'An edition of *Cáin Adomnáin*', p. 201. **84** Ní Dhonnchadha, 'An edition of *Cáin Adomnáin*', p. 202 and p. 205. Thomas Charles-Edwards expresses the view that Adomnán himself 'had no truck with the cult of corporeal relics, trans-

Paragraph 29 is more revealing. It purports to be a statement of what has been conceded to Adomnán in return for his law. However, quite patently, it is incomplete. In contrast to the paragraphs in the main body of the law, which are most explicit in including children, clerics and church property, only women are mentioned. This is strange, particularly when viewed in a context where paragraphs 1–27, 33 and 50–3, which also include only women, have been excluded. If 28–32 formed part of the original *LxI*, there is no possible reason why the author would confine 29 to women, to the exclusion of the other innocents mentioned a few paragraphs further on. While it is correct that *LxI* provides exceptional protection for women, as it does for young men between seven years and manhood, we must conclude that 29 did not form part of the law as drafted by Adomnán. There is a further point about paragraph 29 worth mentioning. It discloses an anxiety to ensure that fines be paid to the heirs of Adomnán who occupy his seat. This could be taken as referring to Iona, or, possibly, to his coarb in Raphoe.[85] On the assumption, as mentioned in the last chapter, that Raphoe was not founded up to a hundred years after his death, there are clear implications for the dating of paragraph 29 and the entire stratum.[86] Máirín Ní Dhonnchadha argues, on linguistic grounds, that a foundation of Adomnán's is intended.[87] Was Raphoe claiming to be such a foundation? It is important to note that there are no substantive legislative provisions contained in this stratum, nor are its charter-like clauses necessarily characteristic of the *cáin* genre.[88] Taken all in all, therefore, paragraphs 28–32 must be excluded from consideration of the law as presented by Adomnán at Birr in 697.

It can be no coincidence that all of the paragraphs excluded from our estimation of what would have constituted *LxI* at the time of its promulgation refer specifically and solely to women. It is clear that, at some point or points in time after 697, a decision was made to bolster its female orientation and to dilute its original target, the broader population of innocents. When, why and how this happened will be studied in the next chapter. However, by way of preliminary explanation, it is important now to note the following. In *Félire Óengusso*, dating from approximately a century after *LxI*, Adomnán is credited with 'the lasting liberation of the women of the Gaels'.[89] In a commentary to the same source

---

lated and enshrined…', seeing their use in the renewal and proclamation of *cána* as first arising at the renewal of *LxI* in 727. See *Early Christian Ireland*, pp 564–5. For a comprehensive treatment of the use of relics in the early medieval Irish context see N. Wycherley, *The cult of relics in early medieval Ireland* (Turnhout, 2015). **85** Ní Dhonnchadha, 'An edition of *Cáin Adomnáin*', pp 18–19 and p. 197. **86** Lacey, *Kingdoms*, p. 245; idem, 'Adomnán and Donegal', p. 35. On Raphoe see also Chapter 6. **87** Ní Dhonnchadha, 'An edition of *Cáin Adomnáin*', p. 17, on the basis that the words *ina suidiu* can only mean 'in his seat', with the implication that 'his foundation' is intended because *suidiu* comes from the verbal noun *saidid* meaning 'seats, sets up'. If Raphoe was not founded until after Adomnán's death, it follows that this reference must have been made sometime after. **88** Charles-Edwards, *Early Christian Ireland*, pp 566–9. **89** W. Stokes (ed. and trans.), *Félire Óengusso Céli Dé: The martyrology of Oengus the Culdee* (London, 1905), p. 196. See also Hughes, *Sources*, pp 205–8; Márkus, *Adomnán's*

there is reference to the four *cána* of Ireland: Patrick's law, not to kill clergy; Adomnán's law, not to kill women; Dáire's law, not to kill cattle; and the law of Sunday, not to transgress thereon.[90] First mention of *Cáin Phátraic* appears in the annals in 734 and we learn that it was in force throughout Ireland in 737.[91] It would appear that Iona, willingly or, more likely, unwillingly, lost possession of the clerical ball to Armagh, who took it for themselves. In 753 the annals record the promulgation of *Cáin Cholmcille* and it features again in 757 and 778.[92] We do not know its terms or objectives as no text survives.[93] But Iona involvement with *LxI* is not mentioned after 730,[94] and the question will be asked, was the protection of women delegated to Raphoe? While these matters are relevant to the dating of the different segments of the text, they will, more appropriately, be considered in the next chapter.

THE CORE TEXT

In paragraphs 34–49, what Thomas Charles-Edwards calls 'the sober legal text of the original edict',[95] is immediately evident. The language used and the tightly drawn legal phraseology mark these paragraphs out from the others. The law is stated in sixteen precise sections (in the modern legal sense of the term as applied to a section of an act). For instance, the term *forus cána,* or a derivation of it, meaning 'the enactment of the law', is used in five of the paragraphs to tell the reader the content of the law.[96] This direct terminology is not used in any of the other strata of the text. In its language, the approach taken is, what would be referred to today as, a no-nonsense approach. We do not know the procedure followed in Birr in 697. It is likely that these paragraphs were read out to the assembly from a platform, erected in a suitable location outside the curtilage of the monastery.[97] This would be the only means by which the contents could be made known to those attending. *Cáin* law was, in fact, written down and read out.[98] For instance, the annals relate that the abbot of Armagh went to Connacht with *Cáin Phátraic* in 811,[99] and it was brought there again in 836.[100] *Cáin Domnaig* states that it is the judge's duty to read the text of the law aloud constantly.[101] The precise wording of a *cáin* is important, in that, as in modern statute law as distinct from common law made and interpreted by judges, it is the letter of the law that counts.[102] It has been suggested that, even by the date of *LxI*, there was in existence, as standard,

---

'Law of the Innocents', p. 3. **90** Stokes, *Martyrology*, p. 211; Kenney, *Sources,* p. 237. **91** AU s. a. 734 and 737. **92** AU s. a. 753, 757 and 778. **93** Herbert, *Iona, Kells and Derry,* p. 64. **94** AU s. a. 730. **95** Charles-Edwards, 'Early Irish law', p. 337. **96** Charles-Edwards, *Early Christian Ireland,* p. 562, n. 134. *LxI*, paragraphs 34, 36, 39, 41 and 48. **97** It is thought that the ruined church in Church Lane, Birr, is the location of the early monastery. See C. O'Brien, *Stories from a sacred landscape: Croghan Hill to Clonmacnoise* (Offaly, 2006), p. 73. **98** Ní Dhonnchadha, 'An edition of *Cáin Adomnáin*', p. 43. **99** AU s. a. 811. **100** Ibid., s. a. 836. **101** V. Hull (ed.), '*Cáin Domnaig*', *Ériu,* 20 (1966), pp 166–9; Ní Dhonnchadha, 'An edition of *Cáin Adomnáin*', p. 43. **102** Ní Dhonnchadha, '*Lex Innocentium*', pp 58–9.

an approved form and technical vocabulary.[103] It is reasonable, therefore, to conclude that a written document containing the provisions of the law was produced in Birr and a list made of the names of those who were its guarantors.[104]

> 34. This is the enactment of the Law of Adomnán in Ireland and in Britain: the immunity of the church of God with her *familia* and her insignia and her sanctuaries and all the property, animate and inanimate, and her law-abiding laymen, with their legitimate spouses who abide by the will of Adomnán and a proper wise and holy confessor. The enactment of this Law of Adomnán enjoins a perpetual law for clerics, and females, and innocent youths until they are capable of killing a person, and of taking their place in the *túath*, and until their drove be known.[105]

Before specifying crimes and penalties, paragraph 34 sets out the objective of the law. It is to provide immunity from violence for stated classes of persons, namely, clerics, females, innocent youths until they reach manhood,[106] along with laypeople, presumably penitents,[107] who are subject to a confessor, and church property. All of these categories are clearly recognizable as non-combatants or innocents because they do not bear arms.[108] Clearly, church property also requires protection.[109] This paragraph explains and, indeed, defines the meaning of the term *LxI* used in the annals. For anybody asking, either today or thirteen centuries ago, what was the Law of the Innocents, this is the answer. This is its view of itself. It purported to be, and saw itself as, a law for the protection of non-combatants and contains, it would appear, the first legislative definition of what today is referred to as a 'non-combatant' and was then called an 'innocent'. A modern statute, incidentally, is drafted in much the same way, by usually providing a preliminary paragraph or preamble indicating the intention of the legislation.

This paragraph also stipulates the territorial jurisdiction of the law, Ireland and Britain. Presumably, by Britain is meant only those parts of the island of

---

103 Charles-Edwards, 'Early Irish law', p. 336, n. 28.   104 A beautifully scripted and decorated manuscript, bound in leather and written on vellum, containing the terms of the law, is housed in Birr library and is available for public viewing. It was made by a local artist Margret Maher, under the tutelage of calligrapher, Timothy O'Neill, on the occasion of the 1300th anniversary of the promulgation of *LxI* in 1997 and was intended to replicate, as far as possible, how a written manuscript of the law would have looked in 697.   105 Ní Dhonnchadha, 'The Law of Adomnán: a translation', p. 62.   106 *For-tá forus inna Cána-sae Adomnáin bithcáin for clérchu ocus banscála ocus maccu encu co-mbat ingníma fri guin duine ocus co-mbat inbuithi fri tuaith ocus con-festar a n-immérgi* (Ó Néill/Dumville, *Cáin Adomnáin*, p. 37).   107 For Adomnán's inclusion of penitents among his innocents see Fraser, 'Morality of war', p. 98.   108 See Bede, *HE* 3.18, where he recounts how the East Anglian king, Sigbert, having retired to a monastery, was persuaded by his people, against his will, to lead them in battle. He refused to bear arms, in accordance with his vows, and was killed.   109 Ní Dhonnchadha, 'An edition of *Cáin Adomnáin*', p. 24. She seems to take a different view of the immunity offered in the opening portion of the paragraph seeing it as referring to an immunity from secular imposts.

Britain over which Iona had influence.[110] That it was no idle claim to jurisdiction is supported by the inclusion in the list of guarantors of a number from Britain including, Bishop Céti (21), of Iona, Bishop Curetán (22), of Rosemarkie in Scotland and Bishop Conamail mac Conainn (23), a future abbot of Iona.[111] To these can possibly be added Feradach úa Artúr (30) and Ioain the Sage mac in Gobann (38), abbot of Eigg.[112] Another noteworthy guarantor with roots from outside Ireland is the Englishman Bishop Uuictberct (29). He is identified with the Uuictberct who followed Wilfrid, sometime in the 680s, on the failed Frisian mission which left from Ireland. He returned to Ireland to the monastery of an English colony in Ráth Máelsigi, probably Clonmelsh, Co. Carlow, where, according to Bede, he 'gave himself up to a life of devotion'.[113] Among the lay guarantors giving support to the claims of extra-territorial jurisdiction are Euchu úa Domnaill (85), identified as king of Scottish Dál Riada,[114] and Bruide mac Derilei (91), king of the Picts (Cruithentúath).[115]

> 35. Whoever wounds and kills a clerical student or an innocent youth in transgression of the Law of Adomnán, eight *cumals* and eight years of penance for it for every hand involved, up to three hundred, one *cumal* and one year of penance for it for each one from three hundred to a thousand, and it is the same fine for the one who commits it and the one who sees it and does not prevent it to the best of his ability. If there be inadvertence or ignorance, half-fine for it, and there shall be an oath-equivalent that it is inadvertence and ignorance.[116]

Paragraph 35 imposes penalties for offences committed against two of the categories indicated in 34, clerical students and youths.[117] These penalties are designed to fill the lacunae in the protection offered by existing law, whether secular, ecclesiastical or mixed, as mentioned in Chapter 3. With regard to clerics, as we have seen, those of full age, as freemen, enjoy the protection of the *éraic* in addition to the applicable honour-price. Under this paragraph, clerical students not old enough to be freemen in their own right would have the protection of an eight-*cumal* fine, seven to their church and one to Adomnán and

---

110 See Richter, *Neighbours*, pp 48–108; Ní Dhonnchadha, 'Lex Innocentium', p. 58. 111 Ní Dhonnchadha, 'Guarantor-list', pp 192–3; eadem, 'Lex Innocentium', p. 64. 112 Ní Dhonnchadha, 'Guarantor-list', pp 194–6. 113 Bede, *HE* 5.9; Ní Dhonnchadha, 'An edition of *Cáin Adomnáin*', p. 192, in which she corrects the identification in 'Guarantor-list; eadem, 'Lex Innocentium', p. 64; D. Ó Cróinín, 'Pride and prejudice', *Peritia*, 1 (1982), p. 359; idem, 'Rath Melsigi, Willibrord, and the earliest Echternach manuscripts', *Peritia*, 3 (1984), pp 21–4. 114 Ní Dhonnchadha, 'Guarantor-list', p. 212. 115 Ibid., p. 214. 116 Ní Dhonnchadha, 'The Law of Adomnán: a translation', pp 62–3. 117 It will be noted that Ní Dhonnchadha's translation reads 'wounds and kills', whereas Meyer, Márkus and Ó Néill/Dumville all read 'wounds or slays (kills)'. She explains her wording by pointing out that the penalties refer to death not to injury ('An edition of *Cáin Adomnáin*', p. 214). The text in Old Irish reads '*Nech gonus ocus marbus ...*'. It is easier to make sense of the provision following Ní Dhonnchadha.

his *familia*,[118] regardless of status. This would appear to be the explanation for 'clerical student' as distinct from 'cleric'.[119] By the same token, the vulnerable position of children between the age of seven and manhood is dramatically improved by prescribing an eight-*cumal* penalty for their killing.[120] *Lex Innocentium*, being a quasi-ecclesiastical law, also provides for penance by way of penalty, in addition to fines.[121]

It is of particular interest that the law covers, not only violence carried out by individuals, but also by large numbers, making specific provision for armies of up to 300 men and of between 300 and a 1000. The involvement of these numbers, it is suggested, having regard to population and the nature of battle in our period, would constitute warfare by any definition of the term,[122] and there is no doubt that *LxI* was an *in bello* law.

It is a measure of the comprehensive nature of this paragraph that it goes on to anticipate and provide for onlooker's liability, even to the extent of stipulating a penalty for a defaulting onlooker. Provision is also made for the taking of oaths if an offender claims inadvertence or ignorance as an excuse for his crime, whether it be the actual killing or the failure to intervene.[123] In the *sellach* text, the onlooker who does not intervene, as distinct from the more serious onlooker, who 'instigates and accompanies and escorts and exults', incurs half-penalty.[124] Here, the onlooker who merely fails to intervene is liable for the full penalty, the same as if he had committed the offence himself;[125] there is a stiffening of the law when it comes to offences against innocents.

Paragraph 36 fulfils the objective in 34 to provide protection for the church and churches. Uniquely among the core paragraphs, this is done by way of honour-price, with the extent of penalty being greater or lesser depending on the importance of the offended church.[126] It is also implicit that the penalties are to be in addition to a myriad of other penalties that could be due, for instance, to an injured cleric, or, if killed, to his kin or superior, or compensation for theft or damage to property.[127] The target here is the outrage to the church and its lands on which the crimes occur, with a lessening of penalty for crimes committed outside the immediate curtilage of the church.[128] It would appear that there was concern for the safety of relics when outside the church where they

---

118 Ní Dhonnchadha, '*Lex Innocentium*', pp 65–6. **119** See Ní Dhonnchadha, 'An edition of *Cáin Adomnáin*', pp 214–15 for a different explanation. It is often difficult to reconcile the information contained in different sources. See Kelly, *Guide*, p. 126. **120** For a discussion of the position of children under early Irish law generally, see B. Ní Chonnaill 'Child-centred law in medieval Ireland'. **121** Is this the first such joint-law, or was penance inserted into the paragraph at a later date? **122** Halsall, *Warfare*, pp 119–33. **123** Kelly understands the reference to inadvertence to apply to the actual killing rather than to the onlooker. See *Guide*, pp 152–3; Ní Dhonnchadha, 'An edition of *Cáin Adomnáin*', p. 216. **124** See Chapter 3, p. 74; Kelly, *Guide*, p. 353. **125** See Kelly, *Guide*, p. 156; Ní Dhonnchadha, 'An edition of *Cáin Adomnáin*', pp 216–17. **126** Ní Dhonnchadha, 'An edition of *Cáin Adomnáin*', p. 219. **127** Ibid., pp 217–18. **128** Ibid., pp 218–19. On the division of property surrounding a church see *Hib* 43.4.

were normally kept and full fines are stipulated if they are violated, with a clear provision that the fines are to be paid to the church to which they belong.[129]

The next three paragraphs might be loosely called enabling clauses. Essentially they are procedural and they facilitate the operation of the law. They do not specify offences or impose penalties. Paragraph 37 provides for the appointment of the judges who will determine the guilt or otherwise of alleged offenders and prescribe penalties. It is a feature of *cáin* law that special judges are appointed to adjudicate cases arising under its provisions,[130] although it has been pointed out that this reference is a century earlier than the first annalistic reference to such judges.[131] It is the *familia* of Adomnán who will appoint the judges, in every church and every *tuath* in which there is an allegation of an offence. Paragraph 38 deals with the pledges that are required of a person accused of an offence under the *cáin*. Vernacular Irish law had an elaborate system of pledges which, at its simplest, provided for the delivery by a defendant in a legal suit, whether civil or criminal, of something of value to his accuser, as a pledge for his compliance with the judgment in due course.[132] The accuser had a lien on the property pending satisfaction of the judgment. If judgment was in the defendant's favour, it was returned to him. Pledges were a normal part of the process of litigation and this paragraph specifies the appropriate pledges under *LxI*. It would appear that the amount of the pledge should be one-third of the applicable penalty. In the normal course of litigation, as mentioned in the text, the pledge is to be given within three days of the offence, judgment within five days and payment within ten. In *LxI* the law is again stiffened by providing for payment of the pledge immediately, judgment within three days and payment within five.[133]

The next paragraph, 39, also covers a standard aspect of litigation procedure, the appointment of a hostage-surety. This is somebody who guarantees compliance with his own person. He swears to surrender himself to the injured party, to be held by him, in case of default.[134] The appointment is to be made and an announcement made,[135] and the force of the *cáin* will be projected into the future, even after the death of Adomnán.[136] Paragraph 40 is in a different category from the foregoing three. It is a simple blunt statement to the effect that fines payable under the *cáin* in respect of the killing of clerics and youths, other than the one *cumal*, which goes to Adomnán's community, are to be paid to the churches who bury them. The fines payable under secular law only are to be paid as appropri-

---

129 Ní Dhonnchadha, 'An edition of *Cáin Adomnáin*', pp 222–3. She mentions the practice of some churches giving a portion of their relics to a dependent church in order to bind them and she cites C. Doherty, 'The cult of Patrick and the politics of Armagh in the seventh century' in J.-M. Picard (ed.), *Ireland and Northern France, AD 600–850* (Dublin, 1991), pp 53–94 at p. 79, where he draws attention to a gift of relics from Armagh to Dún Sobairche in Antrim. See also Wycherley, *Relics*, p. 115. **130** Charles-Edwards, *Early Christian Ireland*, p. 567. **131** AU s. a. 802; Ní Dhonnchadha, 'An edition of *Cáin Adomnáin*', p. 223. **132** Kelly, *Guide*, pp 164–7. **133** For an outline of the procedure see Kelly, *Guide*, p. 191. **134** Ibid., p. 172. See also Binchy, 'Celtic suretyship', pp 360–72. **135** Ní Dhonnchadha, 'An edition of *Cáin Adomnáin*', p. 229, where she draws an analogy with *Cáin Domnaig*. **136** Ibid., p. 229.

ate to the deceased's lord and kin. This provision, presumably, was to put the question beyond doubt.[137]

> 41. The enactment of the Law enjoins that payment in full fines is to be made for every woman that has been killed, whether a human had a part in it, or animals or dogs or fire or a ditch or a building. For in *cáin*-law every construction is to be paid for, including ditch and pit and bridge and hearth and step and pool and kiln and every hardship besides, if a woman should die on account of it. But one-third is remitted for fore-maintenance if it be a senseless person that die on account of it. Of the other two-thirds, one-third belongs to whomsoever is entitled to it.
>
> 42. Whatever violent death a woman die, excepting that which results from an act of God or proper lawful union, it is to be paid for in full fines to Adomnán, including slaying and drowning and burning and poison and crushing and submerging and wounding by domesticated animals, and pigs and cattle. If it be the first crime on the part of the cattle, or the pigs, or the dogs, they are to be killed at once and half-due of a human hand for it. If it be not the first crime, payment is made in full fines.[138]

Paragraphs 41 and 42 deal with violent deaths of women and address the commitment given in 34 to legislate for their protection. Paragraph 41 appears to be concerned with the killing of women inadvertently.[139] In both paragraphs the payment of 'full fines' is stipulated for the killing of a woman. It could be argued that this means that the full fine applicable to the honour-price of the woman's husband or other guardian should be paid rather than the normal half. If that were the case the word *díre* would have been used as it was in paragraph 36. Furthermore, it would mean that no special additional fine was being imposed under the *cáin*. It can only mean the full seven *cumals* fine. There appears to be some doubt as to whether the *éraic*, the fixed penalty of seven *cumals* for the killing of a freeman, regardless of rank,[140] was payable for the killing of a woman.[141] One way or the other, the introduction of a seven *cumal* fine by Adomnán was a major step in the provision of protection for women.[142] It is also of the utmost significance that under the terms of paragraph 42, this fine, in its entirety, was to be

---

137 Ibid., pp 229–30. **138** Ní Dhonnchadha, 'The Law of Adomnán: a translation', pp 64–5 for both paragraphs 41 and 42. **139** There may be some question about this. While eDIL would suggest that the word used in the text, *ro-marbthar*, would translate 'has been slain', which would appear to exclude inadvertence, and this is followed by both Meyer and Ó Néill/Dumville, Ní Dhonnchadha prefers 'has been killed' (An edition of *Cáin Adomnáin*, p. 230), as does Márkus, which does not necessarily exclude inadvertence, thus enabling a distinction to be made between paragraphs 41 and 42. **140** Kelly, *Guide*, p. 126. **141** Ní Dhonnchadha, 'Birr and the Law of the Innocents', p. 22. Payment of the *éraic* for the killing of women is mentioned in the law tracts, for instance, *CIH* 441.6–7 (Kelly, *Guide*, p. 78, n. 79), *CIH* 42.1 (Kelly, *Guide*, p. 134, n. 71). **142** If it was already payable, this new fine would be in addition.

payable to Adomnán, thus bringing women's welfare, in a special way, under his protection. By virtue of this revolutionary provision, women are given at least equal status with men in terms of the value of their lives under the law. The struggle to change attitudes must have been immense and, as we shall see in the next chapter, is reflected in the Middle Irish preface to the text.

In paragraph 42, 'Adomnán envisioned a panoply of horrors arising from war',[143] which he lists out in detail. This is required, it is suggested, to pre-empt possible excuses or defences. It is noteworthy that no provision is made in paragraph 42 for deaths caused by large numbers as was done for clerics and youths in paragraph 35. In view of Adomnán's obvious concern for women, it is unlikely that this was omitted by design. It is possible that the provisions of 35 carry over into 42. Alternatively, paragraph 33, which does cover the involvement of large numbers, could be viewed as amending legislation, designed to correct an omission in the original law. It is unlikely that these questions can be answered with any certainty. While it is a little confusing that Adomnán deals with deaths caused by dangerous domestic animals in 42 rather than 41, it is interesting to note that he makes the same distinction between animals that attack for the first time and those that have exhibited a prior 'vicious propensity' as was made in modern Irish law of dogs up to recent times.[144] Though paragraph 41 appears to be concerned only with the inadvertent killing of women, and therefore somewhat marginal for us, it does illustrate Adomnán's attitudes. It is remarkable that he is concerned with 'the workplaces of women, and of servile women in particular'.[145] It is most noteworthy that Adomnán stipulates that the full fine will not be paid to him in the case of the death of a senseless woman, and directs that one-third of it should go to those who have cared for her in life and one-third to whoever would be entitled under the law (as distinct from Adomnán's law).[146] Apart from compassion, this illustrates Adomnán's concern not to undermine the position of the mentally disturbed in society and of those who care for them.

Paragraph 43 refers to two concepts found in vernacular early Irish law. The first is what would be called today, counterclaiming, referred to in the law texts as *folud* or *frithfholud* .[147] This involves the procedure whereby, if a debt is owing, whether in contract or on foot of a judgment for a wrong done, or otherwise, by one person to another, and subsequently the debtor becomes entitled to a

---

143 Fraser, 'Morality of war', p. 95. **144** Up to the enactment of the Control of Dogs Act in 1986 common law provided no compensation for a person injured by a dog unless the animal had demonstrated a propensity for viciousness on some prior occasion. See R.F.V. Heuston, *Salmond on the law of torts* (13th ed., London, 1961), pp 607–8. **145** Ní Dhonnchadha, 'An edition of *Cáin Adomnáin*', p. 230. **146** Ibid., p. 232. She compares these provisions with those contained in an Old Irish text (*CIH* 1276.18–1277.13) relating to the use of land belonging to an insane person, an *esconn*. See R.M. Smith (ed. and trans.), 'The advice of Doidin', *Ériu*, 11 (1932), pp 66–85 at p. 68 and p. 70. The word used in the text is *escond* (Ó Néill/Dumville, *Cáin Adomnáin*, p. 41), trans. in eDIL as witless or senseless person. **147** Kelly, *Guide*, pp 313–14.

payment from the creditor, the two debts can be set off against one another. A balancing is done, thereby reducing the net debt. If this was done in respect of fines due under *LxI*, the super-levies due to Adomnán's *familia* would be significantly reduced. For this reason the law makes it clear that such counter-balancing will not be possible, and each offender must pay the fines in respect of the offences committed by him.[148] The second concept is the one by which an agent often collected a debt or a fine on behalf of those entitled. This agent was usually the injured party's lord or superior and he would be entitled to a proportion of the debt for his services, perhaps one-third, known as the *forbach*.[149] Under *LxI*, Adomnán takes on the task of collecting fines, but in that case, an additional sum is added to the fine to cover the collector's fee, rather than it being payable out of the principal. This is of benefit to both the person entitled to the fine, who is not obliged to pay an agent, and to Adomnán. Furthermore, society benefited by replacing feud, or the law of self-help, as a means of enforcing judgments, with the *cáin*'s own system, under the aegis of Adomnán.[150] The amount of the super-levy is stipulated in the paragraph and is payable in all cases except the killing of women,[151] where there is no super-levy because the entire seven *cumal* fine goes to Adomnán.

> 44. One eighth of everything small and large to the *familia* of Adomnán for the wounding of clerics and innocent youths. If it be a non-mortal wound that anyone inflict on a woman or a cleric or an innocent youth, half seven *cumals* from him, fifteen *sets* from [related] *fine* and unrelated *fine* for their accompliceship. Three *sets* for every white blow, five *sets* for every spilling of blood, seven *sets* for every wound requiring a staunch, a *cumal* for every injury requiring attendance and the leech's fee besides. It amounts to half of the fines for murdering someone if it be more serious than that. If it be a blow with the palm or the fist, an ounce of silver for it. If it be a livid or red mark or a swelling, six *scripuli* and one ounce [of silver] for it. Women's hair-fights, five wethers for it. If it be woman-combat with degradation, three wethers for it.[152]

Paragraph 44 is notable in that it again, like 34, pulls together the three main categories of innocents, women, clerics and youths and sets out the penalties that are to be imposed on anyone who uses violence towards them resulting in a variety of injuries short of death. It appears that the general principle for these offences is that one-eighth of the stipulated fine is added on to cover Adomnán's collection-fee, thus ensuring that the injured party enjoys the maximum com-

---

148 Ní Dhonnchadha, 'An edition of *Cáin Adomnáin*', p. 234. **149** Ibid., p. 235; Charles-Edwards, *Early Christian Ireland*, pp 567–8. **150** Charles-Edwards, *Early Christian Ireland*, p. 568. **151** Killing is not specified but is implicit because lesser injuries do attract a superlevy. See Ní Dhonnchadha, '*Lex Innocentium*', pp 65–6. **152** Ní Dhonnchadha, 'The Law of Adomnán: a translation', p. 65.

pensation.[153] The fines are carefully graded according to the gravity of the injury, from the minor offence of a white blow, which leaves no mark, to a serious injury requiring the attendance of a physician, and on to more serious injuries, which attract fines amounting to half the fines for murder.[154] Provision is made for the levying of fines against the kin of the offender and, if they were accomplices, against a remoter kindred.[155] Penalties are provided for the offence of pulling women's hair. In the above translation it is 'Women's hair-fights, five wethers for it'. However, Meyer (p. 29), Márkus (p. 22) and Ó Néill/Dumville (p. 44) translate, 'For seizing women's hair' or 'For seizing the hair of women', which could entail an assault by a man.[156] The three wether fine clearly involves a fight among women.[157]

> 45. Men and women are equally liable, then, for all fines small and large from this up to woman-combat, except [it result in] outright death. For this is the death that a woman deserves for her killing of a man or a woman, or for ministering poison from which one dies, or for arson, or for digging beneath a church, to wit, to be put in a boat of one paddle at a sea-marking out at sea, to [see if she will] go ashore with the winds. Judgment on her in that regard [belongs] with God.[158]

This paragraph continues the theme of crimes committed by women and makes a significant concession to them in respect of penalty for some serious crimes which would, if committed by a man, warrant the death penalty. These crimes include the killing of a man or a woman by a woman, murder by poisoning, arson and undermining the structure of a church (is this a figure of speech?). For lesser crimes men and women are to be liable for the same penalties. It has been suggested that the equivalent of a death penalty for digging under a church must imply a seriously criminal objective,[159] or perhaps it reflected the sacrilege involved. Rather than the death penalty, the offending woman should be put in a boat with

---

153 Ní Dhonnchadha, 'Birr and the Law of the Innocents', p. 27. It will be noted that Ní Dhonnchadha's translation reads 'for the wounding' and she is followed by Ó Néill/Dumville (p. 44), whereas Meyer translates as 'slaying' (p. 29), as does Márkus (p. 22). The sentence in the text reads '*Ochtmath caich bicc ocus caich móir do muntir Adomnán di [do] guin clérech ocus mac n-ennac.*' (Ó Néill/Dumville, *Cáin Adomnáin*, p. 45). From the point of view of making sense of the paragraph, 'slaying' seems correct on the basis that 'wounding' is covered, for women, clerics and children, in the second sentence and it is already clear that the entire fine and not one-eighth is payable to Adomnán (paragraphs 41 and 42) for the killing of women, hence their exclusion from the first sentence. See Kelly, *Guide*, pp 131–3, for wounding generally. **154** On the penalty of three séts see N. McLeod, '*Di Ércib Fola*', *Ériu*, 52 (2002), pp 123–216, esp. 127. **155** Ní Dhonnchadha, 'An edition of *Cáin Adomnáin*', p. 237. **156** The text reads '*Foltgabál ban, cóic muilt ind*' (Ó Néill/Dumville, *Cáin Adomnáin*, p. 45). **157** Ní Dhonnchadha, 'An edition of *Cáin Adomnáin*', pp 338–9. **158** Ní Dhonnchadha, 'The Law of Adomnán: a translation', p. 66. **159** Ní Dhonnchadha, 'An edition of *Cáin Adomnáin*', pp 239–40.

only one paddle and be towed out to sea for a mile or so,[160] and be set adrift, at the mercy of the winds. The text says that she is to be provided with a pot of gruel.[161] God's judgment will determine her ultimate fate, not man.[162] This is a remarkable concession by Adomnán, surely reflecting some view on his part of an inherent difference in woman's relationship with violence relative to man's.[163]

Under vernacular Irish law secret murder was regarded as a more serious offence than publicly acknowledged killing, and twice the normal penalty was prescribed.[164] Paragraph 46 opens by providing that a similar double penalty will apply for deaths caused by charms, whether in the material form of drugs or the immaterial form of incantations.[165] It goes on to refer to the finding of 'dire mutilations and dismemberments',[166] which seems to be a reference to the hiding of a body after a secret killing. The paragraph then deals with the question of who is liable for the fines when the guilty party cannot be identified. If there is no sufficient evidence forthcoming from the people of the four lands nearest to where the remains are found as to the identity of the culprit or culprits, and they swear an oath to that effect, on pain of destruction of their souls,[167] they themselves must pay the fines. On the other hand, if they have a suspicion and evidence – it is clearly in their interest to be pro-active – then that suspected person, presumably after due process, must pay.[168] If neither of these procedures produces results, then the law provides for the drawing of lots and the detailed procedure to be followed is fully set out.[169] It is evident that Adomnán was determined to ensure that fines be paid, and the vigilance of the local community was harnessed to that end. Provision is also made for payment of the fines in a situation where a known culprit cannot be apprehended, by attaching liability for payment to his kin. This, essentially, is the purpose of paragraph 47. The full fine is to be paid by the kin and the offender is banished. An additional three-and-a-half-*cumal* fine is imposed

---

160 Ibid., pp 240–1; Márkus, *Adomnán's 'Law of the Innocents'*, p. 23, n. 45. **161** This is inadvertently omitted from Ní Dhonnchadha's translation. See her 'An edition of *Cáin Adomnáin*', pp 241–2. It is included in Márkus, *Adomnán's 'Law of the Innocents'*, p. 23 and Ó Néill/Dumville, *Cáin Adomnáin*, p. 44. **162** Ní Dhonnchadha, 'An edition of *Cáin Adomnáin*', p.243; Kelly, *Guide*, pp 219–21 on setting adrift generally and P. O'Neill, 'Landmarks of another kind: setting adrift and early Irish law', *Australia and New Zealand Law and History eJournal* (2006). **163** Ní Dhonnchadha, 'Birr and the Law of the Innocents', pp 28–31 for a discussion of Adomnán's attitude to women. **164** Kelly, *Guide*, p. 128. For how these attitudes to public and secret killing are reflected in contemporary Continental laws see Halsall, *Violence*, pp 15–16. **165** Ní Dhonnchadha, 'An edition of *Cáin Adomnáin*', p. 245. **166** Ibid., pp 245–6; Ó Néill/Dumville, *Cáin Adomnáin*, p. 46 agrees with Ní Dhonnchadha's translation of '*Dubchrecha ocus chnáimchrói*'. Márkus, *Adomnán's 'Law of the Innocents'*, p. 23, n. 46, differs radically, rendering *chnáimchrói* as a young girl's fatal enchantment being related to the words *creecraw* or *crawcree* as used in Tom MacIntyre's poem, 'Field observations on the craw cree' in his *A glance will tell you and a dream confirm* (Dublin, 1994). **167** Markus' translation in *Adomnán's 'Law of the Innocents'*, p. 23. **168** Ní Dhonnchadha, 'An edition of *Cáin Adomnáin*', pp 243–4. **169** Ibid., p. 244; Márkus, *Adomnán's 'Law of the Innocents'*, p. 23, n. 47. On the casting of lots see *Hib* 25; Enright, *Iona, Tara, Soissons*, pp 31–41.

on every member of the kin and more remote kin who is guilty of failing to bring the offender to justice. Anyone who goes further, and maintains and protects and connives, will suffer the same penalties imposed on the offender, including death, if applicable, or the fines imposed in lieu.[170] The beneficial effects for society of banishment have been noted, in that the offender, and the object of any attempt at revenge, is removed from the locality and the field is cleared for the orderly collection of compensation under the procedure laid down by the *cáin*. The anger of the aggrieved kindred is assuaged and peace maintained.[171]

Scholars have drawn attention to the temporal reference in this paragraph, where the term of banishment is to last only until the end of the law. This seems to be at variance with paragraph 34, where the law is stated to be perpetual.[172] It is not clear whether the renewal of the law in 727, which will be mentioned further in the next chapter, was required to revive it, keep it alive or merely to introduce amendments. *Cána* of the eighth and early ninth centuries were usually in force for a limited period, perhaps seven years.[173] This is probably because those individuals who constituted the paraphernalia of the *cáin*, in terms of personnel, including the enacting king, special judges, guarantors and sureties, were essentially finite. Thomas Charles-Edwards offers an explanation: while the framework was temporary, the intention was that the effect would be permanent by establishing the rules of law for the protection of non-combatants, which, after 'the end of the Law', would continue on the statute book, so to speak, but enforced in the traditional way.[174]

The next two paragraphs, 48 and 49, are, like 37, 38 and 39, procedural in nature. They do not contain substantive laws but rather detail a practical aspect of the process of levying and collecting the fines. Paragraph 48 lays down how the steward of the Law and his company are to be fed and maintained. This is a reference to the enforcing officers who collected the penalties for violation of the *cáin*.[175] It would appear that his company would include the hostage-surety and guarantors, all of whom are to be fed according to their rank, whether lord or cleric or layman.[176] If, while the legal process is in progress, but before it is completed, there is a lack of maintenance, those responsible are liable for a fine of one *cumal*. Once guilt of the original offender has been established, he becomes responsible for providing maintenance and if he fails, he is liable for a two-*cumal* fine.[177] Paragraph 49 makes it clear that the hostage-surety has an

---

170 Ní Dhonnchadha, 'An edition of *Cáin Adomnáin*', p. 249. **171** Charles-Edwards, *Early Christian Ireland*, p. 568. **172** Ní Dhonnchadha, 'An edition of *Cáin Adomnáin*', pp 251–2; Charles-Edwards, *Early Christian Ireland*, pp 568–9. **173** Charles-Edwards, *Early Christian Ireland*, p. 563; Chapman Stacey, *The road to judgment*, p. 94. **174** Charles-Edwards, *Early Christian Ireland*, pp 568–9. **175** Idem, p. 567; Kelly, *Guide*, p. 65 for the term *rechtaire*. **176** Ní Dhonnchadha, 'An edition of *Cáin Adomnáin*, p. 253. She points to similar provisions in *Cáin Domnaig*. **177** Ibid., pp 253–4. She again refers to a parallel passage in *Cáin Domnaig*. Markus' translation in *Adomnán's 'Law of the Innocents'*, p. 24 seems to suggest that the two cumal fine refers to the defaulters and not the original offender. See Kelly, *Guide*, pp 139–40, on refusal of hospitality.

immunity from the normal vicarious liability that would attach to him for the crime of a member of his kin.[178] This immunity persists so long as the hostage-surety fulfils the duties of his position and makes his person available to the injured party if the offender absconds.[179] Once again Adomnán is at pains to clarify the finer details of the workings of his law and so to avoid any misunderstandings that might undermine its effectiveness.

* * *

The analysis of any legal document is difficult. The interpretation of a modern statute requires the skills of a legal expert, well versed in the broader legal context in which the statute is intended to operate. It is common for such experts to differ in their interpretations. When the statute in question is thirteen centuries old and survives in incomplete copies often containing errors, made seven and eight centuries after the law's promulgation,[180] and the surviving sources for information on the legal system itself in which the statute was intended to operate are incomplete and inadequate,[181] then interpretation is perilous in the extreme. Add to that the thought processes, attitudes and prejudices accumulated over those thirteen intervening centuries in the modern mindset, and the capacity to understand becomes even harder. It is not surprising, therefore, that at times, contradictions and apparent incoherences are perceived.

There are constants, however, and violence and killing is one of them. The concept of the non-combatant is another, and that such an innocent should have a degree of immunity from violence exists today as it did, without doubt, in the mind of Adomnán in 697. While we must speculate about many aspects of his law and may not be always correct in that speculation, that *LxI* was clearly a law for the protection of those who do not bear arms is manifest. This is clear from the name given to it in the annals, *Lex Innocentium,* and to the declaration of intent in paragraph 34, which was followed through in the subsequent paragraphs with specific provisions for each class of innocent and careful detail on how the law would operate in practice. It is also clear that it envisaged this protection applying, not only in circumstances of general violence, but also in war and in warlike situations, and each of its provisions must be read as applying in all such contexts. Adomnán recognized the difference between warriors, essentially all males of full age,[182] and those in society who did not bear arms, the innocents, the non-combatants. He articulated this difference, defined it by setting out who were innocents, and enshrined it in legislation which was designed to protect them.

178 On kin see Kelly, *Guide*, pp 12–14. **179** Ní Dhonnchadha, 'An edition of *Cáin Adomnáin*', pp 254–5. **180** A quick glance through Ó Néill/Dumville, *Cáin Adomnáin*, where attention is drawn to the differences in the two surviving copies and the omissions and mistakes, clearly illustrates this. **181** Kelly, *Guide*, pp 1–2. **182** See Ní Dhonnchadha, '*Lex Innocentium*', p. 59; Fraser, 'Morality of war', p. 95.

In many ways, Adomnán broke the mould in which pre-existing vernacular law had been cast. While the *éraic* was not based on rank, rank was the underlying principle that underpinned the rest of the entire legal edifice of early Irish law. Adomnán disregarded it, by stipulating fines for death and injury which were to apply equally to all victims. All women and young men between seven and manhood were put on an equal footing with freemen under the law. While all categories were brought under Adomnán's protection, women were, in a special way, by the stipulation in paragraph 42 that all fines for their violent deaths were to be paid to Adomnán.

CHAPTER 6

After 697: a law for women

DID IT MAKE A DIFFERENCE?

The obvious question, asked by all when they first become aware of *LxI*, is how effective was it? Did it succeed in its objective to provide protection for non-combatants at times of conflict? Unfortunately it is a question that the sources do not allow us to answer with any degree of certainty.

As was apparent from the brief study of the annals in Chapter 3 above, they make little or no reference to the fate of innocents, entries for the years 814 and 821 being exceptions.[1] In addition, records of case law and written judgments, broadly speaking, do not exist in early Irish law.[2] Sometimes it is possible to have a glimpse of the workings of the law from other sources such as the vernacular tales or other works.[3] Clearly, judgments were given verbally and not written down. Furthermore, the law was seen as being static or timeless, not as evolving.[4] There was no need, therefore, to have a written record of earlier judgments to act as precedents, because judges did not make new law, as the judgments of superior courts are binding on lower courts in modern common law. This is not to say that there was no legal commentary by lawyers on the pre-existing laws. There was, in fact, ongoing commentary, often in the form of glosses on law texts, which continued into the Middle Irish period and beyond.[5] These did not change the law and were explanatory in nature.[6] While the law tracts with their glosses and the text of *LxI* itself tell us the procedures by which it was intended law cases should proceed, 'it is unquestionable that our inability to resurrect the details of even a single "real-life" lawsuit poses a formidable obstacle to anyone wishing to resurrect the oral world within which disputes arose and were settled'.[7] Robin Chapman Stacey's absorbing study overcomes this obstacle to a remarkable degree, but, in the final analysis, because vernacular Irish law 'remained in essence an oral tradition',[8] there is no means of knowing how the

---

[1] See Chapter 3, p. 67. AU s. a. 814 and 821. [2] Kelly, *Guide*, pp 238–40. [3] Kelly mentions the case involving the Ulster king Congal Cáech, who sought redress for a bee-sting that allegedly blinded him, the well-known story about Columba and the copyright of a manuscript, and the tale about Cormac mac Airt's judgment on the trespassing sheep. [4] Charles-Edwards, 'Early Irish law', p. 332. [5] L. Breatnach, 'Lawyers in early Ireland' in D. Hogan and W.N. Osborough (eds), *Brehons, serjeants and attorneys: studies in the history of the Irish legal profession* (Dublin, 1990), pp 1–13. [6] For more on this see Houlihan, 'Jurisprudence', pp 167–8. [7] Chapman Stacey, *Dark speech*, p. 8. [8] Charles-Edwards, 'Early Irish law', p. 369.

elaborate system of offences, penalties and enforcement established by Adomnán for the protection of innocents worked out in practice.[9]

One can be sure, however, that as those present at the meeting in Birr gathered themselves up and prepared to depart for the four corners of Ireland and beyond, none would be under any illusion that normal 'honourable' warfare would not resume and continue as it had always done. Indeed it is likely that many harboured aggressive intentions as they bade farewell to their fellow attendees. It is tempting to imagine that, as the kings, major and minor, began to take their leave of Birr, one or more of them may have approached Adomnán to ask him, as we are told in *VC* that Rhydderch ap Tudwal and Guaire mac Áedáin asked Columba,[10] whether they were destined to fall into the hands of their enemies, whether they would die in battle or whether they would die peacefully among their own people. Adomnán would have recognized, as would all present at the meeting, lay and clerical, that the chances of a violent death were high.[11] And so it transpired for many. We learn from the annal entries for the years 697 up to and including 704, the year when Adomnán's own death is recorded, that fifteen of the lay attendees at Birr died. Seven of these died peacefully and eight were killed.[12] Violence continued to be a normal part of daily life.

We know from the annals that a battle occurred within five/six years of the meeting in Birr between two of those who had attended. This battle radically changed the political context in which *LxI* operated. The annal entry for the year 703[13] reads as follows:

> The battle of Corran [won by Cellach son of Ragallach and by the Connachta] in which fell Loingsech mac Óengusa, king of Ireland, together with his three sons, and two sons of Colgu and Dub Díbergg son of Dúngal and Fergus Fercraith and Congal of Gabair and many other *duces*. This battle was joined on the 12th of July, at the sixth hour of Saturday.[14]

9 For some indication of how law worked in practice see Adomnán's story of Librán in *VC* II.39; Kelly, *Guide*, p. 240; See also Chapman Stacey, *Dark speech*, pp 67–9 for an analysis of the law tract on sports judgments, *Melbretha* (*CIH* 1589.1–48 and 1338.5–1341.7), where a court hearing is reconstructed, with her emphasis on 'performance', citing D.A. Binchy (ed.), 'Mellbretha', *Celtica*, 8 (1968), pp 144–54; W. Sayers, 'Games, sport and para-military exercise in early Ireland', *Aethlon: Journal of Sport Literature*, 10:1 (1992), pp 105–23, A. and W. O'Sullivan, 'A legal fragment', *Celtica*, 8 (1968), pp 140–5. For a discussion of why 'pragmatic' written legal sources are so scarce, see Chapman Stacey, *Dark speech*, pp 91–4. **10** *VC* 1.15 and 1.47. **11** See treatment of this subject in Chapter 3 and in particular the distinctions made by the annalists in their descriptions of the deaths met by the elite, lay and clerical, as analysed by Thomas Charles-Edwards in *Chronicle* pp 24–32. **12** Died peacefully: nos. 68, 64, 43, 52, 75, 65, 83. Killed: nos. 77, 73, 48, 55, 41, 69, 81, 89. See Charles-Edwards, *Chronicle*, pp 172–80 covering years 696 to 704 and his notes identifying the relevant obits. **13** AU s. a. 703. See Charles-Edwards, *Chronicle*, p. 179, n. 2 and pp 42–3 adjusting the actual date of the battle to 704. For more on the battle, see Byrne, *Kings*, p. 247 and p. 257; Lacey, *Kingdoms*, pp 254–7. **14** See Ní Dhonnchadha, 'Guarantor-list', where Loingsech features at no. 41, Cellach at

After 697: a law for women

With the death of Loingsech in July 704, *LxI* was to lose its main lay champion. The following September saw the death of Adomnán, its inspiration and author.

While *LxI* was, in its conception and actualization, Adomnán's creation, it carried the force of law by virtue of Loingsech's authority, as king of Ireland, as he was described both in the guarantor-list and the annals. The first source after 697 where it is mentioned, *Críth Gablach*, a legal text dating from the early eighth century, makes this clear.[15] In this text, dubbed by Thomas Charles-Edwards as the 'nearest approach among the Irish laws to a text on kingship',[16] *LxI*, described as *recht Adamnáin*, Adomnán's law or edict, later to be referred to as his *cáin*, is cited as an example of the type of enactment 'which is proper for a king to bind upon his peoples by pledge', it being 'a law of religion which inspires'.[17] The king's authority was required to give *LxI* the force of law and that king must be the king of Ireland to make it binding on all the peoples of Ireland. Loingsech's authority to make this law for, not just a province, but for all Ireland and beyond, was accepted by the author of *Críth Gablach* and by all those who guaranteed it.

There are two other scenarios envisaged in *Críth Gablach* as requiring a king to exercise his prerogative to legislate: when he needs the people's help in driving out foreign invaders, such as the Saxons, and when there is an urgent need to sow crops (presumably when sowing has been neglected through warfare or natural disaster).[18] These two situations are clearly crises. It is reasonable to infer that the circumstances warranting the enactment of *LxI* must have been seen as urgent.[19] However, as will become clear, *LxI* differed from the two other scenarios envisaged by the author of *Críth Gablach* in that it will be seen to have been an enduring law rather than a measure to meet a temporary urgent need. While the absence of legal records denies the historian the means of knowing the day-to-day workings of the law and the extent of its implementation, its endurance over the centuries, which will be traced in this chapter, will enable us to suggest that *LxI* was, probably, at least to some degree, effective, although within limitations.

CHANGING EMPHASIS

The sources are unclear as to how the abbacy of Iona devolved in the years immediately following the death of Adomnán.[20] There appears to have been some internal friction. After its resolution in 716 and a series of short terms of abbots up to 726, 'Iona contacts with Ireland resumed their usual course'.[21] The

---

no. 61, Dub Díbergg at no. 69 and Fergus at no. 81. **15** *CIH* 777.6–783.38; 563.1–570.32; D.A. Binchy (ed.), *Críth Gablach* (Dublin, 1941, repr. 1970); Kelly, *Guide*, p. 267; T.M. Charles-Edwards, 'A contract between king and people', *Peritia*, 8 (1994), pp 107–19. **16** Charles-Edwards, 'Early Irish law', p. 332. **17** Binchy, *Críth Gablach*, lines 514–24. See also Herbert, 'The world of Adomnán', pp 37–8; Charles-Edwards, 'Early Irish law', pp 334–5; Bhreathnach, *Medieval world*, p. 69. See in this chapter below for change to use of the word *cáin*. **18** Binchy, *Críth Gablach*, lines 514–24. **19** For emergency context of *cána* see D. Ó Corráin, 'Ireland c.800: aspects of society' in *NHI*, pp 582–4. **20** See Herbert, *Iona, Kells and Derry*, pp 57–62; Sharpe, *Adomnán of Iona*, pp 74–7. **21** Herbert, *Iona, Kells and Derry*, p. 62.

annals relate that in 727 the relics of Adomnán were brought over to Ireland and the Law is promulgated anew ('*Adomnani reliquie transferuntur in Hiberniam 7 Lex renouatur*').[22] Cilléne Droichtech (726–52), the new abbot, accompanied the relics. It is clear that he was following the normal practice of recently appointed abbots of visiting the Columban foundations in Ireland to assert his position as the saint's successor and to collect tribute.[23] There was nothing normal, however, about the annalistic reference to the bringing of relics in support of the Law. This was an innovation. They remained in Ireland for three years, as the annals inform us that they returned to Iona in the month of October 730, and it is reasonable to conclude that they were on circuit in Ireland during this period.[24] The entry for 727 marks the first mention in the annals of the use of relics in connection with the promulgation or renewal of a law.[25] Their role in the Irish church had been expanding gradually over the years from their use in connection with tomb cults,[26] to their use in church consecration,[27] and oath taking.[28] However, in 727, Iona decided to make use of the relics of Adomnán for an entirely new purpose, the renewal of his law. This decision, as will become clear, had consequences, probably unforeseen.

In the first instance there was now a subtle change of emphasis. As Thomas Charles-Edwards has pointed out, the annal 'entry for 727 marks a shift away from the focus upon the beneficiaries to a focus upon the patron saint'.[29] At the renewal, the law was associated with the relics of Adomnán. In this respect a new trend was set that, as we shall see, other laws were to follow during the course of the century, such as the Law of Patrick and the Law of Columba. The relics gave a spiritual authority to the law and their circuit around Ireland served to mark the authority of both the saint's community and the sponsoring king. The question that must be asked now is, whether *LxI* came to be seen more as the law of Adomnán rather than as *LxI*, as it was described in the annals. This change in emphasis would facilitate, perhaps inadvertently, the transition in the perception of the law from a law for non-combatants generally to a law for women primarily. Máirín Ní Dhonnchadha has suggested that it may have been in 727 that paragraph 33, with its exclusive female targeting, was inserted.[30] However, it will be argued below that it is unlikely that anything would have been conceded to Armagh until after 734 and the promulgation of the Law of Patrick. The view has also been expressed that the titles in the guarantor-list may have been added at that time in order to bolster the authority and prestige of the law.[31] Would this

---

22 AU s. a. 727. It is difficult to say what was the exact nature of these relics. They could have been corporeal, such as all or part of Adomnán's body, or incorporeal, consisting of items with which he had been in contact during his life, such as his bell. On the subject generally see Wycherley, *Relics*. **23** Herbert, *Iona, Kells and Derry*, p. 61. **24** AU s. a. 730; Wycherley, *Relics*, pp 145–6; Herbert, *Iona, Kells and Derry*, p. 61. **25** Wycherley, *Relics*, p. 145 and also her n. 104; Charles-Edwards, *Early Christian Ireland*, pp 563–4. **26** Wycherley, *Relics*, pp 37–72. **27** Ibid., pp 102–27. **28** Ibid., pp 130–40. **29** Charles-Edwards, *Early Christian Ireland*, p. 564. **30** Ní Dhonnchadha, 'The law of Adomnán; a translation', p. 56. **31** T.M. Charles-Edwards, 'The Uí Néill, 695–743: the rise and fall of dynasties', *Peritia*, 16 (2002), p. 403.

include also paragraph 29, that forms part of the same discrete segment as the list of names, and that, too, mentions women alone, to the exclusion of the other innocents? One can only speculate. The reference in paragraph 29 to the payment of fines to Adomnán's coarb, with its Raphoe implications, would, perhaps, indicate a later date. On the other hand, paragraph 29 could, itself, have been amended, at a later date, to include a reference to Adomnán's coarb. While scope for speculation is endless, it seems that the change of emphasis that is evident in 727 was followed by the greater stress on women than on innocents in general that occurred during the course of the eighth century. If the law continued to be referred to as the Law of the Innocents, rather than the Law of Adomnán, it is arguable that the exclusive focus on women would have been difficult to justify.

A more direct consequence of Iona's decision to employ relics in support of its law was that it provoked a response on the part of Armagh that, within seven years, would remove the protection of clerics from Iona's jurisdiction and place these particular innocents firmly under Armagh's wing.[32] It is worth examining the political circumstances under which this happened. In 727, in the battle of Druim Fornocht, Cenél Conaill defeated Cenél nÉogain and subsequently, the annals relate, Adomnán's relics were brought over to Ireland and his law renewed.[33] The following year saw the kingship of Tara being taken by Flaithbertach, son of Loingsech mac Óengusso, the Cenél Conaill king of Tara on whose authority *LxI* was promulgated.[34] With Adomnán's relics on circuit in Ireland in support of *LxI*, and Flaithbertach holding the kingship of Tara, the signs were auspicious for Cenél Conaill, Iona and their law. It has been suggested that Cilléne Droichtech, the Iona abbot who brought Adomnán's relics to Ireland, had hoped to broker a peace between Cenél Conaill and Cenél nÉogain. Cilléne's epithet, *droichtech*, means bridgemaker.[35] It is clear from subsequent events that his efforts were unsuccessful. While Flaithbertach may have been in the ascendant in 730, when the relics were returned to Iona, and into 731, in the following year the tide turned dramatically against him. The annals record heavy defeats for Cenél Conaill at the

---

32 There appears to be little doubt that Armagh, in effect, copied Iona. See Herbert, *Iona, Kells and Derry*, p. 63; Charles-Edwards, *Early Christian Ireland*, p. 564. **33** AU s. a. 727. **34** AU s. a. 728. **35** eDIL s. v. drochtech. See Wycherley, *Relics*, pp 146–7. His peace-making is mentioned in the preface to the poem *Scrín Adomnáin*. See R.I. Best, O. Bergin, M.A. O'Brien and A. O'Sullivan (eds), *The Book of Leinster, formerly Lebar na Núachongbála* (6 vols, Dublin, 1954–83), vi, 1684–6. Here is explained that Cilléne brought with him a box or shrine containing all the relics collected by Adomnán. Were these 'Adomnán's relics'? This is also mentioned in *scholia* to both *Félire Óengusso* in Stokes (ed. and trans.), *Féilre Óengusso*, pp 210–11, and the *Martyrology of Donegal* in J. O'Donovan (trans.), J.H. Todd and W. Reeves (eds), *The martyrology of Donegal: a calendar of the saints of Ireland* (Dublin, 1864), pp 184–5. See also L. Gwynn, 'The reliquary of Adamnán', *Archivium Hibernicum*, 4 (1915), pp 199–214; J. Carney (ed. and trans.), 'A Maccucáin, Sruith in Tíag', *Celtica*, 15 (1983), pp 25–41; Herbert, *Iona, Kells and Derry*, p. 61 and p. 63.

hands of Cenél nÉogain in 732, 733 and 734.³⁶ One of these defeats involved the rout of a fleet from Dál Riata that Flaithbertach had brought to assist him.³⁷ It is difficult to discount some involvement on the part of the abbot of Iona, now back on the island, in arranging this intervention by the forces of the kingdom in which Iona is situated.³⁸ The following year, 734, was the decisive year in which is recorded the defeat of Flaithbertach at the battle of Mag nÍtho, the assumption of the kingship of Tara by Áed Allán of Cenél nÉogain, and the taking on circuit of the relics of Peter and Paul and Patrick in support of the Law of Patrick.³⁹ It is unlikely that Flaithbertach would have conceded anything to Cenél nÉogain in 730/1, following the successful circuit of Adomnán's relics, when he seemed to have the upper hand. Why would Cenél Conaill and Iona, at that point, surrender to Cenél nÉogain and Armagh the clerical protection rights which Iona held under decree of the Cenél Conaill king of Tara, Loingsech mac Óengusa, Flaithbertach's father? It is abundantly evident from the warfare between the two branches of the Northern Uí Néill over these few years that their enmity was intense. It is to be noted that Flaithbertach, after his series of defeats, ceded the kingship of Tara to Áed and retired *in clericatu*.⁴⁰ Did this involve some form of an agreement between the two northern kings, and did the agreement extend to the ceding of protection rights over clergy by Iona to Armagh? It seems probable that it was in 734, after the battle of Mag nÍtho, that this was done, at the same time that Flaithbertach handed over the kingship of Tara to Áed.⁴¹ In any event, an entry in the annals for 737 tells us that the Law of Patrick was in force throughout Ireland after a meeting in Terryglass, a monastery 25km south-west of Birr, between Áed Allán and Cathal mac Finguine, king of Munster.⁴² For the moment, Cenél nEogain and their ecclesiastical allies, Armagh, were clearly in the ascendant. It is only to be expected that Armagh would seize the opportunity to claim from Iona protective rights over the clerical population.

The text of the Law of Patrick has not been preserved. Scholars agree that it contained provisions for the protection of the clergy from violence.⁴³ There appears to have been an acceptance among Irish ecclesiastics of the seventh century of some form of primacy of honour for St Patrick.⁴⁴ There is a surviving source, from as far back as the 630s, where Patrick is described by the cleric

---

36 AU s. a. 732, 733, 734. See Charles-Edwards, 'The Uí Néill, 695–743', pp 407–12. **37** AU s. a. 733. See J. Bannerman, *Studies in the history of Dalriada* (Edinburgh and London, 1974), p. 18. **38** Herbert, *Iona, Kells and Derry*, p. 61. **39** AU s. a. 734. See Wycherely, *Relics*, pp 147–8, where she suggests that these are 'the relics discussed by Tírechán and used by Armagh to justify dominion over the Irish church as outlined in *Liber Angeli*'. See her *Relics*, pp 37–72. **40** AU s. a. 765 where his death is recorded. **41** See Charles-Edwards, *Chronicle*, p. 233 n. 4, citing Best et al. (eds), *The Book of Leinster*, i, 96. **42** AU s. a. 737; Charles-Edwards, *Early Christian Ireland*, p. 564. **43** Kenney, *Sources*, pp 335–6; Ryan, 'Cáin Adomnáin', p. 274; Ó Corráin, 'Ireland *c*.800', p. 583. **44** Charles-Edwards, *Early Christian Ireland*, p. 426. This is reflected in the corpus of Patrician documents from the Book of Armagh edited by Bieler, which includes the seventh-century *Vitae* of Patrick by Muirchú and Tírechán. See L. Bieler (ed. and trans.), *The Patrician texts in the Book of Armagh* (Dublin, 1979).

Cummian, in a letter written by him to the abbot of Iona, Ségéne (d. 652), and to the otherwise unknown Beccán the hermit, as *papa noster*.[45] Cummian held no particular brief for Armagh, and certainly Abbot Ségéne did not. Nevertheless, it seemed to be a normal and acceptable way to refer to Patrick. It is particularly striking, also, that the bishop of Armagh is placed first in the guarantor-list of *LxI*. It is also worth noting the special place given to Patrick in the law tracts. He receives special mention in *Cáin Fhuithirbe*, a tract dating from *c*.680 and of Munster origin. He is also accorded primacy in the introduction to the *Senchas Már* and in several of its constituent texts including *Córus Béscnai* and *Di astud chirt 7 dligid*.[46] It is clear, therefore, that Armagh would have been seen by many to have had a natural claim on protection rights over the clergy, and this fits in with the legalistic claims being put forward by Armagh in documents such as *Liber Angeli*, which has been dated to as early as 650.[47] Armagh's supporters may have resented Iona's claim to these rights in *LxI*. In the changed circumstances of 734, would Iona have resisted the Law of Patrick? Perhaps not so strenuously. It will be recalled that *LxI* provided for the payment to Adomnán of significantly larger fines for crimes against women than against clerics.[48] It is not clear, however, whether children remained under Iona's protection. In any event, with the Law of Patrick, the protection of non-combatants as such ceased, to be replaced by separate laws for, at least, two of their constituent parts.

Finally, the decision of Iona in 727 to make use of relics in support of *LxI* had far-reaching consequences. That decision was a major factor in establishing a practice that was to become, over the next century or so among the main players, both lay and ecclesiastical, a new order in the reality of power and its pursuit.[49] As we have noted, in 734, the same year during which Flaithbertach was defeated and Áed Allán took the kingship of Tara, the relics of Peter, Paul and Patrick were taken on circuit, not just in support of the Law of Patrick but as a powerful testament to the claims of Áed, Cenél nÉogain and Armagh. It is hard to over-estimate the power and influence of relics of Roman provenance in early medieval Ireland.[50] They 'represented papal authority and approval'.[51] They

---

45 Cummian, *De Controversia Paschali*, ed. and trans. M. Walsh, and D. Ó Cróinín, *Cummian's Letter De Controversia Paschali and the De Ratione Computandi* (Toronto, 1988), lines 208–9. For a concise discussion on Cummian and others of similar names see E. Johnston, 'Mapping literate networks in early medieval Ireland: quantitative realities, social mythologies?' in R. Kenna et al. (eds), *Maths meets myths: quantitative approaches to ancient narratives* (Cham, 2017), pp 195–211. **46** *CIH* 527.14ff and 226.31ff, 237.35ff, 240. 21ff; L. Breatnach, 'The ecclesiastical element'; K. McCone, 'Dubthach maccu Lugair and a matter of life and death in the pseudo-historical prologue to the *Senchas Már*', *Peritia*, 5 (1986), pp 1–35. **47** The text is edited and translated by Bieler, *Patrician texts*, pp 184–91; R. Sharpe, 'Palaeographical considerations in the study of the Patrician documents in the Book of Armagh', *Scriptorium*, 36 (1982), pp 3–18, suggests that it was composed in or around 640 or 650. Charles-Edwards, *Early Christian Ireland*, pp 432–9 dates it after 678. **48** Chapter 5. **49** Herbert, *Iona, Kells and Derry*, pp 63–7. **50** Wycherley, *Relics*, pp 37–46. **51** Ibid., p. 40.

demanded the allegiance of the people and in 737 the annals inform us that the Law of Patrick was in force throughout Ireland.[52] In 743, however, Áed Allán was defeated and killed by Domnall of Clann Cholmáin of Mide, who assumed the kingship of Tara and proceeded to identify his interests with Iona as opposed to Cenél nÉogain and Armagh.[53] This commonality of interests enabled Iona to counter Armagh by the promulgation of a new law in 753. Significantly, and subject to the speculative rider at the conclusion of this section, Iona reacted, not with a renewal or reassertion of Adomnán's law, but with a law named after its founder, Columba. The annal entry for 753 informs us of the promulgation of the Law of Colum Cille by Domnall Midi.[54] The terms of this law are not known. However, Máire Herbert points out that its enactment coincided with a period of crop failures, famine and disease, occasioning social disturbance and stress, which continued for most of the eighth century.[55] It is significant, although not surprising, that Iona did not try to recover its position in relation to clerical protection, even though it might have been in a position, politically, to do so. Clearly, that was now a dead issue and the cause of innocents per se no longer had a champion. The exigencies of the moment, whatever they may have been, dominated, and determined the agenda.

When Slébéne, the Cenél Conaill abbot of Iona who succeeded Cilléne, came to Ireland in 757, he further promulgated the Law of Colum Cille, presumably in association with Domnall Midi.[56] The latter died in 763 and was buried 'with honour and veneration' in the Columban foundation of Durrow.[57] He was succeeded as king of Tara by Niall Frossach of Cenél nÉogain who renewed the Law of Patrick in 767.[58] The Law of Colum Cille was to be again promulgated in 778, by the Clann Cholmáin king of Tara, Donnchad son of Domnall, and Bresal, abbot of Iona. The annals inform us of further enforcements of the Law of Patrick on various occasions in various locations in 783, 799, 806, 823, 825 and 842.[59] The period from 740 onwards into the early years of the ninth century saw the promulgation of very many laws, apart from those mentioned above, which were almost invariably associated with a founding saint and generally of provincial or local application. Examples of such laws include the Law of the Uí Suanaig in 743 and 748,[60] the Laws of Ciarán of Clonmacnoise and Brendan of Clonfert for Connacht in 744,[61] the Laws of Commán and Áedán for Connacht in 772 and 780,[62] and the Law of Ailbe of Emly for Munster in 793.[63] The Law of Ciarán of Clonmacnoise is mentioned again, for Connacht, in 788 and

---

52 AU s. a. 737. **53** For factors determining the alliance see Herbert, *Iona, Kells and Derry*, p. 65; Charles-Edwards, *Chronicle*, p. 218, n. 2. **54** AU s. a. 753. **55** Herbert, *Iona, Kells and Derry*, p. 64; Ó Corráin, 'Ireland *c*.800', pp 583–4. **56** AU s. a. 757. **57** Herbert, *Iona, Kells and Derry*, p. 66 and n. 44. **58** AU s. a. 767. **59** AU s. a. 783, 799, 806, 823, 825 and 842. See Wycherley, *Relics*, p. 148. **60** Wycherley, *Relics*, pp 148–9; Etchingham, *Church organization*, pp 199–204. **61** AU s. a. 744. **62** AU s. a. 772 and 780. See Charles-Edwards, *Early Christian Ireland*, p. 561. **63** AI s. a. 784. See also AU s. a. 793 and Charles-Edwards, *Chronicle*, p. 256, n. 3.

814.[64] *Cáin Dar Í* (Dáire's Law) was promulgated over Munster in 810,[65] Connacht in 812 and 826,[66] and Ulster in 813.[67] It is clear that, apart from the specific crises prompting these *cána*, they were part of the power game played out between both lay and ecclesiastical rivals during the eighth and into the ninth century.

An essential feature in the struggle for power was the prestige of the founding saint whose authority had to be invoked, sometimes with the assistance of relics.[68] For this reason Iona was obliged to turn to its founding father.[69] The *érlam* or founding saint played a pivotal role in the power structures, both lay and ecclesiastical, of early Christian Ireland. *Érlam* means 'patron saint, patron or founder (of a church or monastery)'.[70] On a local level the identity of a community was defined by its founding saint, its *érlam*. This saint sometimes gave his or her successor monastery its character, as Clonard was renowned for learning and Slane for law.[71] The *érlam* was also politically important, a case in point being St Íte, who fiercely defended her people, the Uí Chonaill, against their west Munster enemies at a time of shifting territorial boundaries in the late seventh and early eighth centuries.[72] The *érlam* concept was not confined to local communities but could be extended to provincial or national level, as in the cases of Ciarán of Clonmacnoise, Brigit of Kildare, Columba and Patrick, where identification was with a mother church.[73] The word *érlam* is thought to be of pre-Christian origin, meaning 'tutelar deity', and may have been one of the native terms incorporated into the Irish church.[74] It has been suggested that 'it was the saint's role as source of ecclesiastical title that introduced the term *érlam* to the vocabulary of the early Irish church'.[75] It was, therefore, a concept of basic importance, deeply rooted in the Irish psyche. Circuits, sometimes with relics or insignia of the founding saint, were conducted, that had the dual role of establishing and maintaining jurisdictional rights and collecting funds for the saint's ecclesiastical successors and their communities.[76]

---

64 AU s. a. 788 and 814. See Charles-Edwards, *Early Christian Ireland*, pp 561–2. **65** AU s. a. 810. **66** AU s. a. 812 and 826. **67** AU s. a. 813. **68** Wycherley, *Relics*, pp 160–8 and 180–90. She succinctly explains how the identity of a community came to be defined by its relationship with the patron or founder saint, the *érlam*, and how this translated into a system of power and control. **69** See Wycherley, *Relics*, pp 95–6, for a discussion on translation and enshrinement of Columba's relics. **70** eDIL s. v. *érlam*. See T.M. Charles-Edwards, '*Érlam*: the patron-saint of an Irish church' in A. Thacker and R. Sharpe (eds), *Local saints and local churches in the early medieval West* (Oxford, 2002), pp 267–90. **71** Wycherley, *Relics*, p. 164; D. Howlett, *The Celtic Latin tradition of Biblical style* (Dublin, 1995), p. 129 for Clonard; Johnston, *Literacy*, Appendix. For Erc of Slane see Wycherely, *Relics*, pp 164–5, in which she cites the many sources acclaiming the legal credentials of Erc and Slane. **72** E. Johnston, 'Íte: patron of her people', *Peritia*, 14 (2000), pp 423–5; Wycherley, *Relics*, pp 163–4. **73** C. Etchingham, 'The implications of *Paruchia*', *Ériu*, 44 (1993), p. 157. **74** D.A. Binchy, 'Patrick and his biographers: ancient and modern', *Studia Hibernica*, 2 (1962), p. 166. **75** P. Ó Riain, 'Conservation in the vocabulary of the early Irish church' in D. Ó Corráin, L Breatnach and K. McCone (eds), *Sages, saints and storytellers: Celtic studies in honour of Professor James Carney* (Maynooth, 1989), p. 360. **76** Wycherley, *Relics*, pp 155–6.

Iona's use of its *érlam*, Columba, in its struggles during the second half of the eighth century does not in any way signify a lessening in the importance of Adomnán, either in Iona's estimation or in the estimation of the wider Irish church, as will become clear below. While his concept of the non-combatant may have become diluted, with the assumption of responsibility for clerics passing to Armagh, it will be seen that he continued to be revered for many centuries, especially as a protector of the weak. But only Columba could meet the requirements of the ultimate symbol of Iona's claims. It is, perhaps, a little inaccurate to see the renewal in 727 as setting the trend for what happened over the ensuing years. It differed in a number of respects in that it was not a renewal of a law ascribed to somebody who had died hundreds of years before. Adomnán had died only twenty-three years earlier. Furthermore, unlike Patrick or Columba or Ciarán, he was the actual author of the law. The Law of Patrick was more typical. Although it was prompted by the renewal of *LxI* in 727, it provided the prototype for the laws that were to follow.

Before leaving the conflicts of the second half of the eighth century between Cenél nÉogain/Armagh and Clann Cholmáin/Iona it might be worth considering an alternative scenario: the possibility that the Law of Colum Cille might have been *LxI* by another name. It is clear that it was not of importance that the person after whom the law was named was not the actual author. The laws tended to be named after the *érlam* during this period: Patrick, Ciarán, Brendán, Commán, Áedán and Ailbe for example, and this was necessary to give them the required authority. The use of Columba's name for *LxI* would, therefore, be understandable. It would also explain the absence of references to *LxI* in the sources since 727. The Law of Colum Cille was promulgated/renewed on three occasions (753, 757, 778), which might indicate a continuing need over a period rather than a momentary emergency. This is very similar to the frequent renewals of the Law of Patrick, a law of a similar nature, broadly speaking, to *LxI*. Furthermore, as will become evident, the name for the law, *Cáin Adomnáin*, does not appear to have become current until much later, possibly originating in Raphoe. It could have been called *Cáin Colum Cille* during the eighth century. If the Law of Colum Cille was one and the same as *LxI*, it is a moot point as to whether it was being promoted in its original form as a law for innocents generally, including clerics, or in an amended form with increased emphasis on women. The latter is more likely in view of the treatment of Adomnán in *Félire Oengusso*, as we shall see below. With regard to this suggested alternative scenario, however, there is nothing conclusive about any of the arguments in its favour. The naming of the law after Columba is consistent with both scenarios. It must be remembered that in the early part of the century, mention of *LxI* was explicitly done by reference to Adomnán and not Columba. It was referred to as *recht Adamnáin* in *Críth Gablach*, and the annal entry for 727 links it most deliberately with Adomnán's relics. Furthermore, there are many possible explanations for absence of references to it in the annals. Why is the absence remarkable? The frequent renewals of the Law of Colum Cille could well be explained, as suggested by Máire Herbert and Donnchadh Ó Corráin, by the prevailing conditions of crop failures, famine and disease throughout the eighth century. While our alternative scenario is possible, and, it is suggested, worth considering, the arguments in its favour are not sufficiently conclusive. It is intended therefore, for the purposes of the remainder of this chapter, to proceed on the basis of the initial scenario, i.e., *LxI* and the Law of Colum Cille were different laws.

TRANSITION COMPLETED

Lex Innocentium, therefore, ceased to be the law under which the clergy of Ireland found their protection. There is no evidence that Iona, at anytime during the ensuing years, tried to recover the position. It is clear also, that the Middle Irish paragraphs 1–27, compiled in the late tenth or early eleventh century, were concerned exclusively with women. Paragraphs 29, 33 and 50–3, however, also target the protection of women exclusively, but, on linguistic grounds, cannot be precluded from having an earlier date of compilation. It is not possible to offer a convincing argument for the date or dates of their insertion into the text of the law. However a source dating from around 830 makes it clear that, by that date, Adomnán's law was seen as a law for women. *Félire Óengusso* (The Martyrology of Oengus) is a text that Pádraig Ó Riain dates between 828 and 833.[77] Kathleen Hughes refers to it as a 'Who's who' of the Irish church, reflecting 'the very solid and detailed tradition which ... the Irish Church had built up about her own past'.[78] It takes the form of a calendar with a quatrain for each day of the year, giving the names of the saints to be commemorated on each day. This is what is said of Adomnán:

> *Do Adamnán Íae*
> *Assa tóidlech tóiden*
> *Ro ír Ísu úasal*
> *Sóerad mhbúan mhban nhGóidel*
>
> To Adomnán of Iona
> Whose troop is radiant,
> Noble Jesus has granted
> The lasting freedom of the women of the Gaels.[79]

There could hardly be a clearer testament, from a more appropriate source, of how Adomnán and his law were regarded c.125 years after his death. Of all his achievements it was his law that Óengus chose to commemorate and, in his eyes, that law was seen as a law for women. Moreover, the compiler, Óengus ua

77 Stokes, *Féilre Óengusso*. For dating, see D. Dumville, '*Féilre Óengusso*: problems of dating a monument of Old Irish', *Éigse*, 33 (2002), pp 19–48; P. Ó Riain, *Feastdays of the saints: a history of Irish martyrologies* (Bruxelles, 2006), pp 75–98, esp. 94–6. 78 Hughes, *Sources*, pp 206–8. 79 Stokes, *Féilre Óengusso*, p. 196; Márkus, *Adomnán's 'Law of the Innocents'*, p. 3.

Oiblén was a bishop associated with the Céli Dé and a person of importance to their community. The Céli Dé were 'a loose yet influential group of clerics with common ascetic and liturgical interests'.[80] Under their primary inspirer, Máel Ruain of Tallaght, they stressed devotional practice and pastoral care. They were at the forefront of a re-invigoration of ascetic and liturgical practice in Ireland.[81] For example, one of their number, Máel Coích, revised the Stowe Missal, a product of one of the Céli Dé monasteries, either Tallaght or Lorrha, in c.812, bringing contemporary Roman practice into the Eucharistic rite.[82] He 'was at the cutting edge of reform in the ninth century'.[83] In fact, the compilation of the martyrology may have been a response to a directive of a council held at Aachen in 817 requiring that every monastery have a martyrology for use at Chapter.[84] In the opinion of this influential segment of the Irish church, Adomnán's main attribute, viewed from c.830, was that he freed women. The other innocents are not mentioned. It may also be significant that the law was seen to be effective in achieving its objective in that women's freedom was lasting. The clear implication here is that *LxI* had done, and was continuing to do, for women, the job that it was designed to do, although admittedly this must remain speculative. With the Law of Patrick providing clerical protection, by 830, *LxI* had made the transition from a law for innocents generally to a law for women specifically. This then is how *LxI* was perceived and operated at the time when the Viking impact was becoming fully manifest in the Irish world. Indeed, as we shall see, this is how *LxI* is treated in the sources, with one notable exception,[85] in all the fleeting references to it over the following centuries.

THE VIKING INTERLUDE

The annals first report the appearance of Vikings in 794 when it is stated that all the islands of Britain were harried by the gentiles.[86] The following year the burning of Rechru (Rathlin or Lambay) is reported.[87] In 802, Iona was burnt and it was again attacked in 806 when sixty-eight of its community were killed.[88] Thus commenced 'a time of dislocation and change',[89] which was to be traumatic and disruptive for Irish society and for the Columban community in particular. The extent of that disruption is the subject of debate among scholars, with, for

---

80 Johnston, 'Literate networks', p. 11. For the Céli Dé, in general, see the key study by W. Follett, *Céli Dé in Ireland: writing and identity in the early Middle Ages* (Woodbridge, 2006). **81** P. O'Dwyer, *Céli Dé: spiritual reform in Ireland, 750–900* (Dublin, 1981) is a little outdated in seeing the Céli Dé as a reform movement. See now, Follett, *Céli Dé in Ireland*; C. Haggart, 'The *Céli Dé* and the early medieval Irish church: a reassessment', *Studia Hibernica*, 34 (2006–7), pp 11–62. **82** Bhreathnach, *Medieval world*, p. 221. **83** B. Coffey, 'The Stowe enigma: decoding the mystery', *Irish Theological Quarterly*, 75:1 (2010), p. 90. **84** Ó Riain, *Feastdays*, p. 75 and pp 96–7. **85** See reference in the *Fragmentary annals of Ireland*, which includes children and women, below, p. 163. **86** AU s. a. 794; See F.J. Byrne, 'The Viking age' in *NHI*, pp 609–34. **87** AU s. a. 795. **88** AU s. a. 802 and 806. **89** Herbert, *Iona, Kells and Derry*, p. 67.

instance, Donnchadh Ó Corráin arguing that the effect of the Viking incursions on the schools was not as catastrophic as usually assumed.[90] Elva Johnston has shown that learned ecclesiastical culture was hardly touched.[91] On the other hand David Dumville has criticized this tendency to minimize the effect of the Vikings, describing it as the 'cuddly Vikings' view.[92] It is important to see the Vikings as impacting on some areas of Irish life to a greater extent than on others and, more specifically, on some religious communities more than on others. We know that Iona suffered serious Viking attacks in 802 and 806 and that, alone among the *paruchiae*, relocated its head monastery over a period to Kells which was founded in 807.[93] It is hard to say how these developments affected its will and capacity to prosecute *LxI*.

The Vikings started settling in Ireland in the 830s with a *longphort* being established in Dublin in the 840s as a permanent trading-cum-piratical base,[94] from which, attacks could be launched even against inland monasteries. Birr was attacked from Dublin in 842,[95] among the first monastic settlements to be attacked from that base. The era of the proclamation of *cána*, 697–842, came to an end with, coincidentally, the last such proclamation occurring in 842. The Annals of Inisfallen inform us that 'The Law of Patrick was brought to Munster by Forannán and by Diarmait'.[96] In fact, the annal entries for 842 neatly illustrate the difficult environment in which any *cáin* would have to operate. In addition to Birr that year, the foreigners attacked the king of Calatruim, Clonmacnoise, Saigir (Seirkieran), Clochar Mac nDaiméni (Clogher), Linn Duachaill (Annagassan) and Dísert Diarmata (Castledermot) and they were still in Dublin and had fleets on the Boyne and at Lind Sailech (not identified) among the Ulstermen.[97] As it is not known how a *cáin* such as *LxI* operated in practice, it is equally impossible to know how the additional violence emanating from the Viking raids affected its implementation. Certainly the Vikings were not bound

---

90 D. Ó Corráin, 'Ireland, Wales, Man and the Hebrides' in P. Sawyer (ed.), *The Oxford illustrated history of the Vikings* (Oxford, 1997), pp 94–7. See also A.T. Lucas, 'Irish Norse relations: time for a reappraisal', *Journal of the Cork Historical and Archaeological Society*, 71 (1966), pp 62–75; D. Ó Corráin, 'High-kings, Vikings and other kings', *Irish Historical Studies*, 21 (1979), pp 283–323; A.P. Smyth, *Scandinavian York and Dublin* (2 vols, Dublin, 1975–9). For the Vikings in Ireland generally see, H.B. Clarke, M. Ní Mhaonaigh and R. Ó Floinn (eds), *Ireland and Scandinavia in the early Viking age* (Dublin, 1998); H.B. Clarke and R. Johnson (eds), *The Vikings in Ireland and beyond: before and after the Battle of Clontarf* (Dublin, 2015) and, in particular, for an overview of developing scholarship, see, in the latter volume, H.B. Clarke and R. Johnson, 'Ireland and the Viking age', pp 1–24. 91 Johnston, *Literacy*, pp 124–8. 92 D. Dumville, 'Review of Dáibhí Ó Cróinín's *Early medieval Ireland, 400–1200*' in *Times Literary Supplement*, 3 January 1997. See A.P. Smyth, 'The effect of Scandinavian raiders on English and Irish churches: a preliminary reassessment' in B. Smith (ed.), *Britain and Ireland, 900–1300: Insular responses to medieval European change* (Cambridge, 1999), pp 1–38. 93 AU s. a. 807; Herbert, *Iona, Kells and Derry*, pp 68–78. 94 P. Wallace, 'The archaeology of Ireland's Viking-age towns' in *NHI*, p. 815. See also E.P. Kelly, 'The *longphort* in Viking-age Ireland: the archaeological evidence' in Clarke and Johnson (eds), *The Vikings in Ireland and beyond*, pp 55–92, esp. 84–91. 95 AU s. a. 842. 96 AI s. a. 842. 97 AU s. a. 842.

by its provisions and were not part of any accepted conventions in the conduct of violent activities that may have become the norm among the Irish. While *LxI* may have continued to be enforced in some inter-Irish situations, the intensity and frequency of Viking raiding, particularly from the 830s to the 870s,[98] was such that it is difficult to see how the intricate mechanisms and procedures established by the *cána* could operate. In short, it is probable that 'After the 830s the stable society needed to enforce the *cána* had for the time ceased to exist'.[99] This is not to say that there was a widespread collapse of society in general; rather a level of disruption that affected the finely balanced implementation of the provisions of *cáin* law in particular. The prosecution of *LxI*, of course, was also affected by the *particular* problems suffered by the Iona community.

The fate of women and children is not known in detail but can be imagined. The annals relate both the killing and taking captive of many during the Viking raids, although it needs to be remembered that the Irish themselves continued to engage in violence among themselves, and it was their violence that had concerned Adomnán in the first place.[100] Gilbert Márkus points to an entry for 814, which is an example of inter-Irish violence towards innocents, 'where many innocent people were killed',[101] as an indication of awareness on the part of the annalist of a violation of rights. However, neither Adomnán nor his law nor, indeed, any *cáin*, feature to any significant extent in our sources during this period. It is likely that the particular problems suffered by the Columban federation played a major role in this scenario.

While *LxI* does not appear to any noticeable extent in ninth-century sources, there is, however, one annal entry in particular worth examining in a little detail. In the year 817 'Máel Dúin son of Cenn Fáelad, *princeps* of Ráith Both, from the community of Columba Cille, was killed', with the following entry reading, 'The community of Colum Cille went to Tara to excommunicate Áed'.[102] This is the first reference to Raphoe in the annals. As was mentioned already, both surviving manuscripts of *LxI* come from the same exemplar, the Old Book of Raphoe. [103] Furthermore, it is clear from paragraph 23 in the Middle Irish preface to the *cáin* that the fines stipulated were to be paid to Raphoe.[104] At some point Raphoe took possession of *LxI* and assumed responsibility for it. Obviously, this could not have happened until after Raphoe was founded and this is the relevance of these entries for 817. The entries themselves relate to a dispute between Áed Oirdnide, the Cenél nÉogain king of Tara, and the

---

98 C. Etchingham, *Viking raids on Irish church settlements in the ninth century* (Maynooth, 1996). **99** Hughes, *Sources*, p. 82, and see also pp 58–9; Charles-Edwards, *Early Christian Ireland*, p. 561. **100** Examples include AU s. a. 821, 836, 869. See A.T. Lucas 'The plundering and burning of churches in Ireland, 7th to 16th century' in E. Rynne (ed.), *North Munster studies: essays in commemoration of Monsignor Michael Moloney* (1967), pp 172–229. **101** AU s. a. 814. See also Byrne, *Kings*, p. 252 for details of the incident concerned. **102** AU s. a. 817. **103** In Chapters 1 and 5. **104** *LxI*, paragraph 23. See Márkus, *Adomnán's 'Law of the Innocents'*, p. 15; Herbert and Ó Riain, *Betha Adamnáin*, p. 2; Ní Dhonnchadha, 'An edition of *Cáin Adomnáin*', pp 18–19; Lacey, *Kingdoms*, pp 248–9; idem, 'Adomnán and Donegal', pp 33–5.

Columban community.[105] It has been suggested that the killing of Máel Dúin was instigated by Áed in retaliation for the killing of his brother by the Cenél Conaill two years earlier,[106] all part of the ongoing struggles between the two northern branches of the Uí Néill which, at this time, seem to have crystallized in the border area of Raphoe. Brian Lacey suggests that Cenél nEogain territorial dominance was being countered by Cenél Conaill through the medium of Columban claims on Raphoe.[107] In response, that community proceeded to Tara to curse Áed for his violation of Máel Dúin's rights as a cleric.[108] They could hardly rely on the Law of Patrick for redress!

There has been considerable scholarly discussion on the description of Máel Dúin in the annals as being from the Columban community. While Máire Herbert takes it at face value,[109] Máirín Ní Dhonnchadha sees it as being unnecessary, unless Raphoe itself was not part of that community, perhaps a separate foundation of Adomnán's.[110] The latter view makes sense if it is understood that Raphoe was of some antiquity in 817, which was the widely held understanding prior to Lacey's research. A more likely explanation for the stress on Máel Dúin's Columban credentials is the annalist's desire to explain why Áed would have been opposed to him.[111] Even more likely is the fact that in 817 Raphoe was a relatively new foundation, appearing in the annals for the first time and therefore needing elaboration as to its Columban provenance. We have no way of knowing exactly how long before 817 Raphoe was founded. Was its foundation in any way associated with the foundation of Kells in 807, perhaps as a counter-balance for the benefit of Cenél Conaill, who may have felt spurned by Iona relative to Clann Cholmáin, adjacent to whose territory Kells is situated?[112] Máire Herbert posits that the foundation of Kells may have been agreed at a meeting of the synods of the Uí Néill in Dún Cuair in 804.[113] It is reasonable to speculate that, like the new monastery of 'Columba Cille at Kells',[114] a new monastery for Raphoe was agreed at the same meeting, but in the name of Adomnán.

While we cannot know with any certainty, we are even less in a position to say when Raphoe took over responsibility for *LxI* or whether or when it had a hand in the additions made to the text in the form of paragraphs 28–32, 33 and 50–3. One tenuous hint may lie in an annal entry for 832, which states that, in that year, one, Tuathal son of Feradach was taken by the Vikings, and the shrine of Adomnán was removed from Domnach Maigen (Donaghmoyne, Co. Monaghan).[115] This may indicate that the relics of Adomnán were on circuit at

---

[105] Herbert, *Iona, Kells and Derry*, p. 71; Lacey, *Kingdoms*, pp 316–17. [106] Byrne, *Kings*, p. 162; Herbert, *Iona, Kells and Derry*, p. 71. [107] Lacey, *Kingdoms*, pp 316–19 for a detailed analysis. [108] AU s. a. 817; Charles-Edwards, *Chronicle*, p. 276; Wycherley, *Relics*, pp 182–3. [109] Herbert, *Iona, Kells and Derry*, p. 80. [110] Ní Dhonnchadha, 'An edition of *Cáin Adomnáin*', p. 19. [111] Lacey, *Kingdoms*, p. 318. [112] AU s. a. 807. See Herbert, *Iona, Kells and Derry*, pp 68–71 on the foundation of Kells. [113] AU s. a. 804. See Herbert, *Iona, Kells and Derry*, p. 70. [114] AU s. a. 807. [115] AU s. a. 832; Ní Dhonnchadha, 'An edition of *Cáin Adomnáin*', p. 34.

that time. It is to be noted that, in the previous year, the relics of Columba were brought to Ireland.[116] There may have been an apportionment made, over time, of Iona's insignia, with Columba's going to Kells and Adomnán's to Raphoe, when their safety could no longer be assured in an Iona constantly under Viking threat. Clearly, Iona would want to preserve Adomnán's legacy. Indeed, it appears that an attempt was being made in the first half of the ninth century, ultimately successful, to build up a tradition of association between Adomnán and Raphoe.[117] Brian Lacey suggests that there may have already been a tradition associating Adomnán with Raphoe through a combination of two factors. First, it is possible that he was confused with a cleric named Adamnán who died in 731 as bishop of Ráith Maige Oínaig,[118] which Lacey identifies as Rateen, a site about 8km north-east of Raphoe. He points out that references in the annals to Rateen disappear about the same time references to Raphoe start. Second, there is a strong possibility that Adomnán of Iona was born and grew up in the east Donegal area near Raphoe, it being his mother's native place.[119] Even at the start of the ninth century there existed a tradition on which the Columban community could build, in order to provide Raphoe with its *érlam*, Adomnán, so vital to its future as custodians and enforcers of his law.

RAPHOE: ADOMNÁN AND HIS LAW ENDURE

It cannot be discounted, of course, that the incident in Donaghmoyne in 832 occurred on an occasion when *LxI* was, in fact, being implemented. While this will never be known with any certainty, the annals do record the death of one charged with just such a task almost a hundred years later, Cáencomhrac, abbot and bishop of the Columban church of Derry in 929. He is described in the Annals of the Four Masters as *maor cána Adhamhnáin* (*máer* of Adomnán's law),[120] which indicates that *LxI* was operational, to a lesser or greater extent, at that time and which provides context for subsequent annal entries.

The annals inform us of the death in 938 of Dubthach, '*comarba* of Colum Cille and Adomnán'.[121] He is described as the successor of, not only Columba, but also of Adomnán. The same title is accorded to Robartach, his successor, on his death in 954.[122] It has been argued that Kells had taken over from Iona as the abbatial seat of the successor of Columba in 927 on the succession of

---

116 AU s. a. 831. With regard to Columba's relics and the references to them in AU s. a. 825 (martyrdom of Bláthmacc for refusing to disclose their whereabouts to the Vikings), s. a. 831, 849 (being brought to Ireland) and s. a. 878 (to Ireland 'in flight from the foreigners'); see Herbert, *Iona, Kells and Derry*, pp 70–3; Wycherley, *Relics*, pp 53–4, for text and translation of Walafrid Strabo's poem describing the martyrdom of Bláthmacc. 117 For a summary of the tradition of Adomnán's association with Raphoe see Lacey, 'Adomnán and Donegal', pp 33–5. 118 AU s. a. 731. 119 Lacey, 'Adomnán and Donegal', p. 35. 120 *Annála Rioghachta Éireann: Annals of the kingdom of Ireland by the Four Masters (AFM)*, ed. and trans. J. O'Donovan (7 vols, Dublin, 1848–51), s. a. 927. See Etchingham, *Church organization*, pp 212–13. 121 AU s. a. 938. See Herbert, *Iona, Kells and Derry*, pp 78–81. 122 AU s. a. 954.

Dubthach.¹²³ But why describe its abbot as the successor of both Columba and Adomnán? Obviously, it is an indication of the high regard in which Adomnán was held and the renewed interest in his works. But was it more than that? Reeves suggested that it is because Dubthach and Robartach held both the abbacy of the Columban community's head house and Raphoe.¹²⁴ To hold two abbacies at once was not unusual, an apposite example being Máel Muire Ua hUchtáin, who was abbot of Kells and Raphoe from 1025 to 1040.¹²⁵ Máire Herbert does not discount that Dubthach could have held the abbacy of Raphoe or another church associated with Adomnán, at sometime before his appointment as *comarba*.¹²⁶ If the tradition of Adomnán's association with Raphoe had taken hold by 938, a minimum of 184 years after its foundation,¹²⁷ it would be understandable that Dubthach would be described as Adomnán's successor, assuming that he was abbot of Raphoe at some time. It is significant that the two following abbots who are given the title *comarba Coluim Cille* in the annals, Dub-Dúin, who died in 959, and Dub-scuile who died in 964, are not described as the successors of Adomnán.¹²⁸ Perhaps this is because they had no association with Raphoe. It is fair to say that the annal entries for 938 and 954, at the very least indicate the importance of Adomnán, over two centuries after his death and, probably, are an indication of the tradition of his association with Raphoe, whereby he was now considered its founder, its *érlam*, and from whence the exemplar for our texts of *LxI* was shortly to emerge.

Colmán's Hymn and Félire Óengusso
Mugrón is recorded as the next holder of the abbacy of Kells, his death being noted in 980.¹²⁹ He was the author of a number of religious pieces that have survived, including a contribution to a work having an earlier origin, Colmán's Hymn.¹³⁰ It is in this work that we find a later commentary of particular interest. The relevant part of the text reads,

> *Cethri primchana na Herend .i. cain Patraic 7 Darí 7 Adomnan 7 domnaig. Cain Patraic, immorro, cen chleirciu do marbad; cain Darí, cen bú do gait; Adomnán, cen (mna) do marbad; domnaig,cen (dul) ar imthecht.*

---

123 Herbert, *Iona, Kells and Derry*, p. 79.   **124** Reeves, *Adamnán*, pp lxi–lxv and pp 276–85. **125** F.J. Byrne, 'Church and politics, *c*.750–*c*.1100' in *NHI*, p. 666. See Herbert's comments on joint abbacies in *Iona, Kells and Derry*, pp 73–4.   **126** Herbert, *Iona, Kells and Derry*, p. 80. **127** Raphoe first mentioned in annals in AU s. a. 814.   **128** AU s. a. 859, 864. See Herbert, *Iona, Kells and Derry*, p. 82.   **129** AU s. a. 980. See Herbert, *Iona, Kells and Derry*, pp 82–3; Ó Corráin, 'Ireland *c*.800', p. 605.   **130** For his verses see: Herbert, *Iona, Kells and Derry*, p. 82; C. Plummer (ed. and trans.), *Irish litanies* (London, 1925), p. xxi and pp 78–84; Kenney, *Sources*, p. 727; G. Murphy, *Early Irish lyrics* (Oxford, 1956), pp 32–5 and pp 186–7; Ó Corráin, 'Ireland *c*.800', p. 605. For Colmán's Hymn see: W. Stokes and J. Strachan (eds), *Thesaurus Paleohibernicus: a collection of old-glosses, scholia, prose and verse* (2 vols, Cambridge, 1901–3), ii, 306; Kenney, *Sources*, pp 726–7 and p. 421; Hughes, *Sources*, pp 80–1; Kelly, *Guide*, pp 275–6.

'four chief laws of Ireland, the law of Patrick and the law of Dare and of Adamnan and of Sunday. The law of Patrick, now, not to slay clerics; the law of Dare, not to steal cattle; of Adamnan, not to slay women; of Sunday, not to travel.[131]

A very similar commentary can be found in the text containing *Félire Óengusso*, referred to above, which is also worth quoting,

> *Eccmaing mordail ind Eirinn, teit dano Adamnan co forgla cleirech n-Eirenn lais 7 sóerais iarum na mna. As éat so dono ceithri cána Eirenn .i. cain Patraic gan [n]a chleirchiu do marbad, 7 cain Adamnain gan [n]a mna do marbad, cain Daire ga[n] bú do marbad, 7 Cain domnaig can toirimtecht etir.*

There chanced to be a great convention in Ireland. So Adamnán with the pick of Ireland's clerics went (thither) and freed the women. Now these are the four Laws of Erin: Patrick's law, not to kill the clerics; and Adamnán's law, not to kill women: Dáire's law, not to kill kine; and the law of Sunday, not to transgress at all (theron).[132]

Pádraig Ó Riain dates the compilation of the commentary attached to *Félire Óengusso*, of which this quote forms part, to between 1170 and 1174.[133] The compiler had, of course, earlier material at his disposal and Ó Riain details many of the sources.[134] These Middle Irish scholia are revealing. In the first instance they are the main sources for our knowledge that the law of Patrick was concerned with the protection of clerics, because, as already noted, no text of that law survives. Furthermore, they give the impression that, not only were the four laws recognized as being the most important *cána* historically, but that they had current application. None of the other *cána*, such as the laws of Columba or Ciarán, is mentioned as being among the chief laws of Ireland. Presumably, this is because these were temporary laws designed to meet some crisis of the moment. Laws protecting clerics and women, providing against the stealing of cattle, and enforcing Sunday observance, are, on the other hand, required on a continuing basis.[135] It is worth speculating that the specific reference to the four *cána* in these sources indicates that they were still considered relevant, even if evidence for them being enforced is lacking. However, it must be remembered that the scholia have many chronological layers and need to be treated with a great deal of care. Nevertheless, there is a definite interest in the origins of *LxI* in this material as it also includes, in a short version, the story about Adomnán and his mother Rónnat on the battlefield of Brega, a more detailed version of which, as we shall see, appears in the preface to *LxI*.[136]

---

131 Stokes and Strachan, *Thes. Pal*, ii, 306. **132** Stokes, *Félire Óengusso*, pp 210–11; Kenney, *Sources*, p. 237 and p. 481. **133** Ó Riain, *Feastdays*, pp 173–203, esp. 202. **134** Ibid., pp 183–95. **135** 'At éat so dono ceithri cána Eirenn ...' (Stokes, *Félire Óengusso*, p. 210). **136** Stokes, *Félire Óengusso*, pp 210–11.

Betha Adamnáin

That interest in Adomnán and his doings was alive and active in the second half of the tenth century is evident from another text, an Irish life of Adomnán, *Betha Adamnáin*.[137] This 'miserable production, full of anachronisms and absurdities',[138] not only 'provides us with a unique view of the monastic power politics of its time',[139] but gives us an indication of how Adomnán and *LxI* were viewed at that particular juncture. With Kells the likely location of its composition, it has been dated to between 956 and 963 by the text's editors,[140] with other scholars suggesting the 970s.[141] While the work purports to be a life of Adomnán and makes reference to contemporary historical figures, it is often outrageously inaccurate. Máire Herbert and Pádraig Ó Riain forensically examined the text by reference to the known historical facts of both Adomnán's time and the tenth century and found it to reflect the latter.[142] They were able to show that many of the described episodes in Adomnán's life were, in fact, occurrences contemporary with the author's own time. For instance, Congal mac Fergusa, a king of Tara, who features in the text, is, in fact, a proxy for Congalach mac Maile Mithig, king of Tara, who died violently in 956. Congalach's interests and those of the Columban community did not coinside and the author sought to capitalize on his death by portraying it, through the medium of Congal's violent death, as being the consequence of his opposition to the interests of the Columban community.[143]

A fundamental feature of the text is the relationship between secular and ecclesiastical areas of authority, with Adomnán being portrayed as having the power to dispose of kings who oppose him.[144] *Betha Adamnáin* is claiming this power, in no uncertain terms, for Columba's current successors. By the tenth century the hagiographer was less concerned with asserting the subject's sainthood and more with establishing his secular power.[145]

The question must be asked as to why the propagandist used as his vehicle a life of Adomnán rather than a life of Columba. Máire Herbert suggests that the decision was partly influenced by the probable availability in Kells of sources on Adomnán's life, including some material brought directly from Iona. Furthermore, the aspect of Adomnán's life that saw him as a statesman in the world of powerful rulers, including his promotion of *LxI*, was the aspect that was important for his successors in the tenth century.[146] On a practical level, the com-

---

137 Herbert and Ó Riain, *Betha Adamnáin*. **138** Reeves, *Adamnán*, p. xl, n. a. **139** Herbert, *Iona, Kells and Derry*, p. 179. **140** Herbert and Ó Riain, *Betha Adamnáin*, p. 8. **141** C. Breatnach, 'Review of Herbert and Ó Riain, *Betha Adamnáin*', *Éigse*, 26 (1992), pp 77–87; M. Ó Briain, 'Herbert and Ó Riain, *Betha Adamnáin*', *Studia Hibernica*, 27 (1993), pp 155–8. See T.O. Clancy, 'Adomnán in medieval Gaelic literary tradition' in Wooding (ed.), *Adomnán of Iona*, pp 112–13. **142** See Herbert and Ó Riain, *Betha Adamnáin*; Herbert, *Iona, Kells and Derry*, pp 151–79. **143** Herbert, *Iona, Kells and Derry*, p. 175. **144** Ibid., p. 174. For observations on the non-political aspects of the text see J. Carey, 'Varieties of supernatural contact in the Life of Adamnán' in J. Carey, M. Herbert and P. Ó Riain (eds), *Studies in Irish hagiography: saints and scholars* (Dublin, 2001), pp 49–62. **145** Herbert, *Iona, Kells and Derry*, p. 176. **146** Ibid., p. 177.

piler of *Betha Adamnáin*, faced with the task of finding or inventing episodes in Adomnán's life to proxy for the events of the tenth century about which he was concerned, would have an easier task than if he was using Columba's life, particularly with the details of the latter being so well known already. It is reasonable to conclude, therefore, that this text reveals the perception of Adomnán among his community in the second half of the tenth century and the perception that they wished to promote. *Lex Innocentium* features at the forefront of their efforts, it being one of only two actual historical realities to feature.[147] Of the text's eighteen paragraphs, the first is introductory and the second relates to Adomnán's banishment of a devil.[148] Paragraph 3 relates a story, set in a meeting where Adomnán 'was promulgating his Law' and, significantly, is confined to its involvement with women.[149] Paragraph 7 deals with a situation where one Conall Oircnech declares that he will 'not accept the Law of Adamnán', with Adomnán responding, 'Conall will have a short life, he will die a dog's death and no ruler of Tethba will ever descend from him'.[150] Adomnán was, therefore, important and it behoved one to respect his law. It has been pointed out that *Betha Adamnáin* was composed in Kells at a time, or thereabouts, when, as we saw above, the annals refer to the abbots as the successors of Columba and Adomnán.[151] The Raphoe connection with Adomnán and *LxI* will, shortly, become manifest. Were the joint abbacies between Kells and Raphoe the cause or the consequence of what was, clearly, a special relationship, particularly concerning Adomnán, between the two houses?

Paragraphs 1–27
In terms of the devolution of *LxI* over the years, the most important source from the tenth/eleventh centuries is, without doubt, the text's Middle Irish first twenty-seven paragraphs. These have been dated, on linguistic grounds, to the second half of the tenth or the beginning of the eleventh century and it has been suggested that the entire text was compiled at the end of the tenth century, or the beginning of the eleventh,[152] and after *Betha Adamnáin*.[153] The text starts by describing the plight of women before Adomnán emancipated them, detailing their domestic travails and their forced involvement in warfare.[154] It goes on to

---

147 Ibid., p. 152. The other event is the Northumbrian attack on Brega in 685, which is depicted in paragraph 12. **148** *Betha Adamnáin* paragraphs 1 and 2. **149** Ibid., paragraph 3. **150** Ibid., paragraph 7. **151** Herbert and Ó Riain, *Betha Adamnáin*, p. 4. **152** Ní Dhonnchadha, 'An edition of Cáin Adomnáin', p. 20, n. 62 and p. 28. **153** Herbert and Ó Riain, *Betha Adamnáin*, p. 21. **154** *LxI*, paragraphs 2 and 3 respectively. See Márkus, *Adomnán's 'Law of the Innocents'*, pp 4–5, where he is of the view that these paragraphs are wildly exaggerated. On the basis of paragraph 52, which is the only other paragraph to mention female involvement in military engagements, he concedes that women may have been involved in certain kinds of warfare. However, we have seen in the last chapter that 52 also was a later addition. It is, therefore, unlikely that women were employed as troops in Adomnán's time. See Máirín Ní Dhonnchadha's discussion in 'An edition of Cáin Adomnáin', pp 29–32, where she agrees with this view.

describe the scene to which we have already referred, where Adomnán and his mother Rónnat come upon the aftermath of a battle in Brega. This incident is described in shorter form in the commentary to *Félire Óengusso*.[155] The text proceeds to inform us that Rónnat reacts to the scene by demanding of her son that he free women from involvement in war. Adomnán is initially reluctant to undertake such a difficult task. However an angel visited him and assured him of the Lord's support in his labours and took him to the Plain of Birr. Adomnán undertook the task of freeing women and overcame the stern opposition of named kings.

This text continues the theme that was touched upon in *Betha Adamnáin*, that it behoved all to abide by Adomnán's law on pain of facing his wrath and, presumably, that of his successors. Not only that, but it would be prudent to make generous contributions also, because Adomnán is quoted as saying,

> If you do not do good to my community on behalf of the women of this world the children you beget will fail, or they will perish in their sins. Scarcity shall fill your larder and the kingdom of heaven will not be yours. You will not flee from Adomnán of Iona by your meanness or falsehood.[156]

It is made quite clear that Raphoe is the church of Adomnán. Raphoe is the site of the stone chest in which Rónnat buried Adomnán in her efforts to persuade him to take up the task of freeing women,[157] and further in the text the expected contributions are mentioned: 'a horse every quarter-year to his relics, to his heir, to be brought to the bath in Raphoe, but that is only for queens. Other women give according to their ability'.[158] It seems clear that by the year 1000 or so, Raphoe had possession of Adomnán, his cult and his law, presumably by agreement within the Columban community and scholars are agreed that the preface was compiled and preserved there.[159] It has been suggested that the entire tract of *LxI*, including the Middle Irish, Latin and Old Irish sections, was, in fact, compiled by the same single individual in Raphoe.[160]

What is most notable, however, is the extent to which the preface is women-orientated. The law is presented as being exclusively for the benefit of women, with no mention of the other innocents. The compiler, in the first paragraph, sets out his stall by contextualizing the law against the background of the history of the world up to the time of Adomnán, during all of which 'Women were in servitude and oppression'.[161] They were granted their freedom, not by virtue of

---

155 Stokes, *Félire Óengusso*, pp 210–11. See also Ní Dhonnchadha, 'An edition of Cáin Adomnáin', pp 29–30. **156** *LxI*, paragraph 27. See Márkus, *Adomnán's 'Law of the Innocents'*, p. 16 for translation of the text. **157** *LxI*, paragraph 14. **158** *LxI*, paragraph 23. See Márkus, *Adomnán's 'Law of the Innocents'*, p. 15, n. 23. **159** Ní Dhonnchadha, 'An edition of Cáin Adomnáin', p. 28 and p. 42; Márkus, *Adomnán's 'Law of the Innocents'*, p. 4; Lacey, *Kingdoms*, pp 248–9. **160** Ní Dhonnchadha, 'An edition of Cáin Adomnáin', p. 28. **161** *LxI*, paragraph 1.

their place as one of the innocents, but because of their womanhood, 'for a mother is a venerable treasure, a mother is a good treasure, the mother of saints and bishops and just men ...'[162] Rónnat, Adomnán's mother, almost steals the show. It is she who first expresses her horror at the scene, graphically describing the slaughter of women and their babes, of the aftermath of the battle in Brega.[163] She initiates the reaction, which through the most forceful persuasion of her son, ultimately leads to the emancipation of women.

There is an implication throughout the text that, at the time of its compilation, women had been successfully emancipated. For instance, it is stated that, 'After the coming of Adomnán now, a good woman is not deprived of her testimony on earth'.[164] If that was not the factual position, the text's credibility would have been seriously undermined because it seems to be addressed directly to women, 'Adomnán suffered much hardship for your sake, O women, so that half of the house is yours and there is a place for your chair in the other half'.[165] But all of these benefits had to be paid for and, as we have seen, to Raphoe. There is no such thing as a free lunch, certainly not from Raphoe anyway, for:

> Women said and promised that they would give half their household to Adomnán for delivering them from the bondage and oppression in which they had been. Adomnán would take only a little from them i.e. a white tunic with a black border from each penitent spouse, a scruple of gold from each ruler's wife, a linen cloth from each sub-chieftian's wife, seven loaves from each unfree woman, a wether from every small flock, and the first lamb that is born in every house, whether it be black or white, for God and for Adomnán.[166]

The message is clear: Adomnán's law freed women, and their continued privileges will be ensured by his successors, provided women fulfil their obligations to the community of Raphoe. Máirín Ní Donnchadha points out that the word *cáin* primarily means regulation, but that its secondary meaning is punishment (by fine or otherwise) for breach of regulation.[167] On reading paragraphs 1–27 it is this latter implication, with its emphasis on the payment of dues to Raphoe, which appears foremost, while the former is suggested by the core provisions, which were examined in the last chapter. We do not know when the *LxI* of the annals was first given the name *Cáin Adomnáin*. The sources do not disclose use of that specific terminology until the Middle Irish period, when, it is suggested, the secondary meaning of *cáin* may have been its intended meaning.[168]

---

162 Ibid., paragraph 4. See Ní Dhonnchadha, 'Birr and the Law of the Innocents', pp 20–31 for a detailed treatment of women and the law, crimes against women and Adomnán's expectations of women. **163** *LxI*, paragraph 7. **164** Ibid., paragraph 4. **165** Ibid., paragraph 5. See Márkus, *Adomnán's 'Law of the Innocents'*, p. 5, n. 11. **166** *LxI*, paragraph 24. **167** Ní Dhonnchadha, 'Birr and the Law of the Innocents', p. 16. **168** There has been scholarly debate as to whether the *cána* were primarily income-gathering mechanisms or genuine meas-

Paragraph 33

The dating of paragraph 33 of *LxI* presents a problem. In the last chapter we concluded that it was a later addition to the text. It is not possible to say how much later. As we saw, Máirín Ní Dhonnchadha tentatively suggested that it may have been added around the time when the law was being renewed in 727.[169] However, because it is concerned exclusively with protecting women, it is unlikely that it would have been added until, at least, 734, when the Law of Patrick was first promulgated. In fact, it could have originated at any time between then and 1000 when the text of *LxI* was compiled in Raphoe. It is being treated here as a tenth-/eleventh-century text solely because of certain similarities with the Middle Irish preface and it is acknowledged that it could have originated earlier. The visit of the angel is rather similar to the visits of angels described in paragraph 15, and the mention of Mary and motherhood echo paragraphs 9 and 4.[170] Again it is womanhood rather than innocence that is the defining factor. There is a certain intemperance of tone, especially in the penalties provided, which is reminiscent of the exaggerated tone, to our ears, of paragraphs 1–27. All in all, it is hard to disagree with the comparisons drawn by Gilbert Márkus between these two sections of the text.[171] What is important, however, is that paragraph 33 is another later text, whether tenth/eleventh century or somewhat before that, confirming the move away from innocents in general to women exclusively.

The Fragmentary annals *and* Fís Adomnáin

There are some further snippets to be found in the tenth-/eleventh-century sources that throw some light on the perception of Adomnán and *LxI* at that time. Of particular interest is the annal entry for the year 697 contained in the *Fragmentary annals of Ireland*.[172] The relevant entry reads, 'Adamnán came to Ireland and made known the Law of the Innocents to the Irish people, i.e., not to kill children or women'.[173] These Middle Irish annals are thought to have been compiled towards the middle of the eleventh century, from various sources.[174] It uses the term 'Law of the Innocents', like AU's description, and not *Cáin Adomnáin*, or even 'his law' or some similar term. This could be a carry-over from whatever source the compiler was using for this entry, probably from the Chronicle of Ireland in one of its manifestations. It seems probable that the expla-

---

ures to better society. See Hughes, *Sources*, p. 82; eadem, *The church in early Irish society* (London, 1966), pp 150–3 and 168–9; F. Ó Briain, 'The hagiography of Leinster' in J. Ryan (ed.), *Féilsgríbhinn Eóin Mhic Néill: essays and studies presented to Professor Eoin MacNeill on the occasion of his seventieth birthday, May 15th, 1938* (Dublin, 1940), pp 457–63; C. Doherty, 'The use of relics in early Ireland' in P. Ní Chatháin and M. Richter (eds), *Ireland and Europe in the early Middle Ages: learning and literature* (Stuttgart, 1996), p. 96; Ó Corráin, 'Ireland *c*.800', p. 584. Grigg, 'Aspects', pp 48–50. For a useful summary of views see Wycherley, *Relics*, p. 143 and pp 150–8. **169** Ní Dhonnchadha, 'The Law of Adomnán: a translation', p. 56. **170** *LxI* paragraphs 15, 9 and 4. **171** Márkus, *Adomnán's 'Law of the Innocents'*, p. 6. **172** See Chapter 4, p. 98. **173** ' .i. gan maca gan mna do mbarbhadh'. Radner, *Fragmentary annals*, s. a. 697, pp 44–5. **174** Ibid., p. xxvi.

nation of what the law was, 'not to kill children or women', was the compiler's own gloss. If it was a statement of his understanding of the law, it is significant that he includes children, and indeed puts them first. This was his opinion of what the Law of the Innocents meant. This entry may indicate, therefore, that in the perspective of some in the eleventh century, *LxI* was still a law for innocents and not just for women exclusively.

One final snippet from the Middle Irish period worth mentioning is the work known as *Fís Adomnáin*, or Adomnán's Vision. It purports to be an account of a vision that Adomnán had while attending the meeting in Birr in 697. In fact, it is a description of heaven and hell by a later ecclesiastic who chose to ascribe it to Adomnán.[175] James F. Kenney speculated that the author may have been a member of the Columban community, with a special devotion to Adomnán, who was drawing on a tradition that Adomnán had had such a vision.[176] It is another indication of the high regard in which Adomnán was held in the Middle Irish period and an illustration of the continuing awareness of *LxI* three centuries after its enactment, by locating the vision in Birr.

It is reasonable to conclude, therefore, that the tenth/eleventh centuries saw a revival of interest in *LxI*. The evidence of the sources is that this interest was not merely academic, but that the law was seen as having practical application. It is unlikely that so much emphasis would have been placed on a fossil. The Columban community seem to have delegated responsibility for the law to Raphoe, an opportunity which the northern church was determined to exploit. With the exception of the *Fragmentary annals* entry, all references to *LxI* over this period are as a law for the protection of women solely. They are seen as having merited Adomnán's protection, not because they do not bear arms, but by virtue of their womanhood.

SIXTEENTH- SEVENTEENTH-CENTURY AFTERLIFE

Rawlinson MS B 512

Whether our next encounter with *LxI* had a practical objective is less clear. The last chapter noted that one of the surviving manuscripts containing the terms of the law, R, is believed to have been made in the fifteenth/sixteenth century and that scholars are of the opinion that it derives from the Old Book of Raphoe.[177] It is not part of a collection of manuscripts containing mainly legal material, such

---

175 R.I. Best and O. Bergin (eds), *Lebor na hUidre: the Book of the Dun Cow* (Dublin, 1929), pp 67. See also M. McNamara, *The Apocrypha in the Irish church* (Dublin, 1975), p. 126 (no. 100); D. Dumville, 'Towards an interpretation of *Fís Adamnáin*', *Studia Celtica*, 12/13 (1977–8), pp 62–77; J. Carey, E. Nic Cárthaigh and C. Ó Dochartaigh (eds), *The end and beyond: medieval Irish eschatology* (2 vols, Aberystwyth, 2014), for a treatment of *Fís Adamnáin*, throughout the work, in the context of a comprehensive study of medieval Irish texts devoted to themes of death, judgment and afterlife generally. **176** Kenney, *Sources*, pp 444–5. **177** Ibid., p. 245; Márkus, *Adomnán's 'Law of the Innocents'*, p. 4; Ní Dhonnchadha, 'Birr and the Law of the Innocents', p. 16.

as might be required by a lawyer, being preceded by an Old Irish treatise on the Psalter and followed by the poem *Sreth a salmaib súad slán*. As mentioned in the last chapter, the manuscript is thought to have been written by members of the Ó Maoil Chonaire family in Cullentragh, Rathmolyon, Co. Meath.[178] It could be mistaken, however, to impose modern ideas on the division of labour on fifteenth-/sixteenth-century Ireland. It is not inconceivable that a member of the learned class of that time would have had wide interests such as would require a manuscript containing material of many and various genres, including a copy of a *cáin* which still formed part of the corpus of Irish law. While it is highly unlikely that *LxI* was enforced in these later centuries, due to ecclesiastical reform and political change, it was still remembered as an institution of Gaelic society and this is attested by the fact that a copy of its provisions was made by the Uí Maoil Chonaire in or about the year 1500.

O'Clery MS 2324–40

The final source to be examined in this study of the evolution of *LxI*, and how it was perceived in the centuries following 697, is the second surviving manuscript of the text, the copy made by Mícheál Ó Cléirigh, now preserved in the Bibliothèque Royale, Brussels, B. Unlike R, it is possible to have a clear idea of the circumstances surrounding the making of B and, indeed, the mindsets of those involved.

Ó Cléirigh returned to Ireland from Leuven (Louvain) in 1626.[179] His superiors, Patrick Fleming and Hugh Ward, saw an urgent need to promote a positive image of Ireland and, in particular, its Christian heritage by bringing to the attention of European readers the lives of Irish saints. They also envisaged the preparation of a secular history of Ireland to compliment the ecclesiastical, but the first step was to gather and publish hagiographical material.[180] The 'essential precursor' to the achievement of their objectives was the seeking out and copying of old manuscripts all over Ireland,[181] and so 'Irish lives rescued from oblivion at this stage were deliberately collected and transcribed'.[182] Father Valentine Browne, Ó Cléirigh's contemporary and provincial of the Franciscan order, wrote to him on 15 May 1632 commending him on his efforts in rescuing 'the antiquities of our nation ... from the most stygian darkness in which they were enshrouded'.[183]

The earliest dated transcription by Mícheál Ó Cléirigh is from 28 March 1627: an extract from a book written by Tadhg Ó Cianáin.[184] This is followed

---

178 Chapter 5, p. 120. **179** B. Jennings, 'Míchael Ó Cléirigh, chief of the Four Masters, and his associates' in N. Ó Muraíle (ed.), *Míchael Ó Cléirigh, his associates and St Anthony's College, Louvain* (Dublin, 2008), p. 43. **180** See letter from Patrick Fleming to Hugh Ward dated 24 August 1624, printed in B. Jennings (ed.), 'Documents from the archives of St Isidore's College, Rome', *Analecta Hibernica*, 6 (1934), pp 2, 16; B. Cunningham, *The Annals of the Four Masters* (Dublin, 2010), pp 27–8. On the hagiographical researchers generally see R. Sharpe, *Medieval Irish saints' lives: an introduction to 'Vitae Sanctorum Hiberniae'* (Oxford, 1991), pp 39–74. **181** Cunningham, *Four Masters*, p. 41. **182** Sharpe, *Medieval Irish saints' lives*, p. 40. **183** Jennings, 'Míchael Ó Cléirigh, chief of the Four Masters', p. 95. **184** P. Walsh, 'The trav-

by his copy of *LxI* made on 31 March 1627.[185] He subsequently, in May 1628, made copies of the *Betha Adamnáin* and *Fís Adamnáin*.[186] As we have seen, it is probable that manuscripts relating to Adomnán were readily available to him in his own locality, and indeed Adomnán's, in Donegal and, in particular, the Old Book of Raphoe or a copy of it. When sending his copies of *Betha Adamnáin* and *Fís Adamnáin* to Leuven, Ó Cléirigh appended a note to the effect that he also had a copy of *LxI* but that he wished to retain it for the moment with a view to consulting Flann son of Cairbre Mac Aodhagáin relating to difficult legal matters in it. The text of the note and a translation are quoted hereunder:

> *Atá Cain Adhamnain agam (amhail ro shaer mná ar fhecht agus sluaigheadh agus o gach moghsaine) agus dá rabhtai aga hiarraidh, cuireadh fios cugam ar a ceand, agus is aire atu aga congbháil an tan-so d'eagla nach budh eidir do Bhaothghalach o 'na sduider aire do thabairt dhi, agus a nuinighin go ffaicfinn Flann mac Cairpre Meic Aedhagain da fechain an ccuirfeadh urlannacha ar na neithibh cruaidhe bheanus le breitheamhnus fileat innte.*

> I have Cáin Adhamnáin (which freed women from military expeditions and hosting and from every slavery) and if it be required, let him send to me for it, and the reason I am keeping it now is for fear that Baothghalach being engaged in study, might not be able to look after it, and in the expectation that I might see Flann son of Cairbre Mac Aodhagáin in the hope that he might clarify [*lit.* give a handle on] some of the difficult matters relating to [legal] judgment that are in it.[187]

It is clear from the foregoing that Ó Cléirigh, like almost all those before him going back to *Félire Oengusso*, saw *LxI* as a law for the welfare of women. It is evident, however, that something of a legal nature bothered him about the law and, more particularly, about his copy of it. Why did he postpone forwarding his manuscript to Leuven, pending a consultation with Mac Aodhagáin? This is too intriguing a question to ignore and an attempt to answer it may, just possibly, yield some insight into attitudes to *LxI* in the first half of the seventeenth century, particularly among the class of person to which Mícheál Ó Cléirigh belonged.

Flann Mac Aodhagáin was a lawyer and historian living in Ballymacegan Castle, now known as Redwood Castle, in the parish of Lorrha in north Co.y Tipperary. He was a member of the Mac Aodhagáin family of lawyers who for

---

els of Míchéal Ó Cléirigh' in Ó Muraíle (ed.), *Míchéal Ó Cléirigh, his associates and St Anthony's College, Louvain*, p. 137. **185** This is the date given by Ó Cléirigh in the colophon at the end of his manuscript. See references to it in Ní Dhonnchadha, 'Birr and the Law of the Innocents', p. 15, Ó Néill and Dumville, *Cáin Adomnáin*, p. 51, n. 218 and Walsh, 'The travels of Míchéal Ó Cléirigh', p. 137. **186** Herbert and Ó Riain, *Betha Adamnáin*, p. vii; Jennings, 'Míchéal Ó Cléirigh, chief of the Four Masters', pp 49–50. **187** Ó Cléirigh, MS 4190–200, Bibliothèque Royale, Brussels, folio 46v; Jennings, 'Míchéal Ó Cléirigh, chief of the Four Masters', p. 50.

centuries had acted as lawyers for many of the ruling families of western and central Ireland, including McCarthy More of Desmond, Butler of Ormond, O'Kennedy of Ormond, Burke of Clanricard, O'Connor of Offaly, Mageoghegan of Kenelagh, O'Farrell of Annaly, O'Connor Roe, O'Conor Don, O'Rourke of Brefny, O'Connor Sligo, O'Dowd of Tireagh and Barret of Tirawley.[188] In fact, they were the most active and influential of the post-Norman legal families. They had a number of law schools, including one in Ballymacegan Castle. Mícheál Ó Cléirigh had strong personal and family connections with the Meic Aodhagáin. It appears that he had studied in one of their schools,[189] possibly even Ballymacegan.[190] Bernadette Cunningham points out that there should be no surprise at the contact between the Ó Cléirigh and the Mac Aodhagáin families as a century earlier 'there was already a tradition of Ó Cléirigh and Mac Aodhagáin co-operation on historical projects, as evidenced by the manuscript miscellany now known as Bodleian Library MS Laud Misc 610, produced in the 1450s for Edmund Mac Richard Butler' in which the two main scribes were Seaán Buidhe Ó Cléirigh and Giolla na Naomh Mac Aodhagáin.[191] A meeting of Mícheál Ó Cléirigh and Flann Mac Aodhagáin did take place towards the end of 1628 or early in 1629. A letter dated January/February 1629 from Malachy O'Queely, then vicar apostolic of Killaloe, to Fr Hugh Ward in Leuven mentions that he had sent Mícheál to Ormond 'parte of my diocese to write there for a time'.[192] It has been suggested that Ó Cléirigh may, in fact, have remained in the south over the entire winter of 1628–9, giving him the opportunity to carry out substantial research on the manuscripts in the possession of Flann Mac Aodhagáin and elsewhere in the north Munster region.[193] Ó Cléirigh may have brought his copy of *LxI* to Ballymacegan with him. In any event, after completing his discussions with Mac Aodhagáin, at some point in time, it was duly transmitted to Leuven where it was retained, ultimately ending up in the book now known as O'Clery MS 2324–40, carefully preserved in the Bibliothèque Royale in Brussels.

This is a collection of Ó Cléirigh copy manuscripts that have been bound into book form containing 356 folios.[194] The book measures approximately 15cm by 18cm and is approximately 6cm in thickness. For the most part there is text on each side of each folio. *Lex Innocentium* commences on folio 76r and ends on folio 82v. There are 22 lines of text on each of the folios, including the first folio, where the 22 lines are in addition to the colophon, already mentioned, at the top of the page, and the last folio where the final two lines of the 22 comprise of the colophon giving the date that the copy was made. The only exception is folio 80v. The last two lines of paragraph 31 (clauses of malediction) appear at the top of folio 80v. The last word on the second line is the beginning of the first word

---

188 Kelly, *Guide*, pp 253–4. **189** Cunningham, *Four Masters*, p. 247. **190** Ibid., p. 250. **191** Ibid., p. 251. **192** Jennings, 'Documents from the archives of St Isidore's College, Rome', pp 217–18; idem, 'Mícháel Ó Cléirigh, chief of the Four Masters', p. 53. **193** Cunningham, *Four Masters*, p. 253. **194** Breatnach, *Four Masters*, p. 137, n. 9.

of paragraph 32, which continues onto the end of the third line. From that point the page is blank.[194a] Space for 19 further lines on folio 80v has been left, assuming the norm of 22 per page is followed. At the top of the next page, folio 81r, paragraph 34 commences. However, the remainder of paragraph 32 has not been omitted. It has been copied onto a separate chit measuring approximately 11cm by 4cm. This slip of paper has been bound into the book between folios 80v and 81r. The text is somewhat cramped, and the last sentence, that appears in the Rawlinson manuscript, has been omitted being replaced by the words *et cetera* in abbreviated form *etc*. Paragraph 33 has been omitted entirely. It appears clear that the space was left for the insertion of paragraph 33. It is difficult to envisage any other explanation for leaving such a gap in the text.

In the Rawlinson manuscript paragraph 33 is written in approximately 43 lines of text. By comparing 43 lines of that text, from other portions of the manuscript, with the equivalent portions of the Brussels text, it would appear that approximately 21 lines of text in the Brussels manuscript equate to 43 in Rawlinson. Ó Cléirigh left space for approximately 19 lines on folio 80v. Would this have been sufficient space for paragraph 33? Perhaps it would. The method of calculating a requirement of 21 lines is somewhat imprecise. On the other hand it is possible that sufficient space was not left and this could be the answer to our quandary. This is somewhat unlikely. He could have inserted an extra folio. He had already employed the somewhat untidy use of the inserted chit for part of paragraph 32. If he had put all of 32 on the chit, he would have gained space, in excess of an extra line, to use for the insertion of 33. Surely this would have been sufficient? There are many unanswered questions. However, it is quite clear from any reading of the manuscript that, for some reason, Mícheál Ó Cléirigh decided, quite deliberately, to exclude paragraph 33 from his copy of *LxI*, either temporarily or permanently.

While it will never be possible to know for certain, a persuasive case can be made that it was paragraph 33 that Ó Cléirigh wished to discuss with Mac Aodhagáin and a suggestion can be proffered as to what his concerns might have been. It immediately comes to mind that Ó Cléirigh may have had difficulty with the Latin text of paragraph 33. This is the only part of the text that is not in Irish, Ó Cléirigh's native tongue, apart from portions of paragraph 32. However, he had at his disposal in Donegal men whose knowledge of Latin would have been extensive. These included Fr Bernardino (Maolmhuire) Ó Cléirigh, an older brother of Mícheál, whose seminary education had been in Salamanca and Leuven, and Fr Muiris Ultach, a former provincial of the Franciscan order in Ireland and who, in fact, was able to supply Ó Cléirigh with Irish translations of Latin texts.[195] P.A. Breatnach considered the question of Ó Cléirigh's competence in Latin and concludes 'The understanding that Ó Cléirigh was "ignorant of Latin" … is clearly

---

194a Based on a copy of folio 80v received from the Bibliothèque Royale, Brussels. However, this is not a true copy as the chit mentioned below has been placed over and is covering nine lines of the text of paragraph 32. See www.celt.dias.ie. **195** Cunningham, *Four Masters*, p. 39.

untenable'.[196] Obviously there would be no need to consult Flann Mac Aodhagáin about the Latin text, as such. Might there have been a query relating to the Old Irish of the text? In the preface to his Irish glossary, *Foclóir nó sanasán nua*, which was published in 1643, shortly before his death, Ó Cléirigh acknowledged a number of individuals who gave him scholarly support. Among these he mentions Baothgalach Ruadh Mac Aodhagáin, from whom he had personally learned much about the older forms of the Irish language.[197] It is clear, therefore, that Ó Cléirigh had a good knowledge of Old Irish and it is unlikely that he would have needed to consult Flann Mac Aodhagáin on any query relating to it. On the basis that he had finished his copy before he consulted Mac Aodhagáin, any advice received requiring a change to his copy would require an amendment in the form of an interlineation on the text. On a close examination of the text of paragraphs 1 to 32 and 34 to 53 it is not possible to find an obvious correction or amendment that might have been necessitated arising out of a consultation with Mac Aodhagáin.[198] Of course, it is possible that, having consulted, no amendment was required. In any event Ó Cléirigh is quite explicit that it was on 'difficult matters relating to legal judgment' – *ar na neithibh cruaidhe bhenus le breitheamhnus* – that he wished to consult.[199] It could have been on such a matter, but not connected with paragraph 33. However the same considerations relating to amendments to the text would apply. No such considerations apply if it is accepted that it was something involving paragraph 33 that prompted Ó Cléirigh to hold back his copy of *LxI*. It is quite clear that there was indecision on his part relating to that paragraph. He broke off copying paragraph 32 and finished it on a separate small slip, leaving, probably, just sufficient space on the page to insert paragraph 33. He commenced paragraph 34 on a new page. Clearly, he was between two minds on 33. We also know that he was awaiting advice. These two facts, allied to the fact that there is no indication of any question or indecision in any other part of the text, makes it reasonable to conclude that it is probable that paragraph 33 was the matter that Mícheál Ó Cléirigh wished to discuss with Flann Mac Aodhagáin.

He required an explanation of 'difficult things ... relating to the law', or, 'difficult matters relating to legal judgment that are in it'. Paragraph 33 is quasi-legal. It stipulates a crime, the killing of a woman, and it prescribes penalties, including death and amputation. Paragraphs 41 and 42 also forbid the killing of women and prescribe penalties in the form of full fines. There is clearly a glaring contradiction. It is suggested that it was an explanation of the contradiction that Ó Cléirigh sought from Mac Aodhagáin. This is all the more likely as he saw women at the centre of the law. It is further suggested that the latter advised Ó Cléirigh that paragraphs 41 and 42 better represented the law than paragraph 33 and that therefore Ó Cléirigh did not feel obliged to insert it before he sent his

---

[196] Breatnach, *Four Masters*, p. 140, n. 18. [197] Cunningham, *Four Masters*, p. 248. [198] Minor amendments have been made here and there. For instance in line 21 folio 77r, line 22 folio 78v and lines 6 and 7 folio 80r. It is clear, however, that none of these could have been the subject-matter of the discussion. [199] See Bernadette Cunningham's translation: 'if he could explain difficult things it contains relating to the law'. *Four Masters*, p. 252.

copy of *LxI* to Leuven. Seeing the contradiction within the text, he felt obliged to check it out.

It may, at first sight, seem unlikely that he would concern himself about the content of the manuscript he was tasked with copying. It is necessary to look briefly at his background to see that this is not, in fact, unlikely at all. Mícheál Ó Cléirigh was a member of the *Seanchas* tradition and class in the Ireland of his day. *Seanchas* is the learning and lore of Gaelic Irish civilization and the *modus operandi* of its practitioners. Annals were written in Ireland from the sixth century. Initially this work was carried out in the monasteries, Armagh, Iona, Clonmacnoise and Kildare. After the reform of the monasteries in the twelfth century, a learned class developed who took over this responsibility.[200] In the early medieval period *seanchas* included *seanchas* narrative history and law. Many branches developed, including *scéalsheanchas* 'the lore of stories', *laíodhsheanchas* 'the lore of poetry', *naomhsheanchas* 'the lore of saints' and *dinnsheanchas* 'the lore of places', in short, it comprised the lore of an entire civilization. This was entrusted to a learned class who were taught in specially established schools. They were the possessors and custodians of society's memory of the past. Their knowledge gave them power. It was largely exclusive to them. Their function in society was to know it and to guard it, and when required, to apply it in the resolution of disputes. Its survival was their responsibility and solely theirs. If they, as a class, did not ensure the survival of *seanchas*, no one else would.

Viewed in this light, the work and doings of the Franciscans are seen in their historical context. Many of those involved in the Irish college in Leuven were of the Gaelic Irish learned class. The foundation of the college itself was largely brought about by Flaithrí Ó Maoil Chonaire (Florence Conry), the Franciscan who was a major influence in the Spanish court. He was of the Ó Maoil Chonaire family who were, since *c.*1136, historians to the Síol Muireadhaigh, which included the Uí Chonchobhair of Connaught and their kinsmen. 'As custodians of this literary and cultural landscape [*seanchas*] the Uí Mhaolchonaire were responsible for the preservation of the past'.[201] As we have seen, one of them is thought to have been involved, coincidentally, in the making of R. At least six of the Flaithrí Ó Maoil Chonaire's ancestors were given the title of *ollamh* in the annals. Many of them were involved in the compilation of several of Connacht's most significant annalistic collections. He himself was 'classed among the leading Gaelic scholars of his time'.[202] He experienced the encroachments of the English crown into the milieu of the learned families, during a

---

200 E. Bhreathnach, 'The *seanchas* tradition in late medieval Ireland' in E. Bhreathnach and B. Cunningham (eds), *Writing Irish history: the Four Masters and their world* (Dublin, 2007), pp 19–23, for a succinct yet comprehensive description, from which the outline here is taken. **201** B. Hazard, *Faith and patronage: the political career of Flaithri Ó Maolchonaire, c.1560–1629* (Dublin, 2010), p.11. See also idem, 'Flaithrí, Firbisigh and Maoilechlainn: Three Uí Mhaoil Chonaire brothers in the late sixteenth and early seventeenth centuries' in Purcell et al. (eds), *Clerics, kings and Vikings*, pp 209–16. **202** Hazard, *Faith and patronage*, p. 13.

period which has been identified as a 'point of eclipse' for 'the politically enfranchised literati [who] were being eliminated in Ireland'.[203] His ethos must have affected Leuven and those who worked there.

The Ó Maoil Chonaire family had close links with the Mac an Bháird family of Donegal of which Fr Hugh Ward, Mícheál Ó Cléirigh's superior, was a member.[204] The family had for many years been the historians of the Uí Domhnaill of Tír Chonaill, and the responsibility to preserve the *seanchas* down through the centuries rested on them. The Uí Cléirigh themselves occupied positions of learning with the Uí Domhnaill for generations. Mícheál (Tadhg Cam by birth, Mícheál being his name in religion) was son of Donnchadh, son of Uilliam, son of Tuathal, son of Tadhg Cam, who was son of Dearmaid of the Three Schools, so called because he taught literature, history and poetry.[205] Hugh Ward would possibly have met Mícheál's brother Maolmhuire in Salamanca, the latter subsequently becoming guardian of the Franciscan house in Drowes (on the Donegal/Leitrim border). Because of their education and family traditions stretching back for generations these men would have been acutely aware that they were the custodians of *seanchas* with a heavy responsibility in a time of change and conflict. Many joined the Franciscan order, almost as a substitute for the patrons now scattered abroad, and the order and its foundations in Ireland became part of the learned network.[206] These men had a proprietorial attitude to their culture and learning. It was, therefore, in the nature of the beast that Ó Cléirigh should be concerned with the content of this law; all the more so as it was part of Cenél Conaill legacy, the ancestors of the Uí Domhnaill. If, as suggested above, he had studied in the Mac Aodhagáin law school in Ballymacegan, it is likely that he would have had a particular legal awareness.

Notwithstanding all of the above, Ó Cléirigh's primary purpose was to copy saint's lives and to copy them faithfully. In December 1629, Ó Cléirigh copied a life of St Caimín of Inis Cealtra. In a colophon he described it as 'very corrupt, sad, too short in some verses and too long in others, and a great deal of it utter nonsense, but I make my excuse that it was enjoined on me to follow the track of the old books'.[207] Clearly Ó Cléirigh was under orders to copy faithfully, and unquestioningly. Why did he not follow these instructions when copying *LxI*? The answer to this, it is suggested, is that a law was seen differently from a life of a saint and that the instructions to make an exact copy did not apply to the law. When informing Leuven that he was withholding his copy of *LxI*, Mícheál Ó Cléirigh was at pains to assure his superiors that it was a legal query that necessitated the consultation. It is implicit in this that it was acceptable to his superiors that the manuscript should be withheld in those circumstances. Different

---

203 Ibid., p. 17, citing D. Gardiner, '"These are not the things men live by now a days": Sir John Hartington's visit to the O'Neill, 1599', *Cahiers Élisebéthains*, 55 (1999), pp 1–17. **204** Hazard, *Faith and patronage*, pp 12–13. **205** Cunningham, *Four Masters*, pp 176–8. **206** Ibid., p. 283. **207** Ó Cléirigh, MS 2324–40, Bibliothèque Royale, Brussels, folios 264–273v; Jennings, 'Míchéal Ó Cléirigh, chief of the Four Masters', p. 67.

considerations applied to the making of copies of the lives of saints, as it was intended to use those lives later in the production of more complete, rounded works, in Latin, on the Irish saints.[208] As Ó Cléirigh puts it, 'I was directed to follow closely the old books because only a compilation of everything is being abstracted now'.[209] The law, on the other hand, was seen as a living practical thing with experts on it available for consultation. While it is not suggested that *LxI* was being enforced in the seventeenth century – Fleming and Ward had to be reminded or informed that it was a law for women – it was part of the corpus of unchanging Irish law and it was important to record it accurately. If Ó Cléirigh had concerns about it, he would have felt obliged to address and resolve those concerns, being 'naturally drawn by temperament and disposition' to do so.[210]

The position may, therefore, be summarized as follows. We know that Ó Cléirigh had concerns about *LxI* and that these concerns were legal in nature. We know that these legal issues needed to be resolved before his copy manuscript could be sent on to Leuven because he wrote to that effect to his superiors. The concerns impacted in some way on his copy, otherwise he could have sent it on with the other Adomnán material and satisfied his legal curiosity later. We know that Ó Cléirigh and Mac Aodhagáin met over the winter of 1628–9. We can speculate, on good grounds, that paragraph 33 was the object of his concern and, more specifically, the disparities in the penalties it provided relative to paragraphs 41 and 42. We learn from all of this that, in the year 1627, Ó Cléirigh and his associates, the guardians of *seanchas*, regarded *LxI* as a law for women and as an important example of one of the institutions of Irish society that changed so little 'between the Old Irish period and the Flight of the Earls at the beginning of the seventeenth century'.[211]

Thus has been set the scene for one of the most remarkable legal consultations in the history of Western jurisprudence. In the winter of 1628–9, in an Ireland riven by conflict, where the old order was being transformed, two men met in a castle near the flooded banks of the river Shannon, to discuss the finer points of a law enacted 930 years before. It is impossible to find anything comparable, and very difficult to even suggest a similar hypothetical scenario. Two lawyers meeting in the year 2145 to discuss the Magna Carta (1215) at a time when the Western common law system was on the point of collapse would come close! This consultation is an extraordinary testament to the social memory of Gaelic society over a period of nigh on a thousand years. That it concerned a law for the protection of non-combatants and, in the perception of the time, women in particular, makes it all the more remarkable.

* * *

---

208 P. Ó Riain, 'Saints Lives' in Bhreathnach and Cunningham (eds), *Writing Irish history*, p. 38. **209** Jennings, 'Míchéal Ó Cléirigh, chief of the Four Masters', p. 67. **210** Breatnach, *Four Masters*, p. 166. **211** Kelly, *Guide*, p. 241.

It is clear from the foregoing that within fifty years or so of the departure from Birr of those involved in its enactment, *LxI* ceased to be, in perception and presumably in practice, a law for all who did not bear arms in general and became a law for the protection of women and, possibly, children. The protection of clerics was taken by and ceded to Armagh and the Law of Patrick. We cannot know anything of *LxI*'s implementation, or how successful it was in achieving its objectives, but it seems unlikely, given the organization and effort required for its enactment and the detail of its enabling provisions, that it was a flash in the pan. While it is absent from the sources during much of the Viking period, that it had lasting impact is evidenced by its inclusion, in the Middle Irish period, among the four chief *cána* of Ireland, and it makes a significant impact in the second half of the tenth century and into the eleventh. The era of political change and church reform that characterized the twelfth century meant that the early medieval history and context of *LxI* came to an end. Yet, it is clear that *LxI* remained as part of the memory of Gaelic society until the eclipse of that society in the seventeenth century. It is noteworthy that Míchéal Ó Cléirigh was in a position to assume that the lawyer Flann Mac Aodhagáin would be well versed in Adomnán's law and in a position to give it active legal consideration almost a thousand years after its enactment. He would have viewed it as a law that gave recognition and protection to women in Irish society. It might be appropriate, therefore, to conclude this chapter with the following poem, thought to date from the Old Irish period, which purports to be Columba's foretelling of Adomnán.[212]

> He will take his name from my name,
> He will make a law for women
> from the beautiful many-splendoured *Muir nIcht* [eastwards].
> He will be a sage of learning in body (lit. head) and soul,
> He will surpass my goodly rhetoric
> He will pronounce the great law of Birr
> which will take the kingship of Tara from Fínnachta,
> he who will not rise on the strength of Tara.
> Thirty years he will be in the abbacy,
> Adomnán more wonderful than great tales [can tell].

While the poet was writing of Adomnán with the benefit of hindsight, subsequent history shows that in his 'law for women' his foresight would have astonished even himself.

---

212 Ní Dhonnchadha, 'An edition of Cáin Adomnáin', p. 21, taken from Brussels MS 2324. This poem was published by Meyer in Stokes and Meyer, *Archiv fü celtische Lexikographie III*, p. 231 (from the Brussels MS). It was also published by Reeves, *Adamnán*, p. xlii, citing two different MSS (Laud 615, p. 132, and Brussels 5101–4). Ní Dhonnchadha considers it Old Irish.

CHAPTER 7

Lex Innocentium situated: its place in the medieval history of *jus in bello*

THE PEACE OF GOD

Among those scholars who addressed the issue of non-combatants, many of them, for instance, Gillespie, Hartigan and Russell, pointed to the Peace of God movement as the turning-point when their plight was first recognized and legislated for in the Christian West.[1] While there appears to have been an awareness of non-combatant status among Adomnán's contemporaries outside Ireland – Bede's story of Imma being one example mentioned – there is no evidence of legislation or laws for their protection at times of conflict.[2] How attitudes evolved subsequently, particularly with the Carolingians,[3] is of obvious interest. For instance, Charlemagne's capitularies do not attempt to provide protection for non-combatants, apart from widows, orphans and 'humble folk' or 'less powerful people' being taken under his protection.[4] There is no specific recognition of the non-combatant per se, still less, legislative provision for his or her protection at times of conflict.[5] One must, therefore, in common with the scholars already mentioned, move on to the Peace of God movement and, indeed, in common

---

[1] Gillespie, *Laws of war*, ii, 123; Hartigan, *Civilization*, p. 65; Russell, *Just war*, p. 34. [2] See the examination of the barbarian laws in Chapter 2 and the subsequent mention of the Imma incident p. 56. [3] For the Carolingians and attitudes to violence see Brown, *Violence*, pp 69–96. See also, Fouracre, 'Attitudes towards violence', pp 60–75; idem, 'Conflict, power and legitimation in Francia in the late seventh and eighth centuries' in I. Alfonso, H. Kennedy and J. Escalona (eds), *Building legitimacy: political discourses and forms of legitimacy in medieval societies* (Leiden, 2004), pp 3–26; McKitterick, *History and memory*. [4] H.R. Loyn and J. Percival (eds and trans.), *The reign of Charlemagne: documents on Carolingian government and administration* (London, 1975), where Charlemagne did take widows, orphans and 'humble folk' or 'less powerful people' under his protection, see, for example, the following capitularies: Mantua 1 (781), p. 50; Concerning the Saxons 1 (797), p. 54; General Capitulary for the *missi* 5, 30 and 40 (spring 802), p. 54, pp 76–7 and p. 79; Special Capitularies for the *missi* 15 (802), p. 81; Aix 2 (802–3), p. 82. See also P.J. Geary, *Readings in medieval history* (Peterborough, 2003), pp 315–19; Brown, *Violence*, pp 71–6. For a discussion of Charlemagne's coercive missionary practices and Alcuin's response see S. Stofferahn, 'Staying the royal sword: Alcuin and the conversion dilemma in early medieval Europe', *Historian* (2009), pp 461–80. [5] On *ad bellum* see D.A. Bullough, 'Was there a Carolingian anti-war movement', *Early Medieval Europe*, 12 (2003), pp 365–76.

Lex Innocentium situated

with Mathew Strickland who, as stated in the first chapter, pointed to *LxI* as being alone in anticipating the Peace of God movement. Of the latter he states that 'It has been long recognized that the Peace and Truce of God movement had played a highly significant role in the definition and enunciation of noncombatant status'.[6]

In the final years of the tenth century and into the eleventh, a series of gatherings or councils took place in, primarily, Francia, which, taken together are known as the Peace of God councils and which constitute the Peace of God movement.[7] There are many perspectives on this movement and scholars differ in their interpretations. For the purposes of this study it will be sufficient to see what the councils enacted, what gave rise to them and what were their objectives, with some brief observations on how their enactments compared to *LxI* and, finally, what was their aftermath. Of necessity, answers to these questions will be brief and will focus primarily on how they legislated for non-combatants.

In 975, Bishop Guy of Le Puy called a meeting outside the city to discuss and condemn the pillaging of churches in the diocese. The meeting was attended by a large crowd and the knights and armed peasants present were forced to take an oath to maintain the peace. This meeting is seen as a precursor of the peace movement proper and, in common with other gatherings in the Auvergne area, had the goal of providing protection against unjust aristocratic violence.[8] The first peace council proper, of which canons survive, occurred on 1 June 989, when the archbishop of Bordeaux, Gunbaldus, called together a council of his fellow bishops of Aquitaine at the monastery of Charroux. The council issued a number of decrees: 1. anyone attacking or robbing a church is to be anathema; 2. anyone taking livestock from peasants or other poor people without paying compensation is to be anathema; 3. anyone robbing, seizing or assaulting an unarmed cleric is guilty of sacrilege, and if he does not come forward and make compensation he is to be excluded from the holy church of God.[9] Charroux was

---

6 Strickland, 'Rules of war', p. 115. **7** For a comprehensive introduction to the Peace and Truth of God movement and for a taste of the many and diverse views of its scholars see Head and Landes, *Peace of God* and also Janet Nelson's review of that work, J.L. Nelson, 'Review of Head and Landes (eds) 1992', *Speculum*, 69 (1994), pp 163–9. See also, H.E.J. Cowdrey, 'The Peace and Truth of God in the eleventh century', *Past and Present*, 46 (1970), pp 42–67 and the works listed in the detailed historiography outlined in F.S. Paxton, 'History, historians and the Peace of God' in Head and Landes (eds), *Peace of God*, pp 21–40. For more recent contributions see T. Head, 'The development of the Peace of God in Aquitaine (970–1005)', *Speculum*, 74 (1999), pp 656–86; T. Gergen, 'The Peace of God and its legal practice in the eleventh century', *Cuadernos de Historia del Derecho*, 9 (2002), pp 11–27; D. Barthélemy, *L'an mil et la paix de Dieu, La France Chrétienne et Féodale, 980–1060* (Paris, 1999); idem, 'The Peace of God and Bishops at war in the Gallic lands from the late tenth to the early twelfth century' in C.P. Lewis (ed.), *Anglo-Norman Studies 32, Proceedings of the Battle Conference 2009* (Woodbridge, 2010), pp 1ff. **8** Head and Landes (eds), *Peace of God*, pp 3–4; C. Lauranson-Rosaz, 'Peace from the mountains: the Auvergnat origins of the Peace of God' in Head and Landes (eds), *Peace of God*, p. 106. **9** G. Mansi (ed.), *Sacrorum Conciliorum Nova et Amplissima*

followed by at least six similar councils before the end of the century, scattered throughout the French Midi, including Narbonne (990), Limoges (994), Anse (994), Le Puy (994) and Poitiers (1000–14),[10] with less in the first two decades of the new millennium. However, they were revived in the third and fourth decades, with as many as twenty being held all over Francia.[11]

Often large numbers of the general lay population attended and participated. Relics of saints were sometimes brought and the charged atmosphere is apparent from narrative descriptions.[12] It was not unusual that, in addition to its own specific decrees, a council would reiterate the decrees of Charroux, and gradually '"peace" ideology became the transcendent idiom'.[13] Of particular interest, because it gives a detailed account of the matters of concern at a specific time and place, and is representative of the movement's concerns generally, is the peace oath proposed in 1023 by Bishop Warrin of Beauvais to the Capetian king Robert the Pious.[14] This is a lengthy list of actions which an adherent to the peace movement must swear to abjure. He must not invade a church for any reason or its storehouse, unless it is to catch a person who has committed homicide or somebody who has broken this peace or to catch a horse. He must not assault an unarmed cleric or anyone who is walking with him who is not carrying a spear or a shield or seize their horse, unless they have committed a crime, or it is in recompense for a crime for which they would not make amends, having been given fifteen days notice. Also forbidden is the seizing of a list of domestic animals or, more pertinently, the seizing of villeins of either sex, sergeants or merchants. He is not to burn down houses unless a horseman or a thief is harboured within. There are stipulations regarding the seizing of provisions when on a cavalcade, including for the protection of merchants and pilgrims and their possessions. He must swear not to assault noble women in the absence of their husbands, or their fellow-travellers, unless he should find them committing misdeeds against him, and this also applied to nuns and widows. The assaulting of unarmed horsemen and the taking of their possessions is forbidden from the beginning of Lent to the end of Easter. Finally, these provisions do not apply, it appears, during war authorized by the king. This text gives some flavour of the

---

Collectio, revised by J. Martin and L. Petit (60 vols, Paris, 1899–1927), xix, 89–90 (henceforth, Mansi). See Head and Landes (eds), *Peace of God*, p. 4 and trans., pp 327–8. See also Brown, *Violence*, pp 116–17. **10** See H.-W. Goetz, 'Protection of the Church, defense of the law, and reform: on the purposes and character of the Peace of God' in Head and Landes (eds), *Peace of God*, p. 262, for a list. **11** Head and Landes (eds), *Peace of God*, p. 6. **12** Ibid., pp 4–6. See, for example, the acts of the council of Poitiers, as per translation provided in Head and Landes, *Peace of God*, pp 330–1 (Mansi, xix, 265–8). See also Ademar of Chabannes' description, thought to have been composed c.1026, of the first council of Limoges (994), a translation of which is provided in the same work, pp 329–30. See Ademar of Chabannes, *Chronique d'Ademar de Chabannes*, ed. J. Chavanon in *Collection des textes pour servir l'étude et l'enseignement de l'histoire*, 20 (Paris, 1897). **13** Head and Landes (eds), *Peace of God*, p. 6. **14** Ibid., for translation, pp 332–4; original source to be found in Vatican, Bibliotheca Apostolica, codex Reginensis latinus 566, fol. 38v; Brown, *Violence*, p. 118.

Lex Innocentium *situated*

nature of the Peace of God movement and, along with the Charroux text, some indication of the issues it addressed and its objectives.

Other councils took a somewhat different line. For instance, the council of Poitiers was concerned with the resolution of disputes relating to the unlawful usurpation of possessions in the area within the previous five years or in the future, and stipulated that judgments could be enforced by the forfeit of hostages and/or excommunication. It also provided that a bishop should not demand gifts for penitence or confirmation, and that priests or deacons who have women in their house shall lose their clerical order. While this council did specifically reiterate the decrees of Charroux, it is clear that the abuses of concern to the movement were many and varied.[15] Any comprehenvive study of what produced this movement and of what were the intentions of those involved, would be extensive; we, therefore, will be narrowly focused on non-combatants.

In the late tenth century and the eleventh, central authority as envisioned by Charlemagne and his capitularies did not exist in Francia. While the extent to which it ever existed in practice can be disputed, it is fair to say that power and the exercise of it was significantly fragmented relative to Carolingian times and even more so relative to how people imagined it was in those times.[16] When Hugh Capet took the west Frankish throne in 987 he was little different, apart from his royal anointment, from other major magnates throughout Francia, on whose goodwill he depended. They, in turn, depended for their power on attracting or coercing the support of the lesser lords beneath them. On the ground, power was exercised through what Warren C. Brown has called 'two rather remarkable novelties', the knight and the castle.[17] Contending magnates built castles and stationed mounted, armoured and armed warriors in them, who protected and enforced the lord's power, often with little regard for those, lay or clerical, who were not armed. These knights developed a bad reputation, as is apparent from the ecclesiastical sources.[18] Whatever may have been the underlying causes or historical trends in this phenomenon, it promoted the view that society consisted of two categories of person, those who were armed and could use violence, on the one hand, and those who were not armed and could not use violence on the other.[19] To be more precise, it forced society to re-articulate the roles of its constituent parts as Bishop Gerard I of Cambrai (r. 1012–51)

---

[15] For instance, see R.I. Moore, 'Family, community and cult on the eve of the Gregorian reform' in *Transactions of the Royal Historical Society*, 5th ser., 30 (1980), pp 49–69, and the comments thereon in Paxton, 'History, historians', pp 36–7. [16] The extent to which order had broken down in late tenth and eleventh century Francia, relative to the Carolingian period, and thereby contributed to the emergence of the Peace of God movement, has been hotly debated by scholars. Most of the works already cited join in that debate on one side or the other. For a useful summary, including the relevant historiography, see Brown, *Violence*, pp 99–103. See also, M. Bennett, 'Violence in eleventh-century Normandy: feud, warfare and politics' in Halsall, *Violence*, pp 126–40. [17] Brown, *Violence*, p. 99. [18] Ibid., p. 100. [19] Ibid., p. 100; Paxton, 'History, historians', pp 31–2. For the concept of the arms-bearing free man in early medieval Ireland see Charles-Edwards, *Early Christian Ireland*, p. 69.

did, peculiarly in response to what he saw as excessive zeal on the part of a council, as prayers, farmers and fighters.[20] To limit the fighters to their proper role in society, which was to protect and defend the two other orders, the councils deployed spiritual weapons in the form of oaths to uphold God's peace and the threat of excommunication.[21] In such decrees as those proscribing the use of violence against unarmed clergy and their unarmed companions, widows, noblewomen travelling without their husbands, and even unarmed knights during Lent, they were aimed at the protection of defenceless people.[22] Ignoring issues of whether the movement was church-inspired, lay-inspired or class-inspired one must agree that, by and large, 'The goal of the Peace movement was to protect the "civilian" victims of warrior violence'.[23] In recognizing the innocent, the non-combatant, and in affording him or her a measure of protection in times of strife, it takes its place in the history of *jus in bello*.

It can be folly to compare two phenomena from two very different centuries and societies; but because *LxI* and the Peace of God movement are the only examples of *in bello* law making in the West of which we are aware in the first millennium AD, some observations are demanded. The Peace of God movement grew out of a society where, certainly among the elite, the personal right to violence was accepted. The lay magnates felt entitled to wield violence for such purposes as building up their followings, protecting or extending their power over others, asserting their subjectively perceived rights and honour, and to avenge injury and insult. Many of the clergy felt similarly entitled and used similar violence for the same ends. After the disintegration of the Carolingian imperium and its concomitant norms of violence, the perception of a personal right to violence became the dominant norm. Some saw this as a descent into disorder, others merely as a new order or a change of emphasis onto a norm of violence that was ever-present.[24] Whichever it was, it gave rise to the necessity for an attempt to limit violence, expressed in the Peace of God movement. As we have seen, *LxI* emerged from a world where the personal right to violence was accepted, expected and, indeed, woven into legal structures. In its provision for fines, judgment and enforcement, it slotted into the existing legal system, the existing order. That order, violent as it might have been, was essential to the successful promulgation and implementation of *LxI*. It can be said, therefore, at least superficially, that a breakdown of order begat the Peace of God movement, while existing order enabled *LxI*. While this is true, it is also true that the need for *LxI*, and for special protection for non-combatants, arose because of the endemic violence in late seventh-century Ireland. By the same token, the need for the Peace of God movement arose from the degree and nature of conflict in Frankish society, central to which was the feud. This was, fundamentally, the state of dispute between kindred that was the underlying societal stress line, par-

---

20 *Gesta episcoporum Cameracensium* (1024–1036) in *MGH SS* vii, 475, 585. Translation in Head and Landes (eds), *Peace of God*, pp 335–7. **21** Brown, *Violence*, p. 101. **22** Goetz, 'Protection', p. 266. **23** C. Lauranson-Rosaz, 'Mountains', p. 106. **24** Brown, *Violence*, pp 125–7.

ticularly with the nobility, which understood itself in kinship terms.[25] In this respect there was a similarity between the two societies giving rise to the two *in bello* laws. Some of the factors in the Ireland of Adomnán's time, which facilitated the willingness of that society to legislate for non-combatants, will be considered below. It will be suggested that the absence of any real threat from outside the society was one such factor. It is of particular interest that, at the end of the tenth century and beginning of the eleventh, Europe had ceased to be threatened by periodic foreign invasion and was only just beginning to turn its eyes to the east, where it was to reverse roles and become the aggressor, in the form of the crusades.[26] It had, therefore, a brief window, when it could consider the proper conduct of violence among its own people. In this milieu, as in late seventh-century Ireland, there was the space to recognize, what we call today, the non-combatant and to attempt to provide protection.

To that end, *LxI* was the more focused, its sole function being the protection of innocents and it being so named in the chronicles. As we have seen its core provisions are directly aimed at those in society who do not bear arms. Paragraph 34 is a clear statement of the law's objectives and the ensuing paragraphs go on to enact provisions for the achievement of those objectives. The Peace of God councils were explicitly concerned with wider issues, with society's ills, such as ecclesiastical reform;[27] enactments were promulgated repeatedly and over a wide geographic area. Furthermore, although clearly rooted in an awareness of and concern for the unarmed, they are more circumspect in their enactments. The non-combatant is not defined. One is left to wonder whether it is acceptable to attack a noblewoman who is accompanied by her husband, not to mention a woman who is not noble. Indeed, it is in the protection afforded to women that *LxI* is, relative to Peace of God, quite singular. Another important difference between the two is that the sanctions imposed on offenders by the Peace of God councils are ecclesiastical, such as anathemas and excommunications. *Lex Innocentium*, on the other hand, is, to some degree, incorporated into secular law, on the authority of the king. That said, some of the fines are payable to the Columban community, which has primary responsibility for implementation of the law. One could go on comparing and contrasting but the main point for us is that both, most unusually in the medieval world, recognized and legislated for the non-combatant; both addressed *in bello* concerns.

Ad bellum considerations were, however, quickly to reassert their paramount position in the thinking on violence and warfare in Western society of the

---

25 Head and Landes (eds), *Peace of God*, pp 15–16. For a different view that stresses the predominance of the church in attempting to protect its own interests see E. Magnou-Nortier, 'The enemies of the peace: reflections on a vocabulary, 500–1100' in Head and Landes (eds), *Peace of God*, pp 58–79; Goetz, 'Protection'. See also, Halsall, *Violence*, pp 19–32. **26** Head and Landes (eds), *Peace of God*, p. 10. **27** A.G. Remensnyder, 'Pollution, purity and peace: an aspect of social reform between the late tenth century and 1076' in Head and Landes (eds), *Peace of God*, pp 280–307; Goetz, 'Protection', pp 273–9.

eleventh century. Indeed, it has been argued that the peace movement can be divided into three phases: the first, when it was concerned with the separation of the armed from the unarmed; the second, as the millennium of Christ's death approached in 1033, and the mounting atmosphere of purification and penance, with the formation of the knights into an *ordo* of Christian society; the final, when these *milites Christi* were given the holy purpose of defending Christendom and liberating the Holy Land.[28] The Peace of God movement is often linked with another movement, the Truce of God. While the latter was an extension of the former, and both were concerned with establishing a peaceful society, from the point of view of a just war historian, they, broadly speaking, had different motivations and represent respectively *in bello* and *ad bellum* thinking. The Peace of God was an attempt to protect the unarmed. The Truce of God was an attempt to outlaw all fighting during certain periods of religious importance.[29] One of the ordinances of the council of Elne-Toulouges (1027) was to desist from violence 'from the ninth hour on Saturday to the first hour on Monday, so that everyone would render the honour owed to the Lord's day'.[30] At the synod of Arles (1041) all Christians were prohibited from fighting from Thursday to Monday morning, on important feast days and during Advent and Lent on pain of excommunication. This decree was intended to apply throughout the kingdom of France and was spread to neighbouring kingdoms with the assistance of Cluny.[31] The shedding of Christian blood by Christians was now the target for 'No Christian should kill another Christian, since whoever kills a Christian doubtless sheds the blood of Christ' (council of Narbonne, 1054).[32] The corollary, of course, was that it was legitimate to kill non-Christians. Not only that, but it was pleasing to God that the knight should do battle against God's enemies. Urban II invoked the Truce of God in the council of Clermont in 1095, when he called on the knights of Western Europe to fight for Christ in the First Crusade. As mentioned in the first chapter, the crusades were a manifestation of *ad bellum* thinking at its most extreme.

While an in-depth analysis of developments in the history of *jus in bello*, in the later Middle Ages and subsequently, is beyond the scope of this work, for the purpose of understanding the place of *LxI* in that history, it is worth noting that *in bello* thinking was down, but not entirely out. In *c.*1140, Gratian, a Camaldolese monk and canon lawyer from Bologna, produced his textbook, *Concordia Discordantium Canonum*, usually referred to as the *Decretum*.[33] In this Gratian implicitly opposed the then-current Truce of God and followed the Peace of God movement by exempting pilgrims, clerics, monks, women and the

---

28 Paxton, 'History, historians', pp 31–2; G. Duby (trans. C. Postan), 'Les laïcs et la paix de Dieu' in *The Chivalrous Society* (Berkeley, 1977), pp 123–33 at p. 124. **29** Head and Landes (eds), *Peace of God*, p. 7. **30** Mansi, xix, 483–4. Translation in Head and Landes (eds), *Peace of God*, p. 334. **31** Head and Landes (eds), *Peace of God*, pp 7–9; Lauransson-Rosaz, 'Mountains', p. 105; Goetz, 'Protection', p. 274. **32** Mansi, xix, 827; Head and Landes (eds), *Peace of God*, p. 8. **33** Russell, *Just war*, p. 55.

unarmed poor from violence on pain of excommunication. This, to quote F.H. Russell, 'is as close as he came to upholding some kind of non-combatant immunity'.[34] The tenuous thread of *in bello* thinking survived the centuries, therefore, from its initial bold and explicit articulation in 697 through its more cautious manifestation in the Peace of God movement, to Gratian and on to the writings of Francisco Vitoria, Hugo Grotius and others.[35] Apart from chronology, it is often difficult to say how one may have influenced the thinking of another. It is even more difficult, indeed impossible, to know if *LxI* could have had any influence on the Peace of God movement. In all probability, it had none. It is worth noting, however, that the emergence of the latter in the final quarter of the tenth century coincides with the renewal of active interest in *LxI* in Ireland, as is evident in the last chapter. It is likely that *LxI* and its provisions would have been known in the Irish ecclesiastical diaspora among the Franks, particularly to any from the Columban tradition. Indeed it is possible that a knowledge of *LxI* may have been acquired from Irish clerics active in Carolingian Francia, and this awareness may have survived into the late tenth century.[36] This raises a question that might merit research at another time. To pursue this question and the subsequent devolution of *in bello* thinking is well beyond the scope of this study. The place of *LxI* in the early medieval history of *jus in bello* is, however, becoming clear. After this brief study of the only other *in bello* legislative effort in the first millennium AD, the Peace of God, including the conditions that produced it, it is necessary to explore why was it in Ireland in the late seventh century, uniquely in the Christian West, that *in bello* found such explicit expression. There is an explanation, or series of them, that make this expression acceptable and understandable.

WHY IRELAND? WHY 697?

There were aspects of late seventh-century Ireland that facilitated or encouraged a law for innocents such as *LxI*. For instance, prominent among the power structures of early medieval Ireland were the ecclesiastical *paruchiae*.[37] The higher ranking-churches of these *paruchiae* were multi-functional, often having a resident bishop as well as a monastic community.[38] These were designed, to quote Colmán Etchingham, 'to interact with society as pastor, legislator, judge and tribute-raising lord' and provided 'a springboard from which a wider jurisdictional

---

34 Ibid., p. 70; A. Friedburg (ed.), 'Causa in pars secunda of the *Decretum Gratiani*' in *Corpus Iuris Canonici* (Leipsig, 1879), i, 24 q. 3 cc. 22–5 and 17 q. 4 c. 29. For Gratian and the *Decretum* see also S. Kuttner, 'The father of the science of canon law', *Jurist*, 1 (1941), pp 2–19; P. Landau , 'Gratian and the *Decretum Gratiani*' in W. Hartmann and K. Pennington (eds), *The history of medieval canon law in the Classical period: from Gratian to the Decretals of Pope Gregory IX* (Washington, 2008), pp 22–54; A. Winroth, *The making of Gratian's 'Decretum'* (Cambridge, 2000). See reference in Russell Smith, 'Willing body', p. 82. **35** See Chapter 1, p. 19. **36** I am most grateful to Professor Máire Herbert for her helpful suggestions in this regard. **37** See Chapter 3, pp 59–60. **38** Ó Carragáin, *Churches*, p. 9.

claim could be asserted, as, for example, in the case of the promulgation of *Cáin Adomnáin* by the Columban churches in 697'.[39] This meant that ecclesiastical authority had ambitions, not just over a church and surrounding territory, but over the entire island and beyond. Therefore, for instance, Iona and Armagh could aspire to affect, and felt an obligation to, the Irish world as a whole. The Columban *paruchia*, was a suitable instrument by which acceptance for *LxI* could be won and by means of which it could be enacted and subsequently implemented. If there was an ill in Irish society generally, in ecclesiastical perception, the *paruchia* was there, and had incentive, to cure it, without the necessity of the approval of an episcopal council in the continental sense.[40] Iona and its *paruchia* was an almost ideal institution, providing a network of authority and communication, to handle the *LxI* project.[41] With the confluence of this and the beginning, in 695, of the reign of Loingsech mac Óengusso, Adomnán's cousin, as king of Tara, the necessary power alliances in the form of strong and influential ecclesiastical federation backed by the power and influence of the kingship of Tara were in place for the proclamation of *LxI* in 697. The king of Tara's support was an essential element for the proclamation of a *cáin* that was to apply to the entire island of Ireland and the areas of Britain that were part of the Irish world. As the anniversary of Columba's death approached in 697, Adomnán would have seen this not just as his opportunity but as his divinely ordained duty.[42]

Another aspect of Irish society was the sense of shared descent among the elite, a sense which was, as has been seen,[43] explicitly designed as part of the reconciliation of existing traditions with biblical history and which was actively promoted among the people.[44] This, taken together with a further feature, the lack of any substantial threat to the Irish from outside Ireland, greatly facilitated the making of a law for themselves which would regulate their conduct in warfare *inter se*. As has been pointed out, by 697, with the wars of Uí Néill expansion over, and the emergence of Munster something for the future, generally speaking, violence within Irish society was confined to low-grade warfare and raiding. While external threats occurred, they were rare.[45] Outside Ireland the picture was somewhat different. Wars were frequently internal, as the constant infighting of the Merovingians showed, but could also be fought against other people, people seen as alien.[46] The norms of violence often differ, depending on whether the people involved are considered to be 'inside' the culturally drawn circle or 'outsiders'.[47] Thus, internal fighting took place in a wider context where

---

39 Etchingham, *Church organization*, p. 460.   **40** This is not to say, of course, that ecclesiastical synods did not occur. See Etchingham, *Church organization*, pp 206–10 for an analysis of the sources, both the *Hibernensis* and vernacular sources.   **41** Herbert, *Iona, Kells and Derry*, pp 33–5.   **42** Ibid., pp 50–6.   **43** See Chapter 3, p. 62.   **44** Chapter 3, pp 62–3. touches on this. See also, comments on *Lebor Gabála* in Carney, 'Language and literature to 1169', p. 462.   **45** The English attack on the plain of Brega was clearly exceptional (AU s. a. 685).   **46** See I. Wood, *The Merovingian kingdoms, 450–751* (London, 1994). For some examples of external warfare see below.   **47** Brown, *Violence*, p. 20. See also: Wickham, *Inheritance of Rome*, p. 43; Nelson, 'Violence in the Carolingian world', p. 90.

external wars, often conceptualized in terms of ethnic or dynastic rivalry, were commonplace. Even in Britain at the end of the seventh century the alien existed, from an Anglo-Saxon viewpoint, in the form of British, Irish of Dál Riata and Picts, and coloured the wars of conquest and/or group rivalry which they fought among themselves, in imagined ethnic terms.[48] In Britain there was conflict between the Christian Northumbrians and the pagan king of Mercia, Penda (d. 656), and between Anglo-Saxons and British (Cadwallon d. 634). Both of these dynamics, religious change and ethnic tension, were absent in Ireland.

From the time of the Greeks and Romans, who fought against peoples they saw as barbarians, this had been the norm.[49] There was always 'the other', often in the form of non-Christian or heretic. In Adomnán's own time the papacy was threatened by the Lombards, and Visigothic Spain would shortly be under attack from the forces of Islam and due to collapse in 711.[50] External threat from alien peoples continued to be the norm, whether from the peoples across the Rhine in Carolingian times or, later, the threats posed by the Danes, Swedes, Hungarians and Slavs.[51] No one questioned the justness of the cause in wars against these 'other' peoples. *Jus ad bellum* considerations applied to the exclusion of *jus in bello*. As was apparent above, the Peace of God movement in Francia emerged at a time when, briefly, the warrior class was freed from a preoccupation with any perceived threat from outside. Such violence as existed was among themselves and non-combatants were suffering. This demanded *in bello* legislation and, because of the absence of external threat, society had the space to address it. It is true that Dál Riata, where Iona is situated, was engaged in conflict with the Picts and the English. However Adomán's overall concern and context was, broadly speaking, Irish. It is clear, therefore, that external threat did not produce conditions conducive to *in bello* law-making, whereas conditions in late seventh-century Ireland, as in late tenth-century Francia, where there was no 'enemy at the gates', did.

A further obvious explanation for a law to protect innocents would be if they were being violently exploited on a regular basis in the Ireland of the late seventh century. The descriptions of the treatment of women given in paragraphs 1–27 of the text of *LxI* cannot be relied on as a true reflection of the prevailing conditions in 697, those paragraphs having been compiled approximately 300 years later.[52] The contemporary sources, in the form of the medieval chronicles and archaeology, have been examined to see if wide-scale abuse of innocents was evident, such as would make it imperative that measures be introduced for their protection.[53] The chronicles were found to be, in the main, silent and the likely

---

48 Mayr-Harting, *The Coming*, pp 117–19; T.M. Charles-Edwards, 'Bede, the Irish and the Britons', *Celtica*, 15 (1983), pp 42–52 for Bede's incredibly negative attitude to the Britons. **49** See Chapter 1, pp 15–16. **50** Wickham, *Inheritance of Rome*, pp 139–49. **51** Mayr-Harting, 'The West: the age of conversion (700–1050)' in McManners (ed.), *The Oxford illustrated history of Christianity*, pp 92–3. **52** See Chapter 5, pp 121–2 and Chapter 6, pp 160–2 and comments of Máirín Ní Dhonnchadha on paragraphs 1–15 of *LxI* in her 'An edition of *Cáin Adomnáin*', pp 28–34. **53** Chapter 3.

causes of this have been explored. The archaeological evidence, while being limited, did confirm that slaughter of women and children happened to a significant, if not overwhelming extent. It is unlikely that Adomnán would have undertaken the task of organizing the meeting in Birr, enacting the law and establishing the complex legal paraphernalia for its implementation, unless there was a pressing need. It is reasonable to conclude that this, taken in conjunction with the archaeological evidence, such as it is, is sufficient to establish that violence towards innocents was a significant feature of seventh-century Ireland. It is just not possible to say whether it was more prevalent in Ireland than elsewhere. One way or the other, it must rank as a major explanation for the enactment of *LxI*.

Chapter 3 looked briefly at the system of vernacular law and the legal structures that existed in early medieval Ireland and considered what has been identified as early medieval Europe's largest corpus of vernacular laws.[54] It was possible to conclude that the Ireland of that time was, to a large extent, a law-conscious society.[55] It must now be suggested that this too tended to facilitate the enactment of a law such as *LxI* in that there was a long-standing legal tradition which, in its underlying assumptions, was accepted throughout elite society, on which to build. This was bolstered by an entrenched, deeply established professional juridical class.[56] Furthermore, there already existed, in the *cáin* system, a legal mechanism suitable for the enactment and implementation of laws intended to bind all 'the men of Ireland and Britain'. Indeed, a *cáin* law for the limitation of violence already existed, *Cáin Fhuithirbe*, which sought to limit the incursions of a person enforcing a judgment after adequate compensation had been recovered.[57] It was apparent that there were lacunae in vernacular law, which *LxI* would ultimately fill. In doing so the drafters of *LxI* would appear to have had a quite remarkable precedent in the *sellach* (onlooker) text, which exempted women, clerics, boys and senseless and senile persons from the normal duty to intervene, of those observing wrongdoing.[58] Here there is a recognition of the special position of the non-combatant, if only by virtue of the practical reality of his or her inability to intervene. Nevertheless, it is a legal distinction readily comprehendible by all. It is fair to say, therefore, that the existing legal system in Ireland provided fertile ground for the sowing of the *in bello* seed.

If this can be said of vernacular law, it cannot be similarly said of the two other bodies of normative texts, canon law in the form of the *Hibernensis* and the penitentials. To a degree the former, with its emphasis on the Old Testament and the Fathers, neither of which show any significant concern for the non-combatant, while not excluding other authorities, pulled down the shutters on *in bello*

---

54 Chapter 3, p. 70; Flechner, *A study*. **55** Bhreathnach, *Medieval world*, p. 102. **56** Chapman Stacey, *Dark speech*, p. 54 and p. 153; Wickham, *Inheritance of Rome*, p. 165. Both argue that such a class was, relatively, more available in Ireland than in most other contemporary societies. **57** See Chapter 3, p. 88 above, where *Cáin Fhuithirbe* is mentioned in the context of a discussion of *díbergaig*. **58** See discussion of vernacular law in Chapter 3.

considerations. It is possible that the canon lawyers felt that the laws of war, *in bello*, were not their concern, although this is difficult to argue having regard to the very many areas that they considered were their concern.[59] In the same way, the penitentials, while providing for many different sins of violence and many grades of killing, do not provide for the killing of innocents per se.[60] The significance of the penitentials remains, as considered in Chapter 2, that their prominence in Ireland, as distinct from the Continent where they arrived later, facilitated a more nuanced attitude to the taking of human life rather than was the case elsewhere, where all killing was equally sinful. Indeed, the perceived sinfulness of taking any human life in any circumstances partly explains the absence of special provisions against the killing of innocents in the early church, and this persisted into the early Middle Ages.[61] The penitentials and repeatable penance, in contrast, introduced a scale of killing and, thereby, enabled the killing of innocents to be regarded with special opprobrium. As pointed out however, the penitentials, while distinguishing between all manner of killing, from premeditated to accidental, from the killing of a bishop to the killing of a slave, from suicide to kin-slaying, do not deal with the killing of innocents.[62] The willingness to distinguish between different kinds of killing, however, contrasts with the traditional position of some authorities in the church, which, until relatively late, refused to distinguish, treating all killing as equally sinful. As mentioned, Rob Meens has taken a more nuanced view of penitential practices in Francia and western continental Europe in general in the early medieval period. He argues that penitential practices in continental Europe, before the arrival of the Insular penitential handbooks, were many and varied and that the practice of private penance as distinct from public cannot be entirely excluded, as has been argued by some scholars heretofore.[63] The position remains, however, that the penitential system generally practised in Ireland enabled the forgiveness of even the most serious of sins, the killing of another person, by 'repentance, confession and the performance of a penance and that this could be repeated if the need arose'.[64] A society that produced and used penitential tariff-books in dealing with the sin of killing another person is more likely to produce a law that treated the killing of innocents with special abhorrence than a society with a tradition that tended to regard, over the centuries, the taking of human life, whatever the circumstances, as equally sinful. The capacity to distinguish is another factor that explains the emergence of a law proscribing violence towards innocents and which helps answer the question posed: 'why Ireland – why 697?'.

In a further effort to explain the emergence of an *in bello* law in late seventh-century Irish society, it will be worth looking again at the place of violence in that society. Some answers may be found from an analysis of attitudes to violence and the elite's relationship with it. Irish vernacular law was, to a large

---

[59] Chapter 3. [60] Ibid. [61] See discussion of the church's attitude to killing in Chapter 2. [62] This is considered in some detail in Chapter 3. [63] Meens, 'Irish contribution', pp 131–2. [64] Stancliffe, 'Religion and society', p. 406.

degree, a 'law of self-help'.[65] The law was enforced by individuals, such as the *naidm* or enforcing surety in, for instance, the case of breach of contract.[66] To enforce the law against a killer who refused to pay the appropriate fine, the victim's kinsmen were obliged to carry out a blood-feud.[67] An enforcing surety had extensive powers, under law, to force the offender or defaulter to fulfil his obligations. He can distrain his property or seize and imprison him. He is entitled to use violence. Indeed, the law is explicit in specifying that 'blood spilt by a man who is enforcing his surety (*naidm*)' is one of the seven blood-sheddings of Irish law which do not entail fines or sick-maintenance.[68] What is significant about this, and perhaps unique to Ireland at the time,[69] is that the violence generated is judicially authorized and, indeed, sanctioned by judges, whose authority is broadly accepted throughout Irish society. Fergus Kelly argues that, in spite of the absence of a central enforcing authority, it is likely that the prestige of the judge's office, along with the system of pledges and sureties, would be sufficient to achieve compliance with judgments in most cases.[70] It is quite clear, however, that there would often not be compliance with the court's judgments, and this would give rise to violence. It is only natural that efforts would be made to refine the system so as to minimize the extent of that violence. It has been seen that *Cáin Fhuithirbe* was intended for that purpose, and it is suggested that *LxI* had the same purpose. Regulation of the degree and nature of permitted force is to be expected in a legal system that employed private violence as its enforcement mechanism, so specifically and so extensively. The enactment of *LxI* must be viewed through this prism.

Lex Innocentium should also be seen in the wider context of Irish attitudes to violence, not just the judicially approved. We have distinguished between, what Richard Sharpe called 'honourable warfare', on the one hand, and *díbergaig* violence on the other.[71] *Audacht Morainn*, while cautioning the mythical king Feradach Finn Fechtnach against causing undue bloodshed, urged him to 'remove the shame of his cheeks by arms in battle against other territories'.[72] That a king would conduct campaigns was normal and, to a degree, admirable. That is what kings were expected to do and did. The distinction between acceptable warfare and unacceptable brigandage is best illustrated in the *Vita Prima Sanctae Brigitae*, paragraph 65, where Brigit, having disapproved of Conall's diabolical designs, undermines them, persuades him to righteousness and then proceeds to collaborate with him in his, presumably, 'honourable' warfare, in which he 'inflicted great slaughter'.[73] It is evident that Adomnán was of the same view.[74]

65 Chapter 3, p. 65. The description is Thomas Charles-Edwards' of *Senchas Már* ('Early Irish law', p. 341). **66** Kelly, *Guide,* pp 167–73. See also N. McLeod, *Early Irish contract law* (Sydney, 1999) for fuller treatment of contract law; Binchy, 'Celtic suretyship', for a detailed treatment of the surety in early Irish law; Chapman Stacey, *Dark speech*, pp 20–33. **67** Kelly, *Guide,* p.127. **68** *CIH* 9.5; Kelly, *Guide*, p. 171; Chapman Stacey, *Dark speech*, pp 36–7. **69** Chapman-Stacey, *Dark speech*, p. 54 and p. 153. **70** Kelly, *Guide*, p. 214. **71** Chapter 3. **72** Ibid. **73** This is fully discussed in Chapter 3, pp 88. **74** See discussion of 'Adomnán and violence' in Chapter 4.

The accounts of violence contained in *VC* were divided into two: those that do not include any note of condemnation and those that do. It was found that the matter-of-factness with which the incidents of violence in the first category are described was quite remarkable. It was concluded that Adomnán, in all probability, shared the attitudes apparent in *Audact Morainn* and the *Vita Prima*. In a society where 'honourable warfare' was acceptable, and each king was entitled, as of right, to initiate it, it is not surprising that markers be laid down as to how it should be conducted. One is reminded of the conditions that emerged in eighteenth- and nineteenth-century Europe, the period of *raison d'état*, where it came to be considered legitimate for the sovereign to wage war, almost as an extension of diplomacy, by virtue of his or her sovereignty.[75] This rendered redundant the concept of *jus ad bellum*, and allowed *jus in bello* to be developed. Seventh-century Ireland was similar to the extent that the right of a king to attack his neighbour could not be challenged, thus allowing and encouraging the adoption of a *jus in bello*. It appears that *Cáin Fhuithirbe* may have already taken a step in that direction, with its references to 'intentional wounding on a battlefield' and 'violent taking of hostages'.[76] Again, this is the prism through which *LxI* must be viewed: a coming together of the leaders of a society to make distinctions between what was justified and not justified, to lay down ground rules for the conducting of violent interaction between themselves, an interaction which all of them, without exception, knew would continue. In contrast to some societies, there was little expectation or reliance on a king's peace being imposed from above.[77] In fact, that expectation would inhibit a society coming together to enact a law such as *LxI* because the hoped for king's peace would render it unnecessary.[78]

The above characteristics, some of which may be unique to late seventh-century Ireland and others not, taken together, go some of the way to answering the question posed in the heading to this section. The factors that facilitated the enactment of a law for the protection of innocents can be summarized as follows: the obvious need, the necessary enabling infrastructure in the confluence of lay and ecclesiastical power and in a suitably developed legal system, a united sense of shared descent, the absence of a threat from outside, an uninhibited capacity to distinguish between different victims of killing and violence and, finally, an attitude to violence that accepted its inevitability. There is, of course, one final ingredient, the most important, Adomnán.

---

75 See Chapter 1, p. 20. **76** Chapter 3, pp XX. **77** See for instance Brown, *Violence*, pp 69–96, his chapter entitled 'Charlemagne, God, and the license to kill'. **78** Ibid., p. 71. Brown argues that Charlemagne 'made new claims about the power of central authority to regulate the use of violence' which countered the 'far older norms that were still well entrenched among the Franks, namely the norms surrounding the personal right to violence and violent vengeance'.

ADOMNÁN'S *JUS IN BELLO*: HIS CONCEPT, HIS INSPIRATION AND HIS ACHIEVEMENT

It is clear that there are many aspects of late seventh-century Irish society that would have facilitated the introduction of an *in bello* law. As always, however, these factors are not, in themselves, a sufficient explanation, without the active intervention of an individual. It is probable that there were factors in the 1860s that would have helped in the formation of what became the International Committee of the Red Cross. But an historian of that period would be aware that the decisive factor was the initiative taken by Henry Dunant following his experience of the aftermath of the battle of Solferino in 1859.[79] Similarly, a scholar of *LxI* and the jurisprudence of warfare in general, seeking an explanation for the emergence of a *jus in bello* from late seventh-century Ireland, will see as the primary answer, Adomnán and his intervention in Irish affairs in 697. Whether he acted, like Dunant, in response to a traumatic personal experience cannot be known. This possibility has already been briefly considered,[80] where the Middle Irish tradition, as expressed in paragraphs 6 to 15 of the text of *LxI*, dealing with the battlefield of Brega, was noted. Máirín Ní Dhonnchadha, in considering this, has pointed out that it is probable that the compiler of the text was repeating the same tradition expressed in earlier Middle Irish sources.[81] This has been touched on in reference to the commentary on *Félire Óengusso*.[82] While the historicity of these accounts is questionable, it seems clear that they are evidence of a tradition. Furthermore, it is reasonable to conjecture that only a significant shock, resulting from a first-hand personal encounter, similar to that experienced by Dunant, would be sufficient, in the first instance, to instil in Adomnán his singular awareness of innocents and, second, to motivate him to undertake the exceedingly onerous task of their protection. For Adomnán to be so aware of innocents, he must have experienced for himself, rather than have been informed by others, the horror of their involvement in the carnage of war. That he had a remarkable, and, it would appear, unique sensitivity to the plight of innocents is clear from his accounts of Columba's interaction with them in *VC*. Adomnán refers to innocents again and again, from his heading to chapter II.25 of *VC*, 'Again concerning another persecutor of innocents', to such terminology as '... a pitiless persecutor of innocent folk'.[83] It was clear that particularly severe punishment is suffered by those who offend against innocents, even extending to eternal damnation. Further evidence of his deliberate, conscious awareness of the unarmed is the name he decides for his law, the Law of the Innocents, a name chosen quite contemporaneously with his authorship of *VC*.[84] It was evident that this is particularly remarkable, against a background of the complete absence of any similar awareness being apparent in other sources, Irish or Continental.[85] Here and there provisions for the protection of widows and

---

[79] Referred to in Chapters 1 (p. 20) and 4 (p. 99). [80] Chapter 4, pp 98–9. [81] For a detailed analysis see M. Ní Dhonnchadha, 'An edition of *Cáin Adomnáin*', pp 29–32. [82] Chapter 6. [83] Chapter 4, p. 112. [84] Ibid., p. 112. [85] Ibid., p. 113.

orphans were found, but none for the non-combatant per se until the Peace of God movement.[86] That awareness, that concept, in its explicit expression, belonged to Adomnán.

Inspired by his acute sensitivity to the plight of innocents and his grasp of the concept of the non-combatant, Adomnán took action. In effect, he took on the existing vernacular Irish legal establishment by ignoring honour-price. As we have seen, honour-price is a concept by which the lives of some in society were valued higher than others, depending on rank, and it was at the very core of the existing legal system.[87] By providing for penalties in his law that ignored rank and applied to offences against, say, all women or all clerical students or youths, equally, Adomnán broke the mould in which existing law was formed.[88] To value women on a par, at least, with men, was revolutionary and would have met with strident opposition.[89] Under existing law, society was made up of a large number of categories of person.[90] In essence, Adomnán instituted a new category of person, the non-combatant, and protected them by decreeing that violence towards them was to be abhorred to the same extent as *díbergaig* violence, and was to be punished accordingly.[91] In no other society in the early medieval West and, arguably, for many centuries thereafter, was the non-combatant given such consideration. In the history of *jus in bello* Adomnán stands out as its foremost proponent. In Western European thinking on the laws of war, Augustine will be forever associated with *jus ad bellum*. Adomnán must be similarly associated with *jus in bello*.

***

In this chapter, it has been possible to indicate the place of *LxI* in the history of warfare or, to be more precise, in the history of attitudes to non-combatant involvement in war and the laws attempting to give them protection. We can state that *LxI* was the first such law in the Christian West; in fact, the only one in the first one thousand years of Christian history, followed by the Peace of God movement, which straddled the millennium. This, it must be suggested, is a remarkable conclusion. Some explanation for such a singular conclusion was demanded, and this chapter proceeded in an attempt to provide one. It was found that many factors present in late seventh-century Ireland combined together to facilitate the emergence of a law for innocents, but that by far the most important factor was Adomnán. In Chapter 4 he emerges as a figure of immense talents, many and varied, that fully warranted Jonathon M. Wooding's description of him as 'one of the leading churchmen in these islands in the first millennium' and that 'In the wide reception of his writings, and their enduring

---

86 See Chapter 2 for the barbarian laws and Merovingian capitularies and earlier in this chapter for mention of Charlemagne's capitularies. **87** See discussion in Chapter 3, p. 70. **88** See discussion of paragraphs 42 and 35 in Chapter 5. **89** Chapters 5, p. 134. **90** Kelly, *Guide*, pp 7–12; outline in Chapter 3. **91** Chapter 4.

quality, Adomnán approaches the authority of a father of the church'.[92] But it was his unique awareness of the non-combatant, and his persistent concern, possibly resulting from a traumatic personal experience, that marked him out from others and best explains the very singular events in Birr in 697. It was this, and the law it inspired, that enabled the placing of Adomnán in the history of warfare, as the father of *jus in bello*.

It has been apparent also that, among scholars of early medieval Irish history, *LxI* has received scant attention.[93] The seeming lack of interest is evident from the fact that, of the eighteen contributions to Wooding's volume in commemoration of the thirteenth centenary of Adomnán's death, published in 2010, only one is devoted to his law,[94] with the other seventeen drawing their inspiration, either directly or indirectly, from *VC* or *DLS*. Why this is so is not clear. Guy Halsall expresses the view that academic historians generally have 'shied away from the subject of warfare'.[95] Perhaps this has been a reaction against the days when written history consisted of little else than an account of warfare and battles. In any event, it must now be suggested that *LxI* warrants more consideration from scholars than it has been accorded and it is hoped that this work will provoke further academic interest in the future.

For the true significance of *LxI* one must, however, step outside the cloisters of academia into the harsh world of international violence and warfare. The principles enshrined in the Geneva Conventions, *LxI*'s successor, are not universally accepted and are, of course, widely violated in practice.[96] To that extent, we are concerned with a live issue. Sometimes, historians feel entitled, and even obliged, to articulate the modern relevance of their studies. If the historian cannot learn, or indeed teach, the lessons of history, who can? For instance, Charles Doherty, in his discussion of Irish warriors and kings in the centuries after Adomnán, cautions against thinking of the beheadings, mutilations and general slaughters, including tortures and extreme violence towards non-combatants, as something that only happened in the remote dark past, for 'The dilemmas concerning king, leader, warrior, cleric and layman, women and children in our literature are as relevant today as they ever were'.[97] Ralph O'Connor, in his essay on the warrior's fighting-frenzy or *furor* feels constrained to point out that the phenomenon is not just a feature of past cultures, for 'there are plenty of monsters closer to home'.[98] With regard to *LxI* itself, Gilbert Márkus, in the introduction to his translation of the text, expresses the hope 'that readers will be inspired to learn from Adomnán and from his passionate concern to protect the most vulnerable people from violence and the horrors of war'.[99] It goes without saying that vio-

---

92 Wooding, *Adomnán of Iona*, p. 11. **93** See Chapter 1, pp 25–6. **94** Idem; J.W. Houlihan, review of Wooding et al. (eds), *Adomnán of Iona, Peritia*, 26 (2016), pp 292–4. **95** Halsall, *Warfare*, p. 6. **96** See, for instance, references to My Lai in Chapter 1, pp 23–5, when contextualizing *LxI*. **97** Doherty, 'Warrior and king', p. 148. **98** R. O'Connor, 'Monsters of the tribe: berserk fury, shapeshifting and social dysfunction in *Táin Bó Cúailnge, Egils saga* and *Hrólfs saga kraka*' in Rekdal and Doherty (eds), *Kings and warriors*, p. 236. **99** Márkus,

lence towards non-combatants is an appalling problem in today's world. It is a deliberate feature of many current wars. Their suffering in Syria, Myanmar, Afganistan and Yemen are just a sample. The task of those in the Red Cross and others trying to enforce the rule of international law seems overwhelming. It is important to let those working in the field know that *jus in bello*, their task, has a history. This has been provided, to some extent, from the history of Islam. It has been argued that protection for non-combatants forms part of early Islamic teaching.[100] From a Christian perspective, they should know that in seventh-century Ireland an effort similar to theirs was made by a remarkable and enlightened man. In all societies and at all times there will be violence towards the defenceless, but fair thinking people must continue to strive, in the knowledge that they will be successful in limiting its effects. It is important to give them encouragement, and it is hoped that this study will do so.

Many consider the Geneva Conventions of 1949 as a high point, an enlightened achievement of the modern era, coming, as they did, in the aftermath of the Second World War. James E. Fraser writes 'It is … far from hyperbolic exaggeration to liken *LxI*, concerned as it was with the effects rather than with the fact of war, to the Geneva Conventions'.[101] Far indeed, and, it is suggested, now it is possible to know why. The events in Birr 697 can also be considered as a high point, an enlightened achievement, of early medieval Irish society and, indeed, of the early Middle Ages generally. It would be appropriate, therefore, to conclude with Adomnán's words in the original Old Irish (translation in Chapter 5 and appendix), that, no doubt, rang out across 'the plain of Birr at the confines of the Uí Néill and Munster',[102] the first legislative articulation of *jus in bello*, now preserved in paragraph 34 of the text.

Iss ead inso forus cána Adomnáin for Hérinn ocus Albain sóire ecalsi Dé cona muintir ocus a fethlaib ocus termnaib ocus a n-ule folud béudu ocus mardu ocus a lláichib dligthechaib cona cétmunteraib téchtaidib bite fo réir Adomnáin ocus anamcarat téchtaide ecnaid cráibthig. For-tá foras inna Cána-sae Adomnáin bithcáin for clércu ocus banscála ocus maccu encu co-mbat ingníma fri guin duine ocus co-mbat inbuithi fri tuaith ocus con-festar <a n-immérgi>.[103]

Adomnán's 'Law of the Innocents', p. 8. **100** A. Al-Dawoody, 'IHL and Islam: an overview', *International Review of the Red Cross*, 14 March 2017. **101** Fraser, 'Morality of war', p. 96. **102** Meyer, *Cáin Adamnáin*, p. 9 (paragraph 15). **103** Ó Neill and Dumville, *Cáin Adamnáin*, p. 37.

APPENDIX

Irish Text[1]

28. Iss ead in so forus Cána Adomnán lae. Oc Birraib forurmed a forus sae for feraib Hérenn 7 Alban im bithcháin co bráth a forngairi a maithi, clérech 7 laech, immo flaithi 7 a n-oldamnae 7 a n-epscopu 7 a súthiu 7 a n-anmcharde,

Im Fland Febla súi-epscop Aird Machae
Diblaine
Elnai abb Imlechai Ibair
Cennfaelad abb Bennchuir
Failbe Becc abb Clúana maic Nóis
Conodhar apb Lismóir
Cillíne mac Luibneáin apb Biruir
Colmán mac Sechnusaigh abb Lothrai
Echuidh apb Clúanae Húamae
Forandán Cille Dara
Súadbar Insi Demle
Dibléne ap Tíre Dá Glas
Mochonnui Dairi
Oisíne mac Glais apb Clúanai Ferta Molúa
Maincíne Leith[glinne]
Moacru
Mobeoc Aird
Murchu Balnai
Moling Lúachra
Mend Maiche apb Fernai
Colcu mac Móenaig ap Luscan
Ceti epscop
Curetán epscop
Conamail mac Conáin epscop
Colmán hóa Hoircc apb Clúana hIraird
Áedh Sléibte epscop
Colmán mac Findbair[r]
Cardide Ruis Máir

[1] This is a copy of Meyer, *Cáin Adamnáin*, taken from pp 14, 16, 18, 20, 22, 24, 26, 28, 30 and 32.

Appendix

Togialloic úa Lúain, an t-ecnaid
Ichtbricht epscop
Feradach hóa Artur
Faelchú mac Máile-Rubai
Faelán hó Clúain Ferta Brenaind
Dibc[h]éine mac Fileth
Mosacra
Maelcoisnei mac Conaill
Murchu macúi Machthéine
Maeldub epscop
Ioain ecna mac in Gobann
I[o]hain mac Samuél
Faelán úa Silne
Loingsech mac Óenghusa rí Érenn
Congalach mac Ferghusa rí Ceneóil Conaild
Fland Find mac Máilituile rí Ceneóil Eogain
Conc[h]abur mac Máilidúin rí Ceneóil Coirpri
Eterscél mac Máilehumae rí Muman
Cúdínaisc mac Cellaig rí Irmuman
Cúcercae rí Oseirghi
Conghal mac Suibnei rí inna nDéissiu
Eoganán mac Crundmáil rí Úa Fidginti
Andelaith rí in Déissi túaiscirt
Elodach mac Dúnlaingi rí Desmuman
Ailill mac Concenmáthair rí Muigi Féne
Fíachrai Cossalach rí Cruithne
Béec Boirchi rí Ulad
Níel[l] mac Cernaigh rí Breghmuighi
Ceallach mac Gerthighi rí Diaballaigen
Condalach mac Conaic rí Corcu Duibhne
Corpri mac Concoluimb rí Úa Ceindselaig
Congal Úa Mrachaidi
Conall mac Doinennaig rí Úa [Fidgente]
Cellach mac Ragallaig rí Connacht
Dlúthach mac Fithchellaig rí Úa Maine
Dúnchad rí Úa nAmalgaid 7 Úa Fiachrach Murisg
Muirgios mac Máiledúin
Maicnía rí Arda úa nEchach
Murchad Midi
Colmán mac Rechtabrat rí Fernae
Maelfothartaigh mac Maolduib
Dub-díberg
Mane mac Néill
Maelcáich mac Nóindenaig

Erthuile úa Crundmáil
Aed Odbae
Echuid mac Dúnchadha rí na nDéisi
Aodh mac Dlúthaig rí Cúl
Flaithnía mac Ferghaile
Fíannamuild úa Dúnchatai
Ferathach úa Cíaráin
Fethlimith úa Fergusae
Fallomuin rí Úa Tuirtri
Fergus Forchraidh Fócortach
Garbán rí Mide
Euchu Lemnae rí Úa Cremthain
Euchu úa Domnaill rí
Conall Grant rí deiscirt Breg
Túothal úa Dúnchatha rí Úa Conaill Gabrae
Toicthech mac Cinnfaelad rÍ Lugne
Bodbhcath rí Luighne
Irgalach úa Conaing rí Cíannachtae
Bruide mac Derilei rí Cruithintúathi,
et impidi fer nÉrenn uli etir laochu 7 clérchu.

29. Tocuitchetar tra huli laechaib 7 cléirchibh ógh cána Adomnán do comalnad co brádh. Atropartatar lánéraic a mbanchró do Adomnán 7 do cach comorbuo bías ina suidiu co brádh 7 ní gata Adomnán fíachu ar flaith 7 eclais 7 fine dia mbí dír.

30. Roggádhatar tra nóibecalsi Hérenn ule im Adomnán óentaid inna déachta athar 7 maic 7 spirto nóib 7 muntire nime 7 nóebu in talman, cach óen comaldathar in cáin si etir saigid 7 timmarcain 7 comalnath 7 éraicc, arim sírsaegul somma 7 arop airmitnech féith la Día 7 dóine, arim inducbude in-nim 7 hi talmain.

31. Rogádatar dano nóibeccailsi Hérenn im Adhomnán Día co ngrádaiph nime 7 nóebhaib talman, nach óen loittfis Cháin nAdamnán itir laechu 7 cléirciu, nádasia 7 nádacomallnathar a neort 7 a cumung 7 nátimarr for cách itir flaith 7 eclais, arimm garit a shaegul co n-imniuth 7 dígrád, cen athgabáil nime ná talman úadhibh.

32. Rosuidigestar Adomnán ordd n-escoine dóaib dano .i. psalm cach laithe co fiehit laa 7 apstal nó úasalnóeb cach lái do attach leiss .i. 'Quare' 7 Petar, 'Domine quidh multiplicati' 7 Iohain , 'Uerba mea' 7 Pilip, 'Domine deus meus' 7 Partalon, 'Dixit insipiens' 7 Tomas, 'Deus, deus meus respice' 7 Mathius, 'Iudica me Domine innocentium' 7 Iacob, 'Dixit iniustus' 7 Simon, 'Domine ne qm (in furore B) 7 Tatheus, 'Dixi custodiam' 7 Madian, 'Deus deorum' 7 Marcus, 'Quidh glor[i]aris' 7 Lucas, 'Dixit insipiens' 7 Stefan, 'Exurgat Deus' 7 Ambrois,

Appendix

'Saluum me' 7 Grigair Romae, 'Deus uenerunt gentes' 7 Martan, 'Deus quis similis' 7 Senpól, 'Deus laudem' 7 Giurgius 'Audite caeli quae loquar non nobis Domine, non nobis, sed nomini tuo,' 7 rl.

33. Incipit sententia angeli Adomnano :
Adomnanus post .xiiii. annos hanc legem Deo rogauit 7 causa. Angelus sanctus Domini in nocte pentecosten ad eum 7 post annum in altero pentecosten 7 poculum arripuit 7 percussit latus eius 7 dixit ei : Exi in Hiberniam 7 fac legem in ea ne mulieres ullo more ab homine occidentur iugulatione uel quacunque morte uel ueneno uel in aqua uel in igne uel a quocunque peccode uel in fouea uel canibus nisi in lectulo legitimo. Te oportet perficere legem in Hibernia Britaniaque propter matrem uniuscuiusque, quod mater unumquemque portauerit 7 propter Mariam matrem Iesu Christi per quam totus est. Maria filium suum apud Adomnanum circa hanc legem rogauit. Quicumque enim occiderit mulierem duplici poena damnetur, id est manus eius dextera 7 pes sinister ante mortem abscidetur 7 postea moritur 7 red[d]unt fines eius septem ancellas plenas 7 septimam penitentiae. Quod si fuerit pretium inpositum pro anima 7 pro circumcisione, .xiiii. anni penitentiae 7 .xiiii. ancella[e] red[d]entur; quod si aggmen autem fecerit, quintus uir usque tricentos ista ultione damnetur ; quod si pausi, diuidentur in tres partes. Prima pars ex illis sorte mortificatur 7 circumcidetur manu 7 pede, altera reddet .xiiii. anncellas plenas, tertia iactatur in peregrinationem trans mare sub regula regiminis duri, quod grande peccatum qui matrem 7 sororem matris Christi 7 matrem Christi occidit 7 collum unumquemque portantem 7 omnem hominem uestientem contriuit. Qui autem feminam ab ipso die mortificauerit penitentiam secundum legem non agens non solum Deo 7 Adomnano in aeternum peribit [et] maledictus erit, sed maledicti erunt omnes qui audierint 7 non maledicent 7 non corripient eum secundum iudic[i]um huius legis.

Ista est sententia angeli Adomnano.

34. Iss ead in so forus cána Adomnán for Hérinn 7 Albain: sóire ecalsi Dé cona muintir 7 a fethlaib 7 a termnaib 7 a n-ule folud béudu 7 marbdu 7 al-láichib dligthechaib cona cétmunteraib téchtaidib bíte fo réir Adomnáin 7 anamcharat téchtaide ecnaid cráibthig. Fortá forus inna cána sae Adomnáin bithcáin for clérchu 7 banscála 7 maccu encu co mbat ingníma fri guin duine 7 co mbat inbuithi fri túaith 7 confestar a n-immérgi.

35. Nech gonus 7 marbus maccléreach nó mac endacc a téchtu cána Adomnáin, ocht cumala cacha láma, ocht mblíadna penda ind condice trí chét chumal 7 blíadain penda ind cach óin ó tríb cétaib co míle nó díarim 7 is cummae fiach nech fofich 7 aridaccai 7 nachidanaig a neort. Mád étged nó anfes, lethfiach ind 7 arracuir asn-étged 7 asn-anfes.

36. Fortá forus na cána sa : óghdíriu do cech eclais bís i cáinbéscnu; leithdíre dí ina termund sechtar faithchi; óghdíri dí de cech grád etir guin 7 gait 7 forloscud;

leithdíri da blái-neimthib; leithdíre a foltmaissi clérech namá cen guin, cen gait. Is óghdíri nach eclais fria sárughud a fethtaltae, cip port i ndéntur.

37. It é brithimain cánae Adomnán i cach eclais 7 i cach thúaith .i. clérich dongoat munter Adomnán 7 dia n-aithnet forus a cánae.

38. It é gella na cánu sae: trían gild di humui nó argit fo mes cacha críchiu a tóthucht cacha cainggne. Gell ar trisi, breth ar cóicthi, híc ar dechmaid di caingnib olchenae. Gell a ochtaib, breth ar trisi, híc ar cóicthi isin caingin se.

39. Forthá forus na cána as meise cacha saigte[c]he for aitiri aeter grádu túathi 7 grádu ecalse i críchaib immedón 7 i críchaib díanechtair di fiachaib beccaiph 7 móraibh ar réir Adomnán n a muintire. Apad 7 forais, 7 ní dibdai Cáin Adomnáin nach a muntire.

40. Forthá forus na cánae: día ngontar maic annaic nó cléirich, is dia n-úamaib adnacail tíaguit a féich 7 a féich erradais dia flaithib a finib.

41. Fortá a forus na cánae asn-eirrithi lánfíachaib do Adomnán na banscál romarbthar, acht ropbé cuit duine occa nó cethra nó con nó teined nó claidh nó cumtaigh, ar is eirrithi cach ndénte hi Cáin itir claid 7 cuithe 7 drochat 7 tenlach 7 céim 7 lindi 7 áthi 7 cach ingreim olchena, acht atroilli banscál dé. Acht fácabar trían fri herchomét. Mád escond atbéla ann, in dá trían aile. A trían intí asa dír.

42. Cip aided admbéla banscál, acht chuit Dé nó choiblighe díles théchtaide, asrenar lánfíachaib do Adhomnán etir guin 7 bádudh 7 loscud 7 neim 7 chombach 7 chechrad 7 athcumba ó bíastaib cenntaib 7 mucaib 7 chethruiph. Mád cétchin dono a foluth nó dona muccaib nó dona conaiph, a mmarbath fócétóir 7 lethfíach láma duine ind; mani cétchin, asrenar lánfíachaib.

43. Ní dleghar tra frithfola hi Cáin Adomnáin ná comard cinath, acht asren cách a chinta ar a láim. Na foachta fo[f]echar i Cáin Adomnán, dligith munter Adomnáin forbach dé cenmothá banscála, cit maicc ennaig cit cléirig nó do neoc dian timnat .i. cumal forbaich do muntir Iae airm i n-ícatar secht cumala 7 lethchumal di leth secht cumal. Sé séuit for tríchoit sét, tri seúit for cóic sétaib.

44. Ochtmath caich bicc 7 caich móir do muntir Adomnán di guin clérech 7 mac n-ennac. Máth béoguin rogonae nech banscál nó cléirech nó mac n-ennac, leth secht cumal húad, cóic seúit déac for fine nó anfine dia comláithriu. Trí seúit caich bánbéime, cóic seúit cach teilcthi folae, secht seúit cach inindrigh, cumal cach inuithir 7 fiach legae cenmothá sin. Is for leithfiachu gonae duine dotéitt, mád mó sin. Mádh béim co mbois nó de durn, unga argait ind. Máth glas nó derg nó att, sé scripuil for unga ind. Foltgabál ban, cóic muilt ind. Máth banaugra co sártairbirt, trí muilt ind.

45. It cobfíachaigh tra fir 7 mná hi cacha fíachaib beccaib 7 móraib di sund co banugrai ingi etirbás. Ar is ed bás dlegair do banscáil dia marbad fir nó mná, nó di thabairt neime dia n-abbalar, nó di loscad, nó di fochlaid ecalse .i. cor in-nói

Appendix

óin[s]lúaisti for murchreth hi fairrge do techt le gaeth di thír. Long menathcha do breith lee. La Día brithimnacht furi isin.

46. Mát epthai dia n-apallar dabera nech do alailiu, féich dunetáiti ind. Dubchrecha 7 chnáimchrói foreccattar hi ceth[a]rardi, mani rucae in ceth[a]rarta docom neich sainriud, datongat fo altbu anme nandfetatar for neoch 7 atrenat fadesin. Má berait dóig dochom neich co túarasndul, is éside bus fiachach. Mád etir díis nó lín bus lia beth in dóchus, scríbtar a n-anman i ndulne, dober[r] cach duilend inna ecrus im chrand 7 dobertar na crunna i cailech for altóir. Intí fora tuit cran[n]char, iss é is fiachach.

47. Mani eirre bidbaid sáraigetar cáin, asren fine al-lánfiachu íar méitt a chinad 7 doberr a ndílsi 7 a n-indarbu íarsin co cend rechtghi. Leth secht cumal dia comláithriu for cach deirbfine 7 anpfine íarsin. Mád lesugud 7 dítiu 7 chomarlécad, is bás tar[a] éissi, acht aní etirbí fiachu etirbí comláidre.

48. Fortá forus na cánae: bíat rechtaire Cána Adomnán lind bís di sóerbíathad a muintiri .i. cóicfer do aitire 7 bíathad cach óin tobó fiachu in[n]a cánae fo maith cáich etir flaith 7 eclais 7 túaith. Cumal fri toichniuth cach ae intan dombongatar féich 7 cintaigh bíathtae 7 folongat comnaidm fiach.mani bíathat side. Dí chumail doaib do cintachaib.

49. Iss í tra sóeri cach aitere dothét frimtobach (*sic*) na cána sae .i. ní téit cin fine forru céine folósat aideri 7 beta tuinidig 7 nádmbat élathaig, acht a cin fadeisin nó cin clainde 7 a compert 7 a n-amus.

50. Mád forc[h]or ingine, leth secht ccumal inn. Mádh lámh fria nó 'na crios, deich n-unga ind. Mád lám fo étach dia meabluccudh, trí uinge for secht cumal[a] ind. Má beith ainim a cinn nó a súil nó i n-aghaid nó i cclúais nó i sróin nó i bfiacail nó i ttengaid 7 i ccois nó il-láimh, it secht cumala ind. Mád ainimh i curp olcena, as leth secht cumal ind. Mád ríacad étaic[h], secht n-unga for cumhail ind.

51. Mád imdherccad dagmná im drúis no im séna a clainne, it secht cumhala ind conici airig désa anall. Let[h] secht cumal, mád ben airech désa. Ó sin anund go muirig it secht n-unga inn.

52. Mád airbert bansgál i n-orgain nó cuire nó feachta, secht cumhal[a] cac[h]a láma co mórseiser 7 cin óinfir ó sin anon[n]. Mád rotoirrched bansgál a ttáidhe cin cor, cin dílsi, cen ellam, cin ursnaidm, lánfiach de. Nach dilim fil fon lámt[h]orad méit loighet, fil fon roid 7 glaisíne 7 sep. Mád rúam in bruit, dirim bruit de.

53. Teóra aitire cac[h]a prímegalsa fri Cáin Adomnáin .i. secnap 7 coic 7 fertiges 7 aitire cána deirbfine fo Éirinn uile 7 dá eitiri cána ardflat[h]a 7 gíalla gabhála dia díl, dia mbé túarasudal bansgál.

TRANSLATION[2]

28

This is the enactment of the Law of Adomnán of Iona. At Birr this enactment has been enjoined upon the men of Ireland and Britain as a perpetual law until doom, by order of their nobles, clerical and lay, along with their lords and *ollams* and bishops and sages and confessors, including:

1. Fland of Febail sage-bishop of Armagh
2. Díblíne of Eilne abbot of Emly
3. Cenn Fáelad abbot of Bangor
4. Faílbe Becc abbot of Clonmacnoise
5. Conodar abbot of Lismore
6. Cillíne macc Luibnén abbot of Birr
7. Colmán macc Sechnasaig abbot of Lorrha
8. Echuid abbot of Cloyne
9. Forandán of Kildare
10. Suadbar of Little Island
11. Díbléne abbot of Terryglass
12. Mochonna of Derry
13. Oisíne macc Galluist abbot of Clonfertmolue
14. Mainchíne of Leighlinbridge
15. Moacru
16. Mobecóc of Ard
17. Murchú of Balla
18. Moling of Lúachair
19. Mend Machae abbot of Ferns
20. Colcu macc Móenaig abbot of Lusk
21. Bishop Céti
22. Bishop Curetán
23. Bishop Conamail macc Conainn
24. Colmán úa Oircc abbot of Clonard
25. Bishop Áed of Sletty
26. Colmán macc Findbairr
27. Cardide of Rossmore
28. Togíallóic úa Lúain the Sage
29. Bishop Uuictberct
30. Feradach úa Artúr
31. Fáelchú macc Maíle Rubai
32. Fáelán from Clonfert
33. Díbchéine macc Fileth

[2] This is a copy of the translation in Ní Dhonnchadha, 'The law of Adomnán: a translation', pp 57–68.

34 Moshacra
35 Máel Coisne macc Dall
36 Murchú moccu Machthéni
37 Bishop Máeldub
38 Ioain the Sage, macc in Gobann
39 Iohain macc Samuél
40 Fáelán úa Silne
41 Loingsech macc Óengusa king of Ireland
42 Congal macc Fergusa king of Cenél Conaill
43 Fland Find macc Maíle Tuile king of Cenél nEogain
44 Conchobur macc Maíle Dúin king of Cenél Coirpri
45 Eterscél macc Maíle hUmai king of Munster
46 Cú Dínisc macc Forchellaich king of West Munster
47 Cú Chercca king of Osraige
48 Congal macc Suibni king of the Déisi
49 Éoganán macc Crundmaíl king of Uí Fhidgeinti
50 Andelaith king of In Déis Túaiscirt
51 Élódach macc Dúnlainge king of South Munster
52 Ailill macc Con cen máthair king of Mag Féni
53 Fíachra Cossalach king of the Cruithni
54 Béc Bóirche king of the Ulaid
55 Nél macc Cernaig king of Bregmag
56 Cellach macc Gerthide king of the two Leinsters
57 Condálach macc Conaing king of Corcu Duibne
58 Coirpre macc Con Coluimb king of Uí Chendselaig
59 Conamail macc Brachaide
60 Conall macc Doinendaich king of Uí Fhidgeinti
61 Cellach macc Ragallaig king of Connacht
62 Dlúthach macc Fithchellaig king of Uí Maini
63 Dúnchad king of Uí Amalgaid and Uí Fhíachrach Muirisc
64 Muirges macc Maíle Dúin
65 Maicnia rí Ardae Úa nEchach
66 Murchad of Mide
67 Colmán macc Rechtabrat king of Feórann
68 Máel Fotharthaig macc Máelduib
69 Dub Díbeirg
70 Maine macc Néill
71 Máel Cáich macc Noíndenaig
72 Erthuile úa Crundmaíl
73 Áed Odbae
74 Eochaid macc Dúnchada king of the Déisi
75 Áed macc Dlúthaig king of Cúl [Breg]
76 Flaithnia macc Fergaile
77 Fíanamail úa Dúnchatha

78 Feradach úa Cíaráin
79 Fethelmith úa Fergosso
80 Fallomuin king of Uí Thuirtri
81 Fergus Forcaid
82 Fócartach
83 Garbán of Mide king
84 Euchu Lemnae king of Uí Chremthain
85 Euchu úa Domnaill king
86 Conall Grant king of Deiscert mBreg
87 Túothal úa Dúnchatha king of Uí Chonaill Gabra
88 Toicthech macc Cinn Fháelad king of Luigne
89 Bodbchath king of Luigne
90 Írgalach macc Conaing king of Cíanachta
91 Bruide macc Derilei king of Cruithentúath and the intercession of all the men of Ireland, both laymen and clerics.

29

All have sworn, therefore, both lay persons and clerics, to fulfil the entirety of the Law of Adomnán until Doom. They have offered the whole *éraicc*-fine[3] of their female deaths to Adomnán, and to every heir who will be in his seat until Doom, and Adomnán does not steal fines from lord or church or *fine* to whom [their payment] is due.

30

Now, all the holy churches of Ireland together with Adomnán have besought the unity of the Divinity of Father and Son and Holy Spirit and the Heavenly Host, and the saints of the earth, that whoever fulfils this Law, with respect to exacting and enforcing and effecting and *éraicc*-fine, may be long-lived and prosperous, and held in honour by God and mankind, and may be glorified in Heaven and on earth.

31

Now, all the holy churches of Ireland together with Adomnán have besought God with the orders of Heaven and the saints of the earth, that whoever shall violate the Law of Adomnán, both laypeople and clerics, who shall not exact it nor effect it to the best of his ability and power, and who shall not enforce it on every one, both chieftain and church – that his life may be short, with suffering and dishonour, leaving neither heavenly nor earthly inheritance to those [descended] from them.

---

3 Editor's note: When 'fine' is given in roman type, the term means a legal penalty; when given in italic type, it is the old Irish word for 'family', 'kindred'.

Appendix

32

Adomnán moreover has established an order of malediction for them, to wit, a psalm each day until the end of twenty days and an apostle or a noble saint besides to be invoked each day, that is:

Quare and Peter;
Domine, quid multiplicati and John;
Verba mea and Philip;
Domine Deus meus and Bartholomew;
Dixit insipiens and Thomas;
Deus, Deus meus, respice and Matthew;
Iudica me, Domine and Jacob;
Dixit iniustus and Simon;
Domine, ne in furore and Thaddeus;
Dixi: Custodiam and Madian;
Deus deorum and Mark;
Quid gloriaris and Luke;
Dixit insipiens and Stephen;
Exurgat Deus and Ambrose;
Saluum me and Gregory of Rome;
Deus, uenerunt gentes and Martin;
Deus, quis similis erit and Old Paul;
Deus, laudem meam and George;
Audite, caeli, quae loquor;
Non nobis, Domine, non nobis; sed nomini tuo, et cetera.

33

Here begins the angel's directive to Adomnán.

After fourteen years [as abbot] Adomnán obtained this Law from God and this is the cause. On Pentecost eve a holy angel of the Lord came to him, and again at Pentecost after a year, and took a staff and struck his side and said to him: 'Go forth into Ireland and make a law in that women may not be killed in any manner by man, whether through slaughter or any other death, either by poison or in water or in fire or by any beast or in a pit or by dogs, except [they die in childbirth] in lawful bed. You shall establish a law in Ireland and Britain for the sake of the mother of each one, because a mother has borne each one, and for the sake of Mary, the mother of Jesus Christ through whom the whole [human race] is.' Mary along with Adomnán besought her Son about this Law.

And whoever kills a woman shall be condemned to a twofold punishment, that is, before death, his right hand and his left foot shall be cut off and after that he shall die and his kin shall pay seven full *cumals* and [the price of] seven years' penance. If a payment has been imposed instead of life and amputation, [the payment for] fourteen years of penance and fourteen *cumals* shall be paid. If, however, a multitude have done it, every fifth man up to three hundred shall be condemned to that retribution. If few, they shall be divided into three parts. The first part of them shall be put to death by lot, hand and foot having been cut off. The second shall pay fourteen full *cumals*. The third shall be cast out into alienage beyond the sea, under the rule of hard regimen, for great is the sin when anyone kills the one who is mother, and sister to Christ's mother, and mother of Christ, she who labours in carrying the distaff and in clothing everyone. But from this day forward, he that shall put a woman to death, and not do penance in accordance with this Law, shall not only perish in eternity and be cursed by God and Adomnán, but all that have heard and do not curse him, and do not censure him according to the judgment of this Law, shall be cursed.

This is the angel's directive to Adomnán,

34

This is the enactment of the Law of Adomnán in Ireland and in Britain: the immunity of the church of God with her *familia* and her insignia and her sanctuaries and all the property, animate and inanimate, and her law-abiding laymen with their legitimate spouses who abide by the will of Adomnán and a proper, wise and holy confessor. The enactment of this Law of Adomnán enjoins a perpetual law for clerics, and females, and innocent youths until they are capable of killing a person, and of taking their place in the *túath*, and until their drove be known.

35

Whoever wounds and kills a clerical student or an innocent youth in transgression of the Law of Adonmnán, eight *cumals* and eight years of penance for it for every hand involved, up to three hundred, one *cumal* and one year of penance for it for each one from three hundred to a thousand, and it is the same fine for the one who commits it and the one who sees it and does not prevent it to the best of his ability. If there be inadvertence or ignorance, half-fine for it, and there shall be an oath-equivalent that it is inadvertence and ignorance.

36

The enactment of this Law enjoins full *díre* to every church which is in proper discipline; half-*díre* to it for [crimes in] its confines beyond the *faithche*; full *díre* to it for [crimes against] every grade, with respect to wounding and theft and burning; half-*díre* for its exempt sanctuaries; half-*díre* for merely threatening a cleric, without wounding or theft. Every church deserves full *díre* for the violation of its insignia, no matter where it is done.

37

These are the judges of *Cáin Adomnán* in every church and in every *túath*, to wit, the clerics whom the *familia* of Adomnán choose and to whom they entrust the enactment of his *Cáin*.

38

These are the pledges of this Cáin: a one-third pledge in bronze or silver according to the estimation of each territory from the entitlement of every case. The pledge before [the end of] the three-day period, judgment before [the end of] the five-day period, payment before [the end of] the ten-day period in all other cases. The pledge immediately, judgment before [the end of] the three-day period, payment before [the end of] the five-day period in this case.

39

The enactment of this Law enjoins that a hostage-surety is to be appointed with respect to every suit, both for the grades of the laity and the grades of the church, for dues small and large according to Adomnán's stipulation. [There shall be] proclaiming of enactment and the Law of Adomnán and of his *familia* shall not become extinct.

40

The enactment of this Law enjoins that if innocent youths or clerics are killed, it is to their burial-tombs that their fines come, and their *erradas*-fines to their lords and to their *fine*s.

41

The enactment of the Law enjoins that payment in full fines is to be made for every woman that has been killed, whether a human had a part in it, or animals or dogs or fire or a ditch or a building. For in *cáin*-law every construction is to be paid for, including ditch and pit and bridge and hearth and step and pool and kiln and every hardship besides, if a woman should die on account of it. But one-third is remitted for fore-maintenance if it be a senseless person that die on account of it. Of the other two-thirds, one-third belongs to whomsoever is entitled to it.

42

Whatever violent death a woman die, excepting that which results from an act of God or proper lawful union, it is paid for in full fines to Adomnán, including slaying and drowning and burning and poison and crushing and submerging and wounding by domesticated animals, and pigs and cattle. If it be the first crime on the part of the cattle, or the pigs, or the dogs, they are to be killed at once and half-due of a human hand for it. If it be not the first crime, payment is made in full fines.

43

There shall be no counter-claiming or balancing of liabilities but everyone shall pay for the crimes committed by him. The *familia* of Adomnán is entitled to a superlevy for each trespass which is committed in respect to Adomnán's Law, apart from [that against] women, be it [against] innocent youths or clerics, or [it is owing] from him to whom they commit it, that is, a *cumal* in superlevy to the *familia* of Adomnán where seven *cumals* are paid and one half-*cumal* from half of seven *cumals*. Six *séts* on thirty *séts* and three *séts* on fifteen *séts*.

44

One eighth of everything small and large to the *familia* of Adomnán for the wounding of clerics and innocent youths. It it be a non-mortal wound that anyone inflict on a woman or a cleric or an innocent youth, half seven *cumals*-from him, fifteen *séts* from [related] *fine* and unrelated *fine* for their accomplice-ship.

Three *séts* for every white blow, five *séts* for every spilling of blood, seven *séts* for every wound requiring a staunch, a *cumal* for every injury requiring attendance and the leech's fee besides. It amounts to half of the fines for murdering someone if it be more serious than that.

If it be a blow with the palm or the fist, an ounce of silver for it. If it be a livid or red mark or a swelling, six *scripuli* and one ounce [of silver] for it. Women's hair-fights, five wethers for it. If it be woman-combat with degradation, three wethers for it.

45

Men and women are equally liable, then, for all fines small and large from this up to woman-combat, except [it result in] outright death. For this is the death that a woman deserves for her killing of a man or a woman, or for ministering poison from which one dies, or for arson, or for digging beneath a church, to wit, to be put in a boat of one paddle at a sea-marking out at sea, to [see if she will] go ashore with the winds. Judgment on her in that regard [belongs] with God.

46

Should it be charms from which one dies that anyone give to another, fines for body-concealment for it. Dire mutilation and dismemberments which are found in [one of] the four [nearest] uplands, if [that one of] the four [nearest] uplands cannot charge it to anyone in particular, they deny by oath of soul-death that they know it of anyone and they make payment for it themselves. If they lay a charge of suspicion on a person, having evidence, it is he who will be liable. If the suspicion lie between two or a greater number, their names are written on leaves. Each leaf is fixed around a lot and the lots are put into a chalice on the altar. The one on whom the lot falls, it is he who is liable.

47

If the criminals who violate the Law are not apprehendable, the *fine* pay their full fines in accordance with the extent of their crimes, and thereafter is proclaimed their forfeiture [of legal rights], and their expulsion until the end of the Law. Half of seven *cumals* for their accompliceship upon every member of the *derbfine* or other *fine* after that. If there be maintenance and protection and connivance, it is death for it, but that [same amount] which applies to fines applies to accompliceship.

48

The enactment of the Law enjoins: they shall feed the steward of the Law of Adomnán, for whatever period [is required], with the noble refection of his company, that is, the surety as one of five and refection [also] for every one who shall levy the fines of the Law [shall be provided] according to the rank of each, be he lord or cleric or layman. One *cumal* for refusing food to any one of them while fines are being levied; and [when proven guilty] it is the offenders who must feed them, and they are liable for a joint bond of fines. If they do not feed them, two *cumals* to them [i.e. the leviers] from offenders.

49

This, then, is the immunity of every hostage-surety who takes up the joint levying of this Law: they bear no liability for the *fine*'s crime, so long as they uphold [their] suretyship [if the offenders abscond] and remain *in statu* and do not default, apart from their own crime, or that of the family, or their offspring or their hirelings.

50

If it be forcible rape of a girl, half of seven *cumals* for it. If it be hand [touching] against her or on her belt, ten ounces for it. If it be knocking a woman down with intention to injure, one *cumal* and seven ounces for it. If it be [putting] a hand under her clothing to dishonour her, one *cumal* and three ounces for it. If there be a defect in her head or eye or face or ear or nose or tooth or tongue or foot or hand, there is seven *cumals* for it. If it be a defect in another part of the body, half of seven *cumals* for it.

51

If it be insulting a woman by [accusing her of] lust or by denying her child, there are seven *cumals* for it [for every woman] down to [the wife of] an *aire désa*. Half of seven *cumals* if it be the wife of an *aire désa*. From that down to a castaway, there are seven ounces for it.

52

If it be making use of women in a massacre or a muster or a raid, seven *cumals* for every hand [involved] as far as seven, and [it is reckoned as] the crime of one man from that onwards. If a woman has been made pregnant through fornication, without contract, without property, without bride-price, without betrothal, full fines for it. Whatever reckoning is made for the [finished] hand-produce, however great or small, the same is made for the madder and woad and onion; if it be the red dye of a cloak, the value of a cloak for it.

53

Three hostage-sureties for every principal church for the Law of Admonán, to wit, the prior and the cook and the guest-master, and a hostage-surety for every *derbfhine* throughout Ireland, and two hostage-sureties for noble lords, and a hostage as warrant for levying it, if there be the [collective] evidence of women.

Bibliography

MANUSCRIPT SOURCES

Rawlinson MS B 512 in the Bodleian Library, Oxford, ff 48r–51v.
O'Clery MS 2324–40 in the Bibliothèque Royale, Brussels, ff 76r–82v.
O'Clery, MS, 4190–200 in the Bibliothèque Royale, Brussels, f. 46v.
Generalia 1: *The Schaffhausen Adomnán* in the Stadtbibliothek, Schaffhausen.

PRIMARY SOURCES

Ademar of Chabannes, *Chronique d'Ademar de Chabannes*, ed. J. Chavanon in *Collection des textes pour servir l'étude et l'enseignement de l'histoire* 20 (Paris, 1897).
Adomnán, *DLS*, ed. D. Meehan (Dublin, 1958).
— *DLS*, ed. L. Bieler, 'Adomnán, *De locis sanctis*', *CCSL*, 175 (Turnhout, 1965), pp 185–234.
— *VC*, ed. and trans. W. Reeves, *The Life of St Columba, founder of Hy: written by Adamnán, ninth abbot of that monastery* (Dublin, 1857; 2nd ed. 1874).
— *VC*, ed. P. Geyer, *Adamnanus, Abt von Iona. I. Teil* (Augsburg, 1895).
— *VC*, ed. and trans. A.O. Anderson and M.O. Anderson, *Adomnan's Life of Columba* (Edinburgh, 1961; 2nd ed. Oxford, 1991).
— *VC*, trans. R. Sharpe, *Adomnán of Iona: Life of St Columba* (London, 1995).
— *VC*, eds D. Bracken and E. Graff, *The Schaffhausen Adomnán, Schaffhausen Stadtbibliothek, MS Generalia 1* (2 vols, Cork, 2015).
Annals of St-Bertin, trans. J.L. Nelson in *The Annals of St-Bertin: ninth-century histories* (Manchester, 1991).
Aristotle, *Politics*, trans. E. Barber (Oxford, 1995).
— *De Rhetorica ad Alexandrum*, trans. W.R. Roberts (Oxford, 1959).
— *Nicomachean Ethics*, trans. R. Crisp (Cambridge, 2000).
Asser, *Life of King Alfred*, trans. S.D. Keynes and M. Lapidge in *Alfred the Great* (London, 1983), pp 65–110.
Attenborough, F.L. (ed. and trans.), *The laws of the earliest English kings* (Cambridge, 1922).
Augustine, *De libero arbitrio* (*PL* 44).
— *De Civitate Dei* (*CCSL* 47–8).
— *De consensu evangelistarum* (*CSEL* 43).
— *De Ordine* (*CCSL* 29).
— *Epp* (*MGH Epp*).
— *Opus imperfectum contra Julianum* (*PL* 45).
— *Quaestiones in Heptateuchum* (*CSEL* 28).
— *Contra Faustum* (*CSEL* 25).
Ayala, B. (1582), *Three books on the laws of war*, trans. J.P. Bate (Washington, 1912).

Baldric of Bourgueil, *The Historia Ierosolimitana*, ed. S. Biddlecombe (Woodbridge, 2014).
Bede, *Historia Ecclesiastica*, eds. and trans. B. Colgrave and R.A.B. Mynors in *Bede's ecclesiastical history of the English people* (Oxford, 1969).
Belli, P. (1563), *A treatise on military matters and warfare*, trans. H.C. Nutting (Oxford, 1936).
Best, R.I. & Bergin, O. (eds), *Lebor na hUidre: the Book of the Dun Cow* (Dublin, 1929).
Best, R.I., Bergin, O., O'Brien, M.A. & O'Sullivan, A. (eds), *The Book of Leinster, formerly Lebar na Núachongbála* (6 vols, Dublin, 1954–83).
Bieler, L. (ed. and trans.), *The Irish penitentials* (Dublin, 1963).
Binchy, D.A. (ed. and trans.), 'Bretha Crólige', *Ériu*, 12 (1938), pp 1–77.
— (ed.), 'Melbretha', *Celtica*, 8 (1968), pp 144–54.
— (ed.), *Críth Gablach* (Dublin, 1941, repr. 1970).
— (ed.), *Corpus Iuris Hibernici* (6 vols, Dublin, 1978).
Breatnach, L. (ed. and trans.), *Uraicecht na Ríar: the poetic grades in early Irish law* (Dublin, 1987).
Breen, A., 'Towards a critical edition of *De xii Abusivis*: Introductory essays with a provisional edition of the text and accompanied by an English translation' (PhD, Trinity College, Dublin, 1988).
Brunner, H., *Deutsche Rechtsgeschichte: Systematisches Handbuch der deutchen Rechtwissenshaft* (Leipzig, 1882–92).
Caesarius of Arles, *Sermones*, ed. D. Germani Morin, *CCSL*, 103 (2 vols, Turnhout, 1953), i.
Carney, J. (ed. and trans.), 'A Maccucáin, Sruith in Tíag', *Celtica*, 15 (1983), pp 25–41.
Charles-Edwards, T.W. (ed. and trans.), *The Chronicle of Ireland* (2 vols, Liverpool, 2006).
Cicero, *De Officiis*, trans. P.G. Walsh (Oxford, 2001).
Colgrave, B. (ed. and trans.), *Two Lives of Saint Cuthbert: A Life by an anonymous monk of Lindisfarne and Bede's Prose Life* (Cambridge, 1940).
Connolly, S. (ed. and trans.), '*Vita Prima Sanctae Brigitae*: background and historical value', *JRSAI*, 119 (1989), pp 5–49.
Connolly, S. & Picard, J.-M. (eds and trans.), 'Cogitosus's Life of Brigit: content and value', *JRSAI*, 117 (1987), pp 5–27.
Cummian, *De Controversia Paschali*, ed. and trans. M. Walsh and D. Ó Cróinín, *Cummian's Letter De Controversia Paschali and the De Ratione Computandi* (Toronto, 1988).
De Clercq, C. (ed.), *Conciliae Galliae A.511–A.695*, *CCSL*, 148 A (Turnhout, 1963).
De Vattel, E., *Le Droit des Gens* (1758), trans. J.B. Scott (Oxford, 1916).
De Vitoria, F., *De Iure Belli Relectiones*, ed. A. Pagden, *Vitoria: political writings* (Cambridge, 2012)
Dunant, H., *Un souvenir de Solferino* (Geneva, 1862).
Eddius Stephanus, *Life of Wilfrid*, ed. and trans. B. Colgrave in *The Life of Bishop Wilfrid by Eddius Stephanus* (Cambridge, 1927).
Einhard, *Life of Charlemagne*, ed. and trans. A.J. Grant, *Early Lives of Charlemagne by Eginhard and the Monk of St Gall* (London, 1922).
Eusebius, *Vita Constantini*, ed. F. Winkelman (*GCS*, 1975).
Felix, *Life of Guthlac*, ch. 16 (fifteen), ed. and trans. B. Colgrave in *Felix's Life of Guthlac* (Cambridge, 1956).
Finsterwalder, P.W. (ed.), *Die Canones Theodori Cantuariensis* (Weimar, 1929).
Fischer Drew, K. (trans.), *The Burgundian code* (Philadelphia, 1972).

Bibliography

— (trans.), *The Lombard laws* (Philadelphia, 1973).
— (trans.), *The laws of the Salian Franks* (Philadelphia, 1991).
Flechner, R. (ed.), *A study, edition and translation of the Hibernensis, with commentary* (Dublin, forthcoming).
Fredegar, ed. B. Krusch in *Chronicle, MGH SRM* (Hanover, 1888), ii, 1–193.
Fulcher of Chartres in A.C. Krey (trans.), *The First Crusade: the accounts of eye-witnesses and participants* (Princeton, 1921).
— *A history of the expedition to Jerusalem 1095–1127*, ed. H.S. Fink and trans. F.R. Ryan (Tennessee, 1969).
Gantz, J. (trans.), *Early Irish myths and sagas* (London, 1981).
Gregory I, *Registrum Epistolarum* in *MGH Epp*, eds P. Ewald and M. Hartmann (2 vols, Berlin, 1891–9).
Gregory of Tours, *Historia Francorum*, eds W. Arndt and B. Krusch in *MGH SRM* (Berlin, 1885), 10:1.
— *Histories*, trans. L. Thorpe in *Gregory of Tours: the history of the Franks* (Penguin, 1974).
Grimm, J., *Deutche Rechtsalterthümer* (Göttingen, 1828, repr. Darmstadt, 1983).
Grotius, *De Jure Belli ac Pacis (1625)*, trans. W. Whewell (London, 1913).
Hancock, W.N. et al. (eds), *Ancient laws of Ireland* (6 vols, Dublin, 1865–1901).
Hellmann, S. (ed.), *Ps.-Cyprianus. De xxii abusiuis saeculi* (Leipzig, 1909).
Hennessy, W.M. (ed. and trans.) *Chronicum Scotorum: a chronicle of Irish affairs from the earliest times to AD 1135, with a supplement containing events from 1141–1156* (London, 1866).
Herbert, M. & Ó Riain, P. (eds and trans.), *Betha Adamnáin: The Irish Life of Adamnán* (London, 1988).
Hippolytus, *Apostolic tradition*, ed. G. Dix (London, 1937).
Hull, V. (ed.), 'Cáin Domnaig', *Ériu*, 20 (1966), pp 151–77.
Isidore, *Etymologies*, ed. and trans. S.A. Barney et al. (Cambridge, 2006).
— *Isidori Hispalensis Episcopi Etymologiarum sive Originum Libri XX*, ed. W.M. Lindsay (Oxford, 1911).
Jennings, B., 'Documents from the archives of St Isidore's College, Rome', *Analecta Hibernica*, 6 (1934), pp 203–47.
Jonah, *Vita Columbani*, ed. B. Krusch in *MGH SRM* (Hanover, 1902), iv, 61–152.
Julian of Toledo, *History of King Wamba*, 10, ed. W. Levison in *MGH SRM* (Hanover, 1910), v, 501–56.
— *Historia Wambae Regis*, ed. and trans. J. Martinez Pizarro (Washington, 2005).
Kant, I., *Metaphysek der Sitten, Rechtslehre*, trans. M.J. Gregor (Cambridge, 1991).
Kelly, F. (ed. and trans.), *Audacht Morainn* (Dublin, 1976).
Kinsella, T. (trans), *The Táin* (Oxford, 1969).
Knott, E. (ed.), *Togail Bruidne Da Derga* (Dublin, 1936).
Krusch, B. (ed.), *Liber Historiae Francorum* in *MGH SRM*, ii, 213–328 and trans. in P. Fouracre and R. Gerberding, *Late Merovingian France: history and hagiography, 640–720* (Manchester, 1996).
Kurse, F. (ed.), *Royal Frankish annals* in *MGH SRG* (Hanover, 1895).
Leo I (Pope), *Epistolae*, ed. J.P. Migne (221 vols, Paris, 1844–65), 54, cols 1199–1200.
Loyn, H.R. & Percival, J. (eds and trans.), *The reign of Charlemagne: documents on Carolingian government and administration* (London, 1975).
Maassen, F. (ed.), *MGH, Concilia Aevi Merovingici* (Hanover, 1893).
Mac Airt, S. & Mac Niocaill, G. (eds and trans.), *The Annals of Ulster* (Dublin, 1983).

Mac Mathúna, S. (ed. and trans.), *Immram Brain: the voyage of Bran to the land of women* (Tübingen, 1985).
Mansi, G. (ed.), *Sacrorum Conciliorum Nova et Amplissima Collectio*, revised by J. Martin and L. Petit (60 vols, Paris, 1899–1927).
Mansi, J.P. (ed.), *Sacrorum Conciliorum Nova et Amplissima Collectio* 7 (Florence, 1762).
Márkus, G. (trans.), *Adomnán's 'Law of the Innocents'* (Glasgow, 1997).
— (trans.), *Adomnán's 'Law of the Innocents': Cáin Adomnáin* (Kilmartin, 2008).
Merkel, J. (ed.), *Leges Alamannorum, MGH Legum* (Hanover, 1898), iii, 1–182.
— *Leges Baiuwariorum, MGH Legum* (Hanover, 1898), iii, 183–496.
Meyer, K. (ed. and trans.), *Cáin Adamnáin: an Old Irish treatise on the Law of Adamnán* (Oxford, 1905).
Meyer, K. & Nutt, A. (eds and trans.), *The voyage of Bran son of Febal* (London, 1895).
Migne, J.P. (ed.), *Patrologia Latina* (221 vols, Paris, 1844–65).
Muirchú Moccu Macthéni, *'Vita Sancti Patricii': Life of Saint Patrick*, ed. and trans. D. Howlett (Dublin, 2006).
Murphy, G. (ed. and trans.), *Early Irish lyrics* (Oxford, 1956).
Ní Dhonnchadha, M. (ed. and trans.) 'An edition of *Cáin Adomnáin*' (PhD, University College, Cork, 1992).
— 'The law of Adomnán: a translation' in T. O'Loughlin (ed.), *Adomnán at Birr AD 697, essays in commemoration of the Law of the Innocents* (Dublin, 2001), pp 53–68.
Nicholas I(Pope), *Responsa ad Consulta Bulgarorum*, 41 and 102, ed. E. Perels in *MGH Epp*, VI (Berlin, 1925).
Nithard, *Histories*, in *Carolingian chronicles*, trans. B.W. Scholz (Ann Arbour, 1972).
Notker, *Deeds of Charlemagne*, trans. L. Thorpe in *Einhard and Notker the Stammerer, Two Lives of Charlemagne* (London, 1969).
Ó hAodha, D. (ed. and trans.), *Bethu Brigte* (Dublin, 1978).
Ó Néill, P.P. & Dumville, D.N. (eds and trans.), *Cáin Adomnáin and Canones Adomnani II* (Cambridge, 2003).
Ó Riain, P. (ed.), *Corpus Genealogiarum Sanctorum Hiberniae* (Dublin, 1985).
O'Donovan, J. (ed. and trans.), *Annála Rioghachta Éireann: annals of the kingdom of Ireland by the Four Masters* (7 vols, Dublin, 1848–51).
O'Donovan, J. (trans.), Todd, J.H. and Reeves, W. (eds), *The martyrology of Donegal: a calendar of the saints of Ireland* (Dublin, 1864).
O'Rahilly, C. (ed. and trans.), *Táin Bó Cúailnge: recension I* (Dublin, 1976).
Óengus of Tallaght, *Félire Óengusso*, ed. and trans. W. Stokes, *Félire Óengusso Céli Dé: The martyrology of Oengus the Culdee* (London, 1905).
Origen, *Contra Celsum* VIII, 73 in *GCS, Origenes* II, ed. P Koetschau (Berlin, 1899).
Oskamp, H.P.A. (ed.), '*Echtra Condla*', *Études Celtiques*, 14 (1974/5), pp 207–28.
Plummer, C. (ed. and trans.), *Irish litanies* (London, 1925).
Radner, J.N. (ed. and trans.), *Fragmentary annals of Ireland* (Dublin, 1978).
Raymond of Aguilers, 'On the Fall of Jerusalem' in A.C. Krey (trans.), *The First Crusade: the accounts of eyewitnesses and participants* (Princeton, 1921).
Rivers, T.J. (ed. and trans.), *Laws of the Salian and Ripuarian Franks* (New York, 1986).
Salvian of Marseilles, *Oeuvres*, ed. G. Lagarrigue in *Sources Chrétiennes* 176 (Paris, 1971).
Scott, S. P. (trans.), *The Visigothic code (Forum Iudicum)* (Boston, 1910).
Smith, R.M. (ed. and trans.), 'The advice of Doidin', *Ériu*, 11 (1932), pp 66–85.
Sohm, R. (ed.), *Lex Ribuaria, MGH Legum* (Hanover, 1875–89), v, 185–268.

Stokes, W. (ed. and trans.), *The Annals of Tigernach*, Revue Celtique, 16 (1895), pp 374–419; 17 (1896), pp 6–33 and pp 119–263 and pp 337–420; 18 (1897), pp 9–59 and pp 150–97 and pp 267–303 and pp 374–91 (repr. 2 vols, Felinfach, 1993).

— (ed. and trans.), *The Tripartite Life of Patrick and other documents related to the saint* (2 vols, London, 1887).

— (ed. and trans.), *Félire Óengusso Céli Dé: The martryology of Oengus the Culdee* (London, 1905).

Stokes, W. & Strachan, J. (eds), *Thesaurus Paleohibernicus: a collection of old-glosses, scholia, prose and verse* (2 vols, Cambridge, 1901–3)

Suarez, F., 'De bello' in J.B. Scott, *Selections from three works of Francisco Suarez. Original Latin text* (Oxford, 1944).

Tertullian, *Adversus Marcionem*, ed. and trans. E. Evans (Oxford, 1972).

— *De Idololotria*, 19 in *CSEL* 20, eds A. Riefferscheid and G. Wissowa (Vienna 1890).

— *De Idololotria*, eds and trans. J.H. Waszink and J.C.M. Van Winden (Leiden, 1987).

— *De corona* 11 in *CSEL* 70, ed. E. Kroymann (Vienna, 1942).

Tírechán, '*Collectanea*', ed. and trans. L. Bieler *The Patrician texts in the Book of Armagh* (Dublin, 1979), pp 122–62.

Ussher, J., *The whole works*, ed. C. Elrington (17 vols, Dublin, 1844–64), vi.

Von Clausewitz, C., *On war*, trans. J.J. Graham (London, 1908).

Von Richthofen, K. (ed.), *Lex Frisionum, MGH Legum* (Hanover, 1898), v, 631–711.

Von Richthofen, K. & K.F. (eds), *Leges Saxonum, MGH Legum* (Hanover, 1875–89), v, 1–102.

Von Richthofen, K.F. (ed.), *Lex Thuringorum, MGH Legum* (Hanover, 1875–89), v, 103–42.

Wasserschleben, F.H.W., *Die Bu ordnungen der abendländischen Kirche* (1851, repr. Graz, 1958).

Wasserschleben, H. (ed.), *Die irische Kanonensammlung* (Leipzig, 1885).

Wolff, C. (ed.), *Jus Gentium Methodo Scientifica Pertractatum* (1749), trans. T. James (Oxford, 1934).

Wormald, P. (trans.), *The first code of English law* (Medway, Kent, 2005).

Wu Cheng'en (trans. W.J.F. Jenner), *Journey to the West* (Beijing, 1982).

SECONDARY SOURCES

Abass, A., *Complete international law* (Oxford, 2012).

Abé, R., *The weaving of mantra: Kukai and the construction of esoteric Buddhist discourse* (New York, 1999).

Ahlqvist, A., 'Le Testament de Morann', *Études Celtiques*, 21 (1984), pp 151–70.

Aist, R., 'Adomnán, Arculf and the source material of *De locis sanctis*' in J.M.Wooding et al. (eds), *Adomnán of Iona: theologian, lawmaker, peacemaker* (Dublin, 2010), pp 162–80.

Aitchison, N.B., 'Regicide in early medieval Ireland' in G. Halsall (ed.), *Violence and society in the early medieval West* (Woodbridge, 1998), pp 108–125.

Al-Dawoody, A., 'IHL and Islam: an overview', *International Review of the Red Cross*, 14 March 2017.

Alexander, J.J.G., *Insular manuscripts 6th to the 9th century* (London, 1978).

Allmand, C., 'War and the non-combatant in the Middle Ages' in M. Keen (ed.), *Medieval warfare: a history* (Oxford, 1999), pp 253–72.

Amory, P., 'The meaning and purpose of ethnic terminology in the Burgundian laws', *Early Medieval Europe*, 2:1 (1993), pp 1–28.

Bachrach, D.S., *Religion and the conduct of war* (Woodbridge, 2003).

Bainton, R.H., 'The early church and war', *Harvard Theological Review*, 39 (1946), pp 189–213.

— *Christian attitudes toward war and peace* (Nashville, 1960).

Balzaretti, R., '"These are things that men do, not women": the social regulation of female violence in Langobard Italy' in G. Halsall (ed.), *Violence and society in the early medieval West* (Woodbridge, 1998), pp 175–92.

Bannerman, J., *Studies in the sistory of Dalriada* (Edinburgh and London, 1974).

Barthélemy, D., *L'an mil et la paix de Dieu, La France Chrétienne et Féodale, 980–1060* (Paris, 1999).

— 'The Peace of God and bishops at war in the Gallic lands from the late tenth to the early twelfth century' in C.P. Lewis (ed.), *Anglo-Norman Studies 32, Proceedings of the Battle Conference 2009* (Woodbridge, 2010), pp 1ff.

Bennett, M., 'Violence in eleventh-century Normandy: feud, warfare and politics' in G. Halsall (ed.), *Violence and society in the early medieval West* (Woodbridge, 1998), pp 126–40.

Best, R.I., 'Notes on Rawlinson B.512', *Zeitschrift für celtishe Philologie*, 17 (Halle, 1896–1943), pp 389–402.

Bhreathnach, E. (ed.), *The kingship and landscape of Tara* (Dublin, 2005).

— 'The *seanchas* tradition in late medieval Ireland' in E. Bhreathnach and B. Cunningham (eds), *Writing Irish history: the Four Masters and their world* (Dublin, 2007), pp 19–23.

— *Ireland in the medieval world AD 400–1000: landscape, kingship and religion* (Dublin 2014).

Bilton, M. & Sims, K., *Four hours in My Lai, a war crime and its aftermath* (London, 1992).

Binchy, D.A., 'Patrick and his biographers: ancient and modern', *Studia Hibernica*, 2 (1962), pp 7–173.

— *Celtic and Anglo-Saxon kingship* (Oxford, 1970).

— 'Celtic suretyship, a fossilised Indo-European institution' in J.M. Kelly (ed.), *The Irish Jurist*, 7:2 (Dublin, 1972), pp 360–72.

Bonnaud-Delamare, R., *L'idée de Paix á l'époque Carolingienne* (Paris, 1939).

Bourke, J., *An intimate history of killing* (London, 1999).

Bradley, J., 'Towards a definition of the Irish monastic town' in C. Karkov and H. Damico (eds), *Aedificia Nova: studies in honour of Rosemary Cramp* (Kalamazoo, 2008), pp 325–60.

Breatnach, L., 'The ecclesiastical element in the Old-Irish legal tract *Cáin fhuithirbe*', *Peritia*, 5 (1986), pp 36–52.

— 'Lawyers in early Ireland' in D. Hogan and W.N. Osborough (eds), *Brehons, serjeants and attorneys: studies in the history of the Irish legal profession* (Dublin, 1990), pp 1–13.

— 'Review of Herbert and Ó Riain, *Betha Adamnáin*', *Éigse*, 26 (1992), pp 77–87.

— *The early Irish law text Senchas Már and the question of its date*, E.G. Quiggin Memorial Lectures, 13 (Cambridge, 2011).

Breatnach, P.A., *The Four Masters and their manuscripts: studies in palaeography and text* (Dublin, 2013).

Breen, A., 'The evidence of antique Irish exegesis in Pseudo-Cyprian, *De duodecim abusivis saeculi*', *PRIA*, 87C (1987), pp 71–101.

Broun, D., *Scottish independence and the idea of Britain from the Picts to Alexander III* (Edinburgh, 2007).

Brown, D. & Clancy, T.O. (eds), *Spes Scotorum, hope of Scots: Saint Columba, Iona and Scotland* (Edinburgh, 1999).
Brown, P.R.L., 'St Augustine's attitude to religious coercion', *Journal of Roman Studies*, 54 (1964), pp 107–16.
— *Augustine of Hippo* (London, 1967).
— *Religion and society in the age of Saint Augustine* (New York and London, 1972).
— *The rise of Western Christendom: triumph and diversity, AD 200–1000* (2nd ed., Oxford, 2003).
Brown, W.C., *Violence in medieval Europe* (Harlow, 2011).
Brown, W., *Unjust seizure: Conflict, interest and authority in early medieval society* (Ithaca, 2001).
Bruford, A., 'Why an Ulster cycle?' in J.P. Mallory and G. Stockman (eds), *Ulidia* (Belfast, 1994), pp 23–30.
Brundage, J.A., 'The hierarchy of violence in twelfth- and thirteenth-century canonists', *International History Review*, 17 (Nov. 1995), pp 671–92.
Bull, H., Kingsbury, B. & Roberts, A. (eds), *Hugo Grotius and international relations* (Oxford, 1990).
Bullough, D.A., 'Was there a Carolingian anti-war movement?', *Early Medieval Europe*, 12 (2003), pp 365–76.
Byrne, F.J., *Irish kings and high-kings* (Dublin, 1973).
— 'Church and politics, *c*.750–*c*.1100' in D. Ó Cróinín (ed.), *NHI*, pp 656–79.
Cadoux, C.J., *The early Christian attitude to war* (London, 1919).
— *The early Christian attitude to war: a contribution to the history of Christian ethics* (New York, 1982).
Calley, W.L., *Body count* (London, 1971).
Campbell, J. (ed.), *The Anglo-Saxons* (Oxford, 1982).
— 'The debt of the English church to Ireland' in P. Ní Chatháin and M. Richter (eds), *Irland und Europa: Die Kirche im Frühmittelalter/Ireland and Europe: The early church* (Stuttgart, 1984), pp 332–46.
Carey, J., 'On the interrelationships of some *Cín Dromma Snechtai* texts', *Ériu*, 46 (1995), pp 71–92.
— 'Varieties of supernatural contact in the Life of Adamnán' in J. Carey, M. Herbert and P. Ó Riain (eds), *Studies in Irish hagiography: saints and scholars* (Dublin, 2001), pp 49–62.
Carey, J., Nic Cárthaigh, E. & Ó Dochartaigh, C. (eds), *The end and beyond: medieval Irish eschatology* (2 vols, Aberystwyth, 2014).
Carney, J., 'Language and literature to 1169' in D. Ó Cróinín (ed.), *NHI*, pp 451–510.
Cassese, A., *International law* (Oxford, 2005).
Chadwick, H., 'The early Christian community' in J. McManners (ed.), *The Oxford illustrated history of Christianity* (Oxford, 1990), pp 21–61.
Chapman Stacey, R., *The road to judgment: from custom to court in medieval Ireland and Wales* (Philadelphia, 1994).
— *Dark speech: the performance of law in early Ireland* (Philadelphia, 2007).
Charles-Edwards, T.M., 'Bede, the Irish and the Britons', *Celtica*, 15 (1983), pp 42–5.
— *Early Irish and Welsh kinship* (Oxford, 1993).
— 'The new edition of Adomnán's *Life of Columba*', *CMCS*, 26 (1993), pp 65–73.
— 'A contract between king and people', *Peritia*, 8 (1994), pp 107–19.

— 'The contexts and uses of literacy in early Christian Ireland' in H. Pryce (ed.), *Literacy in medieval Celtic societies* (Cambridge, 1998), pp 62–82.
— *Early Christian Ireland* (Cambridge, 2000).
— '*Érlam*: the patron-saint of an Irish church' in A. Thacker and R. Sharpe (eds), *Local saints and local churches in the early medieval West* (Oxford, 2002), pp 267–90.
— 'The Uí Néill 695–743: the rise and fall of dynasties', *Peritia*, 16 (2002), pp 396–418.
— 'Introduction: prehistoric and early Ireland' in D. Ó Cróinín (ed.), *NHI*, pp lvii–lxxxii.
— 'Early Irish law' in D. Ó Cróinín (ed.), *NHI*, pp 182–234.
— 'Brigit [St Brigit, Brigid](439/452–524/526), patron saint of Kildare', http://www.oxforddnb.com/view/article/3427, accessed 19 Oct. 2015.
Clancy, T.O., 'Adomnán in medieval Gaelic literary tradition' in J.M. Wooding et al. (eds), *Adomnán of Iona: theologian, lawmaker, peacemaker* (Dublin, 2010).
Clarke, H.B. & Johnson, R. (eds), *The Vikings in Ireland and beyond: before and after the Battle of Clontarf* (Dublin, 2015).
— 'Ireland and the Viking age' in H.B. Clarke and R. Johnson (eds), *The Vikings in Ireland and beyond: before and after the Battle of Clontarf* (Dublin, 2015), pp 1–24.
Clarke, H.B., Ní Mhaonaigh, M. & Ó Floinn, R. (eds), *Ireland and Scandinavia in the early Viking age* (Dublin, 1998).
Coffey, B., 'The Stowe enigma: decoding the mystery', *Irish Theological Quarterly*, 75:1 (2010), pp 75–91.
Coker, C., *Humane warfare* (London, 2001).
Collins, R., 'Julian of Toledo and the royal succession in late seventh-century Spain' in P. Sawyer and I. Wood (eds), *Early medieval kingship* (Leeds, 1977), pp 30–49.
Corlett, C. & Potterton, M. (eds), *Death and burial in early medieval Ireland in the light of recent archaeological excavations* (Bray, 2010).
Costambeys, M., *Power and patronage in early medieval Italy: local society, Italian politics and the abbey of Farfa, 700–900* (Stuttgart, 1982).
Cowdrey, H.E.J., 'The Peace and Truth of God in the eleventh century', *Past and Present*, 46 (1970), pp 42–67.
Coyne, F. (with a contribution by L.G. Lynch), 'Corbally, Co. Kildare: the results of the 2003–4 excavations of a secular cemetery' in C. Corlett and M. Potterton (eds), *Death and burial in early medieval Ireland in the light of recent archaeological excavations* (Bray, 2010), pp 77–90.
Cramer, P., *Baptism and change in the early Middle Ages c.200–c.1400* (Cambridge, 1993).
Cunningham, B., *The Annals of the Four Masters* (Dublin, 2010).
Daintree, D., 'Virgil and Virgil scholia in early medieval Ireland', *Romanobarbarica*, 16 (1999), pp 347–61.
Davies, W. & Fouracre, P. (eds), *The settlements of disputes in early medieval Europe* (Cambridge, 1986).
De Jong, M., *The penitential state: authority and atonement in the age of Louis the Pious, 814–880* (Cambridge, 2009).
De Than, C. & Shorts, E., *International criminal law and human rights* (London, 2003).
Deane, H., *The political and social ideas of St Augustine* (New York, 1963).
Degregorio, S. (trans.), *Bede: On Ezra and Nehemiah* (Liverpool, 2006).
Dixon, M., *Textbook on international law* (Oxford, 2013).
Doherty, C., 'Some aspects of hagiography as a source for Irish economic history', *Peritia*, 1 (1982), pp 300–28.

— 'The monastic town in early medieval Ireland' in H. Clarke and A. Simms (eds), *The comparative history of urban origins in non-Roman Europe: Ireland, Wales, Denmark, Germany, Poland and Russia from the ninth to the thirteenth century* (Oxford, 1985), pp 45–75.

— 'The cult of Patrick and the politics of Armagh in the seventh century' in J.-M. Picard (ed.), *Ireland and northern France, AD 600–850* (Dublin, 1991), pp 53–94.

— 'The use of relics in early Ireland' in P. Ní Chatháin and M. Richter (eds), *Ireland and Europe in the early Middle Ages: learning and literature* (Stuttgart, 1996) pp 89–101.

— 'Kingship in early Ireland' in E. Bhreathnach (ed.), *The kingship and landscape of Tara* (Dublin, 2005), pp 3–31.

— 'Warrior and king in early Ireland' in J.E. Rekdal and C. Doherty (eds), *Kings and warriors in early north-west Europe* (Dublin, 2016), pp 88–148.

Douglas, M., *Purity and danger: an analysis of the concepts of pollution and taboo* (London and New York, 1980).

Draper, G.I.A.D., 'Penitential discipline and public wars in the Middle Ages: a medieval contribution to the development of humanitarian law', *International Review of the Red Cross* (1961), pp 4–18 and pp 63–78.

Drew, K., *Law and society in early medieval Europe: studies in legal history* (London, 1988).

Duby, G. (trans. C. Postan), 'Les laïcs et la paix de Dieu' in *The Chivalrous Society* (Berkeley, 1977), pp 123–33.

Dudden, F.H., *Life and times of Saint Ambrose* (2 vols, Oxford, 1935).

Dumville, D., 'Towards an interpretation of *Fís Adamnán*', *Studia Celtica*, 12/13 (1977–8), pp 62–77.

— Review of Dáibhi Ó Cróinín's *Early medieval Ireland, 400–1200* in *Times Literary Supplement*, 3 January 1997.

— '*Félire Óengusso*: Problems of dating a monument of Old Irish', *Éigse*, 33 (2002), pp 19–48.

— Review of T. O'Loughlin (ed.), *Adomnán at Birr AD 697, essays in commemoration of the Law of the Innocents* (Dublin, 2001), *Catholic Historical Revue*, 89:2 (2003), pp 283–4.

Duncan, J.S., *The city as text: the politics of landscape interpretation in the Kandyan kingdom* (Cambridge, 1990).

Elsakkers, M., '*Raptus ultra Rhenum*: Early ninth-century Saxon laws on abduction and rape', *Amsterdamer Beiträge zur Älteren Germanistik*, 52 (1999), pp 27–53.

Elshtain, J.B., *The just war theory* (Oxford, 1992).

Enright, M.J., *Iona, Tara and Soissons: the origin of the royal anointing ritual* (Berlin and New York, 1985).

— 'Further reflection on royal ordinations in the *Vita Columbae*' in M. Richter and J.-M. Picard (eds), *Ogma: essays in Celtic studies in honour of Próinséas Ní Chatháin* (2002), pp 20–35.

Erdmann, C., *The origin of the idea of Crusade* [orig. *Die Entstehung des Kreuzzugsgedankens* (Stuttgart, 1933)], trans. M.W. Baldwin and W. Goffart (Princeton, 1977).

Esposito, M., 'Notes on Latin learning and literature in medieval Ireland, IV: On the early Lives of St Brigid of Kildare', *Hermathena*, 49 (1935), pp 120–65.

Etchingham, C., 'The implications of *Paruchia*', *Ériu*, 44 (1993), pp 139–62.

— *Church organization in Ireland AD 650–1000* (Naas, 1999).

Evans, M.D. (ed.), *International law* (Oxford, 2003).

Evans, M. (ed.), *Just war theory: a reappreasal* (Edinburgh, 2005).

Evans, N., *The present and the past in medieval Irish chronicles* (Woodbridge, 2010).
Falk Moore, S., *Law as process: an anthropological approach* (London and Boston, 1978).
Farr, C., 'The incipit pages of the MacRegol Gospels' in R. Moss (ed.), *Making and meaning in Insular art* (Dublin, 2007), pp 275–87.
Fell, C., *Women in Anglo Saxon England and the impact of 1066* (Bloomington, 1984).
FitzPatrick, E. & O'Brien, C., *The medieval churches of County Offaly* (Dublin, 1998).
FitzPatrick, E., *Royal inauguration in Gaelic Ireland, c.1100–1600: a cultural landscape study* (Woodbridge, 2004).
Flechner, R., 'An insular tradition of ecclesiastical law: fifth to eighth century', *Proceedings of the British Academy*, 157 (2009), pp 23–46.
— 'The Chronicle of Ireland: then and now', *Early Medieval Europe*, 21:4 (2013), pp 422–54.
Flechner, R. & Meeder, S. (eds), *The Irish in early medieval Europe: identity, culture and religion* (London, 2016).
Follett, W., *Céli Dé in Ireland: writing and identity in the early Middle Ages* (Woodbridge, 2006).
Fontaine, J., 'Education and learning' in P. Fouracre (ed.), *The new Cambridge medieval history c.500–c.700* (7 vols, Cambridge, 2005), i, 735–59.
Forde, S., 'Hugo Grotius on ethics and war', *The American Political Science Review*, 92:3 (Sept. 1998), pp 639–48.
Fotion, N., *War and ethics* (London, New York, 2007).
Fouracre, P., 'Attitudes towards violence in seventh and eighth century Francia' in G. Halsall (ed.), *Violence and society in the early medieval West* (Woodbridge, 1998), pp 60–75.
— 'Conflict, power and legitimation in Francia in the late seventh and eighth centuries' in I. Alfonso, H. Kennedy and J. Escalona (eds), *Building legitimacy: political discourses and forms of legitimacy in medieval societies* (Leiden, 2004), pp 3–26.
Frantzen, A., *The literature of penance in Anglo-Saxon England* (New Brunswick, 1983).
— 'Spirituality and devotion in the Anglo-Saxon penitentials', *Essays in Medieval Studies*, 22 (2005), pp 117–28.
Fraser, J.E., 'Adomnán and the morality of war' in J.M. Wooding et al. (eds), *Adomnán of Iona: theologian, lawmaker, peacemaker* (Dublin, 2010), pp 95–111.
— 'Adomnán, Cumméne Ailbe, and the Picts', *Peritia*, 17–18 (2003–4), pp 183–98.
Frend, W.H.C., *Martyrdom and persecution in the early church* (Oxford, 1965).
Friedburg, A. (ed.), 'Causa in pars secunda of the *Decretum Gratiani*' in *Corpus Iuris Canonici* (Leipsig, 1879), i.
García Moreno, L.A., 'Legitimate and illegitimate violence in Visigotic law' in G. Halsall (ed.), *Violence and society in the early medieval West* (Woodbridge, 1998), pp 46–59.
Gardiner, D., '"These are not the things men live by now a days": Sir John Hartington's visit to the O'Neill, 1599', *Cahiers Élisebéthains*, 55 (1999), pp 1–17.
Gaudemet, J., 'L'étrangers au bas empire', *Recueils Bodin*, 9 (1958), pp 207–35.
Geary, P.J., *Readings in medieval history* (Peterborough, 2003).
Geber, J., 'Human remains from Owenbristy' in G. Delaney and J. Tierney (eds), *In the lowlands of south Galway: archaeological excavations on the N18 Oranmore to Gort national road scheme* (Dublin, 2011), pp 88–97.
— 'Comparative study of perimortem weapon trauma in two early medieval skeletal populations (AD 400–1200) from Ireland', *International Journal of Osteoarchaeology*, 25:3 (May/June 2015), pp 253–64.

Gergen, T., 'The Peace of God and its legal practice in the eleventh century', *Cuadernos de Historia del Derecho*, 9 (2002), pp 11–27.
Gillespie, A., *A history of the laws of war* (3 vols, Oxford, 2011).
Gillett, A., *Envoys and political communication in the late antique West, 411–533* (Cambridge, 2003).
Given, J.B., *Society and homicide in thirteenth-century England* (Stanford, 1977).
Glover, J., *Humanity: a moral history of the twentieth century* (New Haven, 2001).
Goetz, H.W., 'Protection of the church, defense of the law, and reform: on the purposes and character of the Peace of God' in T. Head and R. Landes (eds), *The Peace of God: social violence and response in France around the year 1000* (New York, 1992), pp 259–79.
Goldstein, J., Marshall B. & Schwarth J. (eds), *The Peers Commission Report* (New York, 1976).
Gorman, M., 'Adomnán's *De locis sanctis*: the diagrams and the sources', *Revue Bénédictine*, 116 (2006), pp 5–41.
— 'Patristic and pseudo-Patristic citations in the *Collectio Hibernensis*', *Revue Bénédictine*, 121:1 (2011), pp 18–93.
Greenwood, C., 'The relationships between *ius ad bellum* and *ius in bello*', *Internatinal Studies*, 9:4 (October 1983), pp 221–34.
Grigg, J., 'The just king and *De duodecim abusiuis saeculi*', *Parergon*, 27:1 (2010), pp 27–52.
Gwynn, L., 'The reliquary of Adamnán', *Archivium Hibernicum*, 4 (1915), pp 199–214.
Haggart, C., 'The *céli Dé* and the early medieval Irish church: a reassessment', *Studia Hibernica*, 34 (2006–7), pp 11–62.
Haggenmacher, P., *Grotius et la Doctrine de la Guerre Juste* (Paris, 1983).
— 'Mutations du concept de guerre juste de Grotius à Kant', *Cahiers de Philosophie Politique et Juridique*, 10 (1986), pp 107–22.
Halfond, G.I., 'War and peace in the acta of the Merovingian church councils' in idem (ed.), *The medieval way of war: studies in medieval history in honour of Bernard S. Bachrach* (Oxford, 2015), ch. 2.
Halsall, G. (ed.), *Violence and society in the early medieval West* (Woodbridge, 1998).
— *Warfare and society in the barbarian West, 450–900* (Abingdon, 2003).
Hamilton, S., *The practice of penance, 900–1050* (London, 2001).
Harnack A., *Militia Christi: die Christliche Religion und der Soldatenstand in den ersten drei Jahrhunderten* (Tübingen, 1905).
Hartigan, R.S., 'Saint Augustine on war and killing: the problem of the innocent', *Journal of the History of Ideas*, 27:2 (1966), pp 195–204.
— *The forgotten victim: a history of the civilian* (Chicago, 1982).
— *Civilian victims in war: a political history* (Piscataway, NJ, 2010).
Hartmann, U., *Carl von Clausewitz and the making of modern strategy* (Potsdam, 2002).
Harvey, A., 'Problems in dating the origins of the ogham script' in J. Higgitt et al. (eds), *Roman, runes and ogham: medieval inscriptions in the Insular world and on the Continent* (Donnington, 2001), pp 37–50.
Hazard, B., *Faith and patronage: the political career of Flaithri Ó Maolchonaire c.1560–1629* (Dublin, 2010).
— 'Flaithrí, Firbisigh and Maoilechlainn: three Uí Mhaoil Chonaire brothers in the late sixteenth and early seventeenth centuries' in E. Purcell et al. (eds), *Clerics, kings and Vikings: essays on medieval Ireland in honour of Donnchadh Ó Corráin* (Dublin, 2015), pp 209–16.

Head, T. & Landes, R. (eds), *The Peace of God: social violence and response in France around the year 1000* (New York, 1992).

Head, T., 'The development of the Peace of God in Aquitaine (970–1005)', *Speculum*, 74 (1999), pp 656–86.

Hedges, C., *War is a force that gives us meaning* (New York, 2002).

Hemphill, S., 'The gospels of MacRegol of Birr: a study in Celtic illumination', *PRIA*, 29C (1911), pp 1–10.

Herbert, M., *Iona, Kells and Derry: the history and hagiography of the monastic familia of Columba* (Oxford, 1988).

— 'The world of Adomnán' in T. O'Loughlin (ed.), *Adomnán at Birr AD 697, essays in commemoration of the Law of the Innocents* (Dublin, 2001).

Herren, M., 'The authorship, date of composition and provenance of the so-called *Lorica Gildae*', *Ériu*, 24 (1973), pp 35–51.

Heuss, A., 'Die völkerrechtlichen Grundlagen der römischen Aussenpolitik in republikanisher Zeit', *Klio*, supplement 31 (1933).

Heuston, R. F.V., *Salmond on the law of torts* (13th ed., London, 1961).

Hillgarth, J.N., 'Ireland and Spain in the seventh century', *Peritia*, 3 (1984), pp 1–16.

Hogan, M., *The gospel book of Macregol of Birr* (Offaly, 2007).

Holmes, A., *Carl von Clausewitz's 'On War': a modern day interpretation of a strategy classic* (Oxford, 2010).

Hough, C., 'Two Kentish laws concerning women: a new reading of Aethelberht 73 and 74', *Anglia*, 119:4 (2001), pp 554–78.

Houlihan, J.W., review of J.M. Wooding et al. (eds), *Adomnán of Iona: theologian, lawmaker, peacemaker* (Dublin, 2010), *Peritia*, 26 (2015), pp 292–4.

— 'Adomnán's *Lex Innocentium* and the jurisprudence of warfare' (PhD, University College, Dublin, 2019).

Housley, N., *Contesting the Crusades* (Malden, 2006).

— *Fighting for the Cross: crusading in the Holy Land* (New Haven, 2008).

Howlett, D., *The Celtic Latin tradition of Biblical style* (Dublin, 1995).

— '*Vita I Sanctae Brigitae*', *Peritia*, 12 (1998), pp 1–23.

Hubrecht, G., 'La guerre juste dans la doctrine chrétienne, des origins au milieu du XVIe siècle', *Recueil de la Société Jean Bodin*, 15 (1961).

Hughes, K., *The church in early Irish society* (London, 1966).

— *Early Christian Ireland: introduction to the sources* (London, 1972).

— 'The church in Irish society, 400–800' in D. Ó Cróinín (ed.), *NHI*, pp 301–30.

Hyams, N., *Ecgfrith: king of the Northumbrians, high-king of Britain* (Donington, 2015).

Ireland, C., 'Aldfrith of Northumbria and Irish genealogies', *Celtica*, 22 (1991), pp 64–78.

— 'Aldfrith of Northumbria and the learning of a *sapiens*' in K.A. Klar et al. (eds), *A Celtic florilegium: studies in memory of Brendan O Hehir* (Andover, Mass, 1996), pp 63–77.

Jaski, B., 'Marriage laws in Ireland and on the Continent in the early Middle Ages' in C.E. Meek and M.K. Simms (eds), *'The fragility of her sex': medieval Irish women in their European context* (Dublin, 1996), pp 16–42.

Jennings, B., 'Míchéal Ó Cléirigh, chief of the Four Masters, and his associates' in N. Ó Muraíle (ed.), *Míchéal Ó Cléirigh, his associates and St Anthony's College, Louvain* (Dublin, 2008), pp 19–122.

Johnston, E., 'Íte: patron of her people', *Peritia*, 14 (2000), pp 421–28.

— 'Kingship made real? Power and the public world in *Longes mac nUislenn*' in F. Edmonds and P. Russell (eds), *Tome: studies in medieval Celtic history and law in honour*

of Thomas Charles-Edwards (Woodbridge, 2011), pp 193–206.
— *Literacy and identity in early medieval Ireland* (Woodbridge, 2013).
— 'Immacallam Choluim Chille 7 ind Óclaig: language and authority in an early-medieval Irish tale' in E. Purcell et al. (eds), *Clerics, kings and Vikings: essays on medieval Ireland in honour of Donnchadh Ó Corráin* (Dublin, 2015), pp 418–28.
— 'Literacy and conversion on Ireland's Roman frontier: from emulation to assimilation?' in N. Edwards, M. Ní Mhaonaigh and R. Flechner (eds), *Transforming landscapes of belief in the early medieval Insular world and beyond: converting the isles II* (Turnhout, 2017), pp 35–51.
— 'Mapping literate networks in early medieval Ireland: quantitative realities, social mythologies?' in R. Kenna et al. (eds), *Maths meets myths: quantitive approaches to ancient narratives* (Cham, 2017), pp 195–211.
— Review of D. Bracken and E. Graff (eds), *The Schaffhausen Adomnán, Schaffhausen stadt-bibliothek, MS Generalia 1* (2 vols, Cork, 2015), *Irish Literary Supplement* (Spring 2017).
Jotischky, A., *Crusading and the Crusader States* (Harlow, 2004).
Keegan J., *A history of warfare* (London, 1994).
Kelly, F., 'An Old-Irish text on court procedure', *Peritia*, 5 (1986), pp 74–106.
— *A guide to early Irish law* (Dublin, 1988).
Kelly, P., 'The *longphort* in Viking-age Ireland: the archaeological evidence' in H.B. Clarke and R. Johnson (eds), *The Vikings in Ireland and beyond: before and after the Battle of Clontarf* (Dublin, 2015), pp 55–82.
Kenney, J.F., *The sources for the early history of Ireland: ecclesiastical* (New York, 1929, reprs. with corrections, Dublin, 1978 and 1993).
King, P.D., *Law and society in the Visigothic kingdom* (Oxford, 1972).
Kissane, N., *Saint Brigid of Kildare: life, legend and cult* (Dublin, 2017).
Klabbers, J., *International law* (Cambridge, 2013).
Koch, J.T. & Carey, J., *The Celtic heroic age* (3rd ed., Andhover, MA, and Aberystwyth, 2000).
Kolb, R., 'Origin of the twin terms *jus ad bellum/jus in bello*', *International Review of the Red Cross*, 320 (1997), pp 1–8.
Kottje, R., *Die Tötung im Kriege: ein moralisches und rechtliches Problem im frühen Mittelalter* (Barsbüttel, 1991).
— 'Tötung im Krieg als rechtliches und moralisches Problem im früheren und hohen Mittelalter' in H. Hecker, *Krieg in Mittelalter und Renaissance* (Düsseldorf, 2005), pp 17–39.
Kuttner, S., 'The father of the science of canon law', *Jurist*, 1 (1941), pp 2–19.
Lacey, B., *Cenél Conaill and the Donegal kingdoms, AD 500–800* (Dublin, 2006).
— 'Adomnán and Donegal' in J.M. Wooding et al. (eds), *Adomnán of Iona: theologian, lawmaker, peacemaker* (Dublin, 2010), pp 20–35.
— *Medieval and monastic Derry: sixth century to 1600* (Dublin, 2013).
Landau, P., 'Gratian and the *Decretum Gratiani*' in W. Hartmann and K. Pennington (eds), *The history of medieval canon law in the classical period: from Gratian to the Decretals of Pope Gregory IX* (Washington, 2008), pp 22–54.
Langan, J., 'The elements of St Augustine's just war theory', *The Journal of Religious Ethics*, 12:1 (1984), pp 19–38.
Lapidge, M. & Sharpe, R. (eds), *A bibliography of Celtic-Latin literature 400–1200* (Dublin, 1985).
Latham, A.A., 'Theorizing the Crusades: identity, institutions, and religious war in medieval Latin Christendom', *International Studies Quarterly*, 55 (2011), pp 223–43.

Lauranson-Rosaz, C., 'Peace from the mountains: the Auvergnat origins of the Peace of God' in T. Head and R. Landes (eds), *The Peace of God: social violence and response in France around the year 1000* (New York, 1992), pp 104–34.

Lauterpacht, H., 'The problem of the revision of the law of war', *British Yearbook of International Law*, 29 (1952), art. 382, pp 1–46.

Levie, H.S., 'History of the law of war on land', *International Review of the Red Cross*, 838 (2000), pp 1–8.

Levy, E., *West Roman vulgar law: the law of property* (Philadelphia, 1951).

Lucas, A.T., 'Irish Norse relations: time for a reappraisal', *Journal of the Cork Historical and Archaeological Society*, 71 (1966), pp 62–75.

Lupoi, M., *Alle radici del mondo giuridico Europeo* (1994), with trans. by A. Belton as *The origins of the European legal order* (Cambridge, 2000).

Mac Cana, P. & Ó Floinn, T., *Scéalaíocht na Ríthe* (Baile Átha Cliath, 1956).

Mac Niocaill, G., *The medieval Irish annals* (Dublin, 1975).

Mac Shamhráin, A. & Byrne, P., 'Prosopography I: Kings named in *Baile Chuinn Chétchathaig* and *The Airgíalla Charter Poem*' in E. Bhreathnach (ed.), *The kingship and landscape of Tara* (Dublin, 2005), pp 159–224.

MacCotter, P., *Medieval Ireland: territorial, political and economic divisions* (Dublin, 2008).

MacDonald, A.J., 'Two kinds of war? Brutality and atrocity in later medieval Scotland' in J. Rogge (ed.), *Killing and being killed: bodies in battle: perspectives on fighters in the Middle Ages* (Bielefeld, 2017), pp 199–230.

MacIntyre, T., 'Field observations on the craw cree' in his *A glance will tell you and a dream confirm* (Dublin, 1994).

MacQueen, J., 'The saint as a seer: Adomnán's account of Columba' in H.E. Davidson (ed.), *The seer in Celtic and other traditions* (Edinburgh, 1989), pp 37–51.

Magnou-Nortier, E., 'The enemies of the peace: reflections on a vocabulary, 500–1100' in T. Head and R. Landes (eds), *The Peace of God: social violence and response in France around the year 1000* (New York, 1992), pp 58–79.

— 'La tentative de subversion de l'etat sous Louis le Pieux et l'oeuvre des falsificateurs', *Moyen âge*, 105 (1999), pp 331–65 and 615–41.

Markus, R.A., 'Saint Augustine's views on the "just war"', *Studies in Church History*, 20 (1983), pp 1–13.

— *The end of ancient Christianity* (Cambridge, 1990).

Marstrander, C. (ed.), 'The deaths of *Lugaid* and *Derbhforgaill*', *Ériu*, 5 (1911), pp 201–18.

Matthox, J.M., *Saint Augustine and the theory of just war* (London, 2006).

Mayr-Harting, H., *The coming of Christianity to Anglo-Saxon England* (London, 1972).

— 'The West: the age of conversion (700–1050)' in J. McManners (ed.), *The Oxford illustrated history of Christianity* (Oxford, 1990), pp 92–122.

McCarthy, D.P., 'Review of Charles-Edwards' *The Chronicle of Ireland*', *Peritia*, 20 (2008), pp 379–87.

— *The Irish annals: their genesis, evolution and history* (Dublin, 2008).

— 'The genesis and evolution of the Irish annals', *Frühmittelalterliche Studien*, 52 (2018), pp 119–55.

McCone, K., 'Brigit in the seventh century: a saint with three lives?', *Peritia*, 1 (1982), pp 107–45.

— 'Werewolves, cyclopes, *díberga* and *fianna*: juvenile delinquency in early Ireland', *Cambridge Medieval Celtic Studies*, 12 (1986), pp 1–22.

— *Pagan past and Christian present in early Irish literature* (Maynooth, 1990).
— (ed.), *Echtrae Connlai and the beginnings of vernacular narrative writing in Ireland* (Maynooth, 2000).
McCormick, M., *Eternal victory: triumphal rulership in late antiquity, Byzantium, and the early medieval West* (Cambridge, 1986).
McKitterick, R., *The Frankish kingdoms under the Carolingians* (Harlow, 1983).
— 'Knowledge of canon law in the Frankish kingdoms before 789: the manuscript evidence', *Journal of Theological Studies*, 36 (1985), pp 140–68.
— *History and memory in the Carolingian world* (Cambridge, 2004).
McLeod, N., *Early Irish contract law* (Sydney, 1999).
— 'Di Ércib Fola', *Ériu*, 52 (2002), pp 123–216.
McLynn, N.B., *Ambrose of Milan: church and court in a Christian capital* (Berkeley and Los Angeles, 1994).
McManus, D., *A guide to ogam* (Maynooth, 1991).
McNamara, M., *The Apocrypha in the Irish church* (Dublin, 1975), p. 126 (no. 100).
Meens R., 'The Penitential of Finnian and the textual witness of the Penitentiale Vindobonense "B"', *Medieval Studies*, 55 (1993), pp 243–55.
— 'Pollution in the early Middle Ages: the case of the food regulations in penitentials', *Early Medieval Europe*, 4:1 (1995), pp 3–19.
— *Penance in medieval Europe, 600–1200* (Cambridge, 2014).
— 'The Irish contribution to the penitential tradition' in R. Flechner and S. Meeder (eds), *The Irish in early medieval Europe* (London, 2016), pp 131–45.
Miller, D.H., 'Sacral kingship, biblical kingship, and the elevation of Pepin the Short' in T.F.X. Noble and J.J. Contreni (eds), *Religion, culture and society in the early Middle Ages: studies in honour of Richard E. Sullivan* (Michigan, 1987).
Moisl, H., 'The Bernician royal dynasty and the Irish in the seventh century', *Peritia*, 2 (1983), pp 103–26.
Moore, M.E., 'The ancient Fathers: Christian antiquity, patristics and Frankish canon law', *Millennium Yearbook/ Millennium Jahrbuch*, 7 (2010), pp 293–342.
— *A sacred kingdom: bishops and the rise of Frankish kingship 300–800* (Washington, DC, 2011).
Moore, R.I., 'Family, community and cult on the eve of the Gregorian reform', *Translations of the Royal Historical Society*, 5th ser., 30 (1980).
More-Watson, J., 'Adomnán: vanquisher of binary opposition: a structural analysis of the miracles in the second book of Adomnán's *Vita Columbae*', *Northern Studies*, 38 (2004), pp 123–33.
Murray, K., *The early Finn Cycle* (Dublin, 2017).
Nagy J.F., *Conversing with angels and ancients: the literary myth of medieval Ireland* (Dublin, 1997).
Nelson, J.L., 'The church's military service in the ninth century: a contemporary view', *Studies in Church History*, 20 (1983), pp 15–30.
— 'Public *Histories* and private history in the work of Nithard' in *Politics and ritual in early medieval Europe* (London, 1986), pp 195–237.
— 'Review of Head and Landes (eds) 1992', *Speculum*, 69 (1994), pp 163–9.
— 'Violence in the Carolingian world and the ritualization of ninth-century warfare' in G. Halsall (ed.), *Violence and society in the early medieval West* (Woodbridge, 1998), pp 90–107.

Ní Bhrolcháin, M., *An introduction to early Irish literature* (Dublin, 2009).
Ní Chonaill, B., 'Child-centred law in medieval Ireland' in R. Davis and T. Dunne (eds), *The empty throne: childhood and the crisis of modernity* (www.eprints.gla.ac.uk/3812/).
Ní Dhonnchadha, M., 'The guarantor-list of *Cáin* Adomnáin, 697', *Peritia*, 1 (1982), pp 178–215.
— 'The *Lex Innocentium*: Adomnán's law for women, clerics and youths, 697 AD' in M. O'Dowd and S. Wichert (eds), *Chattel, servant or citizen: women's status in church, state and society* (Belfast, 1995), pp 58–69.
— 'Birr and the Law of the Innocents' in T. O'Loughlin (ed.), *Adomnán at Birr AD 697, essays in commemoration of the Law of the Innocents* (Dublin, 2001), pp 13–32.
Nussbaum, A., 'Just war – a legal concept?', *Michigan Law Review*, 42 (1943).
Ó Briain, F., 'The hagiography of Leinster' in J. Ryan (ed.), *Féilsgribhinn Eóin Mhic Néill: essays and studies presented to Professor Eoin MacNeill on the occasion of his seventieth birthday, May 15th, 1938* (Dublin, 1940), pp 457–63.
— 'Brigitana', *ZCP*, 36 (1977), pp 112–37.
Ó Briain, M., 'Herbert and Ó Riain, *Betha Adamnáin*', *Studia Hibernica*, 27 (1993), pp 155–8.
Ó Carragáin, T., *Churches in early medieval Ireland: architecture, ritual and memory* (New Haven and London, 2010).
Ó Cathasaigh, T., 'The concept of the hero in Irish mythology' in R. Kearney (ed.), *The Irish mind* (Dublin, 1985), pp 79–90.
— 'Pagan survivals: the evidence of early Irish narrative' in P. Ní Chatháin and M. Richter (eds), *Irland und Europa: Die Kirche im Frühmittelalter* (Stuttgart, 1987), pp 291–307.
Ó Cathasaigh, T. & Ó Coileáin, S., 'Oral or literary: some strands of the argument', *Studia Hibernica*, 17–18 (1977), pp 7–35.
Ó Corráin, D., *Ireland before the Normans* (Dublin, 1972).
— 'High-kings, Vikings and other kings', *Irish Historical Studies*, 21 (1979), pp 283–323.
— 'Ireland, Wales, Man and the Hebrides' in P. Sawyer (ed.), *The Oxford illustrated history of the Vikings* (Oxford, 1997), pp 83–109.
— 'Ireland *c*.800: aspects of society' in D. Ó Cróinín (ed.), *NHI*, pp 549–608.
— (ed.), *Clavis Litterarum Hibernensium: medieval Irish books and texts (c.400–c.1600)* (3 vols, Turnhout, 2017).
Ó Corráin, D., Breatnach, L. & Breen, A., 'The laws of the Irish', *Peritia*, 3 (1984), pp 382–438.
Ó Cróinín, D., 'Pride and prejudice', *Peritia*, 1 (1982), pp 352–62.
— 'Rath Melsigi, Willibrord, and the earliest Echternach manuscripts', *Peritia*, 3 (1984), pp 17–49.
— *Early medieval Ireland 400–1200* (2nd ed., London, 2017).
— (ed.), *A new history of Ireland, i: prehistoric and early Ireland* (Oxford, 2005) [*NHI*].
— 'Ireland, 400–800' in idem (ed.), *NHI*, pp 182–234.
— 'Hiberno-Latin literature to 1169' in idem (ed.), *NHI*, pp 371–407.
Ó Floinn, R., 'The Shannon Shrine: a suggested provenance' in E. Purcell, P. MacCotter, J. Nyhan and J. Sheehan (eds), *Clerics, kings and vikings: essays on medieval Ireland in honour of Donnchadh Ó Corráin* (Dublin, 2015), pp 291–302.
Ó Mainnin, M.B. & Toner, G. (eds), *Ulidia 4: Proceedings of the Fourth International Conference on the Ulster cycle tales* (Dublin, 2017).

Ó Riain, P., 'Conversion in the vocabulary of the early Irish church' in D. Ó Corráin, L. Breatnach and K. McCone (eds), *Sages, saints and storytellers: Celtic studies in honour of Professor James Carney* (Maynooth, 1989), pp 358–66.

— *Feastdays of the saints: a history of Irish martyrologies* (Bruxelles, 2006).

O'Brien, C., *Stories from a sacred landscape: Croghan Hill to Clonmacnoise* (Offaly, 2006).

O'Brien, C., *Bede's temple: an image and its interpretation* (Oxford, 2015).

O'Brien, F., 'Irish Franciscan College of St Anthony, Louvain' in N. Ó Muraíle (ed.), *Mícheál Ó Cléirigh, his associates and St Anthony's college, Louvain* (Dublin, 2008), pp 155–65.

O'Connor, R., *The destruction of Da Derga's hostel: kingship and narrative artistry in a medieval Irish saga* (Oxford, 2013).

— 'Monsters of the tribe: berserk fury, shapeshifting and social dysfunction in *Táin Bó Cúailnge, Egils saga* and *Hrólfs saga kraka*' in J.E. Rekdal and C. Doherty (eds), *Kings and warriors in early north-west Europe* (Dublin, 2016), pp 180–236.

O'Donovan, O., *The just war revisited* (Cambridge, 2003).

O'Dwyer, P., *Céli Dé: spiritual reform in Ireland, 750–900* (Dublin, 1981).

O'Leary, P., '*Fír Fer*: An internalized ethical concept in early Irish literature?' *Éigse*, 22 (1987), pp 1–14.

O'Loughlin, T., 'The library of Iona in the late seventh century: the evidence of Adomnán's *De Locis Sanctis*', *Ériu*, 45 (1994), pp 33–52.

— (ed.), *Adomnán at Birr AD 697, essays in commemoration of the Law of the Innocents* (Dublin, 2001).

— *Adomnán and the holy places: the perceptions of an Insular monk on the location of the biblical drama* (London, 2007).

— 'The *De locis sanctis* as a liturgical text' in J.M. Wooding et al. (eds), *Adomnán of Iona: theologian, lawmaker, peacemaker* (Dublin, 2010), pp 181–92.

O'Neill, P., 'Landmarks of another kind: setting adrift and early Irish law', *Australia and New Zealand Law and History eJournal* (2006).

O'Neill, T., 'The changing character of early medieval burial at Parknahown 5, Co. Laois, AD 400–1200' in C. Corlett and M. Potterton (eds), *Death and burial in early medieval Ireland in the light of recent archaeological excavations* (Bray, 2010), pp 251–60.

O'Neill, T., *The Irish hand: scribes and their manuscripts from the earliest times* (Cork, 2014).

O'Sullivan, A. and W., 'A legal fragment', *Celtica*, 8 (1968), pp 140–5.

Oliver, L., *The body legal in barbarian law* (Toronto, 2011).

Paxton, F.S., 'History, historians and the Peace of God' in T. Head and R. Landes (eds), *The Peace of God: social violence and response in France around the year 1000* (New York, 1992), pp 21–40.

Payer, P.J., 'Confession and the study of sex in the Middle Ages' in V.L. Bullough and J.A. Brundage (eds), *Handbook of medieval sexuality* (New York, 1996), pp 3–31.

Pereira Farrell, E., 'Taboos and penitence: Christian conversion and popular religion in early medieval Ireland' (PhD, University College, Dublin, 2012).

Philippson, C., *The international law and customs of ancient Greece and Rome* (2 vols, London 1911).

Picard, J.-M., 'The purpose of Adomnán's *Vita Columbae*', *Peritia*, 1 (1982), pp 160–77.

— 'Bede, Adomnán, and the writing of history', *Peritia*, 3 (1984), pp 50–70.

— 'Structural patterns in early Hiberno-Latin hagiography', *Peritia*, 4 (1985), pp 67–82.

— 'The strange death of Guaire Mac Áedáin' in M. Breatnach et al. (eds), *Sages, saints and storeytellers: Celtic studies in honour of Professor James Carney* (Maynooth, 1989), pp 367–75.

— 'Adomnán's *Vita Columbae* and the cult of Colum Cille in continental Europe', *PRIA*, 98C (1998), pp 1–23.

Pierce, R. (McKitterick), 'The "Frankish" penitentials', in D. Baker (ed.), *Studies in Church History*, 11 (Oxford, 1975), pp 31–9.

Poschman, B., *Penance and the annointing of the sick*, trans. and rev., F. Courtney (New York, 1964).

— *Die abendländische Kirchenbu e im frühen Mittelalter* (Breslau, 1930).

Prelog, J., 'Sind die Weihesalbungen insularen Ursprungs?', *Frümittelalterliche Studien*, 13 (1979), pp 303–56.

Regout, R., *La doctrine de la guerre juste de Saint Augustin à nos jours, d'après les théologiens et les canonistes Catholiques* (Paris, 1935).

Rekdal, J.E. & Doherty, C. (eds), *Kings and warriors in early north-west Europe* (Dublin, 2016).

Remensnyder, A.G., 'Pollution, purity and peace: an aspect of social reform between the late tenth century and 1076' in T. Head and R. Landes (eds), *The Peace of God: social violence and response in France around the year 1000* (New York, 1992), pp 280–307.

Riché, P., 'Columbanus, his followers and the Merovingian church' in H.B. Clarke and M. Brennan (eds), *Columbanus and Merovingian monasticism* (Oxford, 1981), pp 59–72.

Richter, M., *Ireland and her neighbours in the seventh century* (Dublin, 1999).

Riley-Smith, J., *Crusades: idea and reality 1095–1274. Documents of Medieval History*, 4 (London, 1981).

— *The First Crusade and the idea of crusading* (Philadelphia, 1991).

— *The Oxford illustrated history of the Crusades* (New York, Oxford, 1995).

— 'Religious warriors, reinterpreting the Crusades', *The Economist* (23 December 1995).

— *The first crusaders, 1095–1131* (Cambridge, 1997).

— *The Crusades: a history* (New Haven, 2005).

Roberts, S., *Order and dispute: an introduction to legal anthropology* (New York, 1979).

Rosenwein, B., *Negotiating space: power, restraint and privileges of immunity in early medieval Europe* (Ithaca, NY, 1999).

Rouillard, P., *Histoire de la Penitence des Origins à Nos Jours* (Paris, 1996).

Russell, F.H., *The just war in the Middle Ages* (Cambridge, 1975).

— 'Love and hate in medieval warfare: the contribution of Saint Augustine', *Nottingham Medieval Studies*, 31 (1987), pp 108–24.

Russell Smith, T., 'Willing body, willing mind: non-combatant culpability according to English combatant writers, 1327–77' in J. Rogge (ed.), *Killing and being killed: bodies in battle: perspectives on fighters in the Middle Ages* (Bielefeld, 2017), pp 79–107.

Ryan, E.A., 'The rejection of military service by the early Christians', *Theological Studies*, 13 (1952), pp 1–32.

Ryan, J., 'The *Cáin Adomnáin*', in R. Thurneysen et al. (eds), *Studies in early Irish law* (Dublin, 1936), pp 269–76.

Sarti L., *Perceiving war and the military in early Christian Gaul* (Leiden, 2013).

Sayers, W., 'Games, sport and para-military exercise in early Ireland', *Aethlon: Journal of Sport Literature*, 10:1 (1992), pp 105–23.

Schindler, D. & Toman J., *The laws of armed conflicts* (Geneva, 1988).

Sharpe, R., 'Hiberno-Latin *laicus*, Irish *láech* and the Devil's men', *Ériu*, 30 (1979), pp 75–92.
— '*Vitae S Brigitae*: the oldest texts', *Peritia*, 1 (1982), pp 81–106.
— *Medieval Irish saints' lives: an introduction to 'Vitae Sanctorum Hiberniae'* (Oxford, 1991).
— *A handlist of Latin writers of Great Britain and Ireland before 1540* (Turnhout, 1997).
Shaw, M.M.N., QC, *International law* (6th ed., Cambridge, 2008).
Slotkin, E.M., 'Medieval Irish scribes and fixed texts', *Éigse*, 17 (1979), pp 437–56.
Smith, C. & Gallen, J., 'Cáin Adomnáin and the laws of war', *JHIL* 16 (2014), pp 63–81.
Smyth, A.P., 'The earliest Irish annals: their first contemporary entries, and the earliest centres of recording', *PRIA*, 72C (1972), pp 1–48.
— *Scandinavian York and Dublin* (2 vols, Dublin, 1975–9).
— *Celtic Leinster: towards an historical geography of early Irish civilization, AD 500–1600* (Dublin, 1982).
— 'The effect of Scandinavian raiders on English and Irish churches: a preliminary reassessment' in B. Smith (ed.), *Britain and Ireland, 900–1300: Insular responses to medieval European change* (Cambridge, 1999), pp 1–38.
Stancliffe, C., 'Kings who opted out' in P. Wormald (ed.), *Ideal and reality in Frankish and Anglo-Saxon society* (Oxford, 1983), pp 154–6.
— 'Religion and society in Ireland' in P. Fouracre (ed.), *The new Cambridge medieval history c.500-c.700* (7 vols, Cambridge, 2005), i, 397–415.
— '"Charity with peace": Adomnán and the Easter question' in J.M. Wooding et al. (eds), *Adomnán of Iona: theologian, lawmaker, peacemaker* (Dublin, 2010), pp 51–68.
Stansbury, M., 'The composition of Adomnán's *Vita Columbae*', *Peritia*, 17–18 (2003–4), pp 154–73.
Stenton, F.M., *Anglo-Saxon England* (Oxford, 1971).
Stifter, D., 'Towards the linguistic dating of early Irish law texts' in A. Ahlqvist and P. O'Neill (eds), *Medieval Irish law: text and context* (Sydney, 2013), pp 163–208.
Stofferahn, S., 'Staying the royal sword: Alcuin and the conversion dilemma in early medieval Europe', *Historian* (2009), pp 461–80.
Strickland, M., 'Rules of war or war without rules? – some reflections on conduct and the treatment of non-combatants in medieval transcultural wars' in H.-H. Kortüm (ed.), *Transcultural wars from the Middle Ages to the 21st century* (Berlin, 2006), pp 107–40.
Swift, C., 'Tírechán's motives in compiling the *Collectanea*: an alternative interpretation', *Ériu*, 45 (1994), pp 53–82.
Tamoto, K. (ed.), *The Macregol gospels or the Rushworth gospels* (Amsterdam, 2013).
Tucker, R.W., *The law of war and neutrality at sea* (Washington, 1957).
Turner Johnson, J., *Ideology, reason and the limitation of war: religious and secular concepts, 1200–1740* (Princeton, 1975).
Tyerman, C., *God's war: a new history of the Crusades* (Cambridge, MA, 2006).
Valante, M. 'Reassessing the Irish "monastic town"', *Irish Historical Studies*, 31 (1998), pp 1–18.
— *The Vikings in Ireland: settlement, trade and urbanization* (Dublin, 2008).
Van-der-Melen, G., *Alberico Gentili and the development of international law* (Amsterdam, 1930).
Vogel, C., *Le pécheur et la penitence dans l'Eglise ancienne* (Paris, 1966).
Von Elbe, J., 'The evolution of the concept of the just war in International Law', *American Journal of International Law*, 33:4 (October 1939), pp 665–88.
Wallace-Hadrill, J.M., 'The bloodfeud of the Franks' in idem (ed.), *Long haired kings and other studies in Frankish history* (London, 1962), pp 459–87.

Wallace, P., 'The archaeology of Ireland's Viking-age towns' in D. Ó Cróinín (ed.), *NHI*, pp 814–41.
Walsh, P., 'The travels of Mícháel Ó Cléirigh' in N. Ó Muraíle (ed.), *Mícháel Ó Cléirigh, his associates and St Anthony's college, Louvain* (Dublin, 2008), pp 134–45.
Walzer, M., *Just and unjust wars* (4th ed., New York, 2006).
Ward, B., *Miracles and the medieval mind: theory, record and event 1000–1215* (Aldershot, 1982).
— *Signs and wonders: saints, miracles and prayers from the fourth century to the fourteenth* (Aldershot, 1992).
Watkins, C., '*Is tre fhír flathemon:* marginalia to *Audacht Morainn*', *Ériu*, 30 (1979), pp 181–98.
Watkins, O.D., *A history of penance* (2 vols, London, 1920), ii.
Wickham, C., *The inheritance of Rome: a history of Europe from 400 to 1000* (London, 2009).
Windass, S. & Newman, J., 'The early Christian attitude to war', *Irish Theological Quarterly*, 29 (1962), pp 235–47.
Windass, S., *Christianity versus violence: a social and historical study of war and Christianity* (London, 1964).
Winroth, A., *The making of Gratian's 'Decretum'* (Cambridge, 2000).
Wood, I., *The Merovingian kingdoms, 450–751* (London, 1994).
Wooding, J.M. with Aist, R., Clancy, T.O. & O'Louhglin, T. (eds), *Adomnán of Iona: theologian, lawmaker, peacemaker* (Dublin, 2010).
Woods, D., 'Four notes on Adomnán's *Vita Columbae*', *Peritia*, 16 (2002), pp 40–67.
— 'Arculf's luggage: the sources for Adomnán's *De locis sanctis*', *Ériu*, 52 (2002), pp 25–52.
— 'On the circumstances of Adomnán's composition of *De locis sanctis*' in J.M. Wooding et al. (eds), *Adomnán of Iona: theologian, lawmaker, peacemaker* (Dublin, 2010), pp 193–204.
Wormald, P., '*Lex Scripta and Verbum Regis*: legislation and Germanic kingship from Euric to Cnut' in P.H. Sawyer and I.N. Wood (eds), *Early medieval kingship* (Leeds, 1977), pp 105–38.
— 'Celtic and Anglo-Saxon kingship: some further thoughts' in P.E. Szarmach (ed.), *Sources of Anglo-Saxon culture* (Kalamazoo, 1986), pp 151–83.
— '"Boni genti suae": law making and peace-keeping in the earliest English kingdoms' in idem, *Legal culture in the early medieval West: law as text, image and experience* (London, 1999), pp 179–200.
— *The making of English law: King Alfred to the twelfth century* (Oxford, 1999).
— 'The *Leges Barbarorum*: law and ethnicity in the medieval West' in H.-W. Goetz, J. Jarnut and W. Pohl (eds), *Regna and gentes: the relationship between late antique and early medieval peoples and kingdoms in the transformation of the Roman world* (Leiden and Boston, 2003), pp 21–55.
Wright, R., *Late Latin and early Romance in Spain and Carolingian France* (Liverpool, 1982), pp 105–18.
Wycherley, N., *The cult of relics in early medieval Ireland* (Turnhout, 2015).
Yorke, B., *Kings and kingdoms of early Saxon England* (London, 1990).
— *Rex Doctissimus: Bede and King Aldfrith of Northumbria*, Jarrow Lectures (Jarrow, 2009).
— 'Adomnán at the court of King Aldfrith' in J.M. Wooding et al. (eds), *Adomnán of Iona: theologian, lawmaker, peacemaker* (Dublin, 2010), pp 36–50.

Index

by Eileen O'Neill

Admonitio Generalis, 46
Adomnán, abbot of Iona, 11–12, 59, 93–114; abbacy of Iona, 59, 66, 96–7; Aldfrith, friendship with, 97, 99, 101; Augustine's writings and, 27, 37, 43, 44, 47; biography, 95–100; Brega battlefield and, 98–9, 158, 161, 162, 188; captives, return of from Britain, 78, 97; Cenél Conaill, kinship with, 62, 94, 95–6, 98; Christian faith, influence of, 28; Columba, kinship with, 96; Columba's sainthood, belief in, 102; commemoration in *Félire Óengusso*, 151; death of, 102; diplomatic missions to Northumbria, 26n99; Irish penitentials and, 79; *jus in bello* and, 47–8, 188–9, 190; kin-slaying, condemnation of, 110; kingship, attitude to, 105–8, 109; Latin and, 93; miracles, belief in, 94, 102; monasteries established by, 59–60; perception of, 93, 101, 159–60, 189–90; Raphoe and, 127, 145, 156, 157, 161; *recht Adomnáin*, 72, 143, 150; relics, 144, 144n22, 145, 155–6; reputation as 'illustrious teacher', 101; sagas, awareness of, 90; sin, rating of gravity, 114; theology and, 93, 93n1; 'thought-world', 94; violence, attitude to, 93, 94, 105–13, 187; war, attitude to, 47; warfare, contemporary attitudes to, 16; *Canones Adomnani*, 103–4, 105; *De locis sanctis* (DLS), 99, 100–1, 190; Virgil, commentary on, 104–5; *see also* Birr; *Lex Innocentium*; *Vita Columbae*
Áed Allán, king of Tara (d. 743), 146, 147, 148
Áed Dub, king (d. 588), 107, 110, 114
Áed Oirdnide, king of Tara, 154–5
Áed Sláine, 110
Áedán mac Gabráin, king of Dál Riata, 106, 107–8, 109

Aethelfrith, king of Northumbria (d. 616), 57
Aist, Rodney, 100
Aldfrith, king of Northumbria (d. 705), 62, 97–8, 99, 101
Alfred, king of Wessex (849–99), 28
Ambrose, bishop of Milan (337–97), 16–17, 38, 45
American Civil War, 21
Anderson, A.O., and Anderson, M.O., 112
Anglo-Saxons, 65, 183
annals, 66, 170; *see also* Annals of the Four Masters; Annals of Inisfallen; Annals of Ulster (AU); *Fragmentary annals of Ireland*
Annals of the Four Masters, 156; *see also* Ó Cléirigh, Mícheál
Annals of Inisfallen, 153
Annals of Metz, 64
Annals of Ulster (AU), 66; abbots of Iona, deaths of, 116, 116n10; Adomnán, 95, 99–100, 142, 144, 144n22; Aldfrith, death of, 101; Brendan of Birr, St, 116; *Cáin Cholmcille*, 128; *cáin* law, judges and, 132; *Cáin Phátraic*, 128; Columba's relics 156n116; Corran, battle of, 142; Domnall mac Áedo, death of, 106; Dorbbéne, death of, 102; Flaithbertach, death of, 146n40; innocents, fate of, 141; Law of Colum Cille (Columba), 148; Law of Patrick, 148; *Lex Innocentium*, 11, 12, 112, 150; Loingsech mac Óengusso, king of Ireland, 62, 95, 98; Mac Riogoil, death of, 116; Raphoe, 154, 155; relics, 144, 144n22, 156n116; Vikings, 116, 152
archaeological excavations, 68–9; evidence of violence, 68–9, 184
Aristotle, 15, 15n19
Armagh, 59, 103, 128, 147, 182; clerical protection rights, 128, 145, 146, 147, 150, 173; Iona and, 128, 145, 148; relics and, 132n129; *see also* Law of Patrick

227

Ashdown, battle of (871), 55
Asser (d. c.909), 55
Audacht Morainn, 81–2, 109, 186, 187
Augustine of Hippo, 16–17, 37–48;
    Christian warfare, attitude to, 37; Collectio
    Canonum Hibernensis citations, 77, 78;
    conversion, 38; evil, views on, 38, 39, 40,
    41; evil of war, 42, 43, 44; God, the
    justice of, 44; guilt and innocence,
    concept of, 43; influence on Adomnán,
    27, 37, 43, 44, 47–8; innocents and, 43,
    47; interpretations of, 44–8; jus ad bellum
    and, 43, 189; jus in bello issues, 27, 37, 42–
    4, 47–8; just cause, 84; just war theories,
    17, 27, 37, 39–44, 113; legacy, 44;
    Manichaeism, rejection of, 38, 39;
    morality of war, 38, 42; neo-Platonist
    writings and, 38; non-combatants and, 43,
    47; Old and New Testaments, unity of,
    39, 40, 42; peace, notion of, 42; religious
    coercion, attitude to, 37, 40; Roman
    Empire, perception of, 40, 41; violence,
    authorization of, 42; war, attitude to, 42,
    47; warfare, Old Testament and, 29, 39,
    40, 43; warriors, inner disposition of, 43,
    44, 47; Confessions, 38, 46; Contra Faustum
    (Against Faustus the Manichee), 39, 40, 41,
    44; De Civitate Dei (City of God), 41; De
    libero arbitrio, 38, 39
Ayala (1548–84), 19

Bainton, R.H., 29
Baíthene, abbot of Iona (d. c.600), 96
Ballymacegan Castle, county Tipperary,
    166, 167, 171
barbarian laws, 48–55; Alamannia, laws of,
    49, 50, 51; Bavarian laws, 49, 50, 52, 53;
    Burgundian laws, 38, 49, 50, 52; children
    and, 52–3; clerics and, 53; Frisia, laws of,
    49, 51; Kent, laws of, 49, 50, 58; Latin,
    written in, 49; Lombardy, laws of, 49, 50;
    LxI and, 53–4; military service and, 53;
    non-combatants and, 54; personal injury
    tariffs, 49; rape and, 51–2; regional codes,
    50; Ripuarian Francia, laws of, 49, 51–2;
    Roman legal model, 49; Salic Francia,
    laws of, 28, 49, 50, 51; Saxon laws, 49,
    51, 53; Thuringia, laws of, 51; violence,
    limitation of, 54; Visigothic laws of Ervig,
    28, 49; Visigothic Spain, laws of, 49, 51;
    Wessex, laws of, 28, 51, 58; women,
    protection of, 50–3, 5; see also canon law;
    cáin law; penitentials, the; Roman law;
    vernacular Irish law
barbarians, 15, 16, 17
Bavarian laws (c.745), 49, 50, 52, 53
Bechbretha, 71
Bede: Adomnán's visits to Northumbria, 99;
    Arculf, Adomnán and, 100; Bible,
    interpretation of, 94, 94n8; De locis sanctis
    and, 101; Easter, date of, 93, 99; Ecgfrith's
    raid on Brega, 98; foreign students,
    Ireland and, 64; Historia Ecclesiastica, 101;
    Imma, story of, 56, 174; miracles, belief
    in, 94; monks killed in Northumbria, 57–
    8; Sigbert's refusal to bear arms, 129n108;
    Uuictberct, bishop, 130
Belli, Piero (1502–75), 19
Betha Adamnáin, 120, 159–60, 161, 166
Bhreathnach, Edel, 62, 84
Bible: Amalekites, 24, 26; Augustine, unity
    of Old and New Testaments, 40;
    Christians, killing and, 28–37; Collectio
    Canonum Hibernensis and, 76, 77; New
    Testament, 29, 30, 77; Old Testament,
    24, 26, 29, 39, 40, 108
Bibliothèque Royale, Brussels, 12, 119, 120,
    165, 167; see also O'Clery MS 2324–40
Bieler, L., 78, 146n44, 147n47
Bilichildis, queen (d. 675), 57
Binchy, D.A., 71, 92
Birr, 25, 26; Adomnán and, 11, 60, 100,
    115–16, 117–18; Clonmacnoise, war
    against, 116; lay attendees, warfare and,
    142; Mac Regol Gospels (Book of Birr),
    116; meeting at, 89, 115, 117–18;
    scriptorium, 116; Seefin stone, 116n8;
    Viking attack, 116, 153; see also Lex
    Innocentium guarantor-list
Bodleian Library, Oxford, 119; Gospels of
    MacRegol, 116, 116n12; MS Laud Misc
    610, 167; see also Rawlinson MS B 512
Book of Armagh, 87, 146n44
Book of Birr, 116
Bourke, Joanna, Intimate history of killing,
    An, 23
Breatnach, Liam, 75
Breatnach, P.A., 168
Brega, 61, 66, 98, 99, 158; Adomnán and,
    98–9, 158, 161, 162, 188

Brendan of Birr, St, 116, 118–19, 119n33
Bresal, abbot of Iona, 148
Bretha Crólige, 71, 73, 74, 92
brigands, 16; see also *díbergaig*
Brigit of Kildare, St, 82, 149; *díbergaig* (brigands) and, 83–4, 86, 88; see also *Vita Prima Sanctae Brigitae*
Britain: Adomnán, return of captives, 78; alien, concept of, 183; Christianity in, 60, 94; conflict, internal, 53, 56, 58, 65, 183
Brown, Peter, 37, 44
Brown, Warren C., 177, 187n77–8
Browne, Valentine, OFM, 165
Bruide mac Derilei, king of the Picts (d. 706), 130
Brunichildis, queen (d. 613), 57
Buddhists, 101, 107
Burgundian laws (517), 28, 49, 50, 52
Byrne, F.J., 65

Cadwallon, king (d. 634), 57–8, 106, 109, 183
Cáencomhrac, abbot/bishop of Derry, 156
Caesarius of Arles (502–42), 33, 34
Caimín of Inis Cealtra, St, 171
Cáin Adomnáin, 12, 150, 162; see also *Lex Innocentium*
'Cáin Adomnáin and the laws of war' (Smith and Gallen), 25
Cáin Cholmcille, 128
Cáin Dar Í, 149
Cáin Domnaig, 128
Cáin Fhuithirbe, 88, 89, 147, 184, 186, 187
Cáin Íarraith, 72–3
cáin law, 71, 72, 128–9; etymology of *cáin*, 15n23, 162; judges and, 132; see also *cána* of Ireland
Cáin Phátraic, 128; see also Law of Patrick
Calley, 'Rusty', 23–5, 26; *Body count*, 24
cána of Ireland (697–842), 128, 157–8; Adomnán's law, 128, 158, 173; in *Colmán's Hymn*, 157–8; Dáire's law, cattle and, 128, 158; eighth and early ninth centuries, 138; end of *cána* era, 153, 154; in *Félire Óengusso*, 158; purpose of 162n168; Sunday, the law of, 128, 158; see also Law of Patrick
canon law, 70, 76–8, 184–5; *Collectio Canonum Hibernensis*, 46, 76–8, 184–5; influence on vernacular law, 71; jurisprudence, 76; *jus in bello* and, 185; see also barbarian laws; *cáin* law; penitentials; Roman law; vernacular Irish law
Canones Adomnani, 103–4, 105
Capet, Hugh see Robert the Pious, king of the Franks
Carolingian era, 178; *Admonitio Generalis* and, 46; Augustine's thinking and, 47, 48; *LxI*, awareness of, 181; non-combatants and, 174; patristic scholarship, 46; public penance and, 34; wars of, 44
Cathal mac Finguine, king of Munster (721–42), 62, 146
Céli Dé, 152
Cenél Coirpri, 106, 125
Cenél Conaill: abbacy of Iona and, 96, 148; Adomnán's kinship with, 62, 94, 95–6, 98; Cenél nEogain and, 145–6, 155; Columba, St and, 94; kings/kingship and, 106, 125, 145, 146; territorial expansion, 95
Cenél Fiachach, 117
Cenél nÉndai, 96
Cenél nEogain, 97, 145–6, 147, 155; kingship of Tara, 146, 147, 148, 154
Céti, bishop of Iona, 130
Chapman Stacey, Robin, 65, 141
Charlemagne, 54n198, 57, 174, 177, 187n78
Charles-Edwards, Thomas: *cána*, temporary, 138; *Chronicle of Ireland*, 66, 67–8; *Early Christian Ireland*, 84n191; 'Early Irish Law', 76; kingship, *Críth Gabhlach* and, 143; 'the law of self-help', 65; original text of *LxI*, 128; penitentials, canon law and, 79; relics, laws and, 144
Childeric II, king of the Franks (d. 675), 57
children: barbarian laws and, 52–3; early Irish law and, 131n120; fines for killing, *LxI* and, 131; honour-price system and, 73; protection of, 11, 25; vernacular Irish law, 72–3, 74; violent deaths of, 69
Chilperic, king of Neustria (d. 584), 58
Christianity/Christians, 27, 36; baptism, postponement of, 33; biblical tradition, killing and, 28–7; Constantine the Great and, 31; criteria of Christian violence, 18; enemy, subjective guilt of, 17; Ireland, arrival in, 62–3; Jerusalem and, 101; Jesus, teachings of, 29; Jewish revolts and, 29; just war theory and, 18; killing, different types of, 36; killing in warfare, attitude to, 36; kingship, Christianization of, 106,

107; military service and, 29–30, 31, 32–6; pacifist traditions of early church, 16; penance, perception of, 27, 27n2, 32–3; persecution of, 31; protection of non-combatants, 26; Roman Empire and, 16–17, 30, 31; Roman model of hostility, 16; saints, power and influence of, 94

Chronicle of Ireland/Irish chronicles, 64, 65–8, 163; battles, 67, 68; clerics, killing of, 66, 67; common people, violence and, 67; deaths, 67–8; innocents, fate of, 67; Uí Néill expansion, 66; violent acts recorded, 66–8; women, abduction of, 67

Church: excommunication of deserters, 31; *homicidio*, killing and, 32; innocent persons, killing of, 32; killing, condemnation of, 32, 33; military service, attitude to, 31, 32; organization in Ireland, 59, 182n39; pacifism, importance of, 30; penance, attitude to, 19, 27, 27n2, 32–4; violence, attempts to limit, 48; war, attitude to, 28; *see also* canon law; Church councils; penitentials, the

Church councils: Council of Aachen (789), 46; Council of Aachen (817), 152; Council of Arles (314), 31; Council of Arles (538), 33; Council of Arles (541), 32; Council of Birr (697), 11, 25, 26; Council of Clermont (1095), 180; Council of Clichy (626–7), 32; Council of Elne-Toulouges (1027), 180; Council of Frankfurt (794), 46; Council of Narbonne (1054), 180; Council of Nicea (325), 33; Council of Toledo, Twelfth (681), 35; Council of Tours (461), 33; Council of Tours (567), *Acta* of, 48, 49; Council of Yenne (517), 33; Merovingian, 46, 48; Synod of Arles (1041), 180; *see also* Peace of God councils

Ciarán of Clonmacnoise, St, 102, 148, 149, 150, 158

Cicero, 16

Cilléne Droichtech, abbot of Iona (726–52), 144, 145, 145n35, 148

civilians: International Humanitarian Law and, 14; massacres of 23n83; modern war directed against, 25; Roman warfare and, 16; UN, prohibition of attacks on, 21; *see also* innocents; non-combatants

Clann Cholmáin of Mide, 61, 148, 150, 155

clerics: arms not borne by, 53; barbarian laws and, 53; *Cáin Phátraic* and, 128; *éraic*, protection of, 130; honour-price system and, 73; killing of, Irish chronicles and, 66, 67; killing of, penitentials and, 35, 36; *LxI* and, 130–1, 132–3, 134; monks, slaughter of, 57–8; penalties for violence towards, 53, 130–1, 132–3; protection of, 11, 25, 53; vernacular Irish law and, 73, 74, 75; war at the behest of, 45; *see also* Law of Patrick

Clonard, 149

Clonmacnoise, 59, 66, 116, 117, 170; *see also* Ciarán of Clonmacnoise, St

Clovis, king of the Franks (d. 511), 58

Cogitosus (d. 650), 83, 85–6; *see also* Vita Prima Sanctae Brigitae

Collectio Canonum Hibernensis, 46, 76–8, 184–5; Augustine and, 77, 78; Bible and, 76, 77, 184; circulation of, 76; influence on the Continent, 76, 77; *jus in bello* issues and, 77; punishment, crimes and, 77–8; *Senchas Már* and, 76, 77; women and, 77

Colmán's Hymn, 157–8

Columba, St, 59, 60, 62, 66, 94, 149; Adomnán's kinship with, 96; Áedán mac Gabráin and, 106, 107–8; copyright judgement, 141n3; Crónán (poet) and, 90, 109; *díbergaig* and, 110, 111; family background, 96; foretelling of Adomnán, 173; intercession with God, 94, 106–7; Iona and, 96, 150; kings/kingship and, 106, 107–8, 109, 142; kinship with Adomnán, 96; ordination of Áedán mac Gabráin, 107–8; prophecies, 107–8, 109, 110–11; relics, 156, 156n116; sainthood, 102, 103; souls consigned to hell by, 111, 112, 113; *see also* Law of Colum Cille; *Vita Columbae*

Columban community, fines payable to, 179; Columban monasteries, 60, 97, 144, 148; Viking attacks and, 152–3, 154; *see also* Iona; Kells; Raphoe

Columban *paruchia*, promulgation of *LxI*, 182

Conamail mac Conainn, bishop, 130

Concilium Veneticum (c. 465), 32

Congal Cáech, king, 141n1

Connacht, 61, 117, 125, 128, 148–9, 170

Connolly, Seán, 84

Constantine the Great (d. 337), 31, 33

Continuations of the Chronicle of Fredegar, 64
Corbally, county Kildare, 69
Cormac mac Airt, high king of Ireland 141n3
Corran, battle of, 142
Críth Gablach, 71–2, 73; *recht Adomnáin* in, 72, 143, 150
Crónán (poet), 90, 109
Crusades, 179, 180; Augustine's influence on, 44; criteria of Christian violence and, 18–19; First Crusade, 17, 18, 180; Jerusalem massacre, 18; *jus ad bellum* and, 19, 180; participation, perception of, 18–19; penance and, 19
Cumméne, abbot of Iona (d. 669), 96, 108
Cummeneus Albus, *Liber uirtutibus sancti Columbae*, 110
Cummian, 147, 147n45
Cunningham, Bernadette, 167, 168n195, 169n199
Curétan, bishop of Rosemarkie, 130
Cuthbert, St, 97

Dál Riata (Dalriada), 72, 106, 107, 130, 146, 183
De duodecim abusivis saeculi, 82
De locis sanctis (DLS) (Adomnán), 99, 100–1, 190
de Vattel, Emerich (1714–1804), 20
death: Adomnán's views, 105, 113; Augustine's thinking, 78; *ceciderunt* (dying in battle), 68; of clerics (*quies* and *mors*), 68; *iugulatio*, 68; manner of, 68, 68n78; spiritual quality of, 67–8
Derry, 60, 112, 156
Diarmait mac Cerbaill, king of all Ireland (d. *c*.565), 107, 110
díbergaig (brigands), 85–9, 92, 186; Adomnán's abhorrence of, 104, 105, 110, 111, 113, 189; attitudes to, 87; banishment from *tuath*, reasons for, 86; Brigit, St and, 83–4, 86, 88; characteristics of, 86; Columba and, 110, 111, 113; *LxI* and, 88; *mac báis* (son of death), 86; *mac mallachtan* (son of malediction), 86; *Männerbund* (warrior-hunters), similarity with, 86; paganism and, 86; penitentials and, 87; sagas and, 87; *signa* worn by, 86, 87, 88; *Togail Bruidne Da Derga* and, 87; vernacular Irish law and, 87
Diocletian, Roman emperor (d. 311), 31

Dlúthach mac Fithchellaig, king of Uí Maine, 126
Doherty, Charles, 107, 190
Domnall mac Áedo, high king of Ireland (d. 642), 106, 108
Domnall Midi, high king of Ireland (d. 763), 148
Donaghmoyne, county Monaghan, 155, 156
Donnchad mac Domnall, king of Tara (d. 1089), 148
Dorbbéne (scribe), 100, 102
Draper, G.I.A.D., 35, 36
Druim Fornocht, battle of (727), 145
Druim Tuama (Drumhome), county Donegal, 95, 97
Dubthach, abbot of Iona (d. 938), 156, 157
Dumville, David, 122, 136, 153
Dunant, Henry, 20, 99, 188; *Memory of Solferino, A*, 20
Dúnchad Muirisce (d. 683), 124–5
Durrow, 60, 97, 117, 148

Easter, date of, 93, 93n1, 99, 102
Ecgfrith, king of Northumbria (d. 685), 97–8
Edict of Thessalonica (381), 17
Einhard (770–840), 57
Eisenhower, General Dwight, 22–3
enemy, the: Christian attitudes to, 17; Greek attitudes to, 15; Roman classification of, 16; subjective guilt of, 17
Enlightenment, the, 20
Enright, M.J., 108
enslavement: captives, Adomnán and, 78, 97; just war and, 15, 16, 56
Eochaid Buide (d. 629), 106
éraic (fine), 140; clerics and, 130; rape and, 72, 73; women, killing of, 133–4, 133n141, 140
Erdmann, C., 45
érlam, concept of, 149–50, 156, 157
Ervig, Visigothic Laws of, 28, 49, 53
Etchingham, Colmán, 59, 60, 181, 182n39
Euchu úa Domnaill, king of Dál Riata, 130
Europe: Augustine's thinking and, 47; penitentials and, 36, 185; *raison d'état*, era of, 20, 187; violence, attitudes to, 54
Faílbe, abbot of Iona (d. 679), 96–7
Faustus, bishop of Riez (d. *c*.500), 33
Fedelmid mac Crimthainn, king of Munster (d. 847), 62

Félire Óengusso, 127–8, 150, 151–2, 158, 166, 188
Feradach úa Artúr, 130
fingal (kin-slaying), 85, 85n195
Finsnechtae Fledach, king of Tara (d. 695), 26n99, 98, 173
First World War, 21, 22
Fís Adomnáin, 120, 164, 166
Fischer Drew, Katherine, 52
Flaithbertach, king of Tara, 145–6, 146n40, 147
Flechner, Roy, 68n78, 71, 76–7
Fleming, Patrick, OFM, 165, 172
Fontenoy, battle of (841), 55
Fouracre, Paul, 57, 57n216, 64, 65
Fragmentary annals of Ireland, 98, 163–4
Francia, 64–5; *Annals of Metz*, 64–5; *Continuations of the Chronicle of Fredegar*, 64–5; knights, reputation of, 177; *Liber Historiae Francorum*, 64; Merovingian era, 46, 48–9, 57, 64; order, breakdown of, 177, 177n16; patristic scholarship/literature, 46; Peace of God movement, 175–6, 183; penitentials, spread of, 35, 185; Ripuarian Francia, laws of, 49, 51–2; Salic laws, 28, 49, 50; society, structure of, 177–8; violence and, 65, 178–9; *see also* Franks
Franciscans, 165, 170, 171
Franks, 54n198, 56, 64–5, 181, 187n78
Fraser, James E., 191; 'Adomnán and the morality of war', 26, 129n107
Fredegar, 64
Fulcher of Chartres, 17n37, 18

Gemmán (Columba's teacher), 112
Geneva Convention (1864), 21
Geneva Convention (1899), 21
Geneva Conventions (1949), 190, 191; Additional Protocols, 14n16, 22; Adomnán's Law, successor to, 25, 191; 'Red Cross' conventions, 14, 14n16, 21
Gentili, Alberico (1552–1608), 19
Gerard I, bishop of Cambrai (r. 1012–51), 177–8
Germanic peoples: barbarian laws of, 48–55; individual identities, sense of, 63; legal practice of ordeal, 45; Roman Empire and, 49; *see also* Anglo-Saxons; Saxons
Gillespie, A., 174; *History of the laws of war, A*, 12n5

Gospels of MacRegol of Birr, 116
Gratian, *Concordia Discordantium Canonum* (Decretum), 180–1
Greeks, barbarians and, 15, 183
Gregory the Great, pope (590–604), 34, 45, 47
Gregory of Tours, 58, 64
Grotius, Hugo (1583–1645), 19, 181
Gunbaldus, archbishop of Bordeaux, 175
Guy, bishop of Le Puy, 175

hagiography, 82–5; Cuthbert, St, life of, 97; innocents, lack of concern for, 84, 85; *jus in bello* issues and, 83; lepers, concern for, 83; O'Cleirigh's copies of saints lives, 171–2; poor people, concern for, 83; violence and, 84–5; *see also Betha Adamnáin*; *Vita Columbae*; *Vita Prima Sanctae Brigitae*
Halsall, Guy, 53, 55, 190
Hartigan, R.S., 12n5, 42, 43, 44, 174
Herbert, Máire: Adomnán's 'thought-world', 94; *Betha Adamnáin*, examination of, 159; Iona, influence of, 103; Kells, foundation of, 155; Law of Colum Cille, 148, 151; Uí Néill kingship of Ireland, 108
heretics, 16, 17, 45, 183
Hillgarth, J.N., 45, 47, 47n145
Hippolytus (c.170–235), 30
honour-price: Adomnán and, 189; churches/church property and, 131–2; concept, 70, 72, 73, 189; *éraic* (fine), 72, 73, 130, 133; *fingal* (kin-slaying) and, 85, 85n195; rank and, 189
hostes, Roman definition of, 16
Hughes, Kathleen, 66, 83, 151

Imma, 56, 174
Ine, king of Wessex, 58; Saxon Laws of, 28, 49, 53
infidels, 16, 17
innocents: Adomnán and, 94, 99, 111–13, 114, 139–40, 154, 188; attacks on, archaeological evidence of, 69; Augustine and, 43, 47; Chronicle of Ireland and, 66–7; concept of, 25, 122, 124, 129; fate of, 67, 141; God, punishment and, 114; inter-Irish violence and, 154; lack of concern for plight of, 84, 85, 90, 92;

penitentials and, 80, 81, 185; protection, need for, 184; war and attacks on, 55, 58, 67; *see also* children; clerics; non-combatants; women
Institute of International Law 21n68
International Committee of the Red Cross (ICRC), 13, 14n16, 20, 188
International Court of Justice, 13n13, 14
International Declaration Concerning the Laws and Customs of War, 21
International Humanitarian Law (IHL), 14, 20, 22; *LxI* and, 25, 26
international law, 13n13–18, 13–14, 19, 22, 191
International Peace Conferences, The Hague (1899, 1907), 21
International Review of the Red Cross, 13
Ioain the Sage mac in Gobann, abbot of Eigg, 130
Ioan mac Conaill maic Domnaill (brigand), 110, 111, 112, 113
Iona, 59, 182; abbacy after Adomnán's death, 143; abbots of, 62, 96, 144; Adomnán's abbacy, 59, 66, 96–7; Armagh and, 128, 145, 148; Chronicle, compilation of, 66; clerical protection rights, 146, 148, 150; Columba, abbey founded by, 59, 66, 96; *comarba* of Colum Cille and Adomnán, 156, 157; conversion of northern England by, 60; expansion in Ireland, 60; *familia*, 81, 97, 99, 113, 118; influence in Ireland, 60; Ireland and, 143–4; Kells, relocation of monastery to, 153; Law of Colum Cille promulgated, 148; library in, 47; *LxI* and, 147, 182; relics, 144, 147; Viking attacks, 152–3, 156
Ireland: central authority, lack of, 65, 186; Christianity, arrival of, 62–3; church organization in, 59, 60, 182–3; external threats, rarity in seventh century, 182, 183; high-kingship of, 62, 108; invasion by the sons of Míl, 63; Iona, influence of, 60, 182; juridical class established in, 184, 186; *jus in bello* law, emergence of, 54, 185–6; language, unity of, 63; Latin and, 63–4; Latin texts from Spain, 46; *Lebor Gabála* (origin tale) and, 62–3; linguistic identity, 63; ogam inscriptions, 63; patristic scholarship and, 46; provinces, 61; Roman Empire and, 59; *tuatha* (political divisions), 60–1; vernacular written literature, 63
Irish language: Virgil, commentary on, 104; *see also Lex Innocentium* languages
Irish society: Adomnán's ideal model, 108; elite in, 63, 67, 182, 185–6; hierarchical structure of, 70, 71; honour-price system, 70, 72, 73, 189; king, bond with his people, 105–6; rank and, 70, 72, 74, 189; Viking attacks, effects of, 152–3; violence, attitudes to, 16, 20, 64, 65, 70, 182–3, 186–7
Isidore of Seville (*c*.560–636), 45, 46, 47, 78; *Etymologies*, 47
Islam, 47, 100, 183, 191
Íte, St, 149

Jerusalem, 17, 18, 100, 101
Jesus, teachings of, 29
Jews, 29, 36
Johnston, Elva, 89, 153
Jonas of Bobbio (600–59), 45–6
Julian of Eclanum (*c*.386–455), 44
Julian of Toledo (642–90), 58
jus ad bellum: adoption of the term, 13; Augustine and, 43, 189; *Collectio Canonum Hibernensis* and, 77; Crusades and, 19; definition, 12–13; external threats and, 183; post-First World War, 21; predomination of, 15; United Nations and, 13–14, 21–2; Western society and, 19, 179–80, 187
jus in bello, 183, 187; Adomnán and, 47–8, 188–9, 190; adoption of the term, 13; Augustine and, 27, 37, 42–3; Bible and, 77; canon lawyers and, 185; Cicero and, 16; definition, 12–13; emergence from Ireland, 54; International Humanitarian Law and, 14; *LxI* and, 13, 26, 89, 131, 179, 181; Peace of God movement, 178, 179, 183, 189; post-First World War, 21; Red Cross and, 13
jus contra bellum see jus ad bellum
just cause, 15, 16, 18, 84
just war, 45; Aristotle and 15, 15n19; Augustine's theories, 17, 27, 37, 39–44, 113; Cicero and, 16; enslavement and, 15, 16, 56; First Crusade, perception of, 17; Grotius, four justifications for, 19; Hellenic Greek approach to, 15; Jerusalem massacre and, 18; just causes,

Romans and, 15; objective of peace and justice, 15; origins of term, 15; religious coercion and, 40, 41, 45; Roman approach to, 15

Kant, Immanuel (1724–1804), 20
Kells, 153, 155, 156–7; *Betha Adamnáin* and, 159, 160
Kelly, Fergus, 70, 71, 73, 85, 186
Kenney, James F., 35, 104, 105, 164
Kent, laws of (*c.*600), 49, 50, 58
Kildare, 59, 66, 85, 92, 170
Killaloe, diocese of, 117, 117n21
kin-slaying, 81, 85, 85n195, 110, 185
kings/kingship, 105–8, 125; Adomnán's attitude to, 105–8; *Audacht Morainn* and, 81–2; Buddhist ideas of, 107; Christianization of, 106, 107; Columba and, 106, 107–8; *fingal* (kin-slaying), 85, 85n195; *fir flathemon* (Ruler's Truth), 81; God's favour and, 106; high kings of Ireland, 62, 108; the just king, 82; ordained by God, 107, 108; *táinisí* (heirs-apparent), 118; of Tara, 61–2, 98, 145, 147, 148; of *tuatha* (political divisions), 61; war, inherent right to wage, 20, 84, 88, 109, 113, 186, 187; wars waged by, attitudes to, 20, 84
Kolb, Robert, 13

Lacey, Brian, 95, 96, 155, 156
Lám Dess (brigand), 110, 112, 113
Langan, J., 42, 43, 44
Latin: Adomnán and, 93; barbarian laws written in, 49; Christianity and, 63; Hiberno-Latin, 122; Irish scholars and, 46, 63–4; texts, 46, 82
Lauterpacht, Sir Herach, 22, 54
law: secular law, 132–3, 179; types of, 78; *see also* barbarian laws; *cáin law*; canon law; International Humanitarian Law; international law; penitentials, the; Roman law; vernacular Irish law
law texts/tracts, 70, 71, 72–3, 76; normative texts, 70–81, 184; Patrick's place in, 147; writers of, 71; *see also* Bretha Crólige; *Cáin Fhuithirbe*; Collectio Canonum Hibernensis; Críth Gablach; *Lex Innocentium*; quasi-legal texts; *sellach* text; Senchas Már
Law of Áedán, 148, 150
Law of Ailbe of Emly, 148, 150
Law of Brendan of Clonfert, 148, 150
Law of Ciarán of Clonmacnoise, 148–9, 150, 158
Law of Colum Cille (Columba), 144, 148, 150–1, 158
Law of Commán, 148, 150
Law of the Innocents *see* Lex Innocentium
Laws of Alamannia (*c.*600), 49, 50, 51
Laws of Frisia (*c.*785–803), 49, 51
Laws of Ine (Saxon) (*c.*696), 28
Laws of Kent, 49, 50, 58
Laws of Lombardy (643), 49, 50
Laws of Ripuarian Francia (*c.*623), 49, 51–2
Laws of Thuringia, 51
Laws of Visigothic Spain (654), 49
Laws of Wessex, 28, 51, 53, 58
Laws of Wihtred (*c.*694), 28, 53, 58
Law of Patrick, 144, 146–7, 153; clerical protection and, 128, 152, 157–8, 173; manuscript sources, 157–8; non-combatants, cessation of protection, 147; relics on circuit in support of, 146; renewals, 148, 150
Laws of Salic Francia, 28, 49, 50, 51
Law of Uí Suanaig, 148
League of Nations, 21
Lebor Gabála, 62–3
Leo I, pope (440–61), 33
Leuven (Louvain), 120, 165, 166, 167, 168, 170, 171
Lex Innocentium, 11–12, 66, 67, 115–40, 187; 1300th anniversary edition, 129n104,, 190; annals, references to *LxI*, 11, 112; children, fines for killing, 131; church property, protection of, 129, 131–2; clerical students/youths, killing/wounding, 130–1, 134; collection fees, Adomnán and, 135–6; comparison with Peace of God movement, 178–9; concept, 12–13, 14; concept in a modern context, 22–5; contemporary barbarian laws and, 53–4; counterclaiming (*folud/frithfholud*), 134–5; deaths caused by charms, 137–8; definition of the term, 129, 191; *díberg*, abhorrence of, 88; eleventh-century perception of, 164; enabling clauses, 132; enactment of, 11, 129, 133, 143, 173, 187; European awareness of, 181; fine collection, agents and, 135; fines, killing

of clerics and youths, 132–3; Gaelic society's memory of, 173; historiography, 25–6; hostage-surety, 132, 138–9; IHL and, 25, 26; implementation of, 173; *jus in bello* and, 13, 26, 89, 131, 179, 181; king of Tara's support for, 62, 95, 118, 143, 182; mentally disturbed persons, 134; name chosen for the law, 188–9; objectives, 129, 179; penance in addition to fines, 131; perceived as law of Adomnán, 144; pledges, 132; procedural issues, 138–9; prologue to, 98; promulgation of, 144, 181–2; renewal of, 150; secret killings, 137–8; secular law, incorporation into, 179; *sellach* (onlooker) text and, 75, 92, 131, 184; seventeenth-century attitudes to, 166–7; significance of, 190–1; tenth-century perception of, 159; territorial jurisdiction of, 129–30; transition to law for women, 144, 152, 163, 164, 173; Vikings and, 153–4; violence, Irish attitudes to, 186; women and, 133–4, 140, 144, 145, 147, 151, 152; women, crimes committed by, 136–7; *see also Cáin Adomnáin*; *Lex Innocentium* guarantor-list; *Lex Innocentium* languages; *Lex Innocentium* manuscripts; *Lex Innocentium* manuscripts, dating of; *recht Adomnáin*

Lex Innocentium guarantor-list, 95, 117–18, 119, 124–6, 129; bishop of Armagh placed first on list, 147; date of, 126; Middle Irish introduction to, 115; names, examination of, 124–5; names of guarantors, 130; titles, addition of, 125–6, 144

Lex Innocentium languages: Hiberno-Latin, 122; Latin, 122, 161; Middle Irish, 120, 121–2, 151, 160–2, 163; Old Irish, 122, 161, 169, 191

Lex Innocentium manuscripts, 12, 128–40; paragraphs 1–27, 120, 121–2, 151, 160–2, 163; paragraph 28 (guarantor-list), 124–6; paragraph 29 (fines, Adomnán's heirs and), 126–7, 145; paragraph 32 (maledictive psalms), 122, 126; paragraph 33 (fines), 122, 144, 163; paragraph 34 (definition of the term *LxI*), 129, 191; paragraph 34 (objectives), 129, 179; paragraph 35 (clerical students/youths, killing/wounding), 130–1, 134; paragraph 36 (church property, protection of), 129, 131–2; paragraphs 37–39 (enabling clauses), 132; paragraph 40 (killing of clerics/youths, fines), 132–3; paragraphs 41–42 (women, killing of), 133–4, 140; paragraph 43 (agents, fine collection and), 135; paragraph 43 (counterclaiming), 134–5; paragraph 44 (collection fees, Adomnán and), 135–6; paragraph 45 (crimes committed by women), 136–7; paragraph 46 (deaths caused by charms), 137–8; paragraph 46 (secret killings), 137–8; paragraphs 48–49 (procedural issues), 138–9; paragraph 49 (hostage-surety), 132, 138–9; provenance, 12, 119–20; *see also* O'Clery MS 2324–40; Rawlinson MS B 512

Lex Innocentium manuscripts, dating of 124–8, 164–5; paragraphs 28–32, 124–8; paragraph 29, 126–7, 145; paragraph 32, 122, 126; paragraph 33, 122, 144, 163; paragraph 34, 122, 138; paragraphs 41 and 42, 122; paragraphs 50–3, 123–4

Lex Ribuaria, 51–2

Liber Angeli (650), 146n39, 147, 147n47

Liber Historiae Francorum, 64

Licinius, Roman emperor (d. 325), 31

Lieber Code, 21

Lindisfarne, 60

literary texts, 81–92; *see also díbergaig*; hagiography; quasi-legal texts; sagas, the

Lóchéne Menn, abbot of Kildare (d.696), 66

Loingsech mac Óengusso, king of Tara (d. 704): clerical protection rights, Iona and, 146; death of, 142, 143; kinship with Adomnán, 96, 98; *LxI* and, 62, 95, 118, 143, 182; succeeded by his son, Flaithbertach, 145

Lorrha, 117, 125, 152

Luxeuil, 46, 47

Mac an Bháird family, 171
Mac Aodhagáin, Baothgalach Ruadh, 169
Mac Aodhagáin family, 166–7, 171
Mac Aodhagáin, Flann, 166–7, 168–9, 172, 173
Mac Aodhagáin, Giolla na Naomh, 167
Mac Regol, abbot of Birr (d. 822), 116
Mac Cana, Prionsias, 90
Maccshlechta, 72–3
Machiavelli, Niccolò, *Art of war, The*, 20

Maél Coích, Stowe Missal, revision of, 152
Maél Dúin, 154, 155
Máel Muire Ua hUchtáin, abbot of Kells and Raphoe, 157
Máel Ruain of Tallaght, 152
Mag nÍtho, battle of (734), 146
Maher, Margret, *LxI* 1300th anniversary edition 129n104
Manichaeism, 38, 39
Márkus, Gilbert, 122, 126, 154, 163, 190; additions to original *LxI*, 126; Augustine's influence, 27; fines, 138n177; innocents, concept of, 25; innocents, inter-Irish violence, 154; *LxI* paragraph 33, views on, 122; *LxI* paragraph 52, views on, 160n154; women, hair-pulling offence, 136
Markus, R.A., 37, 38, 43, 44
Meens, Rob, 34, 104, 185
Merovingian era, 64, 182; Church councils, 46, 48–9; Church property, threats to, 48–9; killing of Queen Brunichildis, 57
Meyer, Kuno, 115, 121, 122, 136
military service: age and, 56; Roman, 29–30, 31; Saxon laws and, 53; Visigothic laws and, 53; *see also* Roman army
Moling, St, 115
monasteries, 116–17; development as urban settlements, 60; established by Adomnán, 59–60; in Ireland, 59, 60; martyrologies and, 152; *paruchiae*, 59, 60, 85, 153, 181–2; patron saints and, 149
Moore, M.E., 46
Mugrón, abbot of Kells (d. 980), 157
Muirchú, 87; life of Patrick, 85
Munster, 61, 117, 182, 191; *Cáin Dar Í* promulgated, 149; *Cáin Fhuithirbe*, origin of, 88, 147; kings of, 62, 125, 146; Law of Ailbe, 148; Law of Patrick, 153
My Lai massacre, 22, 23–4; American attitudes to, 24, 25; perpetrators' attitudes to, 23–4, 26; rape and, 23, 24; *Time* poll and, 24

Neman mac Gruthriche, 110–11
Nero, Roman emperor, 30
Ní Bhrolcháin, Muireann, 89, 90
Ní Chonnaill, B., 131n120
Ní Dhonnchadha, Máirín, 15n23; Augustine, influence on Adomnán, 27; birthplace of Adomnán, 95; Brega battlefield, Adomnán and, 188; compilation of *LxI*, 120; dating *LxI* (paragraphs 1–27), 121–2; guarantor-list (*LxI*), 26, 115, 117, 124–5; *LxI* paragraph 33, views on, 122, 144, 163; Raphoe, 127, 127n87, 155; relics, churches and, 132n129; writings on *LxI*, 26, 26n104; 'Birr and the Law of the Innocents', 15, 136n153; Adomnán at Birr', 115; 'Edition of *Cáin Adomnáin*, An', 129n109, 130n117, 132n129, 134n146, 138n176; 'Guarantor-list', 124, 124n68; 'Law of Adomnán, The; a translation' 115, 115n4
Niall Frossach, king of Tara (718–88), 148
Nithard, 55
Nixon, Richard M., 24
non-combatants: Adomnán's awareness of, 14, 111–13, 139–40, 188–9, 190; barbarian laws and, 50–3, 54; Carolingians and, 174; concept of immunity, 13–14; concept of, 28, 189; *De duodecim abusivis saeculi* and, 82; Enlightenment, effects of, 20; God and, 43; IHL and, 14; immunity and, 13, 43; international law and, 13; Islamic teaching and, 191; *Lieber Code* and, 21; Merovingian councils and, 49; modern world's treatment of, 191; plight of, 36–7; protection of, *LxI* and, 26, 47, 139–40, 150; the rights of, 14, 20; treatment of, Grotius' views on, 19; war and, 12, 12n5, 14, 55, 56–8; *see also* children; clerics; innocents; Peace of God movement; women
normative texts, 70–81, 184; *see also* canon law; penitentials, the; vernacular Irish law
Northumbria, 65, 97–8; Adomnán's visits to, 97, 99; conversion to Christianity, 103; Mercians and, 56; Uí Néill dynasty and, 62, 97
Notker the Stammerer (840–912), 57
Nuremberg trials, 23

Ó Carragáin, Tomás, 59
Ó Cianáin, Tadhg, 165
Ó Cléirigh, Bernardino (Maolmhuire), OFM, 168, 171
Ó Cléirigh, Cúmhumhan, 119
Ó Cléirigh, Mícheál (Tadhg Cam): *Betha Adamnáin*, copy of, 166; family background, 171; *Fís Adamnáin*, copy of, 166; *Foclóir nó sanasán nua*, 169; Irish language and, 168, 169; Latin text and,

168–9; legal issues, *LxI* and, 166, 167, 168, 169–70, 172; legal studies, 167, 171; Leuven and, 165, 166, 171, 172; *LxI* perceived as law for women, 166, 172; Mac Aodhagáin family and, 166–7; Mac Aodhagáin, legal discussions with, 166, 167, 168, 169–70, 172, 173; MS sources available to, 166; O'Clery MS 2324–40, 12, 119, 120, 120–1, 122, 123, 126, 165–72; Old Irish, knowledge of, 169; saints' lives, copies of, 171–2; *seanchas* tradition, member of, 170, 171, 172
Ó Cléirigh, Seaán Buidhe, 167
O'Clery MS 2324–40, 12, 165–72; dating, 123, 126, 165–6; description, 120–1, 167–8; *LxI* copy, 167–8; Old Book of Raphoe and, 166; paragraph 31, 167–8; paragraph 32, 168, 169; paragraph 33, omission of, 122, 126, 168, 169–70, 172; paragraph 34, 126, 168, 169; paragraph 41, 169; paragraph 42, 169; provenance, 119
O'Connor, Ralph, 190
Ó Corráin, Donnchadh, 71, 105, 151, 153
Ó Cróinín, Dáibhí, 85
Óengus mac Áedo Commáin (Óengus Bronbachal), king, 106
Óengus ua Oiblén, bishop, 151–2
Oisíne mac Galluist, abbot, 125
Old Book of Raphoe, 12, 119, 120, 124, 154, 166; Rawlinson MS B 512 and, 164; *see also* Raphoe
Old Irish: poem, 173; treatise on the Psalter, 120, 165
Oliver, L., 49
O'Loughlin, Thomas, 93, 100, 101
Ó Maoil Chonaire family, 120, 165, 170–1
Ó Maoil Chonaire, Flaithrí, OFM, 170–1
O'Neill, Timothy (calligrapher), 129n104
Ó Néill, Pádraig P., and Dumville, David N., 122, 136
O'Queely, Malachy, vicar apostolic of Killaloe (d. 1645), 167
Ó Riain, Pádraig, 151, 158, 159
Origen (*c*.185–253/5), 16, 30
Oswald, king of Northumbria (d. 642), 103, 106, 107, 109
Oswiu, king of Northumbria (642–70), 97
Owenbristy, county Galway, 69
Oxford manual on the laws of war on land, 21n68

pacifist tradition, 17; early Church and, 16, 30; *see also* Peace of God movement; Truce of God movement
pagans/paganism, 34, 36, 38, 57; Christian hostility to, 16, 40, 45, 86; *díbergaig* (brigands) and, 86, 87; kings/kingship and, 106, 107; Romans and, 17, 30, 31
Parknahown, county Laois, 69
paruchiae, 59, 60, 85, 153, 181–2
Patrician texts in the Book of Armagh, The, 146n44
Patrick, St, 84, 85, 146–7, 149; First synod of, 78, 79; *see also* Law of Patrick
patristic literature/scholarship, 46; *Admonitio Generalis*, 46; Irish scholars and, 46, 47; *see also* canon law; *Collectio Canonum Hibernensis*
pax, etymology of, 15, 15n23
Pax Ecclesiae, 48
Pax Romana, 17
Peace of God Councils, 26; Council of Anse (994), 176; Council of Charroux (989), 175–6, 177; Council of Le Puy (994), 176; Council of Limoges (994), 176; Council of Narbonne (990), 176; Council of Poitiers (1000–14), 176, 177; ecclesiastical sanctions, 179; excommunication, threat of, 178, 179; *see also* Church Councils
Peace of God movement, 37, 48, 52, 174–5, 181, 183; comparison with *LxI*, 178–9; *jus in bello*, 178, 179, 183, 189; non-combatants, protection of, 177, 178, 179; peace oath proposal, 176–7; phases of, 180
penance: the Church and, 19, 27, 27n2, 32–4; killing in warfare and, 35, 36; *LxI* and, 131; military service and, 32–3; as once-in-a-lifetime sacrament, 27n2, 32–3, 34; private, 34; public (canonical), 34; *see also* penitentials, the
Penda, king of Mercia (d. 656), 183
penitentials, the, 34–7, 70, 78–81, 185; *anmchara* (soul friend), role of, 79; *Canones* and *leges penitentiae*, 79; confessors, role of, 79, 80; *díbergaig*, penance and, 87; innocents and, 80, 81, 185; Ireland and, 185; Irish penitentials, 78–81; killing, manner of, 185; origins of system, 79; repentance and, 185; sins, penances and,

79–80; Bigotian Penitential, 79, 80; First synod of St Patrick, 78, 79; Irish Canons, 79, 87; Old Irish Penitential, 79, 80–1; Old Irish Table of Commutations, 87; Penitential of Columbanus, 35; Penitential of Cummean, 79, 80, 87; Penitential of Finnian, 78, 80; Penitential of Hatligar of Cambrai, 36; Welsh Canons, 79, 80; *see also* barbarian laws; *cáin* law; canon law; Roman law; vernacular Irish law

Pereira Farrell, Elaine, 79
Picts, 130, 183
Platonism, 38
Plotinus (d. 270), 38
Porphyry (d. c.305), 38
prisoners of war, 14, 14n16, 21, 84, 98

quasi-legal texts, 81–2; *Audacht Morainn*, 81–2, 109, 186; *De duodecim abusivis saeculi*, 82; *fir flathemon* (Ruler's Truth), 81

raison d'état, 20, 187
rape: barbarian laws and, 51–2, 54; *éraic* (fine), 72, 73; fines, barbarian laws and, 51; My Lai massacre and, 23, 24
rapists, killing of, 51–2
rapists, vernacular Irish law and, 72; types of (*forcor* and *sleth*), 72; vernacular Irish law and, 72, 73–4
Raphoe, 119–20, 154, 155, 157; Adomnán and, 156, 157, 161; Adomnán's coarb, 127, 145; *Cáin Adomnáin* and, 150; foundation of, 127, 155; *LxI*, compilation of, 163; *LxI*, (paragraphs 1–27), 161; *LxI*, responsibility for, 154, 155; women, contributions paid to Adomnán, 161, 162; women, law protecting, 128, 161–2; *see also* Old Book of Raphoe
Ráth Máelsigi, county Carlow, 130
Rawlinson MS B 512, 122, 123, 126; comparison with O'Clery MS, 168; dating, 122; description, 120–1; Ó Maoil Chonaire family and, 170; Old book of Raphoe and, 12; paragraph 33, 121, 122, 168; provenance, 119–20
Raymond of Aguilers, First Crusade (1096–99) and, 18
recht Adomnáin, *LxI* perceived as, 72, 143, 150
rechtge r g (royal edict), 72

rechtgi (enacted law), 71–2
Reeves, W., 95, 157
relics: Adomnán and, 144, 144n22, 145, 155–6; Armagh and, 132n129, 145; circuits with, 144, 145, 146, 147, 149, 155–6; Iona's use of, Armagh's response to, 145; Law of Patrick and, 146, 147; *LxI* and, 144, 145, 147; of Peter, Paul and Patrick, 146, 147; power and influence of, 147–8, 149; role in Irish church, 144
Rhydderch ap Tudwal, king, 106, 109, 142
Riley-Smith, Jonathan, 18
Robartach, abbot of Iona, 156, 157
Robert the Pious, king of the Franks (d. 1031), 176, 177
Roman army, 29–30, 31
Roman Empire, 41, 49; Augustine's perception of, 40; Christians/Christianity, attitude to, 30, 31; Ireland and, 59; Jews and, 29
Roman law, 16, 70; *see also* barbarian laws; *cáin* law; canon law; penitentials, the; vernacular Irish law
Romans: enemies, classification of, 16; *fetiales* (college of priests) and, 15; *hostes*, definition of, 16; just causes, war and, 15; private law, 15
Rommel, General Erwin, 23
Rónán (father of Adomnán), 95–6
Rónnat (mother of Adomnán), 96, 98, 158, 161, 162
Ruben of Dairinis (d. 725), 76
Russell, Frederick H., 16, 17, 44, 45, 47, 174, 181
Rusticus, bishop of Narbonne (427–61), 33
Ryan, E.A., 29, 31
Ryan, John, 25

sagas, the, 87, 89–92; Adomnán's awareness of, 90; Cú Chulainn and, 90–1; *echtrai* (adventures), 90, 91; ideal community of, 92; *immrama* (voyages), 90, 91; Otherworld sagas, 90, 91; Ulster Cycle sagas, 90; violence in, 90–1; women, perception of, 92; *Echtrai Condlai*, 91; *Immram Brain maic Febail*, 91; *Táin*, 89, 90; *Togail Bruidne Da Derga*, 87; *Wooing of Emer*, 91
saints: authority of, laws and, 144, 148–9, 150; *érlam* concept, 149–50, 156;

monasteries and, 149; patron saints, 144, 149; politics and, 149; *see also* hagiography
Salonius, bishop of Geneva, 33
Salvian of Marseilles (d. c.480), 33
Saxon laws (c.785), 49
Saxon laws of Ine (c.694), 28, 49, 53
Saxons, Charlemagne's slaughter of, 57
Schaffhausen, Switzerland, 102
seanchas tradition in late medieval Ireland, 170–1, 172
Second World War, 13, 21n69, 22–3, 191
Ségéne, abbot of Iona (d. 652), 96, 147
sellach text, 74–5, 92, 113, 131, 184
Senchas Már, 147
Sétna (ancestor of Adomnán), 95–6, 98
Sharpe, Richard, 86, 87, 88, 95, 186
Shaw, M.M.N., *International Law*, 14n15–16
Sigbert, king of East Anglia, 56, 129n108
sins, 78, 79, 80, 87; gravity, Adomnán and, 114; *see also* penance; penitentials, the
síocháin, etymology of, 15n23
Slane, 149
Slébéne, abbot of Iona (d. 767), 148
Smith, C., and Gallen, J., 25n98, 25–6
Solferino, battle of, 20, 99, 188
Spain, 46, 49, 51, 183
Stowe Missal, revision of, 152
Strickland, Mathew, 26, 58n219, 175
Suarez, Francisco (1548–1617), 19

Tallaght, 152
Tara, kingship of, 61–2, 98, 145, 147, 148
Taran, 111, 112
Terryglass, 117, 146
Tertullian, 16, 30; *De corona*, 30; *De idolatria*, 30
Theodosius, Roman emperor, 38, 40
Theofrid, abbot of Corbie (d. after 683), 47
Thurneysen, R., 104
Tírechán, 85, 87, 146n39; life of Patrick, 84, 84n192
Truce of God movement, 17, 180
tuatha (political divisions), 60–1; banishment from, reasons for, 86; *cáin* law and, 71, 72; kings of, 61; *óenach*, laws enacted at, 71; *rí ruirech* (king of kings), 61; *rí tuaithe* (kings), 61

Uí Domhnaill of Tír Chonaill, 171
Uí Maine, 67, 117, 126

Uí Néill dynasty, 60, 61, 66; Clann Cholmáin Máir, 61; kingship of Ireland, will of God and, 108; kingship of Tara, 61–2; Munster kings and, 62; Northern Uí Néill, 61, 62, 98, 146, 155; Northumbria and, 62, 97; Southern Uí Néill, 61, 62, 98, 117; violence, expansion and, 66; warfare, 146; *see also* Cenél Coirpri; Cenél Conaill; Cenél Fiachach; Cenél nEndaí; Cenél nEógain
Ulpian (d. 228), 16
Ulster, 61, 125, 149
Ultach, Muiris, OFM, 168
United Nations, *jus ad bellum* laws and, 13–14, 21–2
United Nations Charter, 13
United Nations Security Council, 13, 25; *People on war: perspectives from 16 countries* 25n94
Urban II, pope, 17, 17n37, 180
urban settlements, monasteries and, 60
Uuictbercet, bishop, 130

vernacular Irish law, 70–5, 184; *aircsiu* (looking on), offence of, 74; banishment from the *tuath*, reasons for, 86; *bechbretha*, 71; blood-feuds and, 186; *Bretha Crólige*, 71, 73, 74, 92; *Bretha Nemed toísech*, 73; *Cáin Íarraith*, 72; *cáin* law, 71, 72; canon law, influence of, 71; children and, 72–3, 74, 75; clerics and, 73, 74, 75; counter-claiming (*folud/frithfholud*), 134–5; *Críth Gablach*, 71, 72, 143; *díbergaig*, legitimate role for, 87; *éraic*, 73; family murder, 110; judgements, verbal, 141; killing in battle, 109; *Maccshlechta*, 72; non-combatants and, 74–5; oral tradition of, 141–2; perceived as static/timeless, 141; pledges, system of, 132; rape, 72, 73–4; *recht Adomnáin*, 72; *rechtge ríg* (royal edict), 72; *rechtgi* (enacted law), 71–2; secret murder, offence of, 137; self-help, law of, 75, 185–6; *sellach* text, 74–5, 92, 113, 131, 184; *Senchas Már*, 75, 76; *Uraicecht Becc*, 73; women and, 70, 72, 73–4, 75; women, honour-price and, 70, 72, 75; workings in practice, 141, 141n3, 142, 142n9; writers of, 71; *see also* barbarian laws; *cáin* law; canon law; honour-price; penitentials, the; Roman law

Vietnam War, 23–4; *see also* My Lai massacre
Vikings, 152–6; attacks by, 116, 152–3, 156; children, fate of, 154; *LxI* and, 153–4, 173; women, fate of, 154
violence: Adomnán's attitude to, 105–13; archaeological evidence in Ireland, 68–9, 184; Augustine and, 42; barbarian laws and, 54; in Britain, 65; cattle raids and, 88; the chronicles, evidence in, 65–8; Church's attempts to limit, 48; continuation of after Birr meeting, 142; feuding and, 54; honourable warfare, perception of, 87–8, 109–10; illegitimate (*seditio/praesumptio*), 54; inter-Irish violence, 154; Irish attitudes to, 16, 20, 64, 65–8, 70, 88–9, 92, 182–3, 186; kin-slaying (*fingal*), 84–5, 110; right to repulse by force, 78, 82, 84; self-help, law of, 88; self-regulating system, perceived as, 65, 88
Virgil, commentary by Adomnán, 104–5
Visigothic Spain, 49, 51, 183
Visigoths, 41, 58
Vita Columbae (VC) (Adomnán), 82, 100, 101–3, 142; Adomnán's visits to Northumbria, 97, 99; Brendan of Birr, St, 118–19; captives, return from Britain, 78; Columba's death, 95; Columba's family background, 96; Columba's feast-day, 115; Crónán (poet), Columba's meeting with, 90; *díbergaig*, condemnation of, 110; Dorbbéne's copy of, 100, 102; God, Columba's intercession with, 94, 106, 111; innocents, persecution of, 111–13, 188; kings, divine providence and, 106; kingship of Ireland, will of God and, 108; purpose of, 103; synod at Birr, 117–18, 142; violence, condemnation of, 110–11; violence in, 108–13, 187
Vita Prima Sanctae Brigitae, 83, 84, 85, 86, 88, 186, 187
Vitoria, Francisco (1492–1546), 19, 181
von Arnim, General Hans-Jürgen, 22–3
Von Clausewitz, Carl, *On war*, 20

Walzer, Michael, 22–3
Wamba, king of the Visigoths, 35, 53, 58
war crimes: Jerusalem massacre, 18; massacres of civilians, 23n83; My Lai massacre, 22, 23–5

war/warfare: Church property, threats to, 48–9; Church's attitude to, 28, 35; class, combatants/non-combatants and, 56; contemporary accounts of, 55–8; Enlightenment and, 20; honourable warfare, perception of, 87–8, 92, 109–10, 186, 187; humanitarian rules (*Lieber Code*), 21; IHL and, 14; Irish attitudes to, 16, 20; justifications for, Grotius and, 19; killing, penance and, 35, 36; looting, 58; *LxI* and, 12, 89, 131; non-combatants and, 12, 12n5, 14, 55, 56–8, 69, 92; Old Testament, 29, 39, 40, 43; prohibited methods of, 14; regulation of, 20; right behaviour during, 12–13; right to go to war, 12–13; rights and duties relating to, 20; sovereign's inherent right to wage, 20, 84, 88, 109; state's right to wage, 20; warriors, inner disposition of, 43, 44, 47; women, violent deaths of, 57, 69; *see also* just war; prisoners of war
Ward, Hugh, OFM, 165, 167, 171, 172
Warrin, bishop of Beauvais (d. 1030), 176
Wessex, 28, 51, 53, 58, 65
Wihtred, king of Kent (d. 725), 28, 53, 58
Wolff, Christian (1679–1754), 20
women: abduction of, 67; Adomnán, contributions paid to, 161, 162; archaeological evidence for killing of, 69; barbarian laws and, 50–3, 54; *Collectio Canonum Hibernensis* and, 77; crimes committed by, *LxI* and, 114, 136–7; *éraic* (fine) for killing of, 133–4, 133n141, 140; hair, offence of pulling (*LxI*), 136; honour price system and, 70, 72; killing of, barbarian laws and, 50–1; killing of, *LxI* and, 133–4, 140; *LxI* and, 133–4, 140, 144, 145, 161–2, 172; non-combatant status of, 50, 54; protection of, 11, 25; queens, killing of, 57; sagas, depiction in, 92; sexual assaults, fines and, 51, 52, 54; violent deaths of, 57, 69; virgins, killing of, 51; *see also* rape
Wooding, Jonathan M., 189, 190; *Adomnán of Iona* 26, 93n1
Wormald, P., 49
Wycherley, N., 145n35, 149n68–9, 156n116

Xuanzang (*c*.602–64), 101

Yugoslavia, 22, 23n83